Study Guide with Selected Solutions
to accompany

Chemistry
An Introduction to General, Organic, and Biological Chemistry
Eighth Edition

Karen C. Timberlake

Professor Emeritus of Chemistry
Los Angeles Valley College

Benjamin
Cummings

San Francisco • Boston • New York
Capetown • Hong Kong • London • Madrid • Mexico City
Montreal • Munich • Paris • Singapore • Sydney • Tokyo • Toronto

Publisher: Jim Smith
Project Editor: Claudia Herman
Managing Editor: Joan Marsh
Cover Designer: Tony Asaro
Manufacturing Coordinator: Vivian McDougal
Marketing Manager: Christy Lawrence

ISBN 0-8053-3000-3

1 2 3 4 5 6 7 8 9 10–PBT–06 05 04 03 02

www.aw.com/bc

Preface

This Study Guide is intended to accompany *Chemistry: An Introduction to General, Organic, and Biological Chemistry,* Eighth Edition. The purpose of this Study Guide is to provide students with additional learning resources to increase their understanding of the key concepts in the text. Each section in the Study Guide is correlated with a chapter in the text. Within each section, there is one or more Learning Exercise that focuses on problem solving, which promotes an understanding of the chemical principles of that Learning Goal. Following the Learning Exercises, a Check List of learning goals and a multiple choice Practice Test provide a review of the entire chapter content. Finally, the Answers and Solutions to Selected Text Problems section gives the odd-numbered solutions for problems at the end of each chapter in the text.

I hope that this Study Guide will help in the learning of chemistry. If you wish to make comments or corrections or ask questions, you can send me an e-mail message to khemist@aol.com.

Karen C. Timberlake
Los Angeles Valley College
Valley Glen, California

"One must learn by doing the thing;
though you think you know it, you
have no certainty until you try."
—*Sophocles*

Here you are in a chemistry class with your textbook in front of you. Perhaps you have already been assigned some reading or some problems to do in the book. Looking through the chapter, you may see words, terms, and pictures that are new to you. This may very well be your first experience with a science class like chemistry. At this point you may have some questions about what you can do to learn chemistry. This Study Guide is written with those considerations in mind.

Learning chemistry is similar to learning a new sport such as tennis or skiing or diving. If I asked you how you learn to play tennis or ski or drive a car, you would probably tell me that you would need to practice every day. It is the same with learning chemistry. Learning the chemical ideas and learning to solve the problems depends on the time and effort you invest in it. If you practice every day, you will find that learning chemistry is an exciting experience and a way to understand the current issues of the environment, health, and medicine.

Manage Your Study Time

I often recommend a study system to students in which you read one section of the text and immediately practice the questions and problems that go with it. In this way, you concentrate on a small amount of information and actively use what you learned to answer questions. This helps you to organize and review the information without being overwhelmed by the entire chapter. It is important to understand each section because the sections build like steps. Information presented in each chapter proceeds from the basic to the more complex skills. Perhaps you will only study three or four sections of a chapter. As long as you also practice doing some problems at the same time, the information will stay with you.

Form a Study Group

I highly recommend that you form a study group the first week of your chemistry class. Working with your peers will help you use the language of chemistry. Scheduling a time to meet each week helps you study and prepare to discuss problems. You will be able to teach some things to the other students in the group, and sometimes they will help you understand a topic that puzzles you. You won't always understand a concept right away. Your group will help you see your way through it. Most of all, a study group creates a strong support system whereby students can help each other complete the class successfully.

Go to Office Hours

Finally, go to your tutor's or professor's office hours. Your professor wants you to understand and enjoy learning this material and should have office hours. Often a tutor is assigned to a class or there are tutors available at your college. Don't be intimidated. Going to see a tutor or your professor is one of the best ways to clarify what you need to learn in chemistry.

Using This Study Guide

Now you are ready to sit down and study chemistry. Let's go over some methods that can help you learn chemistry. This Study Guide is written specifically to help you understand and practice the chemical concepts that are presented in your class and in your text. Some of the exercises teach basic skills; others encourage you to extend your scientific curiosity. The following features are part of this Study Guide.

1. Study Goals
The Study Goals give you an overview of what the chapter is about and what you can expect to accomplish when you complete your study and learning of a chapter.

2. Think About It
Each chapter in the Study Guide has a group of questions that encourage you to think about some of the ideas and practical applications of the chemical concepts you are going to study. You may find that you already have knowledge of chemistry in some of the areas. That will be helpful to you. Other questions give you an overview of the chemistry ideas you will be learning.

3. Key Terms
Each chapter in the Study Guide introduces Key Terms. As you complete the description of the Key Terms, you will have an overview of the topics you will be studying in that chapter. Because many of the Key Terms may be new to you, this is an opportunity to determine their meaning.

4. Chapter Sections
Each section of the chapter begins with a list of key concepts to illustrate the important ideas in that section. The summary of concepts is written to guide you through each of the learning activities. When you are ready to begin your study, read the matching section in the textbook and review the sample exercises in the text.

5. Learning Exercises
The Learning Exercises give you an opportunity to practice problem-solving related to the chemical principles in the chapter. Each set of Exercises reviews one chemical principle. There is room for you to answer the questions or complete the exercise in this Study Guide. The answers are found immediately following each exercise. (Sometimes they will be located at the top of the next page.) Check your answers right away. If they don't match the answer in the Study Guide, go back to the textbook and review the material again. It is important to make corrections before you go on. In learning tennis, you hit the ball a lot from the baseline before you learn to volley or serve. Chemistry, too, involves a layering of skills such that each one must be understood before the next one can be learned.

At various times, you will notice some essay questions that illustrate one of the concepts. I believe that writing out your ideas is a very important way of learning. If you can put your problem-solving techniques into words, then you understand the patterns of your thinking and you will find that you have to memorize less.

6. Check List
Use the Check List to check your understanding of the Study Goals. This gives you an overview of the major topics in the section. If something does not sound familiar, go back and review. One aspect of being a strong problem-solver is the ability to check your knowledge and understanding as you go along.

7. Practice Test
A Practice Test is found in each chapter. When you have learned the material in a chapter, you can apply your understanding to the Practice Test. If the results of this test indicate that you know the material, you are ready to proceed to the next chapter. If, however, the results indicate further study is needed, you can repeat the Learning Exercises in the sections you still need to work on. Answers for all of the questions are included at the end of the Practice Test.

Contents

Contents

Study Goals

- Learn the units and abbreviations for the metric (SI) system.
- Distinguish between measured numbers and exact numbers.
- Determine the number of significant figures in a measurement.
- Use prefixes to change base units to larger or smaller units.
- Write conversion factors from the units in an equality.
- In problem solving, convert the initial unit of a measurement to another unit.
- Round off a calculator answer to report an answer with the correct number of significant figures.
- Calculate the density of a substance; use density to convert between mass and volume.
- Calculate temperature values in degrees Celsius and kelvin.

Think About It

1. What kind of device would you use to measure each of the following: your height, your weight, and the quantity of water to make soup?

2. How do you determine the amount of money in your wallet?

3. When you do a measurement, why should you write down a number and a unit?

4. Why does oil float on water?

Key Terms

Match each of the following key terms with the correct definition.

a. metric system   **b.** exact number   **c.** significant figures
d. conversion factor   **e.** density   **f.** absolute zero

1. _____ All the numbers recorded in a measurement including the estimated digit.

2. _____ A fraction that gives the equal quantities of a relationship in the numerator and denominator.

3. _____ The relationship of the mass of an object to its volume usually expressed as g/mL.

4. _____ A number obtained by counting items or from a definition.

5. _____ A decimal system of measurement used throughout the world.

6. _____ The lowest temperature possible, which is 0 on the Kelvin scale.

Answers   **1.** C   **2.** D   **3.** E
                4. B   **5.** A   **6.** F

1.1 Units of Measurement

- In the sciences, physical quantities are described in units of the metric or International System (SI).
- Length or distance is measured in meters (m), volume in liters (L), mass in grams (g), and temperature in Celsius (°C) or kelvin (K).
- A number written in scientific notation has two parts: a coefficient between 1 and 10 followed by a power of 10.
- For a large numbers greater than 10, the decimal point is moved to the left to give a positive power of ten. For small numbers less than 1, the decimal point is moved to the right to give a negative power of ten.

◆ **Learning Exercise 1.1A**

Indicate the type of measurement in each of the following measurements:

1. length   2. mass   3. volume   4. temperature

a. _____ 45 g	**b.** _____ 8.2 m	**c.** _____ 215°C
d. _____ 45 L	**e.** _____ 825 K	**f.** _____ 8.8 kg

Answers   a. 2   b. 1   c. 4   d. 3   e. 4   f. 2

- A number written in scientific notation has two parts: a coefficient between 1 and 10 followed by a power of 10.
- For a large numbers greater than 10, the decimal point is moved to the left to give a positive power of ten. For small numbers less than 1, the decimal point is moved to the right to give a negative power of ten.

◆ **Learning Exercise 1.1B**

Study Note
1. The number 2.5×10^3 means that 2.5 is multiplied by 10^3 (1 000). $$2.5 \times 1\,000 = 2\,500$$ The number 8.2×10^{-2} means that 8.2 is multiplied by 10^{-2} (0.01). $$8.2 \times 0.01 = 0.082$$ 2. For a number greater than 10, the decimal point is moved to the left to give a number between 1 and 10 and a positive power of ten. For small numbers less than 1, the decimal point is moved to the right to give a number between 1 and 10 and a negative power of ten.

Write the following measurements in scientific notation:

a. 240 000 cm   _____   **b.** 800 m   _____

c. 230 000 kg   _____   **d.** 50 000 years   _____

e. 0.002 m   _____   **f.** 0.000 0015 g   _____

g. 0.08 kg   _____   **h.** 0.000 1 sec   _____

Answers   a. 2.4×10^5 cm   b. 8×10^2 m   c. 2.3×10^5 kg   d. 5×10^4 years

e. 2×10^{-3} m   f. 1.5×10^{-6} g   g. 8×10^{-2} kg   h. 1×10^{-4} sec

1.2 Measured Numbers and Significant Figures

- A measured number is obtained when you use a measuring device to determine an amount of some item.
- An exact number is obtained by counting items or from a definition that relates units in the same measuring system.
- There is uncertainty in every measured number, but not in exact numbers.
- Significant figures in a measured number are all the reported figures including the estimated digit.
- Zeros written in front of a nonzero number or zeros that are used as placeholders in a large number are not significant digits.

◆ Learning Exercise 1.2A

Are the numbers in each of the following statements measured (M) or exact (E)?

a. _____ There are 7 days in one week.　　b. _____ A concert lasts for 73 minutes.

c. _____ There are 1000 g in 1 kg.　　d. _____ The potatoes have a mass of 2.5 kg.

e. _____ A student has 26 CDs.　　f. _____ The snake is 1.2 m long.

Answers　　a. E (counted)　　b. M (use a watch)　　c. E (metric definition)
　　　　　　　d. M (use a balance)　e. E (counted)　　f. M (use a metric ruler)

◆ Learning Exercise 1.2B

Study Note
Significant figures are all the numbers reported in a measurement including the estimated digit. Zeros are significant unless they are placeholders appearing at the beginning of a decimal number or in a large number without a decimal point.
4.255 g (four sig figs)　　　　0.0042 (two sig figs)　　　　46,500 (three sig figs)

State the number of significant figures in the following measured numbers:

a. 35.24 g _____　　　　　b. 0.000080 m _____

c. 55,000 m _____　　　　d. 805 mL _____

e. 5.025 L _____　　　　　f. 0.006 kg _____

g. 268,200 mm _____　　　h. 25.0°C _____

Answers　　a. 4　b. 2　c. 2　d. 3　e. 4　f. 1　g. 4　h. 3

1.3 Significant Figures in Calculations

- In a calculation with measured numbers, the number of significant digits given in the answer must match the number of significant figures in the measurement with the fewest significant figures.
- When evaluating a calculator answer, it is important to count the significant figures in the measurements, and round off the calculator answer properly.
- Answers in chemical calculations rarely use all the numbers that appear in the calculator. Exact numbers are not included in the determination of the number of significant figures in an answer.

◆ Learning Exercise 1.3A

Study Note

1. To round off a number less than 5, keep the digits you need and drop all the digits that follow.

Round 42.8254 to three significant figures → 42.8 (drop 254)

2. If the first number dropped is 5 or greater, keep the proper number of digits and increase the last retained digit by 1.

Round 8.4882 to two significant figures → 8.5

3. In large numbers, maintain the value of the answer by adding nonsignificant zeros.

Round 356,835 to three significant figures → 357 000

Round off each of the following to give **two** significant figures:

a. 88.75 m _____

b. 0.002923 g _____

c. 50.525 g _____

d. 1.6726 m _____

e. 0.0010558 kg _____

f. 82.08 L _____

Answers   **a.** 89 m   **b.** 0.0029 g   **c.** 51 g   **d.** 1.7 m   **e.** 0.0011 kg   **f.** 82 L

◆ Learning Exercise 1.3B

Study Note

1. An answer from multiplying and dividing has the same number of significant figures as the measurement that has the smallest number of significant figures.

1.5   ×   32.546 = 48.819 → 49   *Answer rounded to 2 significant figures.*

two sig figs   *five sig figs*

2. An answer from adding or subtracting has the same number of decimal places as the initial number with the fewest decimal places.

82.223 + 4.1 = 86.323 → 86.3   *Answer rounded to one decimal place*

Solve each problem and give the answer with the correct number of significant figures:

a. $1.3 \times 71.5 =$

b. $\dfrac{8.00}{4.00} =$

c. $\dfrac{0.082 \times 25.4}{0.116 \times 3.4} =$

d. $\dfrac{3.05 \times 1.86}{118.5} =$

e. $\dfrac{376}{0.0073} =$

f. $38.520 - 11.4 =$

g. $4.2 + 8.15 =$

h. $102.56 + 8.325 - 0.8825 =$

Answers   **a.** 93   **b.** 2.00   **c.** 5.3   **d.** 0.0479
         e. 52 000   **f.** 27.1   **g.** 12.4   **h.** 110.00

1.4 Prefixes and Equalities

- In the metric system, larger and smaller units use prefixes to change the size of the unit by factors of 10. For example, a prefix such as *centi* or *milli* preceding the unit meter gives a smaller length than a meter. A prefix such as *kilo* added to gram gives a unit that measures a mass that is 1000 times greater than a gram.
- Some of the most common metric (SI) prefixes are show below:

Prefix	Symbol	Meaning	Numerical Value	
mega	M	one million	1 000 000	10^6
kilo	k	one thousand	1 000	10^3
deci	d	one-tenth	0.1	10^{-1}
centi	c	one-hundredth	0.01	10^{-2}
milli	m	one-thousandth	0.001	10^{-3}
micro	μ	one-millionth	0.000 001	10^{-6}

- An equality contains two units that measure the *same* length, volume, or mass.
- Some common metric equalities are: 1 m = 100 cm; 1 L = 1000 mL; 1 kg = 1000 g.
- Some useful metric-American equalities are:

2.54 cm = 1 inch   1 kg = 2.20 lb   946 mL = 1 quart

◆ Learning Exercise 1.4A
Match the items in column **A** with those from column **B**.

A

1. _____ kilo-
2. _____ one thousand liters
3. _____ deciliter
4. _____ milliliter
5. _____ centimeter
6. _____ one-tenth centimeter
7. _____ microliter
8. _____ kilogram

B

a. millimeter
b. 0.1 L
c. one-millionth of a liter
d. kiloliter
e. 0.01 m
f. 1000 g
g. one-thousandth of a liter
h. one thousand times

Answers   1. h   2. d   3. b   4. g   5. e   6. a   7. c   8. f

◆ Learning Exercise 1.4B
Place the following units in order from smallest to largest.

a. kilogram   milligram   gram   _____

b. centimeter   kilometer   millimeter   _____

c. dL   mL   L   _____

d. kg   mg μg   _____

Answers   **a.** milligram, gram, kilogram   **b.** millimeter, centimeter, kilometer
                        c. mL, dL, L   **d.** μg, mg, kg

◆ Learning Exercise 1.4C

Complete the following metric relationships:

a. 1 L = _____ mL   **b.** 1 L = _____ dL

c. 1 m = _____ cm   **d.** 1 dL = _____ mL

e. 1 kg = _____ g   **f.** 1 cm = _____ mm

g. 1 mg = _____ μg   **h.** 1 dL = _____ L

i. 1 m = _____ mm   **j.** 1 cm = _____ m

Answers   **a.** 1000   **b.** 10   **c.** 100   **d.** 100   **e.** 1000
                    f. 10   **g.** 1000   **h.** 0.1   **i.** 1000   **j.** 0.01

1.5 Problem Solving Using Conversion Factors

- Conversion factors are used in a chemical calculation to change from one unit to another. Each factor represents an equality that is expressed in the form of a fraction.
- Two forms of a conversion factor can be written for any equality. For example, the metric–U.S. equality 2.54 cm = 1 inch can be written as follows:

$$\frac{2.54 \text{ cm}}{1 \text{ inch}} \quad \text{and} \quad \frac{1 \text{ inch}}{2.54 \text{ cm}}$$

- Conversion factors from metric and/or U.S. relationships, percent and density are used to change a quantity expressed in one unit to a quantity expressed in another unit.

◆ Learning Exercise 1.5A

Study Note
Metric conversion factors are obtained from metric prefixes. For example, the metric equality 1 m = 100 cm gives the factors $$\frac{1 \text{ m}}{100 \text{ cm}} \quad \text{and} \quad \frac{100 \text{ cm}}{1 \text{ m}}$$

Write two conversion factors for each of the following pairs of units:

a. millimeters and meters   **b.** kilogram and grams

c. kilograms and pounds   **d.** inches and centimeters

e. centimeters and meters   **f.** milliliters and quarts

g. deciliters and liters   **h.** millimeters and centimeters

Answers

a. $\dfrac{1000 \text{ mm}}{1 \text{ m}}$ and $\dfrac{1 \text{ m}}{1000 \text{ mm}}$ **b.** $\dfrac{1000 \text{ g}}{1 \text{ kg}}$ and $\dfrac{1 \text{ kg}}{1000 \text{ g}}$

c. $\dfrac{2.20 \text{ lb}}{1 \text{ kg}}$ and $\dfrac{1 \text{ kg}}{2.20 \text{ lb}}$ **d.** $\dfrac{2.54 \text{ cm}}{1 \text{ in.}}$ and $\dfrac{1 \text{ in.}}{2.54 \text{ cm}}$

e. $\dfrac{100 \text{ cm}}{1 \text{ m}}$ and $\dfrac{1 \text{ m}}{100 \text{ cm}}$ **f.** $\dfrac{946 \text{ mL}}{1 \text{ qt}}$ and $\dfrac{1 \text{ qt}}{946 \text{ mL}}$

g. $\dfrac{10 \text{ dL}}{1 \text{ L}}$ and $\dfrac{1 \text{ L}}{10 \text{ dL}}$ **h.** $\dfrac{10 \text{ mm}}{1 \text{ cm}}$ and $\dfrac{1 \text{ cm}}{10 \text{ mm}}$

◆ **Learning Exercise 1.5B**

Study Note
To problem solve, identify the given quantity, write a unit plan, and select the appropriate conversion factors. Arrange the factors in a setup to cancel the starting unit and provide the desired unit.

Use metric-metric conversion factors to solve the following problems:

a. 189 mL = _____ L

    Example: Unit plan: mL → L   Setup: $189 \text{ m\cancel{L}} \times \dfrac{1 \text{ L}}{1000 \text{ m\cancel{L}}} = 0.189 \text{ L}$

b. 2.7 cm = _____ mm

c. 0.0025 L = _____ mL

d. 76 mg = _____ g

e. How many meters tall is a person whose height is 175 cm?

f. There are 285 mL in a cup of tea. How many liters is that?

g. The recommended daily value for calcium is 200 mg. How many g are recommended?

h. You walked 1.5 km on the treadmill at the gym. How many meters did you walk?

Answers	**a.** 0.189 L	**b.** 27 mm	**c.** 2.5 mL	**d.** 0.076 g
	e. 1.75 m	**f.** 0.285 L	**g.** 0.2 g	**h.** 1500 m

◆ Learning Exercise 1.5C

Use metric-U.S. conversion factors to solve the following problems:

a. 18 inches = _____ cm   **b.** 4.0 qts = _____ L

c. 275 mL = _____ qt   **d.** 1300 mg = _____ lb

e. 150 lb = _____ kg   **f.** 840 g = _____ lb

g. 15 ft = _____ cm   **h.** 8.50 oz = _____ g

Answers	**a.** 46 cm	**b.** 3.8 L	**c.** 0.291 qt	**d.** 0.0029 lb
	e. 68 kg	**f.** 1.9 lb	**g.** 460 cm	**h.** 241 g

◆ Learning Exercise 1.5D

<table>
<tr><td colspan="2" align="center">Study Note</td></tr>
<tr><td>1.</td><td>For setups that require a series of conversion factors, it is helpful to write out the unit plan first. Work from the starting unit to the final unit. Then use a conversion factor for each unit change.

 Starting unit → unit (1) → unit (2) = final unit </td></tr>
<tr><td>2.</td><td>To convert from unit to another, select conversion factors that cancel the given unit and provide a unit or the final unit for the problem. Several factors may be needed to work the units towards the final unit.</td></tr>
</table>

$$\text{Starting unit} \times \frac{\text{unit (1)}}{\text{Starting unit}} \times \frac{\text{unit (2)}}{\text{unit (1)}} = \text{final unit}$$

Use conversion factors to solve the following problems:

a. A piece of plastic tubing measures 120 mm. What is the length of the tubing in inches?

b. A statue weighs 240 pounds. What is the mass of the statue in kilograms?

c. Your friend has a height of 6 feet three inches. What is your friend's height in meters?

d. In a triple-by-pass surgery, a patient requires 3.00 pints of whole blood. How many mL of blood were given if 1 quart = 2 pints?

e. A doctor orders 0.450 g of a sulfa drug. On hand are 150-mg tablets. How many tablets are needed?

Answers   **a.** 4.7 inches   **b.** 110 kg   **c.** 1.9 m   **d.** 1420 mL   **e.** 3 tablets

1.6 Density

- The density of a substance is a ratio of its mass to its volume, usually in units of g/mL or g/cm^3 (1 mL is equal to $1\ cm^3$). For example, the density of sugar is 1.59 g/mL and silver is 10.5 g/mL.

$$\text{Density} = \frac{\text{mass of substance}}{\text{volume of substance}}$$

- Specific gravity (sp gr) is a unitless relationship of the density of a substance divided by the density of water, 1.00 g/mL. We can calculate the specific gravity of sugar as

$$\frac{1.59\ \text{g/mL (density of sugar)}}{1.00\ \text{g/mL (density of water)}} = 1.59\ \text{(sp gr of sugar)}$$

Study Note

Density can be used as a factor to convert between the mass (g) and volume (mL) of a substance. The density of silver is 10.5 g/mL. What is the mass of 6.0 mL of silver?

$$6.0\ \text{mL silver} \times \underbrace{\frac{10.5\ \text{g silver}}{1\ \text{mL silver}}}_{Density} = 63\ \text{g silver}$$

What is the volume of 25 g of olive oil, (D = 0.92 g/mL)?

$$25\ \text{g olive oil} \times \underbrace{\frac{1\ \text{mL olive oil}}{0.92\ \text{g olive oil}}}_{Density} = 27\ \text{mL olive oil}$$

◆ Learning Exercise 1.6

Calculate the density or specific gravity, or use density as a conversion factor to solve each of the following:

a. What is the density (g/mL) of glycerol if a 200. mL sample has a mass of 252 g?

b. A person with diabetes may produce 5 to 12 liters of urine per day. Calculate the specific gravity of a 100.0 mL sample that has a mass of 100.2 g.

c. A small solid has a mass of 5.5 oz. When placed in a graduated cylinder with a water level of 25.2 mL, the object causes the water level to rise to 43.8 mL. What is the density of the object in g/mL?

d. A sugar solution has a density of 1.20 g/mL. What is the mass in grams of 0.250 L of the solution?

e. A piece of pure gold weighs 0.26 pounds. If gold has a density of 19.3 g/mL, what is the volume in mL of the piece of gold?

f. Diamond has a density of 3.52 g/mL. What is the specific gravity of diamond?

g. A salt solution has a specific gravity of 1.15 and a volume of 425 mL. What is the mass in grams of the solution?

h. A 50.0-g sample of a glucose solution has a density of 1.28 g/mL. What is the volume in liters of the sample?

Answers	a. 1.26 g/mL	b. 1.002	c. 8.4 g/mL	d. 300. g
	e. 6.1 mL	f. 3.52	g. 489 g	h. 0.0391 L

1.7 Temperature

- In the sciences, temperature is measured in Celsius units, °C, or kelvin, K. In the United States, the Fahrenheit scale, °F, is still in use.
- The equation °F = 1.8°C + 32 is used to convert a Celsius temperature to a Fahrenheit temperature. When rearranged for °C, the equation is used to convert from °F to °C.

$$°C = \frac{(°F - 32)}{1.8}$$

- The temperature on the Celsius scale is related to the Kelvin scale: K = °C + 273.

◆ **Learning Exercise 1.7**

Calculate the temperatures in the following problems:

a. To prepare yogurt, milk is warmed to 68°C. What Fahrenheit temperature is needed to prepare the yogurt?

b. On a cold day in Alaska, the temperature drops to −12°C. What is that temperature on a Fahrenheit thermometer?

c. A patient has a temperature of 39.5°C. What is that temperature in °F?

d. On a hot summer day, the temperature is 95°F. What is the temperature on the Celsius scale?

e. A pizza is cooked at a temperature of 425°F. What is the °C temperature?

f. A research experiment requires the use of liquid nitrogen to cool the reaction flask to −45°C. What temperature will this be on the Kelvin scale?

Answers   **a.** 154°F   **b.** 10°F   **c.** 103.1°F   **d.** 35°C   **e.** 218°C   **f.** 228 K

Check List for Chapter 1

You are ready to take the practice test for Chapter 1. Be sure that you have accomplished the following learning goals for this chapter. If you are not sure, review the section listed at the end of the goal. Then apply your new skills and understanding to the practice test.

After studying Chapter 1, I can successfully:

_____ Write the names and abbreviations for the metric (SI) units of measurement (1.1).

_____ Write large or small numbers using scientific notation (1.1).

_____ Identify a number as a measured number or an exact number (1.2).

_____ Count the number of significant figures in measured numbers (1.2).

_____ Report an answer with the correct number of significant figures (1.3).

_____ Write a metric equality from the numerical values of metric prefixes (1.4).

_____ Use conversion factors to change from one unit to another (1.5).

_____ Calculate the density of a substance, or use the density to calculate the mass or volume (1.6).

_____ Given a temperature, calculate a corresponding temperature on another scale (1.7).

Practice Test for Chapter 1

Instructions: Select the letter preceding the word or phrase that best answers the question.

1. Which of the following is a metric measurement of volume?
   A. kilogram   B. kilowatt   C. kiloliter   D. kilometer   E. kiloquart

2. The measurement 24 000 g written in scientific notation is
   A. 24 g   B. 24×10^3 g   C. 2.4×10^3 g   D. 2.4×10^{-3} g   E. 2.4×10^4 g

3. The measurement 0.005 m written in scientific notation is
   A. 5 m   B. 5×10^{-3} m   C. 5×10^{-2} m   D. 0.5×10^{-4} m   E. 5×10^3 m

4. The measured number in the following is
   A. 1 book   B. 2 cars   C. 4 flowers   D. 5 rings   E. 45 g

5. The number of significant figures in 105.4 m is
   A. 1   B. 2   C. 3   D. 4   E. 5

6. The number of significant figures in 0.00082 g is
   A. 1   B. 2   C. 3   D. 4   E. 5

7. The calculator answer 5.78052 rounded to two significant figures is
   A. 5   B. 5.7   C. 5.8   D. 5.78   E. 6.0

8. The calculator answer 3486.512 rounded to three significant figures is
   A. 4000   B. 3500   C. 349   D. 3487   E. 3490

9. The reported answer for the problem $16.0 \div 8.0$ is
   A. 2   B. 2.0   C. 2.00   D. 0.2   E. 5.0

10. The reported answer for the problem $58.5 + 9.158$ is
    A. 67   B. 67.6   C. 67.7   D. 67.66   E. 67.658

11. The reported answer for the problem $\dfrac{2.5 \times 3.12}{4.6}$ is

    A. 0.54   **B.** 7.8   **C.** 0.85   **D.** 1.7   **E.** 1.69

12. Which of these prefixes has the largest value?

    A. centi   **B.** deci   **C.** milli   **D.** kilo   **E.** micro

13. What is the decimal equivalent of the prefix *centi*?

    A. one-thousandth   **B.** one-hundredth   **C.** one-tenth
    D. ten   **E.** one hundred

14. Which of the following is the smallest unit of measurement?

    A. gram   **B.** milligram   **C.** kilogram   **D.** decigram   **E.** centigram

15. Which volume is the largest?

    A. mL   **B.** dL   **C.** cm^3 **D.** L   **E.** kL

16. Which of the following is a conversion factor?

    A. 12 inches   **B.** 3 feet   **C.** 20 meters   **D.** $\dfrac{1000 \text{ g}}{1 \text{ kg}}$ **E.** 2 cubic centimeters

17. Which is a conversion factor that relates milliliters to liters?

    A. $\dfrac{1000 \text{ mL}}{1 \text{ L}}$ **B.** $\dfrac{100 \text{ mL}}{1 \text{ L}}$ **C.** $\dfrac{10 \text{ mL}}{1 \text{ L}}$ **D.** $\dfrac{0.01 \text{ mL}}{1 \text{ L}}$ **E.** $\dfrac{0.001 \text{ mL}}{1 \text{ L}}$

18. Which is a conversion factor for millimeters and centimeters?

    A. $\dfrac{1 \text{ mm}}{1 \text{ cm}}$ **B.** $\dfrac{10 \text{ mm}}{1 \text{ cm}}$ **C.** $\dfrac{100 \text{ cm}}{1 \text{ mm}}$ **D.** $\dfrac{100 \text{ mm}}{1 \text{ cm}}$ **E.** $\dfrac{10 \text{ cm}}{1 \text{ mm}}$

19. 294 mm is equal to

    A. 2940 m   **B.** 29.4 m   **C.** 2.94 m   **D.** 0.294 m   **E.** 0.0294 m

20. The handle on a tennis racket measures 4.5 inches. What is that size in centimeters?

    A. 11 cm   **B.** 1.8 cm   **C.** 0.56 cm   **D.** 450 cm   **E.** 15 cm

21. What is the volume of 65 mL in liters?

    A. 650 L   **B.** 65 L   **C.** 6.5 L   **D.** 0.65 L   **E.** 0.065 L

22. What is the mass in kg of a 22 lb turkey?

    A. 10. kg   **B.** 48 kg   **C.** 10,000 kg   **D.** 0.048 kg   **E.** 22,000 kg

23. The number of milliliters in 2 deciliters is

    A. 20 mL   **B.** 200 mL   **C.** 2000 mL   **D.** 20,000 mL   **E.** 500,000 mL

24. A person who is 5 feet 4 inches tall would be

    A. 64 m   **B.** 25 m   **C.** 14 m   **D.** 1.6 m   **E.** 1.3 m

25. How many ounces are in 1,500 grams? (1 lb = 16 oz)

    A. 94 oz   **B.** 53 oz   **C.** 24,000 oz   **D.** 33 oz   **E.** 3.3 oz

26. How many quarts of orange juice are in 255 mL of juice?

    A. 0.255 qt   **B.** 270 qt   **C.** 236 qt   **D.** 0.270 qt   **E.** 0.400 qt

27. An order for a patient calls for 0.020 grams of medication. On hand are 4-mg tablets. What dose is needed for the patient?

    A. 2 tablets   **B.** 4 tablets   **C.** 5 tablets   **D.** 8 tablets   **E.** 200 tablets

28. A doctor orders 1500 mg of a sulfa drug. Tablets in stock are 0.500 g. How many tablets are needed?

    A. 1 tablet   **B.** $1^{1}/_{2}$ tablets   **C.** $^{1}/_{3}$ tablet   **D.** $2^{1}/_{2}$ tablets   **E.** 3 tablets

29. What is the density of a bone with a mass of 192 g and a volume of 120 cm^3?

    A. 0.63 g/mL   **B.** 1.4 g/cm^3 **C.** 1.6 g/cm^3 **D.** 1.9 g/cm^3 **E.** 2.8 g/cm^3

30. How many milliliters of a salt solution with a density of 1.8 g/mL are needed to provide 400 g of salt solution?

    A. 220 mL   **B.** 22 mL   **C.** 720 mL   **D.** 400 mL   **E.** 4.5 mL

31. The density of a solution is 0.85 g/mL. Its specific gravity is

    A. 222 mL   **B.** 8.5   **C.** 0.85 mL   **D.** 1.2   **E.** 0.85

32. Three liquids have densities of 1.15 g/mL, 0.79 g/mL and 0.95 g/mL. When the liquids, which do not mix, are poured into a graduated cylinder, the liquid at the top is the one with a density of

    A. 1.15 g/mL   **B.** 1.00 g/mL   **C.** 0.95 g/mL   **D.** 0.79 g/mL   **E.** 0.16 g/mL

33. A sample of oil has a mass of 65 g and a volume of 80.0 mL. What is the specific gravity of the oil?

    A. 1.5   **B.** 1.4   **C.** 1.2   **D.** 0.90   **E.** 0.81

34. What is the mass of a 10.0 mL sample of urine with a specific gravity of 1.04?

    A. 104 g   **B.** 10.4 g   **C.** 1.04 g   **D.** 1.40 g   **E.** 9.62 g

35. Ethyl alcohol has a density of 0.790 g/mL. What is the mass of 0.250 L of the alcohol?

    A. 198 g   **B.** 158 g   **C.** 3.95 g   **D.** 0.253 g   **E.** 0.160 g

36. 105°F = ____ °C

    A. 73°C   **B.** 41°C   **C.** 58°C   **D.** 90°C   **E.** 189°C

37. The melting point of gold is 1064°C. The Fahrenheit temperature needed to melt gold would be

    A. 129°C   **B.** 623°F   **C.** 1031°F   **D.** 1913°F   **E.** 1947°F

38. The average daytime temperature on the planet Mercury is 683 K. What is this temperature on the Celsius scale?

    A. 956°C   **B.** 715°C   **C.** 680°C   **D.** 410°C   **E.** 303°C

Answers to the Practice Test

1. C	**2.** E	**3.** B	**4.** E	**5.** D
6. B	**7.** C	**8.** E	**9.** B	**10.** C
11. D	**12.** D	**13.** B	**14.** B	**15.** E
16. D	**17.** A	**18.** B	**19.** D	**20.** A
21. E	**22.** A	**23.** B	**24.** D	**25.** B
26. D	**27.** C	**28.** E	**29.** C	**30.** A
31. E	**32.** D	**33.** E	**34.** B	**35.** A
36. B	**37.** E	**38.** D		

Answers and Solutions to Selected Text Problems

Note: Many mathematical computations involve the use of a calculator. In some of the following solutions, the calculator display is shown in square brackets, [ ] followed by the correct answer rounded to the proper number of significant figures indicated by an arrow →. The correct units will be attached.

1.1 A student in the United States would use pounds, feet, gallons, and °F while a student in France would use kilograms, meters, liters, and °C to measure weight (mass), length, volume, and temperature, respectively.

1.3 **a.** meters (used to measure length)   **b.** grams (mass)   **c.** milliliters (volume)
d. meters (length)   **e.** Celsius degrees (temperature)

1.5 **a.** Move the decimal point left four decimal places to give 5.5×10^4 m

b. 4.8×10^2 g

c. Move the decimal point right six decimal place to five 5×10^{-6} cm

d. 1.4×10^{-4} s

1.7 Measured numbers are obtained using some kind of measuring tool. Exact numbers are numbers obtained by counting or from a definition in the metric or the American measuring system.

a. measured   **b.** exact   **c.** exact   **d.** measured

1.9 **a.** not significant   **b.** significant   **c.** significant
d. significant   **e.** not significant

1.11 **a.** five   **b.** two   **c.** two   **d.** three
e. four   **f.** three

1.13 Calculators carry out mathematical computations and display without regard to significant figures. Our task is to round the calculator's answer to the number of significant figures allowed by the precision of the original data.

1.15 **a.** 1.85   **b.** 184   **c.** 0.00474 (4.74×10^{-3})
d. 8810 (8.81×10^3)   **e.** 1.83

1.17 **a.** $45.7 \times 0.034 = [1.5538] \rightarrow$ (rounds to) 1.6

  b. $0.00278 \times 5 = [0.0139] \rightarrow 0.01$

  c. $\dfrac{34.56}{1.25} = [27.648] \rightarrow 27.6$

  d. $\dfrac{(0.2465)(25)}{1.78} = [3.462078652] \rightarrow 3.5$

1.19 **a.** $45.48 \text{ cm} + 8.057 \text{ cm} = [53.537] \rightarrow$ (rounds to) 53.54 cm
  b. $23.45 \text{ g} + 104.1 \text{ g} + 0.025 \text{ g} = [127.575] \rightarrow 127.6 \text{ g}$
  c. $145.675 \text{ mL} - 24.2 \text{ mL} = [121.475] \rightarrow 121.5 \text{ mL}$
  d. $1.08 \text{ L} - 0.585 \text{ L} = [0.495] \rightarrow 0.50 \text{ L}$

1.21 The km/hr markings indicate how many kolometers (how much distance) will be traversed in one hour's time if the speed is held constant. The mph markings indicate the same distance traversed *but measured in miles* during the one hour of travel.

1.23 Because the prefix *kilo* means one thousand times, a *kilo*gram is equal to 1000 grams.

1.25 **a.** mg **b.** dL **c.** km **d.** kg **e.** μL

1.27 **a.** 0.01 **b.** 1000 **c.** 0.001 **d.** 0.1 **e.** 1 000 000

1.29 **a.** 100 cm **b.** 1000 m **c.** 0.001 m **d.** 1000 mL

1.31 **a.** kilogram **b.** milliliter **c.** km **d.** kL

1.33 Because a conversion factor is unchanged when inverted, $\dfrac{1 \text{ m}}{100 \text{ cm}}$ and $\dfrac{100 \text{ cm}}{1 \text{ m}}$.

1.35 Learning the relationships between the metric prefixes will help you write the following equalties and their resulting conversion factors.

  a. 1 m = 100 cm $\quad\dfrac{1 \text{ m}}{100 \text{ cm}}$ and $\dfrac{100 \text{ cm}}{1 \text{ m}}$

  b. 1 g = 1000 mg $\quad\dfrac{1 \text{ g}}{1000 \text{ mg}}$ and $\dfrac{1000 \text{ mg}}{1 \text{ g}}$

  c. 1 L = 1000 mL $\quad\dfrac{1 \text{ L}}{1000 \text{ mL}}$ and $\dfrac{1000 \text{ mL}}{1 \text{ L}}$

  d. 1 dL = 100 mL $\quad\dfrac{1 \text{ dL}}{100 \text{ mL}}$ and $\dfrac{100 \text{ mL}}{1 \text{ dL}}$

1.37 When using a conversion factor you are trying to cancel existing units and arrive at a new (desired) unit. The conversion factor must be properly oriented so that unit cancellation (numerator to denominator) can be accomplished.

1.39 **a.** $175 \text{ cm} \times \dfrac{1 \text{ m}}{100 \text{ cm}} = 1.75 \text{ m}$

  b. $5500 \text{ mL} \times \dfrac{1 \text{ L}}{1000 \text{ mL}} = 5.5 \text{ L}$

  c. $0.0055 \text{ kg} \times \dfrac{1000 \text{ g}}{1 \text{ kg}} = 5.5 \text{ g}$

1.41 **a.** Unit plan: qt → mL

$$0.750 \text{ qt} \times \frac{946 \text{ mL}}{1 \text{ qt}} = [709.5] \to \text{(rounds to)} \ 710 \text{ mL}$$

b. Unit plan: lb → kg

$$165 \text{ lb} \times \frac{1 \text{ kg}}{2.20 \text{ lb}} = [75] \to 75.0 \text{ kg}$$

c. Unit plan: in. → cm → mm

$$19.5 \text{ in.} \times \frac{2.54 \text{ cm}}{1 \text{ in.}} \times \frac{10 \text{ mm}}{1 \text{ cm}} = [495.3] \to 495 \text{ mm}$$

1.43 **a.** Unit plan: L → qt → gal

$$250 \text{ L} \times \frac{1.06 \text{ qt}}{1 \text{ L}} \times \frac{1 \text{ gal}}{4 \text{ qt}} = [66.25] \to 66 \text{ gal}$$

b. Unit plan: g → mg → tablet

$$0.024 \text{ g} \times \frac{1000 \text{ mg}}{1 \text{ g}} \times \frac{1 \text{ tablet}}{8 \text{ mg}} = [3] \to 3.0 \text{ tablets (add significant zero)}$$

c. Unit plan: lb → g → kg → mg ampicillin

$$34 \text{ lb body weight} \times \frac{454 \text{ g}}{1 \text{ lb}} \times \frac{1 \text{ kg}}{1000 \text{ g}} \times \frac{115 \text{ mg ampicillin}}{1 \text{ kg body weight}} = [1775.14] \to 1.8 \times 10^3 \text{ mg}$$

1.45 Density is the mass of a substance divided by its volume. The densities of solids and liquids are usually stated in g/ml or g/cm³.

$$\text{Density} = \frac{\text{mass (grams)}}{\text{Volume (mL)}}$$

a. $\dfrac{24.0 \text{ g}}{20.0 \text{ mL}} = [1.2] \to 1.20 \text{ g/mL}$

b. $\dfrac{1.65 \text{ lb}}{170 \text{ mL}} \times \dfrac{454 \text{ g}}{1 \text{ lb}} = [4.406470588] \to 4.4 \text{ g/mL}$

c. gem's volume: 34.5 mL total − 20.0 mL water = 14.5 mL

gem's density: $\dfrac{45.0 \text{ g}}{14.5 \text{ mL}} = [3.103448276] \to 3.10 \text{ g/mL}$

1.47 **a.** $150 \text{ mL} \times \dfrac{1.4 \text{ g}}{1 \text{ mL}} = [210] \to 2.1 \times 10^2 \text{ g}$

b. Unit plan: L → mL → g

$$0.500 \text{ L} \times \frac{1000 \text{ mL}}{1 \text{ L}} \times \frac{1.15 \text{ g}}{1 \text{ mL}} = [575] \to 575 \text{ g}$$

c. Unit plan: mL → g → lb → oz

$$225 \text{ mL} \times \frac{7.8 \text{ g}}{1 \text{ mL}} \times \frac{1 \text{ lb}}{454 \text{ g}} \times \frac{16 \text{ oz}}{1 \text{ lb}} = [61.85022026] \to 62 \text{ oz}$$

1.49 a. $\dfrac{1.030 \; \cancel{\text{g/mL}}}{1.000 \; \cancel{\text{g/mL}} \; (H_2O)} = 1.030$

b. $\dfrac{45.0 \text{ g}}{40.0 \text{ mL}} = [1.125] \rightarrow \dfrac{1.13 \; \cancel{\text{g/mL}}}{1.000 \; \cancel{\text{g/mL}} \; (H_2O)} = 1.13$

c. $0.85 \text{ (sp gr of oil)} \times 1.000 \text{ g/mL } (H_2O \text{ density}) = 0.85 \text{ g/mL density of oil}$

1.51 The Fahrenheit temperature scale is still used in the United States. A normal body temperature is 98.6°F on this scale. To convert her temperature to the equivalent reading on the Celsius scale, the following calculation must be performed:

$$\frac{(99.8°F - 32)}{1.8} = 37.7°C$$

Because a normal body temperature is 37.0 on the Celsius scale, her temperature of 37.7°C would be a mild fever.

1.53 a. $1.8 \, (37.0°C) + 32 = 66.6 + 32 = 98.6°F$

b. $\dfrac{(65.3°F - 32°)}{1.8} = \dfrac{33.3}{1.8} = 18.5°C$

c. $-27°C + 273 = 246 \text{ K}$

d. $62°C + 273 = 335 \text{ K}$

e. $\dfrac{(114°F - 32)}{1.8} = \dfrac{82}{1.8} = 46°C$

f. $\dfrac{(72°F - 32)}{1.8} = \dfrac{40}{1.8} = 22°C; \; 22°C + 273 = 295 \text{ K}$

1.55 a. $\dfrac{(106°F - 32)}{1.8} = \dfrac{74}{1.8} = 41°C$

b. $\dfrac{(103°F - 32)}{1.8} = \dfrac{71}{1.8} = 39°C$

No, there is no need to phone the doctor. The child's temperature is less than 40.0°C.

1.57 This problem requires several conversion factors. Let's take a look first at a possible unit plan. When you write out the unit plan, be sure you know a conversion factor you can use for each step.

ft → in. → cm → m → min

$$7500 \; \cancel{\text{ft}} \times \frac{12 \; \cancel{\text{in.}}}{1 \; \cancel{\text{ft}}} \times \frac{2.54 \; \cancel{\text{cm}}}{1 \; \cancel{\text{in.}}} \times \frac{1 \; \cancel{\text{m}}}{100 \; \cancel{\text{cm}}} \times \frac{1 \text{ min}}{55.0 \; \cancel{\text{m}}} = [41.56363636] \rightarrow 42 \text{ min}$$

1.59 $\dfrac{1.40 \; \cancel{\text{Euro}}}{1 \; \cancel{\text{kg}}} \times \dfrac{1 \; \$}{1.10 \; \cancel{\text{Euro}}} \times \dfrac{1 \; \cancel{\text{kg}}}{2.20 \text{ lb}} = [0.5785124] \rightarrow \$0.58/\text{lb}$

1.61 $4.0 \; \cancel{\text{lb}} \times \dfrac{454 \; \cancel{\text{g}}}{1 \; \cancel{\text{lb}}} \times \dfrac{1 \text{ onion}}{115 \; \cancel{\text{g}}} = [15.79130435] \rightarrow 16 \text{ onions}$

1.63 **a.** $8.0 \ \text{oz} \ \times \ \dfrac{\text{o crackers}}{0.50 \ \text{oz}} = [96] \rightarrow 96 \ \text{crackers}$

b. $10 \ \text{crackers} \times \dfrac{1 \ \text{serving}}{6 \ \text{crackers}} \times \dfrac{4 \ \text{g fat}}{1 \ \text{serving}} \times \dfrac{1 \ \text{lb}}{454 \ \text{g}} \times \dfrac{16 \ \text{oz}}{1 \ \text{lb}} = [0.234948605] \rightarrow 0.2 \ \text{oz fat}$

c. $50 \ \text{boxes} \times \dfrac{8.0 \ \text{oz}}{1 \ \text{box}} \times \dfrac{1 \ \text{serving}}{0.50 \ \text{oz}} \times \dfrac{140 \ \text{mg sodium}}{1 \ \text{serving}} \times \dfrac{1 \ \text{g}}{1000 \ \text{mg}} = [112] \rightarrow 110 \ \text{g sodium}$

1.65 **b.** $10 \ \text{days} \times \dfrac{4 \ \text{tablets}}{1 \ \text{day}} \times \dfrac{250 \ \text{mg amoxicillin}}{1 \ \text{tablet}} \times \dfrac{1 \ \text{g}}{1000 \ \text{mg}} \times \dfrac{1 \ \text{lb}}{454 \ \text{g}} \times \dfrac{16 \ \text{oz}}{1 \ \text{lb}}$

$= [0.352422907] \rightarrow 0.35 \ \text{oz amoxicillin}$

1.67 This problem has two units. Convert g to mg, and convert L in the denominator to dL.

$$\dfrac{1.85 \ \text{g}}{1 \ \text{L}} \times \dfrac{1000 \ \text{mg}}{1 \ \text{g}} \times \dfrac{1 \ \text{L}}{10 \ \text{dL}} = 185 \ \text{mg/dL}$$

1.69 The difference between the initial volume of the water and its volume with the lead object will give us the volume of the lead object.

285 mL total − 215 mL water = 70 mL lead

Using the density of lead, we can convert mL to the mass in grams of the lead object.

$$70 \ \text{mL lead} \times \dfrac{11.3 \ \text{g lead}}{1 \ \text{mL lead}} = [791] \rightarrow 790 \ \text{g lead}$$

1.71 Unit plan: L gas → mL gas → g gas → g oil → mL oil → cm³ oil

$1.00 \ \text{L gas} \times \dfrac{1000 \ \text{mL gas}}{1 \ \text{L gas}} \times \dfrac{0.66 \ \text{g gas}}{1 \ \text{mL gas}} \times \dfrac{1 \ \text{g oil}}{1 \ \text{g gas}} \times \dfrac{1 \ \text{mL oil}}{0.92 \ \text{g oil}} \times \dfrac{1 \ \text{cm}^3}{1 \ \text{mL}}$

$= [717.3913043] \rightarrow 720 \ \text{cm}^3 \ \text{oil}$

1.73 $3.0 \ \text{L fat} \times \dfrac{1000 \ \text{mL}}{1 \ \text{L}} \times \dfrac{0.94 \ \text{g fat}}{1 \ \text{mL fat}} \times \dfrac{1 \ \text{lb}}{454 \ \text{g}} = [6.211453744] \rightarrow 6.2 \ \text{lb fat}$

1.75 **a.** $1.012 \ \text{(sp. gr. urine)} \times 1.000 \text{g/mL} \ (\text{H}_2\text{O density}) = 1.012 \ \text{g/mL (urine density)}$

b. $1.022 \ \text{(sp. gr. urine)} \times 1.000 \text{g/mL} \ (\text{H}_2\text{O density}) = 1.022 \ \text{g/mL (urine density)}$

$5.00 \ \text{mL urine} \times \dfrac{1.022 \ \text{g urine}}{1 \ \text{mL urine}} = [5.11] \rightarrow 5.11 \ \text{g urine}$

Atoms and Elements

Study Goals

♦ Write the name of an element from its symbol or its period and group number.
♦ Classify an element as a metal or nonmetal.
♦ Describe the three important particles in the atom, their location, charges, and relative masses.
♦ Describe Rutherford s gold-foil experiment and how it led to the current model of the atom.
♦ Use atomic number and mass number of an atom to determine the number of protons, neutrons, and electrons in the atom.
♦ Understand the relationship of isotopes to the atomic mass of an element on the periodic table.
♦ Write the electron shell arrangements for elements 1—18 in the periodic table.
♦ Explain the relationship between electron arrangement, group number and periodic law.

Think About It

1. Name some of the elements you have seen today.

2. How are the symbols of the elements related to their names?

3. What are some elements that are part of your vitamins?

4. On a dry day, you walk across a carpet and touch a doorknob. You feel a spark. What happened?

Key Terms

Match each the following key terms with the correct definition.

a. element   **b.** atom   **c.** atomic number   **d.** mass number   **e.** isotope

1. _____ The number of protons and neutrons in the nucleus of an atom.

2. _____ The smallest particle of an element.

3. _____ A primary substance that cannot be broken down into simpler substances.

4. _____ An atom of an element that has a different number of neutrons than another atom of the same element

5. _____ The number of protons in an atom.

Answers   **1.** d   **2.** b   **3.** a   **4.** e   **5.** c

2.1 Elements and Symbols

- Elements are the primary substances of matter.
- Chemical symbols are one- or two-letter abbreviations for the names of the elements.
- The physical properties of an element are those characteristics such as color, density, melting and boiling point that we can observe or measure without changing the identity of the element.

◆ Learning Exercise 2.1A

> **Study Note**
> Now is the time to learn the names of the elements and their symbols. Practice saying and writing the names of the elements in the periodic table with atomic number 1-54 and Cs, Ba, Hg, Au, and Pb. Cover the symbols in the lists of elements and practice writing the symbols for the elemental names.

Write the symbols for each of the following elements:

1. carbon _____
2. iron _____
3. sodium _____
4. phosphorus _____
5. oxygen _____
6. nitrogen _____
7. iodine _____
8. sulfur _____
9. potassium _____
10. lead _____
11. calcium _____
12. gold _____
13. copper _____
14. neon _____
15. chlorine _____

Answers
1. C   2. Fe   3. Na   4. P   5. O
6. N   7. I   8. S   9. K   10. Pb
11. Ca   12. Au   13. Cu   14. Ne   15. Cl

◆ Learning Exercise 2.1B

Write the names of the elements represented by each of the following symbols:

1. Mg _____
2. K _____
3. Au _____
4. F _____
5. Cu _____
6. Be _____
7. Ag _____
8. Br _____
9. Zn _____
10. Al _____
11. Ba _____
12. Li _____

Answers
1. magnesium   2. potassium   3. gold
4. fluorine   5. copper   6. beryllium
7. silver   8. bromine   9. zinc
10. aluminum   11. barium   12. lithium

◆ **Learning Exercise 2.1C**

Gold (Au, *aurum,* atomic number 79) has been highly valued from ancient times. Gold, which has a density of 19.3 g/mL melts at 1064°C and boils at 2857°C. It is found free in nature usually along with quartz or pyrite deposits. Gold is a beautiful metal with a yellow color. It is a soft metal that is also the most malleable metal, which accounts for it use in jewelry and gold leaf. Gold is also a good conductor of heat and electricity. List all the physical properties that describe gold.

Answer   density 19.3 g/mL   melting point 1064°C
              boiling point 2857°C   metal
              yellow color   soft
              highly malleable   good conductor of heat and electricity

2.2 The Periodic Table

- The periodic table is an arrangement of the elements by increasing atomic number.
- Each vertical column contains a *group* of elements, which have similar properties.
- A horizontal row of elements is called a period.
- On the periodic table, the *metals* are located on the left of the heavy zig-zag line, the nonmetals are to the right, and metalloids are next to the zig-zag line.

◆ **Learning Exercise 2.2A**

Study Note
1.   The periodic table consists of horizontal rows called *periods* and vertical columns called *groups*.
2.   Elements in Group 1A are the *alkali metals*. Elements in Group 2A are the *alkaline earth metals*, and Group 7A contains the *halogens*. Elements in Group 8A are the *Noble gases*.

Indicate whether the following elements are in a group (G), period (P), or neither (N):

a. Li, C, and O   _____   **b.** Br, Cl, and F _____

c. Al, Si, and Cl   _____   **d.** C, N, and O   _____

e. Mg, Ca, and Ba   _____   **f.** C, S, and Br _____

g. Li, Na, and K   _____   **h.** K, Ca, and Br _____

Answers   **a.** P   **b.** G   **c.** P   **d.** P
               e. G   **f.** N   **g.** G   **h.** P

◆ **Learning Exercise 2.2B**

Complete the list of elements, group numbers, and period numbers in the following table:

Element and Symbol	Group Number	Period Number
	2A	3
Silicon, Si		
	5A	2
Aluminum, Al		
	4A	5
	1A	6

Answers

Element Symbol	Group Number	Period Number
Magnesium, Mg	2A	3
Silicon, Si	4A	3
Nitrogen, N	5A	2
Aluminum, Al	3A	3
Tin, Sn	4A	5
Cesium, Cs	1A	6

◆ Learning Exercise 2.2C

Identify each of the following elements as a metal (M) or nonmetal (NM):

1. Cl _____   2. N _____   3. Fe _____   4. K _____   5. Al _____

6. C _____   7. Ca _____   8. Zn _____   9. Ag _____   10. Mg _____

Answers   1. NM   2. NM   3. M   4. M   5. M
             6. NM   7. M   8. M   9. M   10. M

◆ Learning Exercise 2.2D

Match the names of the chemical groups with the elements, K, Cl, He, Fe, Mg, Ne, Li, Cu, and Br.

1. Halogens   _____

2. Noble gases   _____

3. Alkali metals   _____

4. Alkaline earth metals   _____

5. Transition metals   _____

Answers   1. Cl, Br   2. He, Ne   3. K, Li   4. Mg   5. Fe, Cu

2.3 The Atom

- An atom is the smallest particle that retains the characteristics of an element.
- Atoms are composed of three subatomic particles. Protons have a positive charge (+), electrons carry a negative charge (−), and neutrons are electrically neutral.
- The protons and neutrons each with a mass of about 1 amu are found in the tiny, dense nucleus. The electrons are located outside the nucleus.

◆ Learning Exercise 2.3A

Indicate whether each of the following statements is consistent with atomic theory (true or false):

1. All matter is composed of atoms.

2. All atoms of an element are identical.

3. Atoms combine to form compounds.

4. Most of the mass of the atom is in the nucleus.

Answers   1. true   2. false   3. true   4. true

◆ **Learning Exercise 2.3B**

Match the following terms with the correct statements:

a. proton   **b.** neutron   **c.** electron   **d.** nucleus

1. _____ Found in the nucleus of an atom   **2.** _____ Has a –1 charge

3. _____ Found outside the nucleus   **4.** _____ Has a mass of 1 amu

5. _____ The small, dense center of the atom   **6.** _____ Is neutral

Answers   **1.** a and b   **2.** c   **3.** c   **4.** a and b   **5.** d   **6.** B

2.4 Atomic Number and Mass Number

- The *atomic number* is the number of protons in every atom of an element. In neutral atoms, the number of electrons is equal to the number of protons.
- The mass number is the total number of protons and neutrons in an atom.

◆ **Learning Exercise 2.4A**

Give the number of protons in each of the following neutral atoms:

a. An atom of carbon   _____

b. An atom of the element with atomic number 15   _____

c. An atom with a mass number of 40 and atomic number 19   _____

d. An atom with 9 neutrons and a mass number of 19   _____

e. A neutral atom that has 18 electrons   _____

Answers   **a.** 6   **b.** 15   **c.** 19   **d.** 10   **e.** 18

◆ **Learning Exercise 2.4B**

Study Note
1. The *atomic number* is the number of protons in every atom of an element. In neutral atoms, the number of electrons equals the number of protons.
2. The *mass number* is the total number of neutrons and protons in the nucleus of an atom.
3. The number of neutrons is *mass number – atomic number.*

Find the number of neutrons in each of the following atoms:

a. A mass number of 42 and atomic number 20.   _____

b. A mass number of 10 and 5 protons.   _____

c. $^{30}_{14}\text{Si}$ _____

d. A mass number of 9 and atomic number 4.   _____

e. A mass number of 22 and 10 protons.   _____

f. A zinc atom with a mass number of 66.   _____

Answers   **a.** 22   **b.** 5   **c.** 16   **d.** 5   **e.** 12   **f.** 36

◆ **Learning Exercise 2.4C**

Study Note
In the atomic symbol for a particular atom, the mass number appears in the upper left corner and the atomic number in the lower left corner.   Atomic mass → $^{32}_{16}$S $^{26}_{13}$Al
Atomic number →

Complete the following table for neutral atoms.

Symbol	Atomic Number	Mass Number	Number of Protons	Number of Neutrons	Number of Electrons
	12			12	
			20	22	
		55		29	
	35			45	
		35	17		
$^{120}_{50}$Sn					

Answers

Symbol	Atomic Number	Mass Number	Number of Protons	Number of Neutrons	Number of Electrons
$^{24}_{12}$Mg	12	24	12	12	12
$^{42}_{20}$Ca	20	42	20	22	20
$^{55}_{26}$Fe	26	55	26	29	26
$^{80}_{35}$Br	35	80	35	45	35
$^{35}_{17}$Cl	17	35	17	18	17
$^{120}_{50}$Sn	50	120	50	70	50

2.5 Isotopes

- Atoms that have the same number of protons, but different numbers of neutrons are called isotopes.
- The atomic mass of an element is the average mass of all the isotopes in a naturally occurring sample of that element.

◆ **Learning Exercise 2.5A**

Identify the sets of atoms that are isotopes.

A. $^{20}_{10}$X   **B.** $^{20}_{11}$X   **C.** $^{21}_{11}$X   **D.** $^{19}_{10}$X   **E.** $^{19}_{9}$X

Answer   Atoms A and D are isotopes (At. No. 10); atoms B and C are isotopes (At. No. 11)

◆ Learning Exercise 2.5B

ESSAY: Copper has two naturally occurring isotopes, ^{63}Cu and ^{65}Cu. If that is the case, why is the atomic mass of copper listed as 63.35 on the periodic table?

Answer   Copper in nature consists of two isotopes with different atomic masses. The atomic mass is the average of the individual masses of the two isotopes and their percent abundance in the sample. The atomic mass does not represent the mass of any individual atom.

2.6 Electron Energy Levels

- In an atom, the electrons of similar energy are grouped in specific energy levels or shells. The first level nearest the nucleus can hold 2 electrons, the second level can hold 8 electrons, the third level will take up to 18 electrons.
- The electron shell arrangement is the number of electrons in each energy level beginning with the lowest energy level.
- The periodic law states that physical and chemical properties of elements will be repeated as the atomic number increases.
- The group number of an element gives the number of electrons in the outermost shell.
- Representative elements in a group have similar behavior because they have the same number of electrons in their outermost shells.

◆ Learning Exercise 2.6A

Write the electron shell arrangements for the following elements:

Element	Electron Level 1 2 3 4	Element	Electron Level 1 2 3 4
a. beryllium	_____	b. carbon	_____
c. potassium	_____	d. sodium	_____
e. phosphorus	_____	f. nitrogen	_____
g. chlorine	_____	h. silicon	_____

Answers   a. 2, 2   b. 2, 4   c. 2, 8, 8,1   d. 2, 8, 1   e. 2, 8, 5
f. 2, 5   g. 2, 8, 7   h. 2, 8, 4

◆ **Learning Exercise 2.6B**

State the number of electrons in the outermost energy level and the group number of each element.

Element	Electrons in the Outer energy level	Group number
a. sulfur	_____	_____
b. oxygen	_____	_____
c. magnesium	_____	_____
d. hydrogen	_____	_____
e. fluorine	_____	_____
f. aluminum	_____	_____
g. boron	_____	_____
h. chlorine	_____	_____

Answers
a. $6e^-$, Group 6A **b.** $6e^-$, Group 6A **c.** $2e^-$, Group 2A **d.** $1e^-$, Group 1A
e. $7e^-$, Group 7A **f.** $3e^-$, Group 3A **g.** $3e^-$, Group 3A **h.** $7e^-$, Group 7A

Check List for Chapter 2

You are ready to take the practice test for Chapter 2. Be sure that you have accomplished the following learning goals for this chapter. If you are not sure, review the section listed at the end of the goal. Then apply your new skills and understanding to the practice test.

After studying Chapter 2, I can successfully:

_____ Write the correct symbol or name for an element (2.1).

_____ Use the periodic table to identify the group and period of an element, and describe it as a metal or nonmetal (2.2).

_____ State the electrical charge, mass, and location of the protons, neutrons, and electrons in an atom (2.3).

_____ Given the atomic number and mass number of an atom, state the number of protons, neutrons, and electrons (2.4).

_____ Identify an isotope and describe the atomic mass of an element (2.5).

_____ Explain the periodic law (2.6).

_____ Write the electron shell arrangements for elements with atomic number 1–18 (2.6).

Practice Test for Chapter 2

Write or select the correct answer for each of the following questions.

Write the correct symbol for each of the elements listed:

1. potassium _____

2. phosphorus _____

3. calcium _____

4. carbon _____

5. sodium _____

Write the correct name for each of the symbols listed below:

6. Fe _____

7. Cu _____

8. Cl _____

9. Pb _____

10. Ag _____

11. The elements C, N, and O are part of a
  A. period   **B.** family   **C.** neither

12. The elements Li, Na, and K are part of a
  A. period   **B.** family   **C.** neither

13. What is the classification of an atom with 15 protons and 17 neutrons?
  A. metal   **B.** nonmetal   **C.** transition element   **D.** noble gas   **E.** halogen

14. What is the group number of the element with atomic number 3?
  A. 1   **B.** 2   **C.** 3   **D.** 7   **E.** 8

For questions 15 through 18, consider an atom with 12 protons and 13 neutrons.

15. This atom has an atomic number of
  A. 12   **B.** 13   **C.** 23   **D.** 24   **E.** 25

16. This atom has a mass number of
  A. 12   **B.** 13   **C.** 23   **D.** 24   **E.** 25

17. This is an atom of
  A. carbon   **B.** sodium   **C.** magnesium   **D.** aluminum   **E.** manganese

18. The number of electrons in this atom is
  A. 12   **B.** 13   **C.** 23   **D.** 24   **E.** 25

For questions 19 through 22, consider an atom of calcium with a mass number of 42.

19. This atom of calcium has an atomic number of
  A. 20   **B.** 22   **C.** 40   **D.** 41   **E.** 42

20. The number of protons in this atom of calcium is
  A. 20   **B.** 22   **C.** 40   **D.** 41   **E.** 42

21. The number of neutrons in this atom of calcium is
  A. 20   **B.** 22   **C.** 40   **D.** 41   **E.** 42

22. The number of electrons in this atomof calcium is
  A. 20   **B.** 22   **C.** 40   **D.** 41   **E.** 42

23. Platinum, ^{195}Pt, has
  A. 78 p^+, 78e^-, 78n   **B.** 195 p^+, 195e^-, 195n   **C.** 78p^+, 78e^-, 195n
  D. 78p^+, 78e^-, 117n   **E.** 78p^+, 117e^-, 117n

For questions 24 through 25, use the following list of atoms.

$^{14}_{7}V$ $^{16}_{8}W$ $^{19}_{9}X$ $^{16}_{7}Y$ $^{18}_{8}Z$

24. Which atoms(s) are isotopes of an atom with 8 protons and 9 neutrons?
  A. W   **B.** W, Z   **C.** X, Y   **D.** X   **E.** Y

25. Which atom(s) are isotopes of an atom with 7 protons and 8 neutrons?
  A. V   **B.** W   **C.** V, Y   **D.** W, Z   **E.** none

26. Which element would you expect to have properties most like oxygen?
  A. nitrogen   **B.** carbon   **C.** chlorine   **D.** argon   **E.** sulfur

27. Which of the following is an isotope of nitrogen?

    A. $^{14}_{8}N$ **B.** $^{7}_{3}N$ **C.** $^{10}_{5}N$ **D.** $^{4}_{2}He$ **E.** $^{15}_{7}N$

28. Except for helium, the number of electrons in the outer shells of the noble gases is

    A. 3   **B.** 5   **C.** 7   **D.** 8   **E.** 12

29. The electron shell arrangement for an oxygen atom is

    A. 2,4   **B.** 2,8   **C.** 2,6

    D. 2,4,2   **E.** 2,6,2

30. The electron shell arrangement for aluminum is

    A. 2,11   **B.** 2,8,5   **C.** 2,8,3

    D. 2,10,1   **E.** 2,2,6,3

Answers for the Practice Test

1. K	**2.** P	**3.** Ca	**4.** C	**5.** Na
6. iron	**7.** copper	**8.** chlorine	**9.** lead	**10.** silver
11. A	**12.** B	**13.** B	**14.** A	**15.** A
16. E	**17.** C	**18.** A	**19.** A	**20.** A
21. B	**22.** A	**23.** D	**24.** B	**25.** C
26. E	**27.** E	**28.** D	**29.** C	**30.** C

Answers and Solutions to Selected Text Problems

2.1   **a.** Cu   **b.** Si   **c.** K   **d.** N
        e. Fe   **f.** Ba   **g.** Pb   **h.** Sr

2.3   **a.** carbon   **b.** chlorine   **c.** iodine   **d.** mercury
        e. fluorine   **f.** argon   **g.** zinc   **h.** nickel

2.5   **a.** sodium and chlorine
        b. calcium, sulfur, and oxygen
        c. carbon, hydrogen, chlorine, nitrogen, and oxygen
        d. calcium, carbon, and oxygen

2.7   **a.** Period 2   **b.** Group 8A   **c.** Group 1A   **d.** Period 2

2.9   **a.** alkaline earth metal   **b.** transition element   **c.** noble gas
        d. alkali metal   **e.** halogen

2.11 **a.** C   **b.** He   **c.** Na   **d.** Ca   **e.** Al

2.13 On the periodic table, metals are elements located to the left of the heavy zigzag line, while the nonmetals are elements to the right.

        a. metal   **b.** nonmetal   **c.** metal   **d.** nonmetal
        e. nonmetal **f.** nonmetal   **g.** metal   **h.** metal

2.15 **a.** electron   **b.** proton   **c.** electron   **d.** neutron

2.17 The two most massive subatomic particles, protons and neutrons, are located in a very small region of the atom, which is called the nucleus.

2.19 Selection b (a proton and an electron) is the only one with a pair of particles having opposite charges.

2.21 Because the hair strands repel one another, there must be like electrical charges on each strand.

2.23 **a.** atomic number **b.** both   **c.** mass number   **d.** atomic number

2.25 **a.** lithium, Li   **b.** fluorine, F **c.** calcium, Ca **d.** zinc, Zn
        e. neon, Ne   **f.** silicon, Si   **g.** iodine, I   **h.** oxygen, O

2.27 **a.** 12 **b.** 30 **c.** 53 **d.** 19

2.29

Name of Element	Symbol	Atomic Number	Mass Number	Number of Protons	Number of Neutrons	Number of Electrons
Aluminum	Al	13	27	13	14	13
Magnesium	Mg	12	24	12	12	12
Potassium	K	19	39	19	20	19
Sulfur	S	16	31	16	15	16
Iron	Fe	26	56	26	30	26

2.31 **a.** Since the atomic number of aluminum is 13, every Al atom has 13 protons. An atom of aluminum with a mass number 27 and an atomic number 13 has 14 neutrons.
27 − 13 = 14 n Therefore, 13 protons, 14 neutrons, 13 electrons
   b. 24 protons, 28 neutrons, 24 electrons
   c. 16 protons, 18 neutrons, 16 electrons
   d. 26 protons, 30 neutrons, 26 electrons

2.33 **a.** $^{31}_{15}P$ **b.** $^{80}_{35}Br$ **c.** $^{27}_{13}Al$ **d.** $^{35}_{17}Cl$

2.35 **a.** $^{32}_{16}S$ $^{33}_{16}S$ $^{34}_{16}S$ $^{36}_{16}S$
   b. They all have the same atomic number, (the same number of protons and electrons).
   c. They have different numbers of neutrons, which is reflected in their mass numbers.
   d. The atomic mass of sulfur on the periodic table is the average atomic mass of all the naturally occurring isotopic masses.

2.37 The electrons surrounding a nucleus have specific energies. Electrons with similar energies will be found grouped together within a specific energy level.

2.39 **a.** 8 **b.** 5 **c.** 8 **d.** 0 **e.** 8

2.41 **a.** 2, 4 **b.** 2, 8, 8 **c.** 2, 8, 6 **d.** 2, 8, 4 **e.** 2, 8, 3 **f.** 2, 5

2.43 **a.** Li **b.** Mg **c.** H **d.** Cl **e.** O

2.45 **a.** boron: 2, 3   aluminum: 2, 8, 3 **b.** Three **c.** Group 3A

2.47 **a.** 2e⁻, Group 2A **b.** 7e⁻, Group 7A
   c. 6e⁻, Group 6A **d.** 5e⁻, Group 5A
   e. 2e⁻, Group 2A **f.** 7e⁻, Group 7A

2.49 Mg, Ca, and Sr have similar properties because they are members of the same group (family) in the periodic table. Chemical properties are related to the number of electrons in the outermost occupied energy level, and these three elements all have two electrons in their outermost shell.

2.51 Any element with a two-letter symbol has the first letter capitalized and the second letter in lower case. CO would indicate a compound made of the two elements carbon and oxygen.

2.53 **a.** Mg, magnesium **b.** Br, bromine **c.** Al, aluminum **d.** O, oxygen

2.55 **a.** The proton is a *positive* particle.
   b. The electrons are found *outside of the nucleus.*
   c. The nucleus is the *smallest* part of the atom.
   d. The *electron* has a negative charge.
   e. Most of the mass of the atom is due to its *protons and neutrons.*

2.57 **a.** 26 protons, 30 neutrons, 26 electrons
   b. $^{51}_{26}Fe$ **c.** $^{51}_{24}Cr$

2.59 **a.** $^{16}_{8}X$ $^{17}_{8}X$ $^{18}_{8}X$ All have 8 protons

     b. $^{16}_{8}X$ $^{17}_{8}X$ $^{18}_{8}X$ All are isotopes of oxygen

     c. $^{16}_{8}X$ $^{16}_{9}X$ Mass number of 16

         $^{18}_{10}X$ $^{18}_{8}X$ Mass number of 18

     d. $^{16}_{8}X$ $^{18}_{10}X$ Both have 8 neutrons

2.61 $1 \text{ in.} \times \dfrac{2.54 \text{ cm}}{1 \text{ in.}} \times \dfrac{1 \text{ atom}}{3.14 \times 10^{-8} \text{ cm}} = 8.09 \times 10^{7} \text{ atoms}$

2.63 Any two of the following in each part are correct responses:
  a. helium, beryllium, magnesium, calcium, strontium, barium, and radium
  b. oxygen, sulfur, selenium, tellurium, and polonium
  c. neon, argon, krypton, xenon, and radon
  d. boron, aluminum, gallium, indium, and thallium

2.65 Any two of the following in each part are correct responses:
  a. fluorine, chlorine, bromine, iodine, and astatine
  b. helium, neon, argon, krypton, xenon, and radon
  c. lithium, sodium, potassium, rubidium, cesium, and francium
  d. beryllium, magnesium, calcium, strontium, barium, and radium

Study Goals

♦ Identify the types of radiation as alpha particles, beta particles or gamma radiation.
♦ Describe the methods required for proper shielding for each type of radiation.
♦ Write an equation for an atom that undergoes radioactive decay.
♦ Identify some radioisotopes used in nuclear medicine.
♦ Calculate the amount of radioisotope that remains after a given number of half-lives.
♦ Describe nuclear fission and fusion.

Think About It

1. What is nuclear radiation?

2. Why do you receive more radiation if you live in the mountains or travel on an airplane?

3. In nuclear medicine, iodine-125 is used for detecting a tumor in the thyroid. What does the number 125 used in the name indicate?

4. What type of radiation is emitted by smoke detectors?

5. How are living cells damaged by radiation?

6. How does nuclear fission differ from nuclear fusion?

7. Why is there a concern about radon in our homes?

Key Terms

Match each the following key terms with the correct definition.

a. radioactive nucleus   **b.** half-life   **c.** curie
d. nuclear fission   **e.** alpha particle

1. _____ A particle identical to a helium nucleus produced in a radioactive nucleus.

2. _____ The time required for one-half of a radioactive sample to undergo radioactive decay.

3. _____ A unit of radiation that measures the activity of a sample.

4. _____ A process in which large nuclei split into smaller nuclei with the release of energy.

5. _____ A nucleus that spontaneously emits radiation

Answers   **1.** e   **2.** b   **3.** c   **4.** d   **5.** a

3.1 Radioactivity

- Radioactive isotopes have unstable nuclei that break down (decay) spontaneously emitting alpha (α), beta (β), and gamma (γ) radiation.
- An alpha particle is the same as a helium nucleus; it contains two protons and two neutrons. A beta particle is a high-energy electron and a gamma ray is high-energy radiation.
- Because radiation can damage the cells in the body, proper protection must be used: shielding, time limitation, and distance.

◆ Learning Exercise 3.1A

Study Note
It is important to learn the symbols for the radiation particles in order to describe the different types of radiation: $\quad\quad\quad _1^1 H$ or $_1^1 p \quad\quad _0^1 n \quad\quad _{-1}^0 \beta$ or $_{-1}^0 e \quad\quad _2^4 He$ or $_2^4 \alpha$ $\quad\quad\quad\quad$ *proton* $\quad\quad$ *neutron* $\quad\quad$ *electron* $\quad\quad$ *alpha particle*

Match the description in column B with the terms in column A:

A		B	
1. ____ $_8^{18}O$		a.	Symbol for a beta particle
2. ____ γ		b.	Symbol for an alpha particle
3. ____ radioactive isotope		c.	An atom that emits radiation
4. ____ $_2^4 He$		d.	Symbol for an atom of oxygen
5. ____ β		e.	Symbol for gamma radiation

Answers   **1.** d   **2.** e   **3.** c   **4.** b   **5.** a

◆ Learning Exercise 3.1B

Discuss some things you can do to minimize the amount of radiation received if you work with a radioactive substance. Describe how each method helps to limit the amount of radiation you would receive.

Answer

Three ways to minimize exposure to radiation are: 1) use shielding, 2) keep time short in the radioactive area, and 3) keep as much distance as possible from the radioactive materials. Shielding such as clothing and gloves stops alpha and beta particles from reaching your skin, while lead or concrete will absorb gamma rays. Limiting the time spent near radioactive samples reduces exposure time. Increasing the distance from a radioactive source reduces the intensity of radiation.

◆ **Learning Exercise 3.1C**

What type(s) of radiation (alpha, beta and/or gamma) would each of the following shielding materials protect you from?

a. clothing _____   b. skin _____

c. paper _____   d. concrete _____

e. lead wall _____

Answers   a. alpha, beta   b. alpha   c. alpha, beta
                    d. alpha, beta, gamma   e. alpha, beta, gamma

3.2 Nuclear Equations

● A balanced nuclear equation is used to represent the changes that take place in the nuclei of the reactants and products.
● The new isotopes and the type of radiation emitted can be determined from the symbols that show the mass numbers and atomic numbers of the isotopes in the nuclear reaction.

Radioactive nucleus → new nucleus + radiation
      Total of the mass numbers are equal

$$^{11}_{6}C \rightarrow \, ^{7}_{4}Be + \, ^{4}_{2}He$$

    Total of the atomic numbers are equal
● A new isotope is produced when a nonradioactive isotope is bombarded by a small particle such as a proton, an alpha, or a beta particle.

$$^{10}_{5}B \quad + \quad ^{4}_{2}He \quad \rightarrow \quad ^{13}_{7}N \quad + \quad ^{1}_{0}n$$

   stable   *bombarding*   *new*   *neutron*
   nucleus   *particle (α)*   *nucleus*   *emitted*

◆ **Learning Exercise 3.2A**

Study Note
When balancing nuclear equations for radioactive decay, be sure that
1. the mass number of the reactant must equal the sum of the mass numbers of the products.
2. the atomic number of the reactant must equal the sum of the atomic numbers of the products.

Write a nuclear symbol that completes each of the following nuclear equations:

a. $^{66}_{29}Cu \rightarrow \, ^{66}_{30}Zn + ?$ a. _____

b. $^{127}_{53}I \rightarrow \, ^{1}_{0}n + ?$ b. _____

c. $^{238}_{92}U \rightarrow \, ^{4}_{2}He + ?$ c. _____

d. $^{24}_{11}Na \rightarrow \, ^{0}_{-1}e + ?$ d. _____

e. $? \rightarrow \, ^{30}_{14}Si + \, ^{0}_{-1}e$ e. _____

Answers   a. $^{0}_{-1}e$ b. $^{126}_{53}I$ c. $^{234}_{90}Th$ d. $^{24}_{12}Mg$ e. $^{30}_{13}Al$

◆ **Learning Exercise 3.2B**

Study Note
In balancing nuclear transmutation equations (bombardment by small particles)
1. The sum of the mass numbers of the reactants must equal the sum of the mass numbers of the products.
2. The sum of the atomic numbers of the reactants must equal the sum of the atomic numbers of the products.

Complete the following equations for bombardment reactions:

a. $^{40}_{20}Ca$ + ? → $^{40}_{19}K$ + $^{1}_{1}H$ a. _____

b. $^{27}_{13}Al$ + $^{1}_{0}n$ → $^{24}_{11}Na$ + ?   b. _____

c. $^{10}_{5}B$ + $^{1}_{0}n$ → $^{4}_{2}He$ + ?   c. _____

d. $^{23}_{11}Na$ + ? → $^{23}_{12}Mg$ + $^{1}_{0}n$ d. _____

e. $^{197}_{79}Au$ + $^{1}_{1}H$ → ? + $^{1}_{0}n$ e. _____

Answers   a. $^{1}_{0}n$ b. $^{4}_{2}He$ c. $^{7}_{3}Li$ d. $^{1}_{1}H$ e. $^{197}_{80}Hg$

3.3 Radiation Measurement

- A Geiger counter is used to detect radiation. When radiation passes through the gas in the counter tube, some atoms of gas are ionized producing an electrical current.
- The activity of a radioactive sample measures the number of nuclear transformations per second. The curie (Ci) is equal to 3.7×10^{10} disintegrations in 1 second.
- The radiation dose absorbed by a gram of material such as body tissue is measured in units of rad and gray.
- The biological damage of different types of radiation on the body is measured in radiation units of rem and sievert.

◆ **Learning Exercise 3.3**

Match each type of measurement unit with the radiation process measured.

a. curie   b. rad   c. gray   d. rem

1. _____ The amount of radiation absorbed by one gram of material.

2. _____ An activity of 3.7×10^{10} disintegrations per second.

3. _____ The biological damage caused by different kinds of radiation.

4. _____ A unit of absorbed dose equal to 100 rads

Answers   1. c   2. a   3. e   4. d

3.4 Half-Life of a Radioisotope

- The half-life of a radioactive sample is the time required for one half of the sample to decay (emit radiation).
- Most radioisotopes used in medicine, such as Tc-99m and I-131, have short half-lives. By comparison, many naturally occurring radioisotopes, such as C-14, Ra-226, and U-238, have long half-lives. For example, potassium-42 has a half-life of 12 hr, whereas, potassium-40 takes 1.3×10^9 years for one-half of the radioactive sample to decay.

◆ Learning Exercise 3.4

a. Suppose you have an 80 mg sample of iodine-125. If iodine-125 has a half-life of 60 days, how many mg are radioactive

    (1) after one half-life?

    (2) after two half-lives?

    (3) after 240 days?

b. ^{99m}Tc has a half-life of 6 hours. If a technician picked up a 16 mg sample at 8 AM, how much of the radioactive sample remained at 8 PM that same day?

c. Phosphorus-32 has a half-life of 14 days. How much of a 240 μg sample will be radioactive after 56 days?

d. Iodine-131 has a half-life of 8 days. How many days will it take for 80 mg of I-131 to decay to 5 mg?

e. Suppose a group of archaeologists digs up some pieces of a wooden boat at an ancient site. When a sample of the wood is analyzed for C-14, scientists determine that 12.5% or 1/8 of the original amount of C-14 remains. If the half-life of carbon-14 is 5730 years, how long ago was the boat made?

Answers   **a.** (1) 40 mg (2) 20 mg (3) 5 mg   **b.** 4.0 mg
              c. 15 μg   **d.** 32 days   **e.** 17 200 years ago

3.5 Medical Applications Using Radioactivity

- In nuclear medicine, radioactive isotopes are given that go to specific sites in the body.
- For diagnostic work, radioisotopes are used that emit gamma rays, and produce nonradioactive products.
- By detecting the radiation emitted by medical radioisotopes, evaluations can be made about the location and extent of an injury, disease, or tumor, blood flow, or the level of function of a particular organ.

◆ **Learning Exercise 3.5**

Write the nuclear symbol for each of the following radioactive isotopes:

a. _____ Iodine-131 used to study thyroid gland activity.

b. _____ Phosphorus-32 used to locate brain tumors.

c. _____ Sodium-24 used to determine blood flow and to locate a blood clot or embolism.

d. _____ Nitrogen-13 is used in positron emission tomography.

Answers   **a.** $^{131}_{53}I$ **b.** $^{32}_{15}P$ **c.** $^{24}_{11}Na$ **d.** $^{13}_{7}N$

3.6 Nuclear Fission and Fusion

- In fission, a large nucleus breaks apart into smaller pieces releasing one or more types of radiation, and a great amount of energy.
- In fusion, small nuclei combine to form a larger nucleus, which releases great amounts of energy.

◆ **Learning Exercise 3.6**

Discuss the nuclear processes of fission and fusion for the production of energy.

Answer   *Nuclear fission* is a splitting of the atom into two or more nuclei accompanied by the release of large amounts of energy and radiation. In the process of *nuclear fusion*, two or more nuclei combine to form a heavier nucleus and release a large amount of energy. However, fusion requires a considerable amount of energy to initiate the process.

Check List for Chapter 3

You are ready to take the practice test for Chapter 3. Be sure that you have accomplished the following learning goals for this chapter. If you are not sure, review the section listed at the end of the goal. Then apply your new skills and understanding to the practice test.

After studying Chapter 3, I can successfully:

_____ Describe alpha, beta, and gamma radiation (3.1).

_____ Write a nuclear equation showing mass number and atomic number for radioactive decay (3.2).

_____ Write a nuclear equation for the formation of a radioactive isotope (3.2).

_____ Describe the detection and measurement of radiation (3.3).

_____ Given a half-life, calculate the amount of radioisotope remaining after one or more half-lives (3.4).

_____ Describe the use of radioisotopes in medicine (3.5).

_____ Describe the processes of nuclear fission and fusion (3.6).

Practice Test for Chapter 3

1. The correctly written symbol for an atom of sulfur would be

   A. $^{30}_{16}Su$ **B.** $^{14}_{30}Si$ **C.** $^{30}_{16}S$ **D.** $^{30}_{16}Si$ **E.** $^{16}_{30}S$

2. Alpha particles are composed of

   A. protons   **B.** neutrons   **C.** electrons
   D. protons and electrons   **E.** protons and neutrons

3. Gamma radiation is a type of radiation that

   A. originates in the electron shells
   B. is most dangerous
   C. is least dangerous
   D. is the heaviest
   E. goes the shortest distance

4. The charge on an alpha particle is

   A. −1   **B.** +1   **C.** −2   **D.** +2   **E.** +4

5. Beta particles formed in a radioactive nucleus are

   A. protons   **B.** neutrons   **C.** electrons
   D. protons and electrons   **E.** protons and neutrons

For questions 6 through 10, select from the following:

   A. $^{0}_{-1}X$ **B.** $^{4}_{2}X$ **C.** $^{1}_{1}X$ **D.** $^{1}_{0}X$ **E.** $^{0}_{0}X$

6. An alpha particle

7. A beta particle

8. A gamma ray

9. A proton

10. A neutron

11. Shielding from gamma rays is provided by

   A. skin   **B.**   paper   **C.**   clothing   **D.**   lead   **E.**   air

12. The skin will provide shielding from

   A. alpha particles   **B.** beta particles   **C.** gamma rays
   D. ultraviolet rays   **E.** X rays

13. The radioisotope iodine-131 is used as a radioactive tracer for studying thyroid gland activity. The symbol for iodine-131 is

   A. I   **B.** $_{131}I$ **C.** $^{131}_{53}I$ **D.** $^{53}_{131}I$ **E.** $^{78}_{53}I$

14. When an atom emits an alpha particle, its atomic mass will

   A. increase by 1.   **B.** increase by 2.   **C.** increase by 4.
   D. decrease by 4.   **E.** not change

15. When a nucleus emits a beta particle, the atomic number of the new nucleus

   A. increases by 1   **B.** increases by 2   **C.** decreases by 1
   D. decreases by 2   **E.** will not change.

16. When a nucleus emits a gamma ray, the atomic number of the new nucleus

   A. increases by 1   **B.** increases by 2   **C.** decreases by 1
   D. decreases by 2   **E.** will not change.

For questions 17 through 20, select the particle that completes each of the equations.

    A. neutron   **B.** alpha particle   **C.** beta particle   **D.** gamma ray

17. $^{126}_{50}Sn \rightarrow {}^{126}_{51}Sb + ?$

18. $^{69}_{30}Zn \rightarrow {}^{69}_{31}Ga + ?$

19. $^{99m}_{43}Tc \rightarrow {}^{99}_{43}Tc + ?$

20. $^{149}_{62}Sm \rightarrow {}^{145}_{60}Nd + ?$

21. What symbol completes the following reaction?

$$^{14}_{7}N + {}^{1}_{0}n \rightarrow ? + {}^{1}_{1}H$$

    A. $^{15}_{8}O$ **B.** $^{15}_{6}C$ **C.** $^{14}_{8}O$ **D.** $^{14}_{6}C$ **E.** $^{15}_{7}N$

22. To complete this nuclear equation, you need to write

$$^{54}_{26}Fe + ? \rightarrow {}^{57}_{28}Ni + {}^{1}_{0}n$$

    A. an alpha particle   **B.** a beta particle   **C.** gamma
    D. neutron   **E.** proton

23. The name of the unit used to measure the number of disintegrations per second is

    A. curie   **B.** rad   **C.** rem   **D.** RBE   **E.** MRI

24. The rem is a unit used to measure

    A. activity of a radioactive sample
    B. biological damage of different types of radiation
    C. radiation absorbed
    D. background radiation

25. Radiation can cause

    A. nausea   **B.** a lower white cell count   **C.** fatigue
    D. hair loss   **E.** all of these

26. Radioisotopes used in medical diagnosis

    A. have short half-lives   **B.** emit only gamma rays
    C. locate in specific organs   **D.** produce nonradioactive nuclei.
    E. all of these

27. The imaging technique that uses the energy emitted by exciting the nuclei of hydrogen atoms is

    A. computerized tomography (CT)
    B. positron emission tomography (PET)
    C. radioactive tracer
    D. magnetic resonance imaging (MRI)
    E. radiation

28. The imaging technique that detects the absorption of x rays by body tissues is

    A. computerized tomography (CT)
    B. positron emission tomography (PET)
    C. radioactive tracer
    D. magnetic resonance imaging (MRI)
    E. radiation

29. The time required for a radioisotope to decay is measured by its

    A. half-life   **B.** protons   **C.** activity   **D.** fusion   **E.** radioisotope

30. Oxygen-15 used in PET imaging has a half-life of 2 min. How many half-lives have occurred in the 10 minutes it takes to prepare the sample?

    A. 2   **B.** 3   **C.** 4   **D.** 5   **E.** 6

31. Iodine-131 has a half-life of 8 days. How long will it take for a 160 mg sample to decay to 10 mg?

    A. 8 days   **B.** 16 days   **C.** 32 days   **D.** 40 days   **E.** 48 days

32. Phosphorus-32 has a half-life of 14 days. After 28 days, how many mg of a 100 mg sample will still be radioactive?

    A. 75 mg   **B.** 50 mg   **C.** 40 mg   **D.** 25 mg   **E.** 12.5 mg

33. The "splitting" of a large nucleus to form smaller particles accompanied by a release of energy is called

    A. radioisotope   **B.** fission   **C.** fusion   **D.** rem   **E.** half-life

34. The process of combining small nuclei to form larger nuclei is

    A. radioisotope   **B.** fission   **C.** fusion   **D.** rem   **E.** half-life

35. The fusion reaction

    A. occurs in the sun
    B. forms larger nuclei from smaller nuclei
    C. requires extremely high temperatures
    D. releases a large amount of energy
    E. all of the these

Answers to the Practice Test

1. C	**2.** E	**3.** B	**4.** D	**5.** C
6. B	**7.** A	**8.** E	**9.** C	**10.** D
11. D	**12.** A	**13.** C	**14.** D	**15.** A
16. E.	**17.** C	**18.** C	**19.** D	**20.** B
21. D	**22.** A	**23.** A	**24.** B	**25.** E
26. E	**27.** D	**28.** A	**29.** A	**30.** D
31. C	**32.** D	**33.** B	**34.** C	**35.** E

Answers and Solutions to Selected Problems

3.1 a. An α-particle and a helium nucleus both contain 2 protons and 2 neutrons. However, an α-particle has no electrons and carries a 2+ charge. Alpha-particles are emitted from unstable nuclei during radioactive decay.

    b. α, $_2^4\text{He}$

3.3 a. $_{19}^{39}\text{K}$, $_{19}^{40}\text{K}$, $_{19}^{41}\text{K}$

    b. Each isotope has 19 protons and 19 electrons, but they differ in the number of neutrons present. Potassium-39 has 20 neutrons, potassium-40 has 21 neutrons, and potassium-41 has 22 neutrons.

3.5

Medical Use	Nuclear Symbol	Mass Number	Number of Protons	Number of Neutrons
Heart imaging	$^{201}_{81}\text{Tl}$	201	81	120
Radiation therapy	$^{60}_{27}\text{Co}$	60	27	33
Abdominal scan	$^{67}_{31}\text{Ga}$	67	31	36
Hyperthyroidism	$^{131}_{53}\text{I}$	131	53	78
Leukemia treatment	$^{32}_{15}\text{P}$	32	15	17

3.7 **a.** α, $^{4}_{2}\text{He}$ **b.** $^{1}_{0}\text{n}$ **c.** β, $^{0}_{-1}\text{e}$ **d.** $^{15}_{7}\text{N}$ **e.** $^{125}_{53}\text{I}$

3.9 **a.** β (or e) **b.** α (or He) **c.** n **d.** Na **e.** C

3.11 **a.** Because β-particles move faster than α-particles, they can penetrate further into tissue.
   b. Ionizing radiation breaks bonds and forms reactive species that cause undesirable reactions in the cells.
   c. X-ray technicians leave the room to increase their distance from the radiation source. They are also shielded by a thick wall or one that contains a lead lining.
   d. Wearing gloves shields the skin from α and β radiation.

3.13 The mass number of the radioactive atom is reduced by 4 when an alpha particle is emitted. The unknown product will have an atomic number that is 2 less than the atomic number of the radioactive atom.

   a. $^{208}_{84}\text{Po} \rightarrow {}^{204}_{82}\text{Pb} + {}^{4}_{2}\text{He}$ **b.** $^{232}_{90}\text{Th} \rightarrow {}^{228}_{88}\text{Ra} + {}^{4}_{2}\text{He}$

   c. $^{251}_{102}\text{No} \rightarrow {}^{247}_{100}\text{Fm} + {}^{4}_{2}\text{He}$

3.15 **a.** $^{25}_{11}\text{Na} \rightarrow {}^{25}_{12}\text{Mg} + {}^{0}_{-1}\text{e}$ **b.** $^{20}_{8}\text{O} \rightarrow {}^{20}_{9}\text{F} + {}^{0}_{-1}\text{e}$

   c. $^{92}_{38}\text{Sr} \rightarrow {}^{92}_{39}\text{Y} + {}^{0}_{-1}\text{e}$

3.17 **a.** $^{28}_{13}\text{Al} \rightarrow {}^{28}_{14}\text{Si} + {}^{0}_{-1}\text{e}$

   b. $^{87}_{36}\text{Kr} \rightarrow {}^{86}_{36}\text{Kr} + {}^{1}_{0}\text{n}$

   c. $^{66}_{29}\text{Cu} \rightarrow {}^{66}_{30}\text{Zn} + {}^{0}_{-1}\text{e}$

3.19 **a.** $^{9}_{4}\text{Be} + {}^{1}_{0}\text{n} \rightarrow {}^{10}_{4}\text{Be}$

   b. $^{32}_{16}\text{S} + {}^{0}_{-1}\text{e} \rightarrow {}^{32}_{15}\text{P}$

   c. $^{27}_{13}\text{Al} + {}^{1}_{0}\text{n} \rightarrow {}^{24}_{11}\text{Na} + {}^{4}_{2}\text{He}$

3.21 **a.** When radiation enters the Geiger counter, it ionizes a gas in the detection tube. The ions created in the tube move toward an electrode of opposite charge (recall that opposite electrical charges attract one another). This flow of charge produces an electric current, which is detected by the instrument.
   b. The becquerel (Bq), is the SI unit for activity. The curie (Ci), is the original unit for activity of radioactive samples.
   c. The SI unit for absorbed dose is the gray (Gy). The rad (radiation absorbed dose) is a unit of radiation absorbed per gram of sample. It is the older unit.
   d. A kilogray is 1000 gray (Gy), which is equivalent to 100 000 rads.

3.23 $70.0 \ \text{kg} \times \dfrac{4.20 \ \mu\text{Ci}}{1 \ \text{kg}} = 294 \ \mu\text{Ci}$

3.25 While flying a plane, a pilot is exposed to higher levels of background radiation because there is less atmosphere to act as a shield against cosmic radiation.

3.27 Half-life is the time required for one-half of a radioactive sample to decay.

3.29 **a.** After one half-life, one-half of the sample would be radioactive: $80.0 \ \text{mg} \times \frac{1}{2} = 40.0 \ \text{mg}$

     b. After two half-lives, one-fourth of the sample would still be radioactive

        $80.0 \ \text{mg} \times \frac{1}{2} \times \frac{1}{2} = 80.0 \ \text{mg} \times \frac{1}{4} = 20.0 \ \text{mg}$

     c. $18 \ \text{hr} \times \dfrac{1 \ \text{half-life}}{6.0 \ \text{hr}} = 3.0 \ \text{half-lives}$

        $80.0 \ \text{mg} \times \frac{1}{2} \times \frac{1}{2} \times \frac{1}{2} = 80.0 \ \text{mg} \times \frac{1}{8} = 10.0 \ \text{mg}$

     d. $24 \ \text{hr} \times \dfrac{1 \ \text{half-life}}{6.0 \ \text{hr}} = 4.0 \ \text{half-lives}$

        $80.0 \ \text{mg} \times \frac{1}{2} \times \frac{1}{2} \times \frac{1}{2} \times \frac{1}{2} = 80.0 \ \text{mg} \times \frac{1}{16} = 5.00 \ \text{mg}$

3.31 The radiation level in a radioactive sample is cut in half with each passing half-life. To answer the question we must first determine the number of half-lives. $\frac{1}{4} = \frac{1}{2} \times \frac{1}{2} = 2$ half-lives

Because each half-life is 64 days, it will take 128 days for the radiation level of strontium-85 to fall to one fourth of its original value. 2 half-lives × 64 days/half-life = 128 days

To determine the amount of time for the strontium-85 to drop to one-eight its original activity, we calculate the number of half-lives. $\frac{1}{8} = \frac{1}{2} \times \frac{1}{2} \times \frac{1}{2} = 3$ half-lives

Because each half-life is 64 days, it will take 192 days for the radiation level of strontium-85 to fall to one eighth of its original value. 3 half-lives × 64 days/half-life = 192 days

3.33 **a.** Because the elements calcium and phosphorus are part of bone, any calcium and/or phosphorus atom, regardless of isotope, will be carried to and become part of the bony structures in the body. Once there, the radiation emitted by the radioisotope can be used for diagnosis or treatment of bone diseases.

     b. Strontium is chemically similar to calcium, so it too will be carried to the bones. Once in the bone, the radiation emitted can destroy healthy bone and bony structures.

3.35 $4.0 \ \text{mL} \times \dfrac{45 \ \mu\text{Ci}}{1 \ \text{mL}} = 180 \ \mu\text{Ci}$

3.37 Nuclear fission is the splitting of a large atom into smaller fragments with a simultaneous release of large amounts of energy.

3.39 $^{235}_{92}\text{U} + ^{1}_{0}\text{n} \rightarrow ^{131}_{50}\text{Sn} + ^{103}_{42}\text{Mo} + 2 \ ^{1}_{0}\text{n}$

3.41 **a.** fission   **b.** fusion   **c.** fission   **d.** fusion

3.43 Both carbon-12 and carbon-14 contain 6 protons and 6 electrons, but there are only 6 neutrons in a carbon-12 nucleus while a carbon-14 nucleus has 8. Carbon-12 is a stable isotope, but carbon-14 is radioactive and will emit radiation.

3.45 **a.** Alpha (α) and beta (β) radiation consist of particles emitted from an unstable nucleus, while gamma (γ) rays are radiation emitted as pure energy.

    b. Alpha radiation is abbreviated as α, $^4_2\alpha$, and ^4_2He. Beta radiation is abbreviated as β, β^-, $^0_{-1}\beta$, and $^0_{-1}\text{e}$. Gamma radiation is abbreviated as γ and $^0_0\gamma$.

    c. Alpha particles cannot penetrate skin, beta particles penetrate 4 to 5 mm into body tissue, and gamma radiation easily passes through body tissues.

    d. Lightweight clothing or a piece of paper will shield against alpha particles, heavy clothing and gloves shield against beat particles, thick concrete and lead will shield against gamma rays.

3.47 **a.** $^{225}_{90}\text{Th} \rightarrow {}^{221}_{88}\text{Ra} + {}^4_2\text{He}$ **b.** $^{210}_{83}\text{Bi} \rightarrow {}^{206}_{81}\text{Tl} + {}^4_2\text{He}$

    c. $^{137}_{55}\text{Cs} \rightarrow {}^{137}_{56}\text{Ba} + {}^0_{-1}\text{e}$ **d.** $^{126}_{50}\text{Sn} \rightarrow {}^{126}_{51}\text{Sb} + {}^0_{-1}\text{e}$

3.49 **a.** $^{14}_7\text{N} + {}^4_2\text{He} \rightarrow {}^{17}_8\text{O} + {}^1_1\text{H}$

    b. $^{27}_{13}\text{Al} + {}^4_2\text{He} \rightarrow {}^{30}_{14}\text{Si} + {}^1_1\text{H}$

    c. $^{235}_{92}\text{U} + {}^1_0\text{n} \rightarrow {}^{90}_{38}\text{Sr} + 3\,{}^1_0\text{n} + {}^{143}_{54}\text{Xe}$

3.51 **a.** $^{16}_8\text{O} + {}^{16}_8\text{O} \rightarrow {}^4_2\text{He} + {}^{28}_{14}\text{Si}$

    b. $^{249}_{98}\text{Cf} + {}^{18}_8\text{O} \rightarrow {}^{263}_{106}\text{Sg} + 4\,{}^1_0\text{n}$

    c. $^{222}_{86}\text{Rn} \rightarrow {}^4_2\text{He} + {}^{218}_{84}\text{Po}$

Then the polonium-218 decays as follows:

    $^{218}_{84}\text{Po} \rightarrow {}^4_2\text{He} + {}^{214}_{82}\text{Pb}$

3.53 Half of a radioactive sample decays with each half-life:

    ½ lives   (1)   (2)
         1.2 g $\rightarrow$ 0.60 g $\rightarrow$ 0.30 g

Therefore, the amount of phosphorus-32 will drop to 0.30 g in two half-lives, which is 28 days. One half-life is 14 days. 28 days/2 half-lives = 14 days/half-life

3.55 **a.** $^{131}_{53}\text{I} \rightarrow {}^0_{-1}\text{e} + {}^{131}_{54}\text{Xe}$

    b. First we must determine the number of half-lives.

$$40 \text{ days} \times \frac{1 \text{ half-life}}{8.0 \text{ days}} = 5.0 \text{ half-lifes}$$

Now we can calculate the number of grams of Iodine-131 remaining:
12.0 g × (½ × ½ × ½ × ½ × ½) = 12.0 g × ¹⁄₃₂ = 0.375 g

    c. One-half of a radioactive sample decays with each half-life:

    ½ lives (1)   (2)   (3)   (4)
         48 g $\rightarrow$ 24 g $\rightarrow$ 12 g $\rightarrow$ 6.0 g $\rightarrow$ 3.0 g

When 3.0 g remain, four half-lives must have passed. Because each half-life is 8.0 days, we can calculate the number of days that the sample required to decay to 3.0 g.

$$4 \text{ half-lives} \times \frac{8.0 \text{ days}}{1 \text{ half-life}} = 32 \text{ days}$$

3.57 First, calculate the number of half-lives that have passed since the nurse was exposed:

$$36 \text{ hrs} \times \frac{1 \text{ half-life}}{12 \text{ hrs}} = 3.0 \text{ half-lives}$$

Because the activity of a radioactive sample is cut in half with each half-life, the activity must have been double its present value prior to each half-life. For 3.0 half-lives, we need to double the value 3 times. $\quad 2.0 \ \mu\text{Ci} \times (2 \times 2 \times 2) = 16 \ \mu\text{Ci}$

3.59 First, calculate the number of half-lives:

$$24 \text{ hrs} \times \frac{1 \text{ half-life}}{6.0 \text{ hrs}} = 4.0 \text{ half-lives}$$

And now calculate the amount of technetium-99^m that remains after 4 half-lives have passed:
$120 \text{ mg} \times (\frac{1}{2} \times \frac{1}{2} \times \frac{1}{2} \times \frac{1}{2}) = 120 \text{ mg} \times \frac{1}{16} = 7.5 \text{ mg}$

3.61 Irradiating foods kills bacteria that are responsible for food borne illnesses and food spoilage. As a result, shelf life of the food is extended.

3.63 Nuclear fission is the splitting of a large atom into smaller fragments with a simultaneous release of large amounts of energy. Nuclear fusion occurs when two (or more) nuclei combine (fuse) to form a larger species, with a simultaneous release of large amounts of energy.

3.65 Fusion reactions naturally occur in the stars, such as our sun.

Compounds and Their Bonds

Study Goals

♦ Write an electron dot formula for an atom of a representative element.
♦ Use the octet rule to determine the ionic charge of ions for representative elements.
♦ Use charge balance to write an ionic formula.
♦ Draw the electron dot structure for covalent compounds.
♦ Write the correct names for ionic and covalent compounds.
♦ Write ionic formulas and names of compound with polyatomic ions.
♦ Use VSEPR theory to determine the shape and bond angles of a molecule.
♦ Identify a covalent compound as polar or nonpolar.

Think About It

1. What are the valence electrons in an atom?

2. How does a compound differ from an element?

3. What are some compounds listed on the labels of your vitamins, toothpaste, and foods?

4. What makes salt an ionic compound?

Key Terms

Match each the following key terms with the correct definition.

a. valence electrons   **b.** ion   **c.** ionic bond
d. covalent bond   **e.** octet

1. _____ A sharing of valence electrons by two atoms.

2. _____ An arrangement of 8 electrons in the outer shell.

3. _____ The attraction between positively and negatively charged particles.

4. _____ The electrons that make up the outmost energy level (shell) of an atom.

5. _____ An atom or group of atoms with a positive or negative charge.

Answers   **1.** D   **2.** E   **3.** C   **4.** A   **5.** B

4.1 Valence Electrons

● The electrons located in the outermost energy level of an atom play a major role in determining its chemical properties.
● An electron-dot structure represents the valence electrons in an atom.

◆ Learning Exercise 4.1A
Add dots to represent the valence electrons of each atom:

1. O	2. Cl	3. Na	4. Ca	5. Li
6. H	7. P	8. S	9. Mg	10. C

Answers

1. $:\ddot{O}\cdot$ 2. $:\ddot{\underset{\cdot\cdot}{C}l}\cdot$ 3. $Na\cdot$ 4. $\dot{C}a\cdot$ 5. $Li\cdot$

6. $H\cdot$ 7. $\cdot\dot{\underset{\cdot\cdot}{P}}\cdot$ 8. $:\ddot{S}\cdot$ 9. $Mg\cdot$ 10. $\cdot\dot{C}\cdot$

◆ **Learning Exercise 4.1B**

For each of the following elements, write the electron shell arrangement and the number of valence electrons. Indicate the elements that have octets.

Element	Electron Shell Arrangements	Number of Valence Electrons	Octet? (yes/no)
C			
Ne			
Ca			
Ar			
N			

Answers

Element	Electron Shell Arrangement	Number of Valence Electrons	Octet? (yes/no)
C	2,4	4	No
Ne	2,8	8	Yes
Ca	2,8,8,2	2	No
Ar	2,8,8	8	Yes
N	2,5	5	No

4.2 Octet Rule and Ions

- The stability of the noble gases is associated with 8 electrons, an octet, in their valence shells. Helium is stable with 2 electrons in its valence shell.

  He 2   Ar   2-8-8   Ne   2-8

  Atoms of elements other than the noble gases achieve stability by losing, gaining or sharing their valence electrons with other atoms in the formation of compounds.

- A metal of the representative elements in Groups 1, 2 and 3 achieves a noble gas electron arrangement by losing its valence electrons to form a positively charged cation 1+, 2+, or 3+.
- When a nonmetal forms ions, electrons add to the valence shell to give an octet, and form a negatively charged anion with a charge of 3–, 2–, or 1–.

◆ **Learning Exercise 4.2A**

Study Note

When an atom loses or gains electrons, it acquires the electron arrangement of its nearest nobel gas. For example, sodium loses 1 electron, which gives the Na^+ ion a arrangement like neon. Oxygen gains 2 electrons to give an oxide ion O^{2-} a arrangement like neon.

The following elements lose electrons when they form ions. Indicate the group number, the number of electrons lost and the ion (symbol and charge) for each of the following:

Element	Group Number	Electrons Lost	Ion Formed
Magnesium			
Sodium			
Calcium			
Potassium			
Aluminum			

Answers

Element	Group Number	Electrons Lost	Ion Formed
Magnesium	2A	2	Mg^{2+}
Sodium	1A	1	Na^+
Calcium	2A	2	Ca^{2+}
Potassium	1A	1	K^+
Aluminum	3A	3	Al^{3+}

◆ **Learning Exercise 4.2B**

Study Note

The valence electrons are the electrons in the outermost shell (energy level) of an atom. For representative elements, you can determine the number of valence electrons by looking at the group number.

The following elements gain electrons when they form ions. Indicate the group number, the number of electrons gained and the ion (symbol and charge) for each of the following:

Element	Group Number	Electrons Gained	Ion Formed
Chlorine			
Oxygen			
Nitrogen			
Fluorine			
Sulfur			

Answers

Element	Group Number	Electrons Gained	Ion Formed
Chlorine	7A	1	Cl^-
Oxygen	6A	2	O^{2-}
Nitrogen	5A	3	N^{3-}
Fluorine	7A	1	F^-
Sulfur	6A	2	S^{2-}

4.3 Ionic Compounds

- In the formulas of ionic compounds, the total positive charge is equal to the total negative charge. For example, the compound magnesium chloride, $MgCl_2$, contains Mg^{2+} and 2 Cl^-. The sum of the charges is zero: $(2+) + 2(-) = 0$.
- When two or more ions are needed for charge balance, that number is indicated by subscripts in the formula.

◆ Learning Exercise 4.3A

For this exercise, you may want to cut pieces of paper that represent typical positive and negative ions as shown below. To determine an ionic formula, place the pieces together (positive ion first). Add more positive ions or negatives to complete a geometric shape. Write the number of positive ions and negative ions as the subscripts for the formula.

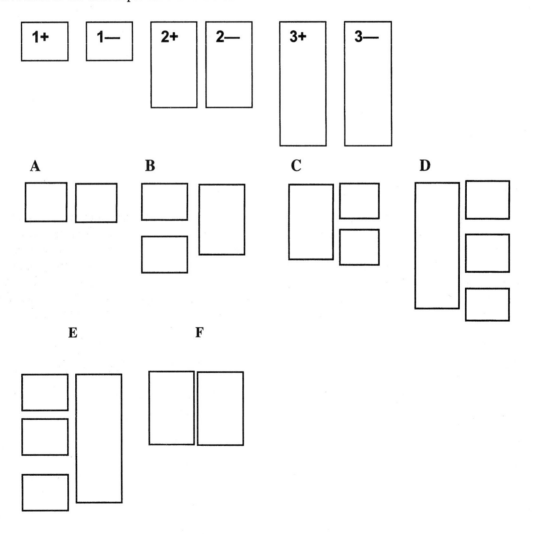

Give the letter (A, B, C, etc.) that matches the arrangement of ions in the following compounds:

Compound	Combination		Compound	Combination
1. $MgCl_2$	_____		2. Na_2S	_____
3. LiCl	_____		4. CaO	_____
5. K_3N	_____		6. $AlBr_3$	_____
7. MgS	_____		8. $BaCl_2$	_____

Answers   1. C   2. B   3. A   4. F
            5. E   6. D   7. F   8. C

◆ **Learning Exercise 4.3B**

Study Note
You can check that the formula you write is electrically neutral by multiplying each of the ionic charges by their subscripts. When added together, their sum should equal zero. For example, the formula Na_2O gives $2(1+) + 1(2-) = (2+) + (2-) = 0$

Write the correct ionic formula for the compound formed from the following pairs of ions:

1. Na^+ and Cl^- _____   2. K^+ and S^{2-} _____

3. Al^{3+} and O^{2-} _____   4. Mg^{2+} and Cl^- _____

5. Ca^{2+} and S^{2-} _____   6. Al^{3+} and Cl^- _____

7. Li^+ and N^{3-} _____   8. Ba^{2+} and P^{3-} _____

Answers   1. NaCl   2. K_2S 3. Al_2O_3 4. $MgCl_2$
            5. CaS   6. $AlCl_3$ 7. Li_3N 8. Ba_3P_2

4.4 Naming Ionic Compounds

- In naming ionic compounds, the positive ion is named first, followed by the name of the negative ion. The name of a representative metal ion (Group 1A, 2A, or 3A) is the same as its elemental name. The name of a nonmetal ion is obtained by replacing the end of its element name with *ide*.
- Most transition metals form cations with two or more ionic charges. Then the ionic charge must be written as a Roman numeral after the name of the metal. For example, the cations of iron, Fe^{2+} and Fe^{3+}, are named iron(II) and iron(III). The ions of copper are Cu^+, copper (I), and Cu^{2+}, copper (II).
- The only transition elements with fixed charges are zinc, Zn^{2+}, silver, Ag^+, and cadmium, Cd^{2+}.

◆ **Learning Exercise 4.4A**

Many of the transition metals form two or more ions with positive charge. Complete the table:

Name of ion	Symbol of ion		Name of ion	Symbol of ion
1. iron(III)	_____		2. _____	Cu^{2+}
3. zinc	_____		4. _____	Fe^{2+}
5. copper(I)	_____		6. _____	Ag^+

Answers   1. Fe^{3+} 2. copper(II)   3. Zn^{2+}
         4. iron(II)   5. Cu^+ 6. Silver

◆ Learning Exercise 4.4B

Write the ions and the correct ionic formula for the following ionic compounds:

Compound	Positive ion	Negative ion	Formula of compound
Aluminum sulfide			
Copper(II) chloride			
Magnesium oxide			
Iron(II) bromide			
Silver oxide			

Answers

Compound	Positive ion	Negative ion	Formula of compound
Aluminum sulfide	Al^{3+}	S^{2-}	Al_2S_3
Copper (II) chloride	Cu^{2+}	Cl^-	$CuCl_2$
Magnesium oxide	Mg^{2+}	O^{2-}	MgO
Iron (II) bromide	Fe^{2+}	Br^-	$FeBr_2$
Silver oxide	Ag^+	O^{2-}	Ag_2O

◆ Learning Exercise 4.4C

Write the name of each of the following ions:

1. Cl^- _____   2. Fe^{2+} _____

3. Cu^+ _____   4. Ag^+ _____

5. O^{2-} _____   6. Ca^{2+} _____

7. S^{2-} _____   8. Al^{3+} _____

9. Fe^{3+} _____   10. Ba^{2+} _____

11. Cu^{2+} _____   12. N^{3-} _____

Answers   1. chloride   2. iron(II)
         3. copper(I)   4. silver
         5. oxide   6. calcium
         7. sulfide   8. aluminum
         9. iron(III)   10. barium
        11. copper(II)   12. nitride

◆ **Learning Exercise 4.4D**

> **Study Note**
> The ionic charge of a metal that forms more than one positive ion is determined from the total negative charge in the formula. For example, in $FeCl_3$, the 3 Cl^- = 3(−). Therefore, the iron ion has an ionic charge of 3+ or Fe^{3+}, which is named iron (III).

Write the ions and a correct name for each of the following ionic compounds:

Formula	Ions	Name
1. $BaCl_2$	_____ _____	_____
2. $FeBr_3$	_____ _____	_____
3. Na_3P	_____ _____	_____
4. Al_2O_3	_____ _____	_____
5. CuO	_____ _____	_____
6. Mg_3N_2	_____ _____	_____

Answers
1. Ba^{2+}, Cl^-, barium chloride
2. Fe^{3+}, Br^-, iron(III) bromide
3. Na^+, P^{3-}, sodium phosphide
4. Al^{3+}, O^{2-}, aluminum oxide
5. Cu^{2+}, O^{2-}, copper(II) oxide
6. Mg^{2+}, N^{3-}, magnesium nitride

4.5 Polyatomic Ions

- A polyatomic ion is a group of nonmetal atoms that carries an electrical charge, usually negative, 1−, 2−, or 3−.
- Polyatomic ions cannot exist alone, but are combined with an ion of the opposite charge.
- Ionic compounds containing three elements (polyatomic ions) end with -*ate* or -*ite*.

> **Study Note**
> Learn the most common polyatomic ions: nitrate NO_3^-, carbonate CO_3^{2-}, sulfate SO_4^{2-}, and phosphate PO_4^{3-}. From these, you can derive the related polyatomic ions. For example, the nitrite ion, NO_2^-, has one oxygen atom less than the nitrate.

◆ **Learning Exercise 4.5A**
Write the polyatomic ion (symbol and charge) for each of the following:

1. sulfate ion	_____	2. hydroxide ion	_____
3. carbonate ion	_____	4. sulfite ion	_____
5. ammonium ion	_____	6. phosphate ion	_____
7. nitrate ion	_____	8. nitrite ion	_____

Answers:
1. SO_4^{2-}
2. OH^-
3. CO_3^{2-}
4. SO_3^{2-}
5. NH_4^+
6. PO_4^{3-}
7. NO_3^-
8. NO_2^-

◆ Learning Exercise 4.5B

Write the formula of each ion or polyatomic ion, and the correct formula for the following compounds:

Compound	Positive ion	Negative Ion	Formula
Sodium phosphate			
Iron(II) hydroxide			
Ammonium carbonate			
Silver bicarbonate			
Iron(III) sulfate			
Ferrous nitrate			
Potassium sulfite			
Barium phosphate			

Answers

Compound	Positive ion	Negative Ion	Formula
Sodium phosphate	Na^+	PO_4^{3-}	Na_3PO_4
Iron(II) hydroxide	Fe^{2+}	OH^-	$Fe(OH)_2$
Ammonium carbonate	NH_4^+	CO_3^{2-}	$(NH_4)_2CO_3$
Silver bicarbonate	Ag^+	HCO_3^-	$AgHCO_3$
Iron(III) sulfate	Fe^{3+}	SO_4^{2-}	$Fe_2(SO_4)_3$
Iron(II) nitrate	Fe^{2+}	NO_3^-	$Fe(NO_3)_2$
Potassium sulfite	K^+	SO_3^{2-}	K_2SO_3
Barium phosphate	Ba^{2+}	PO_4^{3-}	$Ba_3(PO_4)_2$

4.6 Covalent Compounds

- In a covalent bond, atoms of nonmetals share electrons to achieve an octet. For example oxygen with six valence electrons shares electrons with two hydrogen atoms to form the covalent compound water (H_2O).

$$H : \overset{..}{\underset{..}{O}} :$$
$$\overset{..}{H}$$

- In a double bond, two pairs of electrons are shared between the same two atoms. In a triple bond, three pairs of electrons are shared.
- Covalent compounds are composed of nonmetals bonded together to give discrete units called molecules.
- The formula of a covalent compound is written using the symbol of the nonmetals in the name following by subscripts given by the prefixes.

◆ Learning Exercise 4.6A

Write the electron dot structures for the following covalent compounds (the central atom is underlined):

H_2 $\underline{N}Cl_3$ HCl

Cl_2 $H_2\underline{S}$ $\underline{C}Cl_4$

Answers   H:H   :C̈l:N̈:C̈l: H:C̈l: :C̈l:C̈l: H:S̈:   :C̈l: C̈ :C̈l:
:C̈l: H   :C̈l: :C̈l:

◆ Learning Exercise 4.6B

Study Note

Two nonmetals can form two or more different covalent compounds. In their names, prefixes are used to indicate the subscript in the formula. Some typical prefixes are mono (1), di (2), tri (3), tetra (4) and 5 (penta). The ending of the second nonmetal is changed to *-ide*.

Use the appropriate prefixes in naming the following covalent compounds:

1. CS_2 _____   **2.** CCl_4 _____

3. CO _____   **4.** SO_2 _____

5. N_2O_4 _____   **6.** PCl_3 _____

Answers   **1.** carbon disulfide   **2.** carbon tetrachloride   **3.** carbon monoxide
4. sulfur dioxide   **5.** dinitrogen tetroxide   **6.** phosphorus trichloride

◆ Learning Exercise 4.6C

Write the formula of each of the following covalent compounds:

1. dinitrogen oxide _____   **2.** silicon tetrabromide _____

3. nitrogen trichloride _____   **4.** carbon dioxide _____

5. sulfur hexafluoride _____   **6.** oxygen difluoride _____

Answers   **1.** N_2O **2.** $SiBr_4$ **3.** NCl_3
4. CO_2 **5.** SF_6 **6.** OF_2

Summary of Writing Formulas and Names

- In both ionic and covalent compounds containing *two* different elements, the name of the element written first is named as the element. The ending of the name of the second element is replaced by "ide". For example, $BaCl_2$ is named *barium chloride*. If the metal is variable and forms two or more positive ions, a Roman numeral is added to its name to indicate the ionic charge in the compound. For example, $FeCl_3$ is named *iron(III) chloride*.
- In naming covalent compounds, a prefix before the name of an element indicates the numerical value of a subscript. For example, N_2O_3 is named *dinitrogen trioxide*.
- In ionic compounds with three or more elements, a group of atoms is named as a polyatomic ion. The names of negative polyatomic ions end in "ate" or "ite", except for hydroxide. For example, Na_2SO_4 is named *sodium sulfate*.
- When a polyatomic ion occurs two or three times in a formula, its formula is placed inside parenthesis, and the number of ions are shown as a subscript after the parenthesis $Ca(NO_3)_2$.

◆ Learning Exercise 4.6D

Indicate the type of compound (ionic or covalent) formed from each pair of elements. If it is ionic, write the ions; if covalent, write the structure of the molecule. Then give a formula and name for each.

Components	Ionic or covalent?	Ions or structure of molecule	Formula	Name
Mg and Cl				
N and Cl				
K and SO_4				
Li and O				
C and Cl				
Na and PO_4				
H and S				
Ca and HCO_3				

Answers

Mg and Cl	Ionic	Mg^{2+}, Cl^-	$MgCl_2$	Magnesium chloride
N and Cl	Covalent	$Cl-N-Cl$ with Cl below	NCl_3	Nitrogen trichloride
K and SO_4	Ionic	K^+, SO_4^{2-}	K_2SO_4	Potassium sulfate
Li and O	Ionic	Li^+, O^{2-}	Li_2O	Lithium oxide

C and Cl	Covalent	$Cl-C-Cl$ with Cl above and below	CCl_4	Carbon tetrachloride
Na and PO_4	ionic	Na^+, PO_4^{3-}	Na_3PO_4	Sodium phosphate
H and S	covalent	$H-S-H$	H_2S	Dihydrogen sulfide
Ca and HCO_3	ionic	Ca^{2+}, HCO_3^-	$Ca(HCO_3)_2$	Calcium hydrogen Carbonate (bicarbonate)

4.7 Bond Polarity

- Electronegativity indicates the ability of an atom to attract electrons. In general, metals have low electronegativity values and nonmetals have high values.
- When atoms sharing electrons have the same electronegativity values (usually atoms of the same element), the pair is shared equally and the bond is nonpolar covalent.
- Electrons are shared unequally in polar covalent bonds because they are attracted to the more electronegative atom.

◆ Learning Exercise 4.7

Identify the bonding between the following pairs of elements as (I) ionic , (P) polar covalent, (N) nonpolar covalent, or none.

1. H and S _____   2. P and O _____   3. Mg and O _____

4. Li and F _____   5. H and Cl _____   6. Cl and Cl _____

7. S and F _____   8. He and He _____

Answers   1. P   2. P   3. I   4. I
              5. P   6. N   7. P   8. none

4.8 Shapes and Polarity of Molecules

- Valence-shell electron-pair repulsion (VSEPR) theory predicts the geometry of a molecule by placing the electron pairs around a central atom as far apart as possible.
- A tetrahedral molecule has a central atom bonded to four atoms and no lone pairs. In a pyramidal molecule (109°), a central atom is bonded to three atoms and one lone pair. In a bent molecule at 109°, a central atom is bonded to two atoms and two lone pairs.
- A polar bond with its charge separation is called a dipole.
- Nonpolar molecules can have polar bonds when the dipoles are in a symmetrical arrangement.
- In polar molecules, the dipoles do not cancel each other.

Study Note

Guidelines for predicting the shaping of molecules:
1. Write the electron dot structure.
2. Use VSEPR theory to predict the arrangement of the electron groups around the central atom.
3. Identify the shape of the molecule from the number of atoms bonded to the central atom.

◆ Learning Exercise 4.8A

Match the shape of a molecule with the following descriptions of the electron groups around the central atoms and the number of bonded atoms.

A. tetrahedral   B. pyramidal   C. bent (109°)

1. four electron groups with three bonded atoms   _____

2. four electron groups with four bonded atoms   _____

3. four electron groups with two bonded atoms   _____

Answers   1. B   2. A   3. C

◆ Learning Exercise 4.8B

For each of the following, write the electron dot structure, state the number of electron groups and bonded atoms, and predict the shape and angles of the molecule:

Molecule or Ion	Electron dot structure	Number of electron groups	Number of bonded atoms	Shape and angle
CH_4				
PCl_3				
H_2S				

Answers

Molecule or Ion	Electron dot structure	Number of electron groups	Number of bonded atoms	Shape and angle
CH_4	H H:C:H H	4	4	Tetrahedral, 109°
PCl_3	:Cl: P :Cl: :Cl:	4	3	Pyramidal, 109°
H_2S	H:S: H	4	2	Bent, 109°

◆ Learning Exercise 4.8C

Write the symbols δ^+ and δ^- over the atoms in polar bonds.

1. H—O   2. N—H   3. C—Cl
4. O—F   5. N—F   6. P—Cl

Answers

1. $\overset{\delta^+}{H}—\overset{\delta^-}{O}$ 2. $\overset{\delta^-}{N}—\overset{\delta^+}{H}$ 3. $\overset{\delta^+}{C}—\overset{\delta^-}{Cl}$

4. $\overset{\delta^+}{O}—\overset{\delta^-}{F}$ 5. $\overset{\delta^+}{N}—\overset{\delta^-}{F}$ 6. $\overset{\delta^+}{P}—\overset{\delta^-}{Cl}$

◆ Learning Exercise 4.8D

Indicate the dipoles in each of the following and determine whether the molecule is polar or nonpolar:

1. CF_4
2. HCl

3. NH_3
4. OF_2

Answers

1. CF_4 $F \leftarrow \overset{\overset{F}{\uparrow}}{\underset{\underset{F}{\downarrow}}{C}} \rightarrow F$ dipoles cancel, nonpolar

2. HCl $\overset{\delta^+ \quad \delta^-}{H \rightarrow Cl}$ ⊢────▶   dipole does not cancel, polar

3. NH_3 $H \rightarrow \overset{..}{\underset{\underset{H}{\uparrow}}{N}} \leftarrow N$ ↑ ⊢   dipoles do not cancel, polar

4. OF_2 $\overset{..}{\underset{\underset{F}{\downarrow}}{:O}} \rightarrow F$ ╳↘   dipoles do not cancel, polar

Check List for Chapter 4

You are ready to take the self-test for Chapter 4. Be sure that you have accomplished the following learning goals for this chapter. If you are not sure, review the section listed at the end of the goal. Then apply your new skills and understanding to the practice test.

After studying Chapter 4, I can successfully:

_____ Write the electron-dot structure for the representative elements (4.1).

_____ Illustrate the octet rule for the formation of ions (4.2).

_____ Write the formulas of compounds containing the ions of metals and nonmetals of representative elements (4.3).

_____ Use charge balance to write an ionic formula (4.4).

_____ Write the name of an ionic compound (4.4).

_____ Write the formula of a compound containing a polyatomic ion (4.5).

_____ Write the electron dot structure of a covalent compound (4.6).

_____ Write the name and formula of a covalent compound (4.6).

_____ Classify a bond as nonpolar covalent, polar covalent, or ionic (4.7).

_____ Classify a molecular as a polar or nonpolar molecule (4.8).

Practice Test for Chapter 4

For questions 1 through 4, consider an atom of phosphorus.

1. It is in group

   A. 2A   **B.** 3A   **C.** 5A   **D.** 7A   **E.** 8A

2. How many valence electrons does it have?

   A. 2   **B.** 3   **C.** 5   **D.** 8   **E.** 15

3. To achieve an octet, the phosphorus atom will

   A. lose 1 electron   **B.** lose 2 electrons   **C.** lose 5 electrons
   D. gain 2 electrons   **E.** gain 3 electrons

4. As an ion, it has an ionic charge (valence) of

   A. 1+   **B.** 2+   **C.** 5+   **D.** 2–   **E.** 3–

5. To achieve an octet, a calcium atom

   A. loses 1 electron   **B.** loses 2 electrons   **C.** loses 3 electrons
   D. gains 1 electron   **E.** gains 2 electrons

6. To achieve an octet, a chlorine atom

   A. loses 1 electron   **B.** loses 2 electrons   **C.** loses 3 electrons
   D. gains 1 electron   **E.** gains 2 electrons

7. Another name for a positive ion is

   A. anion   **B.** cation   **C.** proton   **D.** positron   **E.** sodium

8. The correct ionic charge (valence) for calcium ion is

   A. 1+   **B.** 2+   **C.** 1–   **D.** 2–   **E.** 3–

9. The silver ion has a charge of

   A. 1+   **B.** 2+   **C.** 1–   **D.** 2–   **E.** 3–

10. The correct ionic charge (valence) for phosphate ion is

    A. 1+   **B.** 2+   **C.** 1–   **D.** 2–   **E.** 3–

11. The correct ionic charge (valence) for fluoride is

    A. 1+   **B.** 2+   **C.** 1–   **D.** 2–   **E.** 3–

12. The correct ionic charge (valence) for sulfate ion is

    A. 1+   **B.** 2+   **C.** 1–   **D.** 2–   **E.** 3–

13. When the elements magnesium and sulfur are mixed,

    A. An ionic compound forms.
    B. A nonpolar covalent compound forms.
    C. No reaction occurs.
    D. The two repel each other and won't combine.
    E. None of the above.

14. An ionic bond typically occurs between

    A. Two different nonmetals.
    B. Two of the same type of nonmetals.
    C. Two noble gases.
    D. Two different metals.
    E A metal and a nonmetal.

15. A nonpolar covalent bond typically occurs between

    A. Two different nonmetals.
    B. Two of the same type of nonmetals.
    C. Two noble gases.
    D. Two different metals.
    E. A metal and a nonmetal.

16. A polar covalent bond typically occurs between

    A. Two different nonmetals.
    B. Two of the same type of nonmetals.
    C. Two noble gases.
    D. Two different metals.
    E. A metal and a nonmetal.

17. The formula for a compound between carbon and chlorine is

    A. Cl **B.** CCl_2 **C.** C_4Cl **D.** CCl_4 **E.** C_4Cl_2

18. The formula for a compound between sodium and sulfur is

    A. SoS **B.** NaS **C.** Na_2S **D.** NaS_2 **E.** Na_2SO_4

19. The formula for a compound between aluminum and oxygen is

    A. AlO **B.** Al_2O **C.** AlO_3 **D.** Al_2O_3 **E.** Al_3O_2

20. The formula for a compound between barium and sulfur is

    A. BaS **B.** Ba_2S **C.** BaS_2 **D.** Ba_2S_2 **E.** $BaSO_4$

21. The correct formula for iron (III) chloride is

    A. $FeCl$ **B.** $FeCl_2$ **C.** Fe_2Cl **D.** Fc_3Cl **E.** $FeCl_3$

22. The correct formula for ammonium sulfate is

    A. AmS **B.** $AmSO_4$ **C.** $(NH_4)_2S$ **D.** NH_4SO_4 **E.** $(NH_4)_2SO_4$

23. The correct formula for copper (II) chloride is

    A. $CoCl$ **B.** $CuCl$ **C.** $CoCl_2$ **D.** $CuCl_2$ **E.** Cu_2Cl

24. The correct formula for lithium phosphate is

    A. $LiPO_4$ **B.** Li_2PO_4 **C.** Li_3PO_4 **D.** $Li_2(PO_4)_3$ **E.** $Li_3(PO_4)_2$

25. The correct formula for silver oxide is

    A. AgO **B.** Ag_2O **C.** AgO_2 **D.** Ag_3O_2 **E.** Ag_3O

26. The correct formula for magnesium carbonate is

    A. $MgCO_3$ **B.** Mg_2CO_3 **C.** $Mg(CO_3)_2$ **D.** $MgCO$ **E.** $Mg_2(CO_3)_3$

27. The correct formula for copper (I) sulfate is

    A. $CuSO_3$ **B.** $CuSO_4$ **C.** Cu_2SO_3 **D.** $Cu(SO_4)_2$ **E.** Cu_2SO_4

28. The name of $AlPO_4$ is

    A. aluminum phosphide   **B.** alum phosphate   **C.** aluminum phosphate
    D. aluminum phosphorus oxide   **E.** aluminum phosphite

29. The name of CuS is

    A. copper sulfide   **B.** copper (I) sulfate   **C.** copper (I) sulfide
    D. cuprous sulfide   **E.** copper (II) sulfide

30. The name of $FeCl_2$ is

    A. ferric chloride   **B.** iron (II) chlorine   **C.** iron (II) chloride
    D. iron chlorine   **E.** iron (III) chloride

31. The name of $ZnCO_3$ is

    A. zinc(III) carbonate   **B.** zinc (II) carbonate   **C.** zinc bicarbonate
    D. zinc carbon trioxide   **E.** zinc carbonate

32. The name of Al_2O_3 is

    A. aluminum oxide   **B.** aluminum (II) oxide   **C.** aluminum trioxide
    D. dialuminum trioxide   **E.** aluminum oxygenate

33. The name of NCl_3 is

    A. nitrogen chloride   **B.** nitrogen trichloride   **C.** trinitrogen chloride
    D. nitrogen chlorine three   **E.** nitrogen chloride (III)

34. The name of CO is

    A. carbon monoxide   **B.** carbonic oxide   **C.** carbon oxide
    D. carbonious oxide   **E.** carboxide

For questions 35 through 40, indicate the type of bonding expected between the following elements:

    A. ionic   **B.** nonpolar covalent   **C.** polar covalent   **D.** none

35. _____ silicon and oxygen   **36.** _____ barium and chlorine

37. _____ aluminum and chlorine   **38.** _____ chlorine and chlorine

39. _____ sulfur and oxygen   **40.** _____ neon and oxygen

Determine the shape and angles of each of the following molecules as

    A. tetrahedral, 109°   **B.** pyramidal , 109°   **C.** bent, 109°

41. PCl_3 **42.** CBr_4 **43.** H_2S

Answers to the Practice Test

1. C	2. C	3. E	4. E	5. B
6. D	7. B	8. B	9. A	10. E
11. C	12. D	13. A	14. E	15. B
16. A	17. D	18. C	19. D	20. A
21. E	22. E	23. D	24. C	25. B
26. A	27. E	28. C	29. E	30. C
31. E	32. A	33. B	34. A	35. C
36. A	37. A	38. B	39. C	40. D
41. B	42. A	43. C		

Answers and Solutions to Selected Text Problems

4.1   Valence electrons are found in the outermost energy level in an atom.

4.3   The number of dots is equal to the number of valence electrons as indicated by the group number.

    a. Sulfur has 6 valence electrons $\ddot{:}\dot{S}\cdot$ **b.** Nitrogen has 5 valence electrons $\cdot\ddot{\dot{N}}\cdot$

    c. Calcium has 2 valence electrons $\dot{C}a\cdot$ **d.** Sodium has 1 valence electron $Na\cdot$

    e. Potassium has 1 valence electron $K\cdot$

4.5   **a.**   M·   **b.**   ·M·

4.7   Alkali metals are members of Group 1A, and each has one valence electron.

4.9   **a.**   If sodium atom loses its valence electron, its second energy level has a complete octet.

      b.   A neon atom has the same electronic arrangement as a sodium ion.
      c.   Group 1A and Group 2A elements do not have a stable octet until each has lost one or two electrons, respectively. Electrically charged ions are formed when electrons are lost, and these positively-charged ions are attracted to negatively-charged ions resulting in the formation of compounds. Group 8A elements have stable octets while remaining electrically neutral, and thus have no tendency to form compounds.

4.11   Atoms with 1, 2 or 3 valence electrons lose those electrons to form ions.
      a. one   **b.** two   **c.** three   **d.** one   **e.** two

4.13   **a.** Li^+ **b.** F^- **c.** Mg^{2+} **d.** Fe^{3+} **e.** Zn^{2+}

4.15   **a.** Cl^- **b.** K^+ **c.** O^{2-} **d.** Al^{3+}

4.17   **a.** (Li & Cl) and **c.** (K & O) form ionic compounds

4.19   **a.** Na_2O **b.** $AlBr_3$ **c.** BaO **d.** $MgCl_2$ **e.** Al_2S_3

4.21   **a.** Na_2S **b.** K_3N **c.** AlI_3 **d.** Li_2O

4.23   **a.** aluminum oxide   **b.** calcium chloride   **c.** sodium oxide
      d. magnesium nitride   **e.** potassium iodide

4.25   The Roman numeral is used to specify the positive charge on the transition metal in the compound. It is necessary for most transition metal compounds because many transition metals can exist as more than one cation; transition metals have variable ionic charges.

4.27   **a.** iron(II)   **b.** copper(II)   **c.** zinc
      d. lead(IV)

4.29   **a.** tin(II) chloride   **b.** iron(II) oxide
      c. copper(I) sulfide   **d.** copper(II) sulfide

4.31   **a.** +3   **b.** +3   **c.** +4   **d.** +2

4.33   **a.** $MgCl_2$ **b.** Na_2S **c.** Cu_2O **d.** Zn_3P_2 **e.** AuN

4.35   **a.** HCO_3^- **b.** NH_4^+ **c.** PO_4^{3-} **d.** HSO_4^-

4.37   **a.** sulfate   **b.** carbonate   **c.** phosphate   **d.** nitrate

4.39

	OH^-	NO_2^-	CO_3^{2-}	HSO_4^-	PO_4^{3-}
Li^+	$LiOH$	$LiNO_2$	Li_2CO_3	$LiHSO_4$	Li_3PO_4
Cu^{2+}	$Cu(OH)_2$	$Cu(NO_2)_2$	$CuCO_3$	$Cu(HSO_4)_2$	$Cu_3(PO_4)_2$
Ba^{2+}	$Ba(OH)_2$	$Ba(NO_2)_2$	$BaCO_3$	$Ba(HSO_4)_2$	$Ba_3(PO_4)_2$

4.41   **a.** CO_3^{2-}, sodium carbonate   **b.** NH_4^+, ammonium chloride
      c. PO_4^{3-}, lithium phosphate   **d.** NO_2^-, copper(II) nitrite
      e. SO_3^{2-}, iron(II) sulfite

4.43   **a.** $Ba(OH)_2$ **b.** Na_2SO_4 **c.** $Fe(NO_3)_2$ **d.** $Zn_3(PO_4)_2$ **e.** $Fe_2(CO_3)_3$

4.45   **a.** :B̈r:B̈r: **b.** H:H   **c.** H:F̈:   **d.** :F̈:Ö:
                                                                     :F̈:

4.47 **a.** phosphorus tribromide **b.** carbon tetrabromide **c.** silicon dioxide
d. hydrogen fluoride

4.49 **a.** dinitrogen trioxide **b.** nitrogen trichloride **c.** silicon tetrabromide
d. phosphorus pentachloride

4.51 **a.** CCl_4 **b.** CO **c.** PCl_3 **d.** N_2O_4

4.53 **a.** OF_2 **b.** BF_3 **c.** N_2O_3 **d.** SF_6

4.55 **a.** This is an ionic compound with Al^{3+} ion and the sulfate SO_4^{2-} polyatomic ion. The correct name is aluminum sulfate.
b. This is an ionic compound with Ca^{2+} ion and the carbonate CO_3^{2-} polyatomic ion. The correct name is calcium carbonate.
c. This is a covalent compound because it contains two nonmetals. Using prefixes, it is named dinitrogen oxide.
d. This is an ionic compound with sodium ion Na^+ and the PO_4^{3-} polyatomic ion. The correct name is sodium phosphate.
e. This ionic compound contains two polyatomic ions ammonium NH_4^+ and sulfate SO_4^{2-}. It is named ammonium sulfate.
f. This is an ionic compound containing the variable metal ion Fe^{3+} and oxide ion O^{2-}. It is named using the Roman numeral as iron(III) oxide.

4.57 **a.** nonpolar covalent **b.** polar covalent **c.** nonpolar covalent
d. ionic

4.59 **a.** polar covalent **b.** ionic **c.** polar covalent
d. nonpolar covalent **e.** polar covalent

4.61 **a.** F **b.** F **c.** Cl **d.** Br

4.63 In a polar covalent bond, the more electronegative atom is assigned δ^-.

a. $\overset{\delta^+ \quad \delta^-}{H-F}$ **b.** $\overset{\delta^+ \quad \delta^-}{C-Cl}$ **c.** $\overset{\delta^+ \quad \delta^-}{N-O}$ **d.** $\overset{\delta^+ \quad \delta^-}{N-F}$

4.65 Tetrahedral. Four atoms bonded to the central atom froms a tetrahedron.

4.67 The four electron groups in PCl_3 have a tetrahedral arrangement, but three bonded atoms around a central atom give a pyramidal shape.

4.69 In the electron dot structure of PH_3, the central atom P has three bonded atoms and one lone pair, which give PH_3 a pyramidal shape. In the molecule NH_3, the central atom N is bonded to three atoms and one lone pair. The structure of the electron groups is tetrahedral, which gives NH_3 a pyramidal shape.

4.71 **a.** The central oxygen atom has four electron pairs with two bonded to fluorine atoms. Its shape is bent with 109° angles.
b. The central atom C is bonded to four chlorine atoms; CCl_4 has a tetrahedral shape.

4.73 Cl_2 is a nonpolar molecule because there is a nonpolar covalent bond between Cl atoms, which have identical electronegativity values. In HCl, the bond is a polar covalent bond, which is a dipole and makes HCl a polar molecule.

4.75 **a.** polar **b.** dipoles do not cancel; polar
c. four dipoles cancel; nonpolar

4.77 **a.** P **b.** Na **c.** Al **d.** Si

4.79 **a.** 2-8 **b.** 2-8 **c.** 2-8 **d.** 2-8 **e.** 2

4.81 **a.** Group 2A **b.** $\cdot X \cdot$ **c.** Be

4.83   **a.** Sn^{4+} **b.**   50 protons, 46 electrons   **c.** SnO_2 **d.** $Sn_3(PO_4)_4$

4.85   Compounds with a metal and nonmetal are classified as ionic; two nonmetals as covalent.
     a.   ionic   **b.**   covalent   **c.**   covalent   **d.**   covalent
     e.   ionic   **f.**   covalent   **g.**   ionic   **h.**   ionic

4.87   **a.**   iron(III) chloride   **b.**   dichlorine heptoxide
     c.   bromine   **d.**   calcium phosphate
     e.   phosphorus trichloride   **f.**   aluminum carbonate
     g.   lead(IV) chloride   **h.**   magnesium carbonate
     i.   nitrogen dioxide   **j.**   tin(II) sulfate
     k.   barium nitrate   **l.**   copper(II) sulfide

4.89   **a.**   pyramidal, dipoles do not cancel, polar
     b.   bent, dipoles do not cancel, polar

4.91   **a.**   bent, dipoles do not cancel, polar
     b.   pyramidal, dipoles do not cancel, polar

Chemical Reactions and Quantities

Study Goals

- Classify a change in matter as a chemical change or a physical change.
- Show that a balanced equation has an equal number of atoms of each element on the reactant side and the product side.
- Write a balanced equation for a chemical reaction when given the formulas of the reactants and products.
- Classify an equation as a combination, decomposition, replacement and/or combustion reaction.
- Describe the features of oxidation and reduction in an oxidation-reduction reaction.
- Determine the molar mass of a compound from its formula.
- Use the molar mass to convert between the grams of a substance and the number of moles.
- Using a given number of moles and a mole-mole conversion factor, determine the corresponding number of moles for a reactant or a prouduct.
- Using a given mass of a substance in a reaction and the appropriate mole factor and molar masses, calculate the mass of a reactant or a product.

Think About It

1. What causes a slice of apple or an avocado to turn brown?

2. How is a recipe like a chemical equation?

3. Why is the digestion of food a series of chemical reactions?

Key Terms

Match the following terms with the statements below:

a. chemical change **b.** chemical equation **c.** combination reaction **d.** mole
e. molar mass **f.** physical change

1. ___ The amount of a substance that contains 6.02×10^{23} particles of that substance.
2. ___ A change that alters the composition of a substance producing a new substance with new properties.
3. ___ The mass in grams of an element or compound that is equal numerically to its atomic or sum of atomic masses.
4. ___ The type of reaction in which reactants combine to form a single product.
5. ___ A shorthand method of writing a chemical with the formulas of the reactants written on the left side of an arrow and the formulas of the products on the right side.

Answers   **1.** d   **2.** a   **3.** e   **4.** c   **5.** b

5.1 Chemical Changes

- A chemical change occurs when the atoms of the initial substances rearrange to form new substances.
- Chemical change is indicated by a change in properties of the reactants. For example, a rusting nail, souring milk, and a burning match are all chemical changes.
- When new substances form, a chemical reaction has taken place.

◆ Learning Exercise 5.1

Identify each of the following as a chemical (C) or a physical (P) change:

1. _____ tearing a piece of paper
2. _____ burning paper
3. _____ rusting iron
4. _____ digestion of food
5. _____ dissolving salt in water
6. _____ boiling water
7. _____ chewing gum
8. _____ removing tarnish with silver polish

Answers   **1.** P   **2.** C   **3.** C   **4.** C   **5.** P   **6.** P   **7.** P   **8.** C

5.2 Chemical Equations

- A chemical equation shows the formulas of the reactants on the left side of the arrow and the formulas of the products on the right side.
- In a balanced equation, *coefficients* in front of the formulas provide the same number of atoms for each kind of element on the reactant and product sides.
- A chemical equation is balanced by placing coefficients in front of the symbols or formulas in the equation.

  Example: Balance the following equation:

  $$N_2(g) + H_2(g) \longrightarrow NH_3(g)$$

  1. Count the atoms of N and H on the reactant side and on the product side.

     $$N_2(g) + H_2(g) \longrightarrow NH_3(g)$$
     2N, 2H   1N, 3H

  2. Balance the N atoms by placing a coefficient of 2 in front of NH_3. (This increases the H atoms too.) Recheck the number of N atoms and the number of H atoms.

     $$N_2(g) + H_2(g) \longrightarrow 2NH_3(g)$$

  3. Balance the H atoms by placing a coefficient of 3 in front of H_2. Recheck the number of N atoms and the number of H atoms.

     $$N_2(g) + 3H_2(g) \longrightarrow 2NH_3(g)$$
     2N, 6H   2 N, 6H   *The equation is balanced.*

◆ Learning Exercise 5.2A

State the number of atoms of each element on the reactant side and on the product side for each of the following balanced equations:

a. $CaCO_3(s) \longrightarrow CaO(g) + CO_2(g)$

Element	Atoms on reactant side	Atoms on product side
Ca		
C		
O		

b. $2Na\ (s) + H_2O\ (l) \longrightarrow Na_2O\ (s) + H_2\ (g)$

Element	Atoms on reactant side	Atoms on product side
Na		
H		
O		

c. $C_5H_{12}\ (g) + 8O_2\ (g) \longrightarrow 5CO_2\ (g) + 6H_2O\ (g)$

Element	Atoms on reactant side	Atoms on product side
C		
H		
O		

d. $2AgNO_3\ (aq) + K_2S\ (aq) \longrightarrow 2KNO_3\ (aq) + Ag_2S\ (s)$

Element	Atoms on reactant side	Atoms on product side
Ag		
N		
O		
K		
S		

e. $2Al(OH)_3\ (aq) + 3H_2SO_4\ (aq) \longrightarrow Al_2(SO_4)_3\ (s) + 6H_2O\ (l)$

Element	Atoms on reactant side	Atoms on product side
Al		
O		
H		
S		

Answers

a. $CaCO_3\ (s) \longrightarrow CaO\ (g) + CO_2\ (g)$

Element	Atoms on reactant side	Atoms on product side
Ca	1	1
C	1	1
O	3	3

b. $2Na\ (s) + H_2O\ (l) \longrightarrow Na_2O\ (s) + H_2(g)$

Element	Atoms on reactant side	Atoms on product side
Na	2	2
H	2	2
O	1	1

c. $C_5H_{12}(g) + 8O_2(g) \longrightarrow 5CO_2(g) + 6H_2O(g)$

Element	Atoms on reactant side	Atoms on product side
C	5	5
H	12	12
O	16	16

d. $2AgNO_3(aq) + K_2S(aq) \longrightarrow 2KNO_3(aq) + Ag_2S(s)$

Element	Atoms on reactant side	Atoms on product side
Ag	2	2
N	2	2
O	6	6
K	2	2
S	1	1

e. $2Al(OH)_3(aq) + 3H_2SO_4(aq) \longrightarrow Al_2(SO_4)_3(s) + 6H_2O(l)$

Element	Atoms on reactant side	Atoms on product side
Al	2	2
O	18	18
H	12	12
S	3	3

◆ Learning Exercise 5.2B

Balance each of the following equations by placing appropriate coefficients in front of the formulas as needed:

a. _____ $MgO \longrightarrow$ _____$Mg +$ _____O_2

b. _____ $Zn +$ _____ $HCl \longrightarrow$ _____ $ZnCl_2 +$ _____ H_2

c. _____ $Al +$ _____ $CuSO_4 \longrightarrow$ _____$Cu +$ _____$Al_2(SO_4)_3$

d. _____ $Al_2S_3 +$ _____ $H_2O \longrightarrow$ _____ $Al(OH)_3 +$ _____H_2S

e. _____ $BaCl_2 +$ _____ $Na_2SO_4 \longrightarrow$ _____ $BaSO_4 +$ _____ $NaCl$

f. _____ $CO +$ _____ $Fe_2O_3 \longrightarrow$ _____ $Fe +$ _____ CO_2

g. _____ $K +$ _____ $H_2O \longrightarrow$ _____ $K_2O +$ _____ H_2

h. _____ $Fe(OH)_3 \longrightarrow$ _____$Fe_2O_3 +$ _____ H_2O

Answers

a. $2MgO \longrightarrow 2Mg + O_2$

b. $Zn + 2HCl \longrightarrow ZnCl_2 + H_2$

c. $2Al + 3CuSO_4 \longrightarrow 3Cu + Al_2(SO_4)_3$

d. $Al_2S_3 + 6H_2O \longrightarrow 2Al(OH)_3 + 3H_2S$

e. $BaCl_2 + Na_2SO_4 \longrightarrow BaSO_4 + 2NaCl$

f. $3CO + Fe_2O_3 \longrightarrow 2Fe + 3CO_2$

g. $2K + H_2O \longrightarrow K_2O + H_2$

h. $2Fe(OH)_3 \longrightarrow Fe_2O_3 + 3H_2O$

5.3 Types of Reactions

- Reactions are classified as combination, decomposition, replacement and combustion.
- In a *combination* reaction, reactants are combined. In a *decomposition* reaction, a reactant splits into simpler products.
- In *single (or double) replacement* reactions, one (or two) elements in the reacting compounds are replaced with the element(s) from the other reactant(s).
- In a *combustion* reaction, oxygen combines with a reactant to form an oxide product. Compounds of carbon and hydrogen react with oxygen to produce CO_2 and H_2O.

◆ **Learning Exercise 5.3A**

Study Note
Combination reactions combine reactants. *Decomposition* splits compounds into simpler products. In *replacement*, elements in the reacting compounds are replaced with the element(s) from the other reactant(s).

Match each of the following reactions with the type of reaction:

a. combination   b. decomposition   c. single replacement
d. double replacement

1. _____ $N_2 + 3H_2 \longrightarrow 2\,NH_3$

2. _____ $BaCl_2 + K_2CO_3 \longrightarrow BaCO_3 + 2\,KCl$

3. _____ $2H_2O_2 \longrightarrow 2H_2O + O_2$

4. _____ $CuO + H_2 \longrightarrow Cu + H_2O$

5. _____ $N_2 + 2O_2 \longrightarrow 2NO_2$

6. _____ $2NaHCO_3 \longrightarrow Na_2O + 2CO_2 + H_2O$

7. _____ $PbCO_3 \longrightarrow PbO + CO_2$

8. _____ $Al + Fe_2O_3 \longrightarrow Fe + Al_2O_3$

Answers   1. a   2. d   3. b   4. c
              5. a   6. b   7. b   8. c

◆ **Learning Exercise 5.3B**

1. One way to remove tarnish from silver is to place the silver object on a piece of aluminum foil and add boiling water and some baking soda. The unbalanced equation is the following:

$$Al + Ag_2S \longrightarrow Ag + Al_2S_3$$

a. What is the balanced equation?

b. What type of reaction takes place?

2. Octane, C_8H_{18}, a compound in gasoline, burns in oxygen to produce carbon dioxide and water.

   a. What is the balanced equation for the reaction?

   b. What type of reaction takes place?

Answers   **1a.** $2Al + 3Ag_2S \longrightarrow 6Ag + Al_2S_3$ **1b.** single replacement
                       2a. $2C_8H_{18} + 25O_2 \longrightarrow 16CO_2 + 18H_2O$ **2b.** combustion

5.4 Oxidation-Reduction Reactions

- An oxidation-reduction reaction consists of a loss and gain of electrons. In an oxidation, electrons are lost. In a reduction, there is a gain of electrons.
- An oxidation must always be accompanied by a reduction. The number of electrons lost in the oxidation reaction and gained in the reduction reaction are equal.
- In biological systems, the term oxidation describes the gain of oxygen or the loss of hydrogen. The term reduction is used to describe a loss of oxygen or a gain of hydrogen.

◆ Learning Exercise 5.4

For each of the following reactions, indicate whether the underlined element is *oxidized or reduced*.

a. $4\underline{Al} + 3O_2 \longrightarrow 2Al_2O_3$ Al is _____

b. $\underline{Fe}^{3+} + 1e^- \longrightarrow Fe^{2+}$ Fe^{3+} is _____

c. $\underline{Cu}O + H_2 \longrightarrow Cu + H_2O$ Cu^{2+} is _____

d. $2\underline{Cl}^- \longrightarrow Cl_2 + 2e^-$ Cl^- is _____

e. $2H\underline{Br} + Cl_2 \longrightarrow 2HCl + Br_2$ Br^- is _____

f. $2\underline{Na} + Cl_2 \longrightarrow 2NaCl$ Na is _____

g. $\underline{Cu}Cl_2 + Zn \longrightarrow ZnCl_2 + Cu$ Cu^{2+} is _____

Answers   **a.** Al is oxidized to Al^{3+}; loss of electrons (addition of O)

                 b. Fe^{3+} is reduced to Fe^{2+}; gain of electrons

                 c. Cu^{2+} is reduced to Cu; gain of electrons (loss of O)

                 d. $2Cl^-$ is oxidized to Cl_2; loss of electrons

                 e. $2 Br^-$ is oxidized to Br_2; loss of electrons

                 f. Na is oxidized to Na^+; loss of electrons

                 g. Cu^{2+} is reduced to Cu; gain of electrons

5.5 The Mole

- A mole of any element contains Avogadro's number, 6.02×10^{23}, of atoms; a mole of any compound contains 6.02×10^{23} molecules or formula units.
- The subscripts in a formula indicate the number of moles of each element in one mole of the compound.

◆ **Learning Exercise 5.5A**

Consider the formula for vitamin C (ascorbic acid) $C_6H_8O_6$.

a. How many moles of carbon are in 2.0 moles of vitamin C?

b. How many moles of hydrogen are in 5.0 moles of vitamin C?

c. How many moles of oxygen are in 1.5 moles of vitamin C?

Answers   a. 12 moles of carbon (C)   b. 30 moles of hydrogen (H)
                 c. 9 moles of oxygen (O)

◆ **Learning Exercise 5.5B**

For the compound ibuprofen used in Advil™ and Motrin™ ($C_{13}H_{18}O_2$), determine the moles of each of the following:

a. Moles of carbon (C) atoms in 2.20 moles of ibuprofen.

b. Moles of hydrogen (H) in 0.5 moles of ibuprofen.

c. Moles of oxygen (O) in 0.75 mole of ibuprofen.

d. Moles of ibuprofen that contain 36 moles of hydrogen (H).

Answers   a. 28.6 moles of C   b. 9 moles of H
               c. 1.5 moles of O   d. 2 moles of ibuprofen

5.6 Molar Mass

- The molar mass (g/mole) of an element is numerically equal to its atomic mass in grams.
- The molar mass (g/mole) of a compound is the mass in grams equal numerically to the sum of the mass for each element in the formula. $MgCl_2$ has a molar mass that is the sum of the mass of 1 mole of Mg (24.3 g) and 2 moles of Cl (2×35.5 g) = 95.3 g/mole.
- The molar mass is useful as a conversion factor to change a given quantity in moles to grams.

$$\text{moles of substance} \times \frac{\text{number of grams}}{\text{1 mole of substance}} = \text{grams}$$

Study Note

The molar mass of an element or compound is determined as follows:
1. Determine the moles of each element (from subscripts) in the compound.
2. Calculate the total mass contributed by each element.
3. Total the masses of all the elements.

Example: What is the molar mass of silver nitrate, $AgNO_3$?

1 mole Ag	$\times$	107.9 g/mole	=		107.9 g
1 mole N	$\times$	14.0 g/mole	=		14.0 g
3 moles O	$\times$	16.0 g/mole	=		48.0 g
		molar mass $AgNO_3$	=		169.9 g

◆ Learning Exercise 5.6A

Determine the molar mass (to the nearest 0.1 g) for each of the following:

a. K_2O

b. $AlCl_3$

c. $C_{13}H_{18}O_2$ ibuprofen

d. C_4H_{10}

e. $Ca(NO_3)_2$

f. Mg_3N_2

g. $FeCO_3$

h. $(NH_4)_3PO_4$

Answers **a.** 94.2 g **b.** 133.5 g **c.** 206.0 g **d.** 58.0 g
e. 164.1 g **f.** 100.9 g **g.** 115.9 g **h.** 149.0 g

◆ Learning Exercise 5.6B

Study Note

Use the molar mass as a conversion factor to change the number of moles of a substance to its mass in grams. Find the mass in grams of 0.25 mole of Na_2CO_3.

Molar mass
Grams $\longleftrightarrow$ Moles

Example: $0.25 \text{ mole } Na_2CO_3 \times \dfrac{106.0g \; Na_2CO_3}{1 \text{ mole } Na_2CO_3} = 27 \text{ g } Na_2CO_3$

Find the number of grams in each of the following quantities:

a. 0.100 mole SO_2

b. 0.100 mole H_2SO_4

c. 2.50 moles NH_3

d. 1.25 moles O_2

e. 0.500 mole Mg

f. 5.00 moles H_2

g. 10.0 moles PCl_3

h. 0.400 mole S

Answers **a.** 6.41 g **b.** 9.81 g **c.** 42.5 g **d.** 40.0 g
e. 12.2 g **f.** 10.0 g **g.** 1380 g **h.** 12.8 g

◆ **Learning Exercise 5.6C**

Study Note

When the grams of a substance are given, the molar mass is used to calculate the number of moles of substance present.

$$\text{grams of substance} \times \frac{1 \text{ mole}}{\text{grams of substance}} = \text{moles}$$

Example: How many moles of NaOH are in 4.0 g of NaOH?

$$4.0 \text{ g NaOH} \times \frac{1 \text{ mole NaOH}}{40.0 \text{ g NaOH}} = 0.10 \text{ mole NaOH}$$

Molar Mass (inverted)

Calculate the number of moles in each of the following quantities:

a. 32.0 g of CH_4 **b.** 391 g of K

c. 8.00 g of C_3H_8 **d.** 25.0 g of Cl_2

e. 0.220 g of CO_2 **f.** 5.00 g of Al_2O_3

g. The methane burned in a gas heater has a formula of CH_4. If 725 grams of methane are used in 1 month, how many moles of methane were burned?

h. There is 18 mg of iron in a vitamin tablet. If there are 100 tablets in a bottle, how many moles of iron are contained in the vitamins in the bottle?

Answers	**a.** 2.00 moles	**b.** 10.0 moles	**c.** 0.182 mole
	d. 0.352 mole	**e.** 0.00500 mole	**f.** 0.0490 mole
	g. 45.3 moles	**h.** 0.032 mole	

73

5.7 Mole Relationships in Chemical Equations

- The coefficients in a balanced chemical equation describe the moles of reactants and products in the reactions.
- Using the coefficients, mole–mole conversion factors are written for any two substances in the equation.
- For the reaction of oxygen forming ozone, $3O_2(g) \longrightarrow 2O_3(g)$, the mole–mole conversion factors are the following:

$$\frac{3 \text{ moles } O_2}{2 \text{ moles } O_3} \quad \text{and} \quad \frac{2 \text{ moles } O_3}{3 \text{ moles } O_2}$$

◆ Learning Exercise 5.7A

Write the conversion factors that are possible from the following equation:
$$N_2 + O_2 \longrightarrow 2NO$$

Answers

$$\frac{1 \text{ mole } N_2}{1 \text{ mole } O_2} \quad \text{and} \quad \frac{1 \text{ mole } O_2}{1 \text{ mole } N_2} ; \quad \frac{1 \text{ mole } N_2}{2 \text{ moles } NO} \quad \text{and} \quad \frac{2 \text{ moles } NO}{1 \text{ mole } N_2}$$

$$\frac{1 \text{ mole } O_2}{2 \text{ moles } NO} \quad \text{and} \quad \frac{2 \text{ moles } NO}{1 \text{ mole } O_2}$$

Study Note
The appropriate mole factor is used to change the number of moles of the given substance to moles of the desired products.
Example: Using the equation, $N_2 + O_2 \longrightarrow 2NO$, calculate the moles of NO obtained from 3 moles N_2.

$$3 \text{ moles } N_2 \times \frac{2 \text{ moles } NO}{1 \text{ mole } N_2} = 6 \text{ moles } NO$$

Mole–mole factor

◆ **Learning Exercise 5.7B**

Use the equation below to answer the following questions:

$$C_3H_8\,(g) + 5O_2\,(g) \longrightarrow 3CO_2\,(g) + 4\,H_2O\,(g)$$

a. How many moles of O_2 are needed to react with 2.00 moles of C_3H_8?

b. How many moles CO_2 are produced when 4.00 moles O_2 react?

c. How many moles of C_3H_8 react with 3.00 moles O_2?

d. How many moles of H_2O are produced from 0.50 mole C_3H_8?

Answers	**a.** 10.0 moles O_2	**b.** 2.4 mole CO_2
	c. 0.600 mole C_3H_8	**d.** 2.0 moles of H_2O

5.8 Mass Calculations for Reactions

- The grams or moles of one substance in an equation are converted to another using their respective molar masses and mole–mole factors.
- Suppose that a problem asks for the number of grams of O_3 (ozone) produced from 8.0 g O_2. The equation is $3O_2 \longrightarrow 2O_3$.

Step 1	*Step 2*	*Step 3*
Use molar mass of O_2	Use mole factor from coefficients	Use molar mass of O_3

$$8.0\text{ g }O_2 \longrightarrow \text{moles}O_2 \longrightarrow \text{moles }O_3 \longrightarrow \text{g }O_3$$

$$8.0\ \cancel{\text{g }O_2} \times \frac{1\ \cancel{\text{mole }O_2}}{32.0\ \cancel{\text{g }O_2}} \times \frac{2\ \cancel{\text{moles }O_3}}{3\ \cancel{\text{moles }O_2}} \times \frac{48.0\text{ g }O_3}{1\ \cancel{\text{mole }O_3}} = 8.0\text{ g }O_3$$

◆ Learning Exercise 5.8

Consider the equation for the following questions:

$$2C_2H_6(g) + 7O_2(g) \longrightarrow 4CO_2(g) + 6H_2O(g)$$

a. How many grams of oxygen (O_2) are needed to react with 4.00 moles of C_2H_6?

b. How many grams of C_2H_6 are needed to react with 115 g of O_2?

c. How many grams of C_2H_6 react if 2.00 L of CO_2 gas are produced at STP?

d. How many grams of CO_2 are produced when 2.00 moles of C_2H_6 react with sufficient oxygen?

e. How many grams of water are produced when 82.5 g O_2 react with sufficient C_2H_6?

Answers   **a.** 448 g O_2 **b.** 30.8 g C_2H_6 **c.** 1.34 g C_2H_6
              d. 176 g of CO_2 **e.** 39.8 g H_2O

Check List for Chapter 5

You are ready to take the practice test for Chapter 5. Be sure that you have accomplished the following learning goals for this chapter. If you are not sure, review the section listed at the end of the goal. Then apply your new skills and understanding to the practice test.

After studying Chapter 5, I can successfully:

_____ Identify a chemical and physical change (5.1).

_____ State a chemical equation in words and calculate the total atoms of each element in the reactants and products (5.2).

_____ Write a balanced equation for a chemical reaction from the formulas of the reactants and products (5.2).

_____ Identify a reaction as a combination, decomposition, replacement, or combustion reaction (5.3).

_____ Identify an oxidation and reduction reaction (5.4).

_____ State the number of particles in a mole of a substance (5.5).

_____ Calculate the molar mass given the formula of a substance (5.6).

_____ Convert the grams of a substance to moles; moles to grams (5.6).

_____ Use mole-mole factors for the mole relationships in an equation to calculate the moles of another substance in an equation for a chemical reaction (5.7).

_____ Calculate the mass of a substance in an equation using mole factors and molar masses (5.8).

Practice Test for Chapter 5

Indicate whether each change is a (A) physical change or a (B) chemical change:

1. _____ A melting ice cube   2. _____ Breaking glass

3. _____ Bleaching a stain   4. _____ A burning candle

5. _____ Milk turning sour

For each of the *unbalanced equations* in questions 6 through 10, balance and indicate the correct coefficient for the component in the equation written in boldface type.

A. 1   **B.** 2   **C.** 3   **D.** 4   **E.** 5

6. _____ $Sn + \mathbf{Cl_2} \longrightarrow SnCl_4$

7. _____ $Al + H_2O \longrightarrow Al_2O_3 + \mathbf{H_2}$

8. _____ $C_3H_8 + \mathbf{O_2} \longrightarrow CO_2 + H_2O$

9. _____ $\mathbf{NH_3} + O_2 \longrightarrow N_2 + H_2O$

10. _____ $N_2O \longrightarrow N_2 + \mathbf{O_2}$

For questions 11 through 15, classify each reaction as one of the following:

A. combination   **B.** decomposition   **C.** single replacement   **D.** double replacement

11. _____ $S + O_2 \longrightarrow SO_2$

12. _____ $Fe_2O_3 + 3C \longrightarrow 2Fe + 3CO$

13. _____ $CaCO_3 \longrightarrow CaO + CO_2$

14. _____ $Mg + 2AgNO_3 \longrightarrow Mg(NO_3)_2 + 2Ag$

15. _____ $Na_2S + Pb(NO_3)_2 \longrightarrow PbS + 2NaNO_3$

For questions 16 through 20, identify as an (A) oxidation or a (B) reduction.

16. $Ca \longrightarrow Ca^{2+} + 2e^-$ _____

17. $Fe^{3+} + 3e^- \longrightarrow Fe$ _____

18. $Al^{3+} + 3e^- \longrightarrow Al$ _____

19. $Br_2 + 2e^- \longrightarrow 2Br^-$ _____

20. $Sn^{2+} \longrightarrow Sn^{4+} + 2e^-$ _____

21. The moles of oxygen (O) in 2.0 moles of $Al(OH)_3$ is
   A. 1　　　B. 2　　　C. 3　　　D. 4　　　E. 6

22. What is the molar mass of Li_2SO_4?
   A. 55.1 g　B. 62.1 g　C. 100.1 g　D. 109.9 g　E. 103.1 g

23. What is the molar mass of $NaNO_3$?
   A. 34.0 g　B. 37.0 g　C. 53.0 g　D. 75.0 g　E. 85.0 g

24. The number of grams in 0.600 mole of Cl_2 is
   A. 71.0 g　B. 118 g　C. 42.6 g　D. 84.5 g　E. 4.30 g

25. How many grams are in 4.00 moles of NH_3?
   A. 4.00 g　B. 17.0 g　C. 34.0 g　D. 68.0 g　E. 0.240 g

26. How many moles is 8.0 g NaOH?
   A. 0.10 mole　B. 0.20 mole　C. 0.40 mole　D. 2.0 moles　E. 4.0 moles

27. The number of moles of aluminum in 54 g of Al is
   A. 0.50 mole　B. 1.0 mole　C. 2.0 moles　D. 3.0 moles　E. 4.0 moles

28. The number of moles of water in 36 g of H_2O is
   A. 0.50 mole　B. 1.0 mole　C. 2.0 moles　D. 3.0 moles　E. 4.0 moles

29. What is the number of moles in 2.2 g CO_2?
   A. 2.0 moles　B. 1.0 mole　C. 0.20 mole　D. 0.050 mole　E. 0.010 mole

30. 0.20 g H_2 = _____ mole H_2
   A. 0.10 mole　B. 0.20 mole　C. 0.40 mole　D. 0.040 mole　E. 0.010 mole

For questions, 31 to 35, use the reaction: $C_2H_5OH + 3O_2 \rightarrow 2CO_2 + 3H_2O$
　　　　　　Ethanol

31. How many grams of oxygen are needed to react with 1.0 mole of ethanol?
   A. 8.0 g　B. 16 g　C. 32 g　D. 64 g　E. 96 g

32. How many moles of water are produced when 12 moles of oxygen react?
   A. 3.0 moles　B. 6.0 moles　C. 8.0 moles　D. 12.0 moles　E. 36.0 moles

33. How many grams of carbon dioxide are produced when 92 g of ethanol react?
   A. 22 g　B. 44 g　C. 88 g　D. 92 g　E. 176 g

34. How many moles of oxygen would be needed to produce 44 g of CO_2?
   A. 0.67 mole　B. 1.0 mole　C. 1.5 moles　D. 2.0 moles　E. 3.0 moles

35. How many grams of water will be produced if 23 g of ethanol react?

    A. 54 g   **B.** 27 g   **C.** 18 g   **D.** 9.0 g   **E.** 6.0 g

Answers to the Practice Test

1. A	**2.** A	**3.** B	**4.** B	**5.** B
6. B	**7.** C	**8.** E	**9.** D	**10.** A
11. A	**12.** C	**13.** B	**14.** C	**15.** D
16. A	**17.** B	**18.** B	**19.** B	**20.** A
21. E	**22.** D	**23.** E	**24.** C	**25.** D
26. B	**27.** C	**28.** C	**29.** D	**30.** A
31. E	**32.** D	**33.** E	**34.** C	**35.** B

Answers and Solutions to Selected Text Problems

5.1 A chemical change occurs when the atoms of the initial substances rearrange to form new substances. Chemical change is indicated by a change in properties of the reactants. For example, a rusting nail, souring milk, and a burning match are all chemical changes.

    a. physical: the shape changes, but not the substance.
    b. chemical: new substances form
    c. physical: water evaporates forming gaseous water
    d. chemical: the composition of the substances change to give new substances
    e. physical: water freezes
    f. chemical: new substances form

5.3 An equation is balanced when there are equal numbers of atoms of each element on the reactant as on the product side.

    a. not balanced   **b.** balanced   **c.** not balanced   **d.** balanced

5.5 Place coefficients in front of formulas until you make the atoms of each element equal on each side of the equation. Try starting with the formula that has subscripts.

    a. $N_2 + O_2 \rightarrow 2\,NO$ **b.** $2HgO \rightarrow 2Hg + O_2$
    c. $4Fe + 3O_2 \rightarrow 2Fe_2O_3$ **d.** $2Na + Cl_2 \rightarrow 2NaCl$

5.7 **a.** There are two NO_3^- in the product. Balance by placing a 2 before $AgNO_3$.

$$Mg + 2AgNO_3 \rightarrow Mg(NO_3)_2 + 2Ag$$

    b. Start with the formula $Al_2(SO_4)_3$. Balance the Al by writing 2 Al and balance the SO_4^{2-} by writing $3CuSO_4 + 2Al \rightarrow 3Cu + Al_2(SO_4)_3$
    c. $Pb(NO_3)_2 + 2NaCl \rightarrow PbCl_2 + 2NaNO_3$
    d. $2Al + 6HCl \rightarrow 2AlCl_3 + 3H_2$

5.9 **a.** Decomposition. A single reactant splits into two simpler substances (elements).
    b. This is a single replacement reaction. I_2 in BaI_2 is replaced by Br_2.

5.11   **a.** combination   **b.** single replacement   **c.** decomposition
      d. combustion   **e.** decomposition   **f.** double replacement

5.13   **a.** oxidation   **b.** reduction   **c.** oxidation   **d.** reduction

5.15   **a.** Zinc(Zn) is oxidized because it loses electrons to form Zn^{2+}; chlorine (Cl_2) is reduced
      b. Bromide ion ($2Br^-$) is oxidized to Br_2^0; chlorine (Cl_2) is reduced to $2Cl^-$ (gains electrons)
      c. Oxide ion (O^{2-}) is oxidized to O_2^0 (loses electrons); lead(II) ion Pb^{2+} is reduced
      d. Sn^{2+} ion is oxidized to Sn^{4+} (loses electrons); Fe^{3+} ion is reduced to Fe^{2+}(gains electrons)

5.17   **a.** $Fe^{3+} + e^- \rightarrow Fe^{2+}$ is a reduction.   **b.** $Fe^{2+} \rightarrow Fe^{3+} + e^-$ is an oxidation.

5.19   Because the linoleic acid adds hydrogen, the acid has been reduced.

5.21   A mole is the amount of a substance that contains 6.02×10^{23} items. For example, one mole of water contains 6.02×10^{23} molecules of water.

79

5.23 The subscripts indicate the moles of each element in one mole of that compound.
    a. 24 moles of H

    b. 5.0 ~~moles quinine~~ $\times$ $\dfrac{20\ \text{moles C atoms}}{1\ \text{mole quinine}}$ = 100 moles C atoms

    c. 0.020 ~~moles quinine~~ $\times$ $\dfrac{2\ \text{moles N atoms}}{1\ \text{mole quinine}}$ = 0.040 mole N atoms

5.25 a. 1 mole of Na and 1 mole of Cl:
      23.0 g + 35.5 g = 58.5 g/mole NaCl

    b. 2 moles of Fe and 3 moles of O:
      111.8 g + 48.0 g = 159.8 g/mole Fe_2O_3

    c. 2 moles of Li and 1 mole of C and 3 moles of O:
      13.8 g + 12.0 g + 48.0 g = 73.8 g/mole Li_2CO_3

    d. 2 moles of Al and 3 moles of S and 12 moles of O:
      54.0 g + 96.3 g + 192.0 g = 342.3 g/mole $Al_2(SO_4)_3$

    e. 1 mole of Mg and 2 moles of O and 2 moles of H:
      24.3 g + 32.0 g + 2.0 g = 58.3 g/mole $Mg(OH)_2$

    f. 16 moles of C and 19 moles of H and 3 moles of N and 5 moles of O and 1 mole of S:
      192.0 g + 19.0 g + 42.0 g + 80.0 g + 32.1 g = 365.1 g/mole $C_{16}H_{19}N_3O_5S$

5.27 a.   2.00 ~~moles Na~~ $\times$ $\dfrac{23.0\ \text{g Na}}{1\ \text{mole Na}}$ = 46.0 g Na

    b.   2.80 ~~moles Ca~~ $\times$ $\dfrac{40.1\ \text{g Ca}}{1\ \text{mole Ca}}$ = 112 g Ca

    c.   0.125 ~~mole Sn~~ $\times$ $\dfrac{118.7\ \text{g Sn}}{1\ \text{mole Sn}}$ = 14.8 g Sn

5.29 a.   0.500 ~~mole NaCl~~ $\times$ $\dfrac{58.5\ \text{g NaCl}}{1\ \text{mole NaCl}}$ = 29.3 g NaCl

    b.   1.75 ~~moles Na$_2$O~~ $\times$ $\dfrac{62.0\ \text{g Na}_2\text{O}}{1\ \text{mole Na}_2\text{O}}$ = 109 g Na_2O

    c.   0.225 ~~mole H$_2$O~~ $\times$ $\dfrac{18.0\ \text{g H}_2\text{O}}{1\ \text{mole H}_2\text{O}}$ = 4.05 g H_2O

5.31 a.   5.00 ~~moles MgSO$_4$~~ $\times$ $\dfrac{120.4\ \text{g MgSO}_4}{1\ \text{mole MgSO}_4}$ = 602 g $MgSO_4$

    b.   0.25 ~~mole CO$_2$~~ $\times$ $\dfrac{44.0\ \text{g CO}_2}{1\ \text{mole CO}_2}$ = 11 g CO_2

5.33 a. $50.0 \text{ g Ag} \times \dfrac{1 \text{ mole Ag}}{107.9 \text{ g Ag}} = 0.463 \text{ mole Ag}$

b. $0.200 \text{ g C} \times \dfrac{1 \text{ mole C}}{12.0 \text{ g C}} = 0.0167 \text{ mole C}$

c. $15.0 \text{ g NH}_3 \times \dfrac{1 \text{ mole NH}_3}{17.0 \text{ g NH}_3} = 0.882 \text{ mole NH}_3$

d. $75.0 \text{ g SO}_2 \ \dfrac{1 \text{ mole SO}_2}{64.1 \text{ g SO}_2} = 1.17 \text{ moles SO}_2$

5.35 $480 \text{ g NaOH} \times \dfrac{1 \text{ mole NaOH}}{40.0 \text{ g NaOH}} = 12 \text{ moles NaOH}$

5.37 a. $25 \text{ g S} \times \dfrac{1 \text{ mole S}}{32.1 \text{ g S}} = 0.78 \text{ mole of S}$

b. $125 \text{ g SO}_2 \times \dfrac{1 \text{ mole SO}_2}{64.1 \text{ g SO}_2} \times \dfrac{1 \text{ mole S}}{1 \text{ mole SO}_2} = 1.95 \text{ moles of S}$

c. $2.0 \text{ moles Al}_2\text{S}_3 \times \dfrac{3 \text{ moles S}}{1 \text{ mole Al}_2\text{S}_3} = 6.0 \text{ moles of S}$

5.39 a. Two SO_2 molecules react with one O_2 molecule to produce two SO_3 molecules.

Two moles of SO_2 react with one mole of O_2 to produce two moles of SO_3.

b. Four P atoms react with five O_2 molecules to produce two P_2O_5 molecules.

Four moles of P react with five moles of O_2 to produce two moles of P_2O_5.

5.41 a. $\dfrac{2 \text{ moles SO}_2}{1 \text{ mole O}_2}$ and $\dfrac{1 \text{ mole O}_2}{2 \text{ moles SO}_2}$ $\quad$ $\dfrac{2 \text{ moles SO}_2}{2 \text{ moles O}_3}$ and $\dfrac{2 \text{ moles O}_3}{2 \text{ moles SO}_2}$

$\dfrac{1 \text{ mole O}_2}{2 \text{ moles SO}_3}$ and $\dfrac{2 \text{ moles SO}_3}{1 \text{ mole O}_2}$

b. $\dfrac{4 \text{ moles P}}{5 \text{ moles O}_2}$ and $\dfrac{5 \text{ moles O}_2}{4 \text{ moles P}}$ $\quad$ $\dfrac{4 \text{ moles P}}{2 \text{ moles P}_2\text{O}_5}$ and $\dfrac{2 \text{ moles P}_2\text{O}_5}{4 \text{ moles P}}$

$\dfrac{5 \text{ moles O}_2}{2 \text{ moles P}_2\text{O}_5}$ and $\dfrac{2 \text{ moles P}_2\text{O}_5}{5 \text{ moles O}_2}$

5.43 a $\quad 2.0 \text{ moles H}_2 \times \dfrac{1 \text{ mole O}_2}{2 \text{ moles H}_2} = 1.0 \text{ mole O}_2$

b. $\quad 5.0 \text{ moles O}_2 \times \dfrac{2 \text{ moles H}_2}{1 \text{ mole O}_2} = 10.0 \text{ moles H}_2$

c. $\quad 2.5 \text{ moles O}_2 \times \dfrac{2 \text{ moles H}_2O}{1 \text{ mole O}_2} = 5.0 \text{ moles H}_2O$

5.45 a. $\quad 0.500 \text{ mole SO}_2 \times \dfrac{5 \text{ moles C}}{2 \text{ moles SO}_2} = 1.25 \text{ moles C}$

b. $\quad 1.2 \text{ moles C} \times \dfrac{4 \text{ moles CO}}{5 \text{ moles C}} = 0.96 \text{ mole CO}$

c. $\quad 0.50 \text{ mole CS}_2 \times \dfrac{2 \text{ moles SO}_2}{1 \text{ mole CS}_2} = 1.0 \text{ mole SO}_2$

5.47 a. $\quad 2.5 \text{ moles Na} \times \dfrac{2 \text{ moles Na}_2O}{4 \text{ moles Na}} \times \dfrac{62.0 \text{ g Na}_2O}{1 \text{ mole Na}_2O} = 78 \text{ g Na}_2O$

b. $\quad 18.0 \text{ g Na} \times \dfrac{1 \text{ mole Na}}{23.0 \text{ g Na}} \times \dfrac{1 \text{ mole O}_2}{4 \text{ moles Na}} \times \dfrac{32.0 \text{ g O}_2}{1 \text{ mole O}_2} = 6.26 \text{ g O}_2$

c. $\quad 75.0 \text{ g Na}_2O \times \dfrac{1 \text{ mole Na}_2O}{62.0 \text{ g Na}_2O} \times \dfrac{1 \text{ mole O}_2}{2 \text{ moles Na}_2O} \times \dfrac{32.0 \text{ g O}_2}{1 \text{ mole O}_2} = 19.4 \text{ g O}_2$

5.49 a. $\quad 8.0 \text{ moles NH}_3 \times \dfrac{3 \text{ moles O}_2}{4 \text{ moles NH}_3} \times \dfrac{32.0 \text{ g O}_2}{1 \text{ mole O}_2} = 190 \text{ g O}_2$

b. $\quad 6.50 \text{ g O}_2 \times \dfrac{1 \text{ mole O}_2}{32.0 \text{ g O}_2} \times \dfrac{2 \text{ moles N}_2}{3 \text{ moles O}_2} \times \dfrac{28.0 \text{ g N}_2}{1 \text{ mole N}_2} = 3.79 \text{ g N}_2$

c. $\quad 34 \text{ g NH}_3 \times \dfrac{1 \text{ mole HN}_3}{17.0 \text{ g NH}_3} \times \dfrac{6 \text{ moles H}_2O}{4 \text{ moles NH}_3} \times \dfrac{18.0 \text{ g H}_2O}{1 \text{ mole H}_2O} = 54 \text{ g H}_2O$

5.51 **a.** $2Al + 3Cl_2 \rightarrow 2AlCl_3$ $\qquad\qquad$ combination
  b. $2Fe + 3H_2SO_4 \rightarrow Fe_2(SO_4)_3 + 3H_2$ $\quad$ single replacement
  c. $2AgNO_3 + H_2S \rightarrow Ag_2S + 2HNO_3$ $\quad$ double replacement
  d. $Cl_2 + 2KI \rightarrow 2KCl + I_2$ $\qquad\qquad$ single replacement

5.53 **a.** $C_4H_8 + 6O_2 \rightarrow 4CO_2 + 4H_2O$
  b. $C_5H_{12} + 8O_2 \rightarrow 5CO_2 + 6H_2O$
  c. $C_6H_{12}O_6 + 6O_2 \rightarrow 6CO_2 + 6H_2O$

5.55 **a.** $Zn^{2+} + 2e^- \rightarrow Zn$ reduction   **b.** $Al \rightarrow Al^{3+} + 3\,e^-$ oxidation

c. $Pb \rightarrow Pb^{2+} + 2e^-$ oxidation   **d.** $Cl_2 + 2e^- \rightarrow 2Cl^-$ reduction

5.57 **a.** $0.150 \; \text{mole K} \; \times \; \dfrac{39.1 \text{ g K}}{1 \text{ mole K}} \; = 5.87 \text{ g K}$

b. $0.150 \; \text{mole Cl}_2 \; \times \; \dfrac{71.0 \text{ g Cl}_2}{1 \text{ mole Cl}_2} \; = 10.7 \text{ g Cl}_2$

c. $0.150 \; \text{mole Na}_2\text{CO}_3 \times \dfrac{106.0 \text{ g Na}_2\text{CO}_3}{1 \text{ mole Na}_2\text{CO}_3} = 15.9 \text{ g Na}_2\text{CO}_3$

5.59 **a.** $25.0 \; \text{g CO}_2 \; \times \; \dfrac{1 \text{ mole CO}_2}{44.0 \text{ g CO}_2} = 0.568 \text{ mole CO}_2$

b. $25.0 \; \text{g Al(OH)}_3 \; \times \; \dfrac{1 \text{ mole Al(OH)}_3}{78.0 \text{ g Al(OH)}_3} = 0.321 \text{ mole Al(OH)}_3$

c. $25.0 \; \text{g MgCl}_2 \; \times \; \dfrac{1 \text{ mole MgCl}_2}{95.3 \text{ g MgCl}_2} = 0.262 \text{ mole MgCl}_2$

5.61 **a.** $124 \; \text{g C}_2\text{H}_6\text{O} \; \times \; \dfrac{1 \text{ mole C}_2\text{H}_6\text{O}}{46.0 \text{ g C}_2\text{H}_6\text{O}} \; \times \; \dfrac{1 \text{ mole C}_6\text{H}_{12}\text{O}_6}{2 \text{ moles C}_2\text{H}_6\text{O}} = 1.35 \text{ moles C}_6\text{H}_{12}\text{O}_6$

b. $0.240 \; \text{kg C}_6\text{H}_{12}\text{O}_6 \; \times \; \dfrac{1000 \text{ g}}{1 \text{ kg}} \; \times \; \dfrac{1 \text{ mole C}_6\text{H}_{12}\text{O}_6}{180.0 \text{ g C}_6\text{H}_{12}\text{O}_6} \; \times \; \dfrac{2 \text{ moles C}_2\text{H}_6\text{O}}{1 \text{ mole C}_6\text{H}_{12}\text{O}_6} \; \times \; \dfrac{46.0 \text{ g C}_2\text{H}_6\text{O}}{1 \text{ mole C}_2\text{H}_6\text{O}}$

$= 123 \text{ g C}_2\text{H}_6\text{O}$

5.63 $2NH_3 + 5F_2 \rightarrow N_2F_4 + 6HF$

a. $4.00 \; \text{moles HF} \; \times \; \dfrac{2 \text{ moles NH}_3}{6 \text{ moles HF}} = 1.33 \text{ moles NH}_3$

$4.00 \; \text{moles HF} \; \times \; \dfrac{5 \text{ moles F}_2}{6 \text{ moles HF}} = 3.33 \text{ moles F}_2$

b. $1.50 \; \text{moles NH}_3 \; \times \; \dfrac{5 \text{ moles F}_2}{2 \text{ moles NH}_3} \; \times \; \dfrac{38.0 \text{ g F}_2}{1 \text{ mole F}_2} = 143 \text{ g F}_2$

c. $3.40 \; \text{g NH}_3 \; \times \; \dfrac{1 \text{ mole NH}_3}{17.0 \text{ g NH}_3} \; \times \; \dfrac{1 \text{ mole N}_2\text{F}_4}{2 \text{ moles NH}_3} \; \times \; \dfrac{104.0 \text{ g N}_2\text{F}_4}{1 \text{ mole N}_2\text{F}_4} = 10.4 \text{ g N}_2\text{F}_4$

6

Energy and States of Matter

Study Goals

- Describe potential and kinetic energy.
- Calculate the calories lost or gained by a specific amount of a substance for a specific temperature change.
- Determine the kilocalories for food samples.
- Determine the energy lost or gained during a change of state at the melting or boiling point.
- Identify the states of matter and changes of state on a heating or cooling curve.
- Describe the types of forces that hold particles together in liquids and solids.
- Describe the factors that affect the rate of a reaction.
- Use the concept of reversible reactions to explain chemical equilibriium.

Think About It

1. What kinds of activities did you do today that used *kinetic* energy?

2. What are some of the forms of energy you use in your home?

3. Why is the energy in your breakfast cereal *potential* energy?

4. Why is the high specific heat of water important to our survival?

5. How does perspiring during a workout help to keep you cool?

6. During a rain or snowfall, temperature rises? Why?

7. Why is a steam burn much more damaging to skin than a hot water burn?

Key Terms

Match the following terms with the statements below:

a. change of state   b. kinetic energy   c. potential energy
d. calorie

1. _____ The amount of heat needed to raise the temperature of 1 g of water by 1°C.

2. _____ Water boiling at 100°C.

3. _____ The energy of motion.

4. _____ Stored energy.

Answers   1. d   2. a   3. b   4. c

6.1 Energy and Heat

- Energy is the ability to do work.
- Potential energy is stored energy; kinetic energy is the energy of motion.
- Some forms of energy include heat, mechanical, radiant, solar, electrical, chemical, and nuclear.
- Specific heat is the amount of energy required to raise the temperature of 1 g of a substance by 1°C.
- The specific heat for liquid water is 1.00 calorie/g°C or 4.18 joules/g°C.

◆ Learning Exercise 6.1A

Match the words in column A with the descriptions in column B.

A

1. _____ kinetic energy
2. _____ potential energy
3. _____ chemical energy
4. _____ energy

B

a. Inactive or stored energy.
b. The ability to do work.
c. The energy of motion.
d. The energy available in the bonds of chemical compounds.

Answers   **1.** c   **2.** a   **3.** d   **4.** b

◆ Learning Exercise 6.1B

State whether the following statements describe potential (P) or kinetic (K) energy:

1. _____ A potted plant sitting on a ledge.
2. _____ Your breakfast cereal.
3. _____ Logs sitting in a fireplace.
4. _____ A piece of candy.
5. _____ An arrow shot from a bow.
6. _____ A ski jumper at the top of the ski jump.
7. _____ A jogger running.
8. _____ A sky diver waiting to jump.
9. _____ Water flowing down a stream.
10. _____ A bowling ball striking the pins.

Answers   **1.** P   **2.** P   **3.** P   **4.** P   **5.** K
             6. P   **7.** K   **8.** P   **9.** K   **10.** K

◆ Learning Exercise 6.1C

Match the words in column A with the descriptions in column B.

A

1. _____ calorie
2. _____ specific heat
3. _____ kilocalorie

B

a. 1000 calories.
b. The heat needed to raise 1 g of water by 1°C.
c. A measure of the ability of a substance to absorb heat.

Answers   **1.** b   **2.** c   **3.** a

◆ **Learning Exercise 6.1D**

Study Note

The heat lost or gained by a substance is calculated from the mass, temperature change, and specific heat of the substance.
 	
     Heat (calories) = **mass** (g) × **temperature change** (ΔT) × **specific heat** (cal/g°C)
     There are 4.18 joules in one calorie.
     Number of calories × 4.18 = number of joules

Calculate the calories (cal) gained or released during the following:

1. Heating 20. g of water from 22°C to 77°C.

2. Heating 10. g of water from 12°C to 97°C.

3. Cooling 4.00 kg of water from 80.0°C to 35.0°C.

4. Cooling 125 g of water from 45.0°C to 72.0°C.

Answers	**1.** 1100 cal	**2.** 850 cal
	3. 180,000 cal	**4.** 3380 cal

6.2 Energy and Nutrition

- A nutritional Calorie is the same amount of energy as 1 kcal or 1000 calories.
- When a substance is burned in a calorimeter, the water that surrounds the reaction chamber absorbs the heat given off. The calories absorbed by the water are calculated and the caloric value (energy per gram) is determined for the substance

◆ **Learning Exercise 6.2A**

State the caloric value in kcal/g associated with the following:

a. amino acid _____   **b.** protein _____

c. sugar _____   **d.** sucrose _____

e. oil _____   **f.** fat _____

g. starch _____   **h.** lipid _____

i. glucose _____   **j.** lard _____

Answers	**a.** 4 kcal/g	**b.** 4 kcal/g	**c.** 4 kcal/g	**d.** 4 kcal/g	**e.** 9 kcal/g
	f. 9 kcal/g	**g.** 4 kcal/g	**h.** 9 kcal/g	**i.** 4 kcal/g	**j.** 9 kcal/g

86

◆ Learning Exercise 6.2B

Study Note

The caloric content of a food is the sum of calories from carbohydrate, fat, and protein. It is calculated by using their number of grams in a food and the caloric values of 4 kcal/g for carbohydrate and protein, and 9 kcal/g for fat.

Calculate the kcal for the following foods using the following calorimetry data:

Food	Carbohydrate	Fat	Protein	kcal
a. Peas, green, cooked	19 g	1 g	9 g	_____
b. Potato chips, 10 chips	10 g	8 g	1 g	_____
c. Cream cheese, 8 oz	5 g	86 g	18 g	_____
d. Hamburger, lean, 3 oz	0	10 g	23 g	_____
e. Salmon, canned	0	5 g	17 g	_____
f. Snap beans, 1 cup	7 g	2 g	30 g	_____
g. Banana, 1	26 g	0	1 g	_____

Answers   **a.** 120 kcal **b.** 120 kcal **c.** 870 kcal **d.** 180 kcal
e. 110 kcal **f.** 170 kcal **g.** 110 kcal

◆ Learning Exercise 6.2C

Using caloric values, give answers with two significant figures for each of the following problems:

1. How many kcal are in a single serving of pudding that contains 4 g protein, 31 g of carbohydrate, and 5 g of fat?

2. A can of tuna has a caloric value of 200 kcal. If there are 2 g of fat and no carbohydrate, how many grams of protein are contained in the can of tuna?

3. A serving of breakfast cereal provides 220 kcal. In this serving, there are 8 g of protein and 6 g of fat. How many grams of carbohydrates are in the cereal?

4. Complete the following table listing ingredients for a peanut butter sandwich.

	Protein	Carbohydrate	Fat	kcal
2 slices bread	4 g	30 g	0	_____
2 Tbsp peanut butter	8 g	6 g	_____	170 kcal
2 tsp jelly	0	_____	0	40 kcal
1 tsp margarine	0	0	5 g	_____

Total kcal in sandwich _____

Answers

1. protein 16 kcal + carbohydrate 124 kcal + fat 45 kcal = 190 kcal

2. fat 18 kcal; 200 kcal – 18 = protein 182 kcal; 46 g protein

3. protein 32 kcal + fat 54 kcal = 86 kcal protein and fat; 220 kcal – 86 kcal = 134 kcal due to carbohydrate; 134 kcal/4 kcal/g = 34 g carbohydrate.

4. bread, 136 kcal; peanut butter, 13 g fat; jelly, 10 g carbohydrate; margarine, 45 kcal; total = 400 kcal (4.0×10^2 kcal)

6.3 States of Matter

- Matter is anything that has mass and occupies space.
- The three states of matter are solid, liquid, and gas.
- Physical properties such as shape, state, or color can change without affecting the identity of a substance.

◆ Learning Exercise 6.3

State whether the following statements describe a gas (G), a liquid (L), or a solid (S).

1. _____ There are no attractions among the molecules.

2. _____ Particles are held close together in a definite pattern.

3. _____ The substance has a definite volume, but no definite shape.

4. _____ The particles are moving extremely fast.

5. _____ This substance has no definite shape and no definite volume.

6. _____ The particles are very far apart.

7. _____ This material has its own volume, but takes the shape of its container.

8. _____ The particles of this material bombard the sides of the container with great force.

9. _____ The particles in this substance are moving very, very slowly.

10. _____ This substance has a definite volume and a definite shape.

Answers 1. G 2. S 3. L 4. G 5. G
6. G 7. L 8. G 9. S 10. S

6.4 Changes of State

- A substance undergoes a physical change when its shape, size, or state changes, but not the type of substance itself.
- A substance melts and freezes at its melting (freezing) point.
- As long as a substance is changing state during boiling, or condensation, the temperature remains constant.
- The *heat of fusion,* is the heat energy required to change 1 g of solid to liquid. For water to freeze at 0°C, the heat of fusion is 80. calories. This is also the amount of heat lost when 1 gram of water freezes at 0°C.
- Sublimation is the change of state from a solid directly to a gas.
- When water boils at 100°C, 540 calories, the heat of vaporization, is required to change 1 g of liquid to gas (steam); it is also the amount of heat released when 1 g of water vapor condenses at 100°C.
- A heating or cooling curve illustrates the changes in temperature and states as heat is added to or removed from a substance.

◆ Learning Exercise 6.4A

Identify each of the following as

1. melting   2. freezing   3. sublimation.

a. _____ A liquid changes to a solid

b. _____ Ice forms on the surface of a lake in winter.

c. _____ Dry ice in an ice cream cart changes to a gas.

d. _____ Butter in a hot pan turns to liquid.

Answers   a. 2   b. 2   c. 3   d. 1

◆ Learning Exercise 6.4B

Study Note
The amount of heat needed or released during melting or freezing can be calculated using the heat of fusion: Heat (cal) = mass (g) × heat of fusion

Calculate the energy required or released when the following substances melt or freeze:

a. How many calories are needed to melt 15 g ice at 0°C?

b. How much heat in kilocalories is released when 325 g of water freezes at 0°C?

c. How many grams of ice would melt when 4 000 calories of heat were absorbed?

Answers   a. 1200 cal   b. 26 kcal   c. 50 g

◆ **Learning Exercise 6.4C**

Calculate the energy required or released for the following substances undergoing boiling or condensation:

a. How many calories are needed to completely change 10. g of water to vapor at 100°C?

b. How many kilocalories are released when 515 grams of steam at 100°C condense to form liquid water at 100°C?

c. How many grams of water can be converted to steam at 100°C when 272 kcal of energy are absorbed?

Answers   **a.** 5400 cal   **b.** 278 kcal   **c.** 504 g

◆ **Learning Exercise 6.4D**

On each heating or cooling curve, indicate the portion that corresponds to a solid, liquid, gas, and the changes in state.

1. Draw a heating curve for water that begins at –20°C and ends at 120°C. Water has a melting point of 0°C and a boiling point of 100°C.

↑
Temperature (°C)

Heat added ⟶

2. Draw a heating curve for bromine from −25° to 75°C. Bromine has a melting point of −7°C and a boiling point of 59¡C.

Temperature (°C) ↑

Heat added ⟶

3. Draw a cooling curve for sodium from 1000°C to 0°C. Sodium has a freezing point of 98°C and a boiling (condensation) point of 883°C.

Temperature (°C) ↑

Heat removed ⟶

Answers:

1.

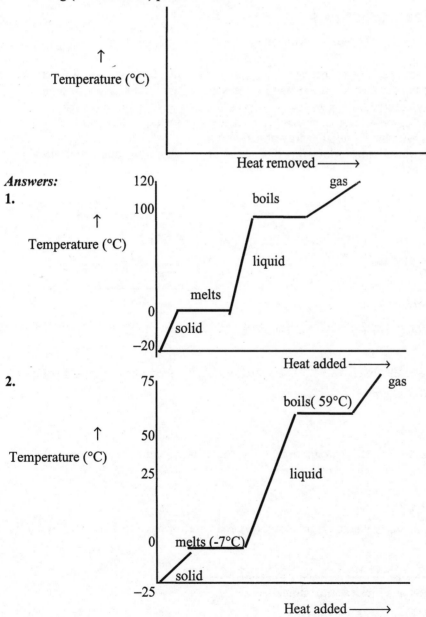

Temperature (°C) ↑

120
100
0
−20

gas
boils
liquid
melts
solid

Heat added ⟶

2.

Temperature (°C) ↑

75
50
25
0
−25

gas
boils(59°C)
liquid
melts (-7°C)
solid

Heat added ⟶

91

3.

6.5 Energy in Chemical Reactions

- In a reaction, molecules (or atoms) must collide with energy equal to or greater than the energy of activation.
- The heat of reaction is the energy difference between the energy of the reactants and the products.
- In exothermic reactions, the heat of reaction is the energy released. In endothermic reactions, the heat of reaction is the energy absorbed.
- At higher temperatures, reaction rates increase because reactants move faster, collide more often, and produce more collisions with the required energy of activation.
- Increasing the concentration of reactants or lowering the energy of activation by adding a catalyst increases the rate of a reaction.
- The reaction rate slows when the temperature or the concentration of reactants is decreased.

◆ Learning Exercise 6.5A
Indicate whether each of the following is an endothermic or exothermic reaction:

1. $2H_2(g) + O_2(g) \longrightarrow 2H_2O(g) + 137$ kcal _____

2. $C_2H_4(g) + 42$ kcal $\longrightarrow H_2(g) + C_2H_2(g)$ _____

3. $2C(s) + O_2(g) \longrightarrow 2CO(g) + 53$ kcal _____

4. $C_6H_{12}O_6(s) + 6 O_2(g) \longrightarrow 6CO_2(g) + 6 H_2O(l) + 1350$ kcal _____
  glucose

5. $C_2H_4(g) + H_2O(g) \longrightarrow C_2H_5OH(l) + 21$ kcal _____

Answers   **1.** exothermic   **2.** endothermic   **3.** exothermic
               4. exothermic   **5.** exothermic

◆ Learning Exercise 6.5B
Indicate whether the following changes would (I) increase, (D) decrease, or have (N) no effect upon the rate of a chemical reaction:

1. _____ adding a catalyst

2. _____ running the reaction at a lower temperature

3. _____ doubling the concentration of the reactants

4. _____ removing a catalyst

5. _____ running the experiment in a different laboratory

6. _____ increasing the temperature

7. _____ using a larger container

8. _____ using a lower concentration of reactants

Answers   **1.** I   **2.** D   **3.** I   **4.** D   **5.** N   **6.** I   **7.** N   **8.** D

6.6 Chemical Equilibrium

- Chemical equilibrium is achieved when the rate of the forward reaction becomes equal to the rate of the reverse reaction.
- A change in the concentration of the reactants or products or the temperature shifts the equilibrium in the direction to relieve the stress.

◆ Learning Exercise 6.6

Identify the effect of each of the following changes on the equilibrium of the reaction

$$N_2(g) + O_2(g) \rightleftarrows 2\,NO(g) + Heat$$

A. Shift toward products   **B.** Shift toward reactants   **C.** No change

1. _____ Adding $O_2(g)$ **2.** _____ Removing $N_2(g)$

3. _____ Removing $NO(g)$ **4.** _____ Adding heat

Answers   **1.** A   **2.** B   **3.** A   **4.** B

Check List for Chapter 6

You are ready to take the practice test for Chapter 6. Be sure that you have accomplished the following learning goals for this chapter. If you are not sure, review the section listed at the end of the goal. Then apply your new skills and understanding to the practice test.

After studying Chapter 6, I can successfully:

_____Describe some forms of energy (6.1).

_____Given the mass of a sample, specific heat, and the temperature change, calculate the heat lost or gained (6.1).

_____Calculate the energy of a food sample (6.2).

_____Identify the physical state of a substance as a solid, liquid, or gas (6.3).

_____Calculate the heat change for the boiling and condensation of a specific amount of a substance (6.4).

_____Draw heating and cooling curves using the melting and boiling points of a substance (6.4).

_____Identify the energy change in a reaction as exothermic or endothermic (6.5).

_____Describe the factors that increase or decreases the rate of a reaction (6.5).

_____Describe the factors that cause a shift in the equilibrium of a reversible reaction (6.6).

Practice Test for Chapter 6

1. Which of the following would be described as potential energy?
   A. A car going around a racetrack. B. A rabbit hopping.
   C. Oil in an oil well. D. A moving merry-go-round.
   E. A bouncing ball.

2. Which of the following would be described as kinetic energy?
   A. A car battery B. A can of tennis balls.
   C. Gasoline in a car fuel tank D. A box of matches
   E. A tennis ball crossing over the net

3. The number of calories needed to raise the temperature of 5.0 g water from 25°C to 55°C is
   A. 5 cal B. 30 cal C. 5 cal D. 80 cal E. 150 cal

4. The number of calories (kcal) released when 150 g of water cools from 58°C to 22°C.
   A. 1.1 kcal B. 4.2 kcal C. 5.4 kcal D. 6.9 kcal E. 8.7 kcal

For questions 5 through 8, consider a cup of milk with a caloric value of 165 kcal. In the cup of milk, there are 9 g of fat, 12 g of carbohydrate, and some protein.

5. The number of kcal provided by the carbohydrate is
   A. 4 kcal B. 9 kcal C. 36 kcal D. 48 kcal E. 81 kcal

6. The number of kcal provided by the fat is
   A. 4 kcal B. 9 kcal C. 36 kcal D. 48 kcal E. 81 kcal

7. The number of kcal provided by the protein is
   A. 4 kcal B. 9 kcal C. 36 kcal D. 48 kcal E. 81 kcal

8. Which of the following describes a liquid?
   A. A substance that has no definite shape and no definite volume.
   B. A substance with particles that are far apart.
   C. A substance with a definite shape and a definite volume.
   D. A substance containing particles that are moving very fast.
   E. A substance that has a definite volume, but takes the shape of its container.

Identify the statements in questions 9 through 12 as:
   A. evaporation B. heat of fusion
   C. heat of vaporization D. boiling

9. _____ The energy required to convert a gram of solid to liquid.

10. _____ The heat needed to boil a liquid.

11. _____ The conversion of liquid molecules to gas at the surface of a liquid.

12. _____ The formation of a gas within the liquid as well as on the surface.

13. Ice cools down a drink because
    A. the ice is colder than the drink and heat flows into the ice cubes.
    B. heat is absorbed from the drink to melt the ice cubes.
    C. the heat of fusion of the ice is higher than the heat of fusion for water.
    D. Both A and B
    E. None of the above

14. The number of kilocalories needed to convert 400 g of ice to liquid at 0°C is
    A. 400 kcal B. 320 kcal C. 80 kcal D. 40 kcal E. 32 kcal

For questions 15 through 18, consider the heating curve below for *p*-toluidine. Answer the following questions when heat is added to *p*-toluidine at 20°C where toluidine is below its melting point.

Heat added ⟶

15. On the heating curve, segment BC indicates
    A. solid   B. melting   C. liquid   D. boiling   E. gas

16. On the heating curve, segment CD shows toluidine as
    A. solid   B. melting   C. liquid   D. boiling   E. gas

17. The boiling point of toluidine would be
    A. 20°C   B. 45°C   C. 100°C   D. 200°C   E. 250°C

18. On the heating curve, segment EF shows toluidine as
    A. solid   B. melting   C. a liquid   D. boiling   E. a gas

Identify the changes in questions 19 through 23 as (A) exothermic or (B) endothermic.

19. _____ The flow of heat from a reaction to the surroundings.

20. _____ The absorption of light energy by green plants to synthesize starches.

21. _____ The energy of the products are lower than the energy of the reactants.

22. _____ $2H_2O\ (l) + 137\ kcal \longrightarrow 2H_2\ (g) + O_2\ (g)$

23. _____ $2NO\ (g) \longrightarrow N_2\ (g) + O_2\ (g) + 43\ kcal$

For questions 24 through 28, indicate how each of the following affects the equilibrium of the reaction shown here.

$$PCl_5\ (g) + Heat \rightleftarrows PCl_3\ (g) + Cl_2\ (g)$$

A. Shift to the right   B. Shift to the left   C. No change

24. _____ Add Cl_2 25. _____ Cool the reaction   26. _____ Remove PCl_3

27. _____ Add PCl_5 28. _____ Remove PCl_5

For questions 29 through 33, indicate whether the rate of reaction would (I) increase, (D) decreases, or (N) not change for the following reaction:

$$Cl_2\ (g) + CHCl_3\ (g) \longrightarrow HCl\ (g) + CCl_4\ (g)$$

29. _____ Add Cl_2 30. _____ Increase temperature

31. _____ Add a catalyst   32. _____ Decrease $CHCl_3$

33. _____ Cool the reaction

95

Answers to the Practice Test

1. C	2. E	3. E	4. C	5. D
6. E	7. C	8. E	9. B	10. C
11. A	12. D	13. D	14. E	15. B
16. C	17. D	18. E	19. A	20. B
21. A	22. B	23. A	24. B	25. B
26. A	27. B	28. B	29. I	30. I
31. I	32. D	33. D		

Answers and Solutions to Selected Text Problems

6.1 At the top of the hill, all of the energy of the car is in the form of potential energy. As it descends down the hill, potential energy is being converted into kinetic energy. When the car reaches the bottom, all of its energy is in the form of motion (kinetic energy).

6.3 **a.** potential **b.** kinetic **c.** potential **d.** potential

6.5 Copper has the lowest specific heat of the samples and will reach the highest temperature.

6.7 **a.** $\Delta T = 25°C - 15°C = 10°C$ $\qquad 25 \text{ g} \times \dfrac{1.00 \text{ cal}}{\text{g°C}} \times 10°C = 250 \text{ cal}$

  b. $150 \text{ g} \times \dfrac{4.18 \text{ J}}{\text{g°C}} \times 75°C = 47\,000 \text{ J}$

  c. $150 \text{ g} \times \dfrac{1.00 \text{ cal}}{\text{g°C}} \times 62°C = 9.3 \text{ kcal}$

6.9 Recall that a Calorie is equivalent to a kilocalorie!

  a. Because the orange juice contains both carbohydrate and protein, two calculations will be needed.

  $$26 \text{ g carbohydrate} \times \dfrac{4 \text{ Cal}}{\text{g carbohydrate}} = 100 \text{ Cal}$$

  $$2 \text{ g protein} \times \dfrac{4 \text{ Cal}}{\text{g protein}} = 8 \text{ Cal}$$

  Total: 100 Cal + 8 Cal = 110 Cal

  b. With only carbohydrate present, a single calculation is all that is required.

  $$72 \text{ kcal} \times \dfrac{1 \text{ g carbohydrate}}{4 \text{ kcal}} = 18 \text{ g carbohydrate}$$

  c. With only fat present, a single calculation is all that is required.

  $$14 \text{ g fat} \times \dfrac{9 \text{ Cal}}{\text{g fat}} = 130 \text{ Cal}$$

  d. Three calculations are needed:

  $$30. \text{ g carbohydrate} \times \dfrac{4 \text{ kcal}}{\text{g carbohydrate}} \times \dfrac{1 \text{ Cal}}{1 \text{ kcal}} = 120 \text{ Cal}$$

$$15 \ \cancel{\text{g fat}} \times \frac{9 \text{ Cal}}{\cancel{\text{g fat}}} \times \frac{1 \text{ Cal}}{\cancel{1 \text{ kcal}}} = 140 \text{ Cal}$$

$$5 \ \cancel{\text{g protein}} \times \frac{4 \text{ kcal}}{\cancel{\text{g protein}}} \times \frac{1 \text{ Cal}}{\cancel{1 \text{ kcal}}} = 20 \text{ Cal} - \text{Total: } 120 \text{ Cal} + 140 \text{ Cal} + 20 \text{ Cal} = 280 \text{ Cal}$$

6.11 Three calculations are needed:

$$9 \ \cancel{\text{g protein}} \times \frac{4 \text{ kcal}}{\cancel{\text{g protein}}} = 40 \text{ kcal}$$

$$12 \ \cancel{\text{g fat}} \times \frac{9 \text{ kcal}}{\cancel{\text{g fat}}} = 110 \text{ kcal}$$

$$16 \ \cancel{\text{g carbohydrate}} \times \frac{4 \text{ kcal}}{\cancel{\text{g carbohydrate}}} = 64 \text{ kcal}$$

Total: 40 kcal + 110 kcal + 64 kcal = 210 kcal

6.13 **a.** gas   **b.** gas   **c.** solid

6.15 **a.** melting   **b.** sublimation   **c.** freezing

6.17 **a.** $65 \ \cancel{\text{g ice}} \times \dfrac{80. \text{ cal}}{1 \ \cancel{\text{g ice}}} = 5200 \text{ cal absorbed}$

       b. $17.0 \ \cancel{\text{g ice}} \times \dfrac{80. \text{ cal}}{1 \ \cancel{\text{g ice}}} = 1400 \text{ cal absorbed}$

       c. $225 \ \cancel{\text{g water}} \times \dfrac{80. \ \cancel{\text{cal}}}{1 \ \cancel{\text{g water}}} \times \dfrac{1 \text{ kcal}}{1000 \ \cancel{\text{cal}}} = 18 \text{ kcal released}$

6.19 **a.** condensation   **b.** evaporation   **c.** boiling   **d.** condensation

6.21 **a.** The liquid water in perspiration absorbs heat and changes to vapor. The heat needed for the change is removed from the skin.
       b. On a hot day, there are more liquid water molecules in the damp clothing that have sufficient energy to become water vapor. Thus, water evaporates from the clothes more readily on a hot day.

6.23 **a.** $10.0 \ \cancel{\text{g water}} \times \dfrac{540 \text{ cal}}{1 \ \cancel{\text{g water}}} = 540 \text{ cal absorbed}$

       b. $50.0 \ \cancel{\text{g water}} \times \dfrac{540 \ \cancel{\text{cal}}}{1 \ \cancel{\text{g water}}} \times \dfrac{1 \text{ kcal}}{1000 \ \cancel{\text{cal}}} = 27 \text{ kcal absorbed}$

       c. $8.0 \ \cancel{\text{kg steam}} \times \dfrac{1000 \ \cancel{\text{g}}}{1 \ \cancel{\text{kg}}} \times \dfrac{540 \ \cancel{\text{cal}}}{1 \ \cancel{\text{g steam}}} \times \dfrac{1 \text{ kcal}}{1000 \ \cancel{\text{cal}}} = 4300 \text{ kcal released}$

6.25

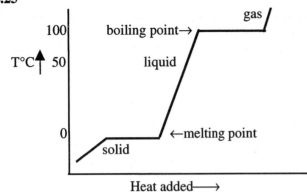

6.27 **a.** The energy of activation is the energy required to break the bonds in the reactants.
   b. A catalyst lowers the activation energy by providing an alternate path, which increases the rate of a reaction.
   c. In exothermic reactions, the energy of the products is lower than the reactants.
   d.

6.29 **a.** exothermic; heat loss **b.** endothermic; heat gain **c.** exothermic; heat loss

6.31 **a.** exothermic   **b.** endothermic   **c.** exothermic

6.33 **a.** The rate of a reaction relates the speed at which reactants are transformed into products.
   b. Because more reactants will have the energy necessary to proceed to products (the activation energy) at room temperature than at refrigerator temperatures, the rate of formation of mold will be higher at room temperature.

6.35 **a.** Addition of a reactant increases the reaction rate.
   b. Increasing the temperature increases the number of collisions with the energy of activation. The rate of reaction will be increased.
   c. Addition of a catalyst increases the reaction rate.
   d. Removal of reactant decreases the reaction rate.

6.37 In a reversible reaction, the forward reaction converts reactants to products and a reverse reaction converts products back to reactants again.

6.39 **a.** Addition of a reactant pushes the reaction toward the product side.
   b. Addition of heat to an exothermic reaction pushes the reaction toward the reactant side.
   c. Removal of a product pulls the reaction toward the product side.
   d. Removal of a reactant pulls the reaction toward the reactant side.

6.41 **a.** Addition of a reactant pushes the reaction toward the product side.
   b. Addition of a product pushes the reaction toward the reactant side.
   c. Addition of heat to an endothermic reaction pushes the reaction toward the product side.
   d. Removal of heat from an endothermic reaction pulls the reaction to the reactant side.

6.43 As gaseous carbon dioxide escapes into the atmosphere, product is removed from the reaction system. According to LeChatelier's principle, the reaction will shift toward the product side in an attempt to re-establish equilibrium. However, the soda is open to the atmosphere and will continue to lose its carbonation.

6.45 From Table 6.1, we see that liquid water has a high specific heat (1.00 cal/g °C), which means that a large amount of energy is required to cause a significant temperature change. Sand, on the other hand, has a low specific heat (0.19 cal/g °C), so even a small amount of energy will cause a significant temperature change in the sand.

6.47 Both water condensation (formation of rain) and deposition (formation of snow) from the gaseous moisture in the air are exothermic processes (heat is released). The heat released in either of these processes warms the surrounding air, and so the air temperature is in fact raised.

6.49 **a.** For 15% of one's total Calories (kcal) to be supplied by protein, a conversion factor of 15 kcal from protein/100 kcal total in the daily diet will be used in the calculation. Similar factors will be used for the carbohydrate (carbs) and fat calculations.

$$1200 \text{ kcal (total)} \times \frac{15 \text{ kcal (protein)}}{100 \text{ kcal (total)}} \times \frac{1 \text{ g protein}}{4 \text{ kcal (protein)}} = 45 \text{ g protein}$$

$$1200 \text{ kcal (total)} \times \frac{45 \text{ kcal (carbs)}}{100 \text{ kcal (total)}} \times \frac{1 \text{ g carbs}}{4 \text{ kcal (carbs)}} = 140 \text{ g carbohydrate}$$

$$1200 \text{ kcal (total)} \times \frac{40 \text{ kcal (fat)}}{100 \text{ kcal (total)}} \times \frac{1 \text{ g fat}}{4 \text{ kcal (fat)}} = 53 \text{ g fat}$$

b. The calculations for part b differ from part a only in the total kcal per day.

$$1900 \text{ kcal (total)} \times \frac{15 \text{ kcal (protein)}}{100 \text{ kcal (total)}} \times \frac{1 \text{ g protein}}{4 \text{ kcal (protein)}} = 71 \text{ g protein}$$

$$1900 \text{ kcal (total)} \times \frac{45 \text{ kcal (carbs)}}{100 \text{ kcal (total)}} \times \frac{1 \text{ g carbs}}{4 \text{ kcal (carbs)}} = 210 \text{ g carbohydrate}$$

$$1900 \text{ kcal (total)} \times \frac{40 \text{ kcal (fat)}}{100 \text{ kcal (total)}} \times \frac{1 \text{ g fat}}{9 \text{ kcal (fat)}} = 84 \text{ g fat}$$

c. The calculations for part c again differ only in the total kcal per day.

$$2600 \text{ kcal (total)} \times \frac{15 \text{ kcal (protein)}}{100 \text{ kcal (total)}} \times \frac{1 \text{ g protein}}{4 \text{ kcal (protein)}} = 98 \text{ g protein}$$

$$2600 \text{ kcal (total)} \times \frac{45 \text{ kcal (carbs)}}{100 \text{ kcal (total)}} \times \frac{1 \text{ g carbs}}{4 \text{ kcal (carbs)}} = 290 \text{ g carbohydrate}$$

$$2600 \text{ kcal (total)} \times \frac{40 \text{ kcal (fat)}}{100 \text{ kcal (total)}} \times \frac{1 \text{ g fat}}{9 \text{ kcal (fat)}} = 120 \text{ g fat}$$

6.51 Because each gram of body fat contains 15% water, a person actually loses 85 grams of fat per hundred grams of body fat. (We considered 1 lb of fat as exactly 1 lb.)

$$1 \text{ lb body fat} \times \frac{454 \text{ g}}{1 \text{ lb}} \times \frac{85 \text{ g fat}}{100 \text{ g body fat}} \times \frac{9 \text{ kcal}}{1 \text{ g fat}} = 3500 \text{ kcal}$$

6.53 $\quad 725 \text{ g} \times \dfrac{1 \text{ cal}}{\text{g°C}} \times 28°\text{C} \times \dfrac{1 \text{ kcal}}{1000 \text{ cal}} = 20. \text{ kcal}$

Study Goals

- Describe the kinetic molecular theory of gases.
- Describe the units of measurement used for pressure, and change from one unit to another.
- Use the gas laws to determine the new pressure, volume, or temperature of a specific amount of gas.
- Describe the relationship between the amount of a gas and its volume.
- Use the combined gas law to find the new pressure, volume, or temperature of a gas when changes in two of these properties are given.
- Use partial pressure to calculate the total pressure of a gas mixture.

Think About It

1. How does a barometer work?

2. What happens to the pressure on a person who is scuba diving?

3. Why are airplanes pressurized?

4. Why does a bag of chips expand when you take it to a higher altitude?

Key Terms

Match the key terms with the statements shown below.

a. Kinetic theory   **b.** Pressure   **c.** Boyle's law
d. Charles' law   **e.** Partial pressure

1. _____ The volume of a gas varies directly with the Kelvin temperature when pressure and amount of gas remain constant.

2. _____ Force exerted by gas particles that collide with the sides of a container.

3. _____ The pressure exerted by the individual gases in a gas mixture.

4. _____ The volume of a gas varies inversely with the pressure of a gas when temperature and amount of gas are constant.

5. _____ A model that explains the behavior of gaseous particles.

Answers   **a.** 4   **b.** 2   **c.** 5   **d.** 3   **e.** 1

7.1 Gases and Kinetic Molecular Theory

- In a gas, particles are so far apart and moving so fast that they are not attracted to each other.
- A gas is described by the physical properties of pressure (P), volume (V), temperature (T), and amount in moles (n).

◆ Learning Exercise 7.1
True or false:

a. _____ Gases are composed of small particles.

b. _____ Gas molecules are usually close together.

c. _____ Gas molecules move rapidly because they are strongly attracted.

d. _____ The distances between gas molecules are great.

e. _____ Gas molecules travel in straight lines until they collide.

Answers   a. T   b. F   c. F   d. T   e. T

7.2 Gas Pressure

- A gas exerts pressure, which is the force of the gas particles on the surface of a container.
- Units of gas pressure include torr, mmHg, and atmosphere.

◆ Learning Exercise 7.2
Complete the following:

a. 1.50 atm = _____ mmHg

b. 550 mmHg = _____ atm

c. 725 mmHg = _____ torr

d. 1520 mmHg = _____ atm

Answers   a. 1140 mmHg   b. 0.72 atm   c. 725 torr
d. 2.00 atm

7.3 Pressure and Volume (Boyle s Law)

- According to Boyle's law, pressure increases if volume decreases; pressure decreases if volume increases.
- The volume (V) of a gas changes inversely with the pressure (P) of the gas when T and n are held constant: $P_1V_1 = P_2V_2$.

◆ Learning Exercise 7.3A
Complete with *increases* or *decreases*:

1. Gas pressure increases (T constant) when volume _____.

2. Gas volume increases at constant T when pressure _____.

Answers   1. decreases 2.   decreases

◆ **Learning Exercise 7.3B**

Calculate the variable in each of the following gas problems using Boyle's Law.

a. Four (4.0) liters of helium gas has a pressure of 800. mmHg. What will be the new pressure if the volume is reduced to 1.0 liter (*n* and *T* constant)?

b. A gas occupies a volume of 360 mL at 750 mmHg. What volume does it occupy at a pressure of (1) 1500 mm Hg? (2) 375 mm Hg? (*n* and *T* constant)

c. A gas sample at a pressure of 5.0 atm has a volume of 3.00 L. If the gas pressure is changed to 760 mm Hg, what volume will the gas occupy (*n* and *T* constant)?

d. A sample of 250. mL of nitrogen is initially at a pressure of 2.50 atm. If the pressure changes to 825 mm Hg, what is the new volume in mL (*n* and *T* constant)?

Answers	**a.** 3200 mmHg	**b.** (1) 180 mL (2) 720 mL	
	c. 15 L	**d.** 576 mL	

7.4 Temperature and Volume (Charles Law)

• The volume (V) of a gas is directly related to its Kelvin temperature (T) when there is no change in the pressure of the gas:

$$\frac{V_1}{T_1} = \frac{V_2}{T_2}$$

• According to *Charles'* Law, temperature increases if the volume of the gas increases; temperature decreases if volume decreases.

◆ **Learning Exercise 7.4A**

Complete with *increases* or *decreases*:

a. When the temperature of a gas increases at constant pressure, its volume _____.

b. When the volume of a gas decreases at constant pressure, its temperature _____.

Answers: **a.** increases   **b.** decreases

◆ **Learning Exercise 7.4B**

Use Charles' law to solve the following gas problems.

a. A large balloon has a volume of 2.5 L at a temperature of 0°C. What is the new volume of the balloon when the temperature rises to 120°C and the pressure remains constant?

b. Consider a balloon filled with helium to a volume of 6600 L at a temperature of 223°C. To what temperature must the gas be cooled to decrease the volume to 4800 L? (*P* constant)

c. A sample of 750 mL of neon is heated from 120°C to 350°C. If pressure is kept constant, what is the new volume?

d. What is the final temperature of 350 mL of oxygen gas at 22°C if its volume increases to 0.80 L? (*P* constant)

Answers   **a.** 3.6 L   **b.** 88°C   **c.** 1200 mL   **d.** 401°C

7.5 Temperature and Pressure (Gay-Lussac s Law)

- The pressure (*P*) of a gas is directly related to its Kelvin temperature (*T*).

$$\frac{P_1}{T_1} = \frac{P_2}{T_2}$$

This means that an increase in temperature increases the pressure of a gas, or a decrease in temperature decreases the pressure, as long as the volume stays constant.

◆ **Learning Exercise 7.5**

Solve the following gas law problems using Gay-Lussac's law.

a. A sample of helium gas has a pressure of 860 mmHg at a temperature of 225 K. At what pressure (mmHg) will the helium sample reach a temperature of 675 K? (*V* constant)

b. A balloon contains a gas with a pressure of 580 mmHg and a temperature of 227°C. What is the new pressure (mmHg) of the gas when the temperature drops to 27°C?
(*V* constant)

c. A spray can contains a gas with a pressure of 3.0 atm at a temperature of 17°C. What is the pressure (atm) in the container if the temperature inside the can rises to 110°C?
(*V* constant)

d. A gas has a pressure of 1200 mmHg at 300.°C. What will the temperature (°C) be when the pressure falls to 1.10 atm?
(*V* constant)

Answers   **a.** 2580 mmHg   **b.** 348 mmHg
              c. 4.0 atm   **d.** 126°C

7.6 The Combined Gas Law

- The gas laws can be combined into a relationship of pressure (*P*), volume (*V*) and temperature (*T*).

$$\frac{P_1 V_1}{T_1} = \frac{P_2 V_2}{T_2}$$

This expression is used to determine the effect of changes in two of the variables on the third.

◆ Learning Exercise 7.6
Solve the following using the combined gas laws:

a. A 5.0 L sample of nitrogen gas has a pressure of 1200 mmHg at 220 K. What is the pressure of the sample when the volume increases to 20.0 L at 440 K?

b. A 10.0 L sample of gas is emitted from a volcano with a pressure of 1.20 atm and a temperature of 150.0°C. What is the volume of the gas when its pressure is 0.900 atm and the temperature is −40.0°C?

104

c. A 25.0-mL bubble forms at the ocean depths where the pressure is 10.0 atm and the temperature is 5.0°C. What is the volume of that bubble at the ocean surface where the pressure is 760.0 mmHg and the temperature is 25°C?

d. A 35.0 mL sample of argon gas has a pressure of 1.0 atm and a temperature of 15°C. What is the final volume if the pressure goes to 2.0 atm and the temperature to 45°C?

e. A 315 L weather balloon is launched at the earth's surface where the temperature is 12°C and the pressure is 0.93 atm. What is the volume of the balloon in the upper atmosphere if the pressure is 116 mmHg and the temperature is −35°C?

Answers　　**a.** 600 mmHg　　**b.** 7.34 L　　**c.** 268 mL　　**d.** 19 mL　　**e.** 1600 L

7.7 Volume and Moles (Avogadro's Law)

- Avogadro's law states that equal volumes of gases at the same temperature and pressure contain the same number of moles. The volume (V) of a gas is directly related to the number of moles of the gas when the pressure and temperature of the gas do not change.

$$\frac{V_1}{n_1} = \frac{V_2}{n_2}$$

- If the moles of gas increase, the volume must increase; if the moles of gas decrease, the volume decreases.
- At STP conditions, standard pressure (1 atm) and temperature (0°C), one mole of a gas occupies a volume of 22.4 L.

Study Note

AT STP, the molar volume factor 22.4 L/1 mole converts between moles of a gas and volume.

Example: How many liters would 2.00 mole N_2 occupy at STP?

Solution: 　　2.00 ~~mole N_2~~ × $\frac{22.4 \text{ L (STP)}}{1 \text{ mole } N_2}$ = 44.8 L (STP)

◆ Learning Exercise 7.7
Use Avogadro's law to solve the following gas problems:

a. A gas containing 0.50 mole of helium has a volume of 4.00 L. What is the new volume when 1.0 mole of nitrogen is added to the container when pressure and temperature remain constant?

b. A balloon containing 1.00 mole of oxygen has a volume of 15 L. What is the new volume of the balloon when 2.00 moles of helium are added (T and P constant)?

c. What is the volume occupied by 28.0 g of nitrogen (N_2) at STP?

d. What is the volume (in liters) of a container that holds 6.40 g O_2 at STP?

Answers: **a.** 12 L   **b.** 45 L   **c.** 22.4 L   **d.**   4.48 L

7.8 Partial Pressures (Dalton's Law)

- In a mixture of two or more gases, the total pressure is the sum of the partial pressures of the individual gases.

$$P_{total} = P_1 + P_2 + P_3 + L$$

- The partial pressure of a gas in a mixture is the pressure it would exert if it were the only gas in the container.

◆ Learning Exercise 7.8A

Use Dalton's law to solve the following problems about gas mixtures:

a. What is the pressure in mmHg of a sample of gases containing oxygen at 0.500 atm, nitrogen (N_2) at 132 torr, and helium at 224 mmHg?

b. What is the pressure (atm) of a gas sample containing helium at 285 mmHg and oxygen (O_2) at 1.20 atm?

c. A gas sample containing nitrogen (N_2) and oxygen (O_2) has a pressure of 1500. mmHg. If the partial pressure of the nitrogen is 0.900 atm, what is the partial pressure (mmHg) of the oxygen gas in the mixture?

Answers   **a.** 736 mm Hg   **b.** 1.58 atm   **c.** 816 mmHg

◆ Learning Exercise 7.8B

Fill in the blanks by writing *I (increases)* or *D (decreases)* for a gas in a closed container.

	Pressure	Volume	Moles	Temperature
a.	_____	increases	constant	constant
b.	increases	constant	_____	constant
c.	constant	decreases	_____	constant
d.	_____	constant	constant	increases
e.	constant	_____	constant	decreases
f.	_____	constant	increases	constant

Answers
a. D		**b.** I		**c.** D	
d. I		**e.** D		**f.** I	

◆ Learning Exercise 7.8C

Complete the table for typical blood gas values for partial pressures.

Gas	Alveoli	Oxygenated blood	Deoxygenated blood	Tissues
CO_2	_____	_____	_____	_____
O_2	_____	_____	_____	_____

Answers

Gas	Alveoli	Oxygenated blood	Deoxygenated blood	Tissues
CO_2	40 mm Hg	40 mm Hg	46 mm Hg	50 mm Hg or greater
O_2	100 mm Hg	100 mm Hg	40 mm Hg	30 mm Hg or less

Check List for Chapter 7

You are ready to take the practice test for Chapter 7. Be sure that you have accomplished the following learning goals for this chapter. If you are not sure, review the section listed at the end of the goal. Then apply your new skills and understanding to the practice test.

After studying Chapter 7, I can successfully:

_____ Describe the kinetic theory of gases (7.1).

_____ Change the units of pressure from one to another (7.2).

_____ Use the pressure-volume relationship (Boyle's law) to determine the new pressure or volume of a fixed amount of gas at constant temperature (7.3).

_____ Use the temperature-volume relationship (Charles' law) to determine the new temperature or volume of a fixed amount of gas at a constant pressure (7.4).

_____ Use the temperature-pressure relationship (Gay-Lussac's law) to determine the new temperature or pressure of a certain amount of gas at a constant volume (7.5)

_____ Use the combined gas law to find the new pressure, volume, or temperature of a gas when changes in two of these properties are given (7.6).

_____ Describe the relationship between the amount of a gas and its volume (AV. Law) and use this relationship in calculations (7.7).

_____ Calculate the total pressure of a gas mixture from the partial pressures (7.8).

Practice Test for Chapter 7

Answer questions 1 through 5 using T (true) or F (false):

1. _____ A gas does not have its own volume or shape.

2. _____ The molecules of a gas are moving extremely fast.

3. _____ The collisions of gas molecules with the walls of their container create pressure.

4. _____ Gas molecules are close together and move in straight-line patterns.

5. _____ We consider gas molecules to have no attractions between them.

6. When a gas is heated in a closed metal container, the

   A. pressure increases.   **B.** pressure decreases.   **C.** volume increases.
   D. volume decreases.   **E.** number of molecules increases.

7. The pressure of a gas will increase when

   A. the volume increases.
   B. the temperature decreases.
   C. more molecules of gas are added.
   D. molecules of gas are removed.
   E. none of these

8. If the temperature of a gas is increased,

   A. the pressure will decrease.
   B. the volume will increase.
   C. the volume will decrease.
   D. the number of molecules will increase.
   E. none of these

9. The relationship that the volume of a gas is inversely related to its pressure at constant temperature is known as

   A. Boyle's law   **B.** Charles' law   **C.** Gay-Lussac's law
   D. Dalton's law   **E.** Avogadro's law

10. What is the pressure (atm) of a gas with a pressure of 1200 mm Hg?

    A. 0.63 atm   **B.** 0.79 atm   **C.** 1.2 atm
    D. 1.6 atm   **E.** 2.0 atm

11. A 6.00 L sample of oxygen has a pressure of 660. mm Hg. When the volume is reduced to 2.00 liters at constant temperature, it will have a new pressure of

    A. 1980 mmHg   **B.** 1320 mmHg   **C.** 330. mmHg
    D. 220. mmHg   **E.** 110. mmHg

12. A sample of nitrogen gas at 180 K has a pressure of 1.0 atm. When the temperature is increased to 360 K at constant volume, the new pressure will be

   A. 0.50 atm   **B.** 1.0 atm   **C.** 1.5 atm
   D. 2.0 atm   **E.** 4.0 atm

13. If two gases have the same volume, temperature, and pressure, they also have the same

   A. density   **B.** number of molecules   **C.** molar mass
   D. speed   **E.** size molecules

14. A gas sample with a volume of 4.00 L has a pressure of 750 mm Hg and a temperature of 77°C. What is its new volume at 277°C and 250 mmHg?

   A. 7.6 L   **B.** 19 L   **C.** 2.1 L
   D. 0.00056 L   **E.** 3.3 L

15. If the temperature of a gas does not change, but its volume doubles, its pressure will

   A. double.
   B. triple.
   C. decrease to one-half the original pressure.
   D. decrease to one-fourth the original pressure.
   E. not change.

16. A sample of oxygen with a pressure of 400 mmHg contains 2.0 moles of gas and has a volume of 4.0 L. What will the new pressure be when the volume expands to 5.0 L, and 3.0 moles of helium gas is added while temperature is constant?

   A. 160 mmHg   **B.** 250 mmHg   **C.** 800 mmHg
   D. 1000 mmHg   **E.** 1560 mmHg

17. A sample of 2.00 moles of gas initially at STP is converted to a volume of 5.0 L and a temperature of 27°C. What is its new pressure in atm?

   A. 0.12 atm   **B.** 5.5 atm   **C.** 7.5 atm
   D. 8.9 atm   **E.** 9.8 atm

18. The conditions for standard temperature and pressure (STP) are

   A. 0 K, 1 atm   **B.** 0°C, 10 atm   **C.** 25°C, 1 atm
   D. 273 K, 1 atm   **E.** 273 K, 0.5 atm

19. The volume occupied by 1.50 moles of CH_4 at STP is

   A. 44.8 L   **B.** 33.6 L   **C.** 22.4 L
   D. 11.2 L   **E.** 5.60 L

20. How many grams of oxygen gas (O_2) are present in 44.8 L of oxygen at STP?

   A. 8.0 g   **B.** 16.0 g   **C.** 32.0 g
   D. 48.0 g   **E.** 64.0 g

21. What is the volume in liters of 0.50 mole of nitrogen gas (N_2) at STP?

   A. 0.50 L   **B.** 1.0 L   **C.** 11.2 L
   D. 22.4 L   **E.** 44.8 L

22. A gas mixture contains helium with a partial pressure of 0.80 atm, oxygen with a partial pressure of 450 mmHg, and nitrogen with a partial pressure of 230 mm Hg. What is the total pressure in atm for the gas mixture?

   A. 1.10 atm   **B.** 1.39 atm   **C.** 1.69 atm
   D. 2.00 atm   **E.** 8.00 atm

23. A mixture of oxygen and nitrogen has a total pressure of 840 mm Hg. If the oxygen has a partial pressure of 510 mm Hg, what is the partial pressure of the nitrogen?

    A. 240 mmHg   **B.** 330 mmHg   **C.** 1.69 mmHg
    D. 1040 mmHg   **E.** 1350 mmHg

24. The exchange of gases between the alveoli, blood, and tissues of the body is a result of

    A. pressure gradients.
    B. different molecular weights.
    C. shapes of molecules.
    D. altitude.
    E. all of these

25. Oxygen moves into the tissues from the blood because its partial pressure

    A. in arterial blood is higher than in the tissues.
    B. in venous blood is higher than in the tissues.
    C. in arterial blood is lower than in the tissues.
    D. in venous blood is lower than in the tissues.
    E. is equal in the blood and in the tissues.

Answers to the Practice Test

1. T	**2.** T	**3.** T	**4.** F	**5.** T
6. A	**7.** C	**8.** B	**9.** A	**10.** D
11. A	**12.** D	**13.** B	**14.** B	**15.** C
16. C	**17.** E	**18.** D	**19.** B	**20.** E
21. C	**22.** C	**23.** B	**24.** A	**25.** A

Answers and Solutions to Selected Text Problems

7.1 a. Gaseous particles have greater kinetic energies at higher temperatures. Because kinetic energy is a measure of the energy of motion, the gaseous particles must be moving faster at higher temperatures than at lower values.

   b. Because particles in a gas are very far apart, gases can be easily compressed without the particles bumping into neighboring gas particles. Neighboring particles are much closer together in solids and liquids, and they will "bump" into each other and repel each other if the sample is compressed.

7.3   **a.** temperature   **b.** volume   **c.** amount of gas   **d.** pressure

7.5   Some units used to describe the pressure of a gas are pounds per square inch (lb/in.^{2} which is also abbreviated as psi), atmospheres (abbreviated atm), torr, mmHg, in. Hg, and pascals.

7.7   **a.** $2.00 \text{ atm} \times \dfrac{760 \text{ torr}}{1 \text{ atm}} = 1520 \text{ torr}$

     b. $2.00 \text{ atm} \times \dfrac{760 \text{ mmHg}}{1 \text{ atm}} = 1520 \text{ mmHg}$

7.9   The gases in the diver's lungs (and dissolved in the blood) will expand because pressure decreases as the diver ascends. Unless the diver exhales, the expanding gases could rupture the membranes in the lung tissues. In addition, the formation of gas bubbles in the bloodstream could cause "the bends."

7.11 **a.** According to Boyle's law, for the pressure to increase while temperature and quantity of gas remains constant, the gas volume must decrease. Thus, cylinder A would represent the final volume.

b.

	Initial	**Final**
P	650 mmHg	1.2 atm
V	220 mL	160 mL

Because $P_1V_2 = P_2V_2$, then $V_2 = P_1V_1/P_2$

$$V_2 = 220 \text{ mL} \times \frac{650 \text{ mmHg}}{1.2 \text{ atm}} \times \frac{1 \text{ atm}}{760 \text{ mmHg}} = 160 \text{ mL}$$

7.13 **a.** The pressure doubles when the volume is halved.
b. The pressure falls to one-third the initial pressure when the volume expands to three times its initial volume.
c. The pressure increases to ten times the original pressure when the volume decreases to 1/10 of its initial volume.

7.15 From Boyle's law we know that pressure is inversely related to volume. (For example, the pressure increases when the volume decreases.)
a. Volume increases; pressure must decrease.

$$655 \text{ mmHg} \times \frac{10.0 \text{ L}}{20.0 \text{ L}} = 328 \text{ mmHg}$$

b. Volume decreases; pressure must increase.

$$655 \text{ mmHg} \times \frac{10.0 \text{ L}}{2.50 \text{ L}} = 2620 \text{ mmHg}$$

c. The mL units must be converted to L for unit cancellation in the calculation, and because the volume decreases; pressure must increase.

$$655 \text{ mmHg} \times \frac{10.0 \text{ L}}{1500 \text{ mL}} \times \frac{1000 \text{ mL}}{1 \text{ L}} = 4400 \text{ mmHg}$$

7.17 From Boyle's Law we know that pressure is inversely related to volume.
a. Pressure increases; volume must decrease.

$$50.0 \text{ L} \times \frac{760 \text{ mmHg}}{1500 \text{ mmHg}} = 25 \text{ L}$$

b. The mmHg units must be converted to atm for unit cancellation in the calculation.

$$50.0 \text{ L} \times \frac{760 \text{ mmHg}}{2.0 \text{ atm}} \times \frac{1 \text{ atm}}{760 \text{ mmHg}} = 25 \text{ L}$$

c. The mmHg units must be converted to atm for unit cancellation in the calculation.

$$50.0 \text{ L} \times \frac{760 \text{ mmHg}}{0.500 \text{ atm}} \times \frac{1 \text{ atm}}{760 \text{ mmHg}} = 100. \text{ L}$$

7.19 Pressure decreases; volume must increase.

$$5.0 \text{ L} \times \frac{5.0 \text{ atm}}{1.0 \text{ atm}} = 25 \text{ L}$$

7.21 a. Inspiration begins when the diaphragm flattens causing the lungs to expand. The increased volume reduces the pressure in the lungs such that air flows into the lungs.

   b. Expiration occurs as the diaphragm relaxes causing a decrease in the volume of the lungs. The pressure of the air in the lungs increases and air flows out of the lungs.

   c. Inspiration occurs when the pressure in the lungs is less than the pressure of the air in the atmosphere.

7.23 According to Charles' law, there is a direct relationship between temperature and volume. For example, volume increases when temperature increases while the pressure and amount of gas remains constant.

   a. Diagram C describes an increased volume corresponding to an increased temperature.
   b. Diagram A describes a decreased volume corresponding to a decrease in temperature.
   c. Diagram B shows no change in volume, which corresponds to no change in temperature.

7.25 Heating a gas in a hot air balloon increases the volume of gas, which reduces its density and allows the balloon to rise above the ground.

7.27 According to Charles' law, gas volume is directly proportional to Kelvin temperature when P and n are constant. In all gas law computations, temperatures must be in Kelvin units. (Temperatures in °C are converted to K by the addition of 273.)

   a. When temperature decreases, volume must also decrease.

   $$75°C + 273 = 348 \text{ K} \qquad 55°C + 273 = 328 \text{ K}$$

   $$2500 \text{ mL} \times \frac{328 \text{ K}}{348 \text{ K}} = 2400 \text{ mL}$$

   b. When temperature increases, volume must also increase.

   $$2500 \text{ mL} \times \frac{680 \text{ K}}{348 \text{ K}} = 4900 \text{ mL}$$

   c. $-25°C + 273 = 248 \text{ K}$

   $$2500 \text{ mL} \times \frac{248 \text{ K}}{348 \text{ K}} = 1800 \text{ mL}$$

   d. $2500 \text{ mL} \times \dfrac{240 \text{ K}}{348 \text{ K}} = 1700 \text{ mL}$

7.29 Because gas pressure increases with an increase in temperature, the gas pressure in an aerosol can may exceed the tolerance of the can when it is heated and cause it to explode.

7.31 When the temperature of the oxygen in the tanks increases, the pressure also increases, which may cause the tanks to explode.

7.33 According to Gay-Lussac's law, temperature is directly related to pressure. For example, temperature increases when the pressure increases. In all gas law computations, temperatures must be in Kelvin units. (Temperatures in °C are converted to K by the addition of 273.)

   a. When temperature decreases, pressure must also decrease.

   $$155°C + 273 = 428 \text{ K} \qquad 0°C + 273 = 273 \text{ K}$$

   $$1200 \text{ torr} \times \frac{273 \text{ K}}{428 \text{ K}} = 700 \text{ torr}$$

   b. When temperature increases, pressure must also increase.

   $$12°C + 273 = 285 \text{ K} \qquad 35°C + 273 = 308 \text{ K}$$

   $$1.40 \text{ atm} \times \frac{308 \text{ K}}{285 \text{ K}} = 1.51 \text{ atm}$$

7.35 $T_1 = 325$ K; $V_1 = 6.50$ L; $P_1 = 845$ mmHg (1.11 atm)

    a. $T_2 = 125°C + 273 = 398$ K; $V_2 = 1.85$ L

$$1.11 \text{ atm} \times \frac{6.50 \text{ L}}{1.85 \text{ L}} \times \frac{325 \text{ K}}{298 \text{ K}} = 4.25 \text{ atm}$$

    b. $T_2 = 12°C + 273 = 285$ K; $V_2 = 2.25$ L

$$1.11 \text{ atm} \times \frac{6.50 \text{ L}}{2.25 \text{ L}} \times \frac{285 \text{ K}}{298 \text{ K}} = 3.07 \text{ atm}$$

    c. $T_2 = 47.°C + 273 = 320$ K; $V_2 = 12.8$ L

$$1.11 \text{ atm} \times \frac{6.50 \text{ L}}{12.8 \text{ L}} \times \frac{320 \text{ K}}{298 \text{ K}} = 0.605 \text{ atm}$$

7.37 $T_1 = 225°C + 273 = 498$ K; $P_1 = 1.80$ atm; $V_1 = 100.0$ mL
$T_2 = -25°C + 273 = 248$ K; $P_2 = 0.80$ atm

$$100.0 \text{ atm} \times \frac{1.80 \text{ L}}{0.80 \text{ L}} \times \frac{248 \text{ K}}{498 \text{ K}} = 110 \text{ mL}$$

7.39 Addition of more air molecules to a tire or basketball will increase its volume.

7.41 According to Avogadro's law, a change in a gas's volume is directly proportional to the change in the number of moles of gas.

    a. When moles decrease, volume must also decrease. (One half of 4.00 mole = 2.00 moles)

$$8.00 \text{ L} \times \frac{2.00 \text{ mole}}{4.00 \text{ mole}} = 4.00 \text{ L}$$

    b. When moles increase, volume must also increase.

$$25.0 \text{ g neon} \times \frac{1 \text{ mole neon}}{20.2 \text{ g neon}} = 1.24 \text{ mole Ne added}$$

(1.50 mole + 1.24 mole = 2.74mole)

$$8.00 \text{ L} \times \frac{2.74 \text{ mole}}{1.50 \text{ mole}} = 14.6 \text{ L}$$

7.43 At STP, the molar volume of any gas is 22.4 L per mole.

    a. $44.8 \text{ L} \times \dfrac{1 \text{ mole } O_2}{22.4 \text{ L}} = 2.00 \text{ mole } O_2$

    b. $4.00 \text{ L} \times \dfrac{1 \text{ mole } O_2}{22.4 \text{ L}} = 0.179 \text{ mole } CO_2$

    c. $6.40 \text{ g } O_2 \times \dfrac{1 \text{ mole } O_2}{32.0 \text{ g } O_2} \times \dfrac{22.4 \text{ L}}{1 \text{ mole } O_2} = 4.48 \text{ L}$

    d. $50.0 \text{ g Ne} \times \dfrac{1 \text{ mole Ne}}{20.2 \text{ g Ne}} \times \dfrac{22.4 \text{ L}}{1 \text{ mole Ne}} \times \dfrac{1000 \text{ mL}}{1 \text{ L}} = 55\,400 \text{ mL}$

7.45 Each gas particle in a gas mixture exerts a pressure as it strikes the walls of the container. The total gas pressure for any gaseous sample is thus a sum of all of the individual pressures. When the portion of the pressure due to a particular type of gaseous particle is discussed, it is only part of the total. Accordingly, these "portions" are referred to as "partial" pressures.

7.47 To obtain the total pressure in a gaseous mixture, add up all of the partial pressures (provided each carries the same pressure unit).

$$P_{total} = P_{Nitrogen} + P_{Oxygen} + P_{Helium}$$
$$= 425 \text{ torr} + 115 \text{ torr} + 225 \text{ torr} = 765 \text{ torr}$$

7.49 Because the total pressure in a gaseous mixture is the sum of the partial pressures (provided each carries the same pressure unit), addition and subtraction is used to obtain the "missing" partial pressure.

$$P_{Nitrogen} = P_{total} - (P_{Oxygen} + P_{Helium)}$$
$$= 925 \text{ torr} - (425 \text{ torr} + 75 \text{ torr}) = 425 \text{ torr}$$

7.51 a. If oxygen cannot readily cross from the lungs into the bloodstream, then the partial pressure of oxygen will be lower in the blood of an emphysema patient.
   b. An increase in the partial pressure of oxygen in the air supplied to the lungs will result in an increase in the partial pressure of oxygen in the bloodstream (addition of reactant causes the formation of more product). Because an emphysema patient has a lower partial pressure of oxygen in the blood, the use of a portable oxygen tank helps to bring the oxygenation of the patient's blood to a more desirable level.

7.53 a. The volume of the chest and lungs will decrease when compressed during the Heimlich maneuver.
   b. A decrease in volume causes the pressure to increase. A piece of food would be dislodged with a sufficiently high pressure.

7.55 Recall that all temperatures *must* be in kelvins in computations involving gas laws!

$$10. \text{ atm} \times \frac{348 \text{ K}}{298 \text{ K}} = 12 \text{ atm}$$

7.57 Remember to use Kelvin temperature units in the calculation and convert to Celsius degrees after completing the calculation!

$$400 \text{ K} \times \frac{0.25 \text{ atm}}{2.00 \text{ atm}} = 50 \text{ K} \qquad\qquad 50 \text{ K} - 273 = -223°C$$

7.59 The partial pressure of each gas is proportional to the number of particles of each type of gas that is present. Thus, a ratio of partial pressure to total pressure is equal to the ratio of moles of that gas to the total number of moles of gases that are present:

$$P_{Helium}/P_{total} = n_{Helium}/n_{total}$$

Solving the equation for the partial pressure of helium yields:

$$P_{Helium} = 2400 \text{ torr} \times \frac{2.00 \text{ mole}}{8.0 \text{ mole}} = 600 \text{ torr (or } 6.0 \times 10^2 \text{ torr to show two sig figs)}$$

And for oxygen:

$$P_{Oxygen} = 2400 \text{ torr} \times \frac{6.0 \text{ mole}}{8.0 \text{ mole}} = 1800 \text{ torr}$$

7.61 Because the partial pressure of nitrogen is to be reported in torr, the atm and mmHg units (for oxygen and argon, respectively) must be converted to torr, as follows:

$$0.60 \text{ atm} \times \frac{760 \text{ torr}}{1 \text{ atm}} = 460 \text{ torr}$$

$$425 \text{ mmHg} \times \frac{1 \text{ torr}}{1 \text{ mmHg}} = 425 \text{ torr}$$

and P_{Nitrogen} $= P_{\text{total}} - (P_{\text{Oxygen}} + P_{\text{Argon}})$

$= 1250 \text{ torr} - (460 \text{ torr} + 425 \text{ torr}) = 370 \text{ torr}$

7.63 $D = \dfrac{\text{mass}}{\text{volume}} = \dfrac{32.0 \text{ g } O_2}{1 \text{ mole}} \times \dfrac{1 \text{ mole}}{22.4 \text{ L (STP)}} = 1.43 \text{ g/L}$

7.65 a. The partial pressure of oxygen in the lungs is greater than what is present in blood in the alveoli.

b. Arterial blood picks up oxygen in the lungs and delivers oxygen to body tissues. Arterial blood has a higher partial pressure of oxygen than venous blood.

c. Because carbon dioxide is generated in body tissues, the partial pressure of CO_2 will be greater in the tissues than in arterial blood.

d. The venous blood is returning to the lungs from body tissues. Venous blood, which has a higher partial pressure of carbon dioxide than the lungs, transports the excess CO_2 to the lungs to be exhaled.

7.67 The mole-mole conversion factor is obtained from the reaction and used to convert to moles of gas, and the STP molar volume conversion factor is used to convert moles of gas into liters of gas, as shown below:

$$2.00 \text{ mole } CaCO_3 \times \frac{1 \text{ mole } CO_2}{1 \text{ mole } CaCO_3} \times \frac{22.4 \text{ L}}{1 \text{ mole } CO_2} = 44.8 \text{ L } CO_2$$

7.69 $425 \text{ mL} \times \dfrac{745 \text{ mmHg}}{0.115 \text{ atm}} \times \dfrac{1 \text{ atm}}{760 \text{ mmHg}} \times \dfrac{178 \text{ K}}{297 \text{ K}} = 2170 \text{ mL}$

7.71 $5.4 \text{ g } AL \times \dfrac{1 \text{ mole } AL}{27.0 \text{ g } AL} \times \dfrac{3 \text{ moles } O_2}{4 \text{ moles } Al} \times \dfrac{22.4 \text{ L } O_2 \text{ (STP)}}{1 \text{ mole } H_2} = 3.4 \text{ L } O_2 \text{ (g)}$

8
Solutions

Study Goals

- Identify the solute and solvent in a solution
- Describe hydrogen bonding in water.
- Describe electrolytes in a solution.
- Define solubility.
- Calculate the percent concentrations and molarity of a solution
- Distinguish between a solution, a colloid, and a suspension.
- Describe the behavior of a red blood cell in hypotonic, isotonic, and hypertonic solutions.

Think About It

1. Why is salt used to preserve foods?

2. Why do raisins or dried prunes swell when placed in water?

3. Why are pickles made in a brine solution with a high salt concentration?

4. Why can't you drink seawater?

5. How do your kidneys remove toxic substances from the blood but retain the usable substances?

Key Terms

Match the following terms with the correct statement shown below:

a. solution   **b.** concentration   **c.** molarity
d. osmosis   **e.** electrolyte

1. _____ A substance that dissociates into ions when it dissolves in water.

2. _____ The flow of solvent through a semipermeable membrane into a solution with a higher solute concentration.

3. _____ The amount of solute that is dissolved in a specified amount of solution.

4. _____ The number of moles of solute in one liter of solution.

5. _____ A mixture of at least two components called a solute and a solvent.

Answers   **1.** e   **2.** d   **3.** b   **4.** c   **5.** a

8.1 Types of Solutions

- A polar solute is soluble in a polar solvent; a nonpolar solute is soluble in a nonpolar solvent; "like dissolves like."
- A solution forms when a solute dissolves in a solvent.
- The partial positive charge of hydrogen and the partial negative charge of oxygen permits water molecules to hydrogen bond to other water molecules.

◆ Learning Exercise 8.1A

Indicate the solute and solvent in each of the following:

		Solute	**Solvent**
a.	10 g KCl dissolved in 100 g of water.	_____	_____
b.	Soda water: $CO_2(g)$ dissolved in water.	_____	_____
c.	An alloy composed of 80% Zn and 20% Cu.	_____	_____
d.	A mixture of O_2 (200 mm Hg) and He (500 mm Hg).	_____	_____
e.	A solution of 40 mL CCl_4 and 2 mL Br_2.	_____	_____

Answers   **a.** KCl; water   **b.** CO_2; water   **c.** Cu; Zn
            d. oxygen; helium   **e.** Br_2; CCl_4

◆ Learning Exercise 8.1B

ESSAY: How does the polarity of the water molecule allow it to hydrogen bond?

Answer   The O-H bonds in water molecules are polar because the hydrogen atoms are partially positive and the oxygen atoms are partially negative. Hydrogen bonding occurs because the partially positive hydrogen atoms in one water molecule are attracted to partially negative oxygen atoms of other water molecules.

8.2 Formation of Solutions

- An ionic solute dissolves in water, a polar solvent, because the polar water molecules attract and pull the positive and negative ions into solution. In solution, water molecules surround the ions dues to a process called hydration.
-

◆ Learning Exercise 8.2

Water is polar and hexane is nonpolar. In which solvent is each of the following soluble?

a. Bromine, Br_2, nonpolar _____   **b.** HCl, polar _____

c. Cholesterol, nonpolar _____   **d.** Vitamin D, nonpolar _____

e. Vitamin C, polar _____

Answers   **a.** hexane **b.** water **c.** hexane **d.** hexane **e.** water

8.3 Solubility and Saturated Solutions

- The amount of solute that dissolves depends on the nature of the solute and solvent.
- Solubility describes the maximum amount of a solute that dissolves in 100 g of solvent at a given temperature.
- A saturated solution contains the maximum amount of dissolved solute at a certain temperature.
- An increase in temperature increases the solubility of most solids, but decreases the solubility of gases in water.

◆ Learning Exercise 8.3A

Identify each of the following as a saturated solution (S) or an unsaturated solution (U):

1. A sugar cube dissolves when added to a cup of coffee.　　　　_____

2. A KCl crystal added to a KCl solution does not change in size.　　_____

3. A layer of sugar forms in the bottom of a glass of ice tea.　　_____

4. The rate of crystal formation equals the rate of solution.　　_____

5. Upon heating, all the sugar dissolves.　　_____

Answers　　　**1. U**　　**2. S**　　**3. S**　　**4. S**　　**5. U**

◆ Learning Exercise 8.3B

Use the KNO_3 solubility chart for the following problems:

Solubility of KNO_3

Temperature (°C)	g KNO_3/100 g H_2O
0	15
20	30
40	65
60	110
80	170
100	250

a. How many grams of KNO_3 will dissolve in 100 g of water at 40°C?

b. How many grams of KNO_3 will dissolve in 300 g of water at 60°C?

c. A solution is prepared using 200 g of water and 350 g of KNO_3 at 80°C. Will any solute remain undissolved? If so, how much?

d. Will 200 g of KNO_3 dissolve when added to 100 g of water at 100°C?

Answers　　　**a.** 65 g　　　　　　　　**b.** 330 g
　　　　　　　　c. Yes, 10 g of KNO_3 will not dissolve.
　　　　　　　　d. Yes, all 200 g of KNO_3 will dissolve.

8.4 Electrolytes

- Electrolytes conduct an electrical current because they produce ions in aqueous solutions.
- Strong electrolytes are nearly completely ionized, whereas weak electrolytes are slightly ionized. Nonelectrolytes do not form ions in solution but dissolve as molecules.
- An equivalent is the amount of an electrolyte that carries 1 mole of electrical charge.
- There are 1, 2, or 3 equivalents per mole of a positive or negative ion depending on the charge.

◆ Learning Exercise 8.4A

Write an equation for the formation of an aqueous solution of each of the following strong electrolyes:

a. $LiCl$ _____

b. $Mg(NO_3)_2$ _____

c. Na_3PO_4 _____

d. K_2SO_4 _____

e. $MgCl_2$ _____

Answers

a. $LiCl(s) \xrightarrow{H_2O} Li^+(aq) + Cl^-(aq)$

b. $Mg(NO_3)_2(s) \xrightarrow{H_2O} Mg^{2+}(aq) + 2NO_3^-(aq)$

c. $Na_3PO_4(s) \xrightarrow{H_2O} 3Na^+(aq) + PO_4^{3-}(aq)$

d. $K_3SO_4(s) \xrightarrow{H_2O} 2K^+(aq) + SO_4^{2-}(aq)$

e. $MgCl_2(s) \xrightarrow{H_2O} Mg^{2+}(aq) + 2Cl^-(aq)$

◆ Learning Exercise 8.4B

Indicate whether an aqueous solution of each of the following contains mostly ions, molecules only, or mostly molecules with some ions. Write an equation for the formation of the solution:

a. glucose, $C_6H_{12}O_6$, a nonelectrolyte

b. NaOH, a strong electrolyte

c. K_2SO_4, a strong electrolyte

d. HF, a weak electrolyte

Answers

a. $C_6H_{12}O_6(s) \longrightarrow C_6H_{12}O_6(aq)$ — molecules only

b. $NaOH(s) \longrightarrow Na^+(aq) + OH^-(aq)$ — mostly ions

c. $K_2SO_4(s) \longrightarrow 2K^+(aq) + SO_4^{2-}(aq)$ — mostly ions

d. $HF + H_2O \rightleftarrows H_3O^+ + F^-$ — mostly molecules and a few ions

◆ Learning Exercise 8.4C

Calculate the following:

a. Number of equivalents in 1 mole of Mg^{2+}

b. Number of equivalents of Cl^- in 2 moles of Cl^-

c. Number of equivalents of Ca^{2+} in 2.0 moles of g of Ca^{2+}

Answers   a. 2 equivalents   b. 2 equivalents   c. 4.0 equivalents

8.5 Percent Concentration

- The concentration of a solution is the relationship between the amount of solute (g or mL) and the amount (g or mL) of solution.
- A mass percent (mass/mass) expresses the ratio of the mass of solute to the mass of solution multiplied by 100.

$$\text{Percent (m/m)} = \frac{\text{grams of solute}}{\text{grams of solution}} \times 100$$

- Percent concentrations can also be expressed as a mass/volume ratio.

$$\text{Percent (m/v)} = \frac{\text{grams of solute}}{\text{mL of solution}} \times 100$$

Study Note

Calculate mass percent concentration (% m/m) as

$$\frac{\text{grams of solute}}{\text{grams of solution}} \times 100$$

Example: What is the percent (mass/mass) when 2.4 g of $NaHCO_3$ dissolves in 120 g of solution?

Solution: $\dfrac{2.4 \text{ g } NaHCO_3}{120 \text{ g solution}} \times 100 = 2.0\% \text{ (m/m)}$

◆ Learning Exercise 8.5A

Determine the percent concentration of the following solutions:

a. The mass/mass % of 18.0 g NaCl in 90.0 g of solution.

b. The mass/volume % of 5.0 g KCl in 2.0 liters of solution.

c. The mass/mass % of 1.0 g KOH in 25 g of solution.

d. The mass/volume % of 0.25 kg glucose in 5.0 liters of solution.

Answers   **a.** 20.0%   **b.** 0.25%   **c.** 4.0%   **d.** 5.0%

Study Note

In solution problems, the percent concentration is useful as a conversion factor. The factor is obtained by rewriting the % as g solute/100 g (or mL) solution.

Example 1:   How many g of KI are needed to prepare 250 mL of a 4% (m/v) KI solution?

Solution: $250 \ \cancel{\text{mL solution}} \times \dfrac{4 \text{ g KI}}{\underset{\% \ (m/v) \ factor}{100 \ \cancel{\text{mL solution}}}} = 10 \text{ g KI}$

Example 2:   How many grams of a 25% (m/m) NaOH solution can be prepared from 75 g NaOH?

Solution: $75 \ \cancel{\text{g NaOH}} \times \dfrac{100 \text{ g NaOH solution}}{\underset{\% \ (m/m) \ factor \ (inverted)}{25 \ \cancel{\text{g NaOH}}}} = 300 \text{ g NaOH solution}$

◆ Learning Exercise 8.5B

Calculate the number of grams of solute needed to prepare each of the following solutions:

a. How many grams of glucose are needed to prepare 400. mL of a 10.0% (m/v) solution?

b. How many grams of lidocaine hydrochloride are needed to prepare 50.0 g of a 2.0% (m/m) solution?

c. How many grams of KCl are needed to prepare 0.80 liter of a 0.15% (m/v) KCl solution?

d. How many grams of NaCl are needed to prepare 250 mL of a 1.0% (m/v) solution?

Answers   **a.** 40.0 g   **b.** 1.0 g   **c.** 1.2 g   **d.** 2.5g

◆ **Learning Exercise 8.5C**

Use percent-concentration factors to calculate the volume (mL) of each solution that contains the amount of solute stated in each problem.

a. 2.00 g NaCl from a 1.00% (m/v) NaCl solution.

b. 25 g glucose from a 5% (m/v) glucose solution.

c. 1.5 g KCl from a 0.50% (m/v) KCl solution.

d. 75.0 g NaOH from a 25.0% (m/v) NaOH solution.

Answers   **a.** 200. mL   **b.** 500 mL   **c.** 300 mL   **d.** 300. mL

8.6 Molarity and Dilutiion

- Molarity is a concentration term that describes the number of moles of solute dissolved in 1 L (1000 mL) of solution.

$$M = \frac{\text{moles of solute}}{\text{L solution}}$$

- *Dilution* is the process of mixing a solution with solvent to obtain a lower concentration.
- For dilutions, use the expression $C_1V_1 = C_2V_2$ and solve for the unknown value.

◆ **Learning Exercise 8.6A**

Calculate the molarity of the following solutions:

a. 2.0 mole HCl in 1.0 liter

b. 10.0 mole glucose ($C_6H_{12}O_6$) in 2.0 liters

c. 80.0 g NaOH in 4.0 liters (Hint: Find moles NaOH.)

Answers   **a.** 2.0 M HCl   **b.** 5.0 M glucose   **c.** 0.50 M NaOH

Study Note

Molarity can be used as a conversion factor to convert between the amount of solute and the volume of solution.

Example 1:　How many grams of NaOH are in 0.20 L of a 4.0 M NaOH solution?

Solution:　The concentration 4.0 M can be expressed as the conversion factors:

$$\frac{4.0 \text{ mole NaOH}}{1 \text{ L NaOH}} \quad \text{and} \quad \frac{1 \text{ L NaOH}}{4.0 \text{ mole NaOH}}$$

$$0.20 \text{ L NaOH} \times \frac{4.0 \text{ mole NaOH}}{1 \text{ L NaOH}} \times \frac{40.0 \text{ g NaOH}}{1 \text{ mole NaOH}} = 32 \text{ g NaOH}$$

Example 2:　How many mL of a 6 M HCl solution will provide 0.36 mole HCl?

Solution:　$0.36 \text{ mole HCl solution} \times \dfrac{1 \text{ L}}{\underset{\textit{Molarity factor (inverted)}}{6 \text{ mole HCl}}} \times \dfrac{1000 \text{ mL}}{1 \text{ L}} = 60 \text{ mL HCl solution}$

◆ Learning Exercise 8.6B

Calculate the quantity of solute in the following solutions:

a.　How many moles of HCl are in 1.0 liter of a 4.0 M HCl solution?

b.　How many moles of KOH are in 5.0 liters of a 2.0 M KOH solution?

c.　How many grams of NaOH are needed to prepare 0.50 L of a 6.0 M NaOH solution? (Hint: Find moles of NaOH.)

d.　How many grams of NaCl are in 200. mL of a 1.00 M NaCl solution?

Answers　　**a.**　4.0 moles HCl　　**b.**　10. moles KOH　**c.**　120 g NaOH　　**d.** 11.7 g NaCl

◆ Learning Exercise 8.6C

Calculate the milliliters needed of each solution to obtain the quantity of solute:

a. 1.0 mole of $Mg(OH)_2$ from a 2.0 M $Mg(OH)_2$ solution

b. 0.50 mole of glucose from a 5.0 M glucose solution

c. 0.20 mole of KI from a 4.0 M KI solution

d. 8.0 g NaOH from a 1.0 M NaOH solution

Answers   a. 500 mL   b. 100 mL   c. 50. mL   d. 200 mL

◆ Learning Exercise 8.6D

Solve each of the following dilution problems (assume the volumes add):

a. What is the final concentration after 100 mL of a 5.0 M KCl solution is diluted with water to give a final volume of 200 mL?

b. What is the final concentration of the diluted solution if 5.0 mL of a 15% (m/v) KCl solution is diluted to 25 mL?

c. What is the final concentration after 250 mL of an 8% (m/v) NaOH is diluted with 750 mL of water?

d. 160 mL of water is added to 40 mL of an 1.0 M NaCl solution. What is the final concentration?

e. What volume of water must be added to 2.0 L of 12% (m/v) KCl to obtain a 4.0 %(m/v) KCl solution? What is the total volume of the solution?

f. What volume of 6.0 M HCl is needed to prepare 300. mL of 1.0 M HCl? How much water must be added?

Answers	**a.** 2.5 M	**b.** 3.0 % (m/v)	**c.** 2% (m/m)
	d. 0.20 M	**e.** add 4.0 L; $V_2 = 6.0$ L	**f.** $V_1 = 50$ mL; add 250 mL water

125

8.7 Colloids and Suspensions

- Colloids contain particles that do not settle out and pass through filters but not through semipermeable membranes.
- Suspensions are composed of large particles that settle out of solution.

◆ Learning Exercise 8.7

Identify each of the following as a solution, colloid, or suspension:

1. _____ Contains single atoms, ions, or small molecules.

2. _____ Settles out with gravity.

3. _____ Retained by filters.

4. _____ Cannot diffuse through a cellular membrane.

5. _____ Aggregates of atoms, molecules, or ions larger in size than solution particles.

6. _____ Large particles that are visible.

Answers   **1.** solution   **2.** suspension   **3.** suspension
                          4. colloid   **5.** colloid   **6.** suspension

8.8 Osmosis and Dialysis

- In the process of osmosis, water (solvent) moves through a semipermeable membrane from the solution that has a lower solute concentration to a solution where the solute concentration is higher.
- Osmotic pressure is the pressure that prevents the flow of water into a more concentrated solution.
- Isotonic solutions have osmotic pressures equal to that of body fluids. A hypotonic solution has a lower osmotic pressure than body fluids; a hypertonic solution has a higher osmotic pressure.
- A red blood cell maintains its volume in an isotonic solution, but it swells (hemolysis) in a hypotonic solution and shrinks (crenation) in a hypertonic solution.
- In dialysis, water and small solute particles can pass through a dialyzing membrane, while larger particles are retained.

◆ Learning Exercise 8.8A

Fill in the blanks:

In osmosis, the direction of solvent flow is from the (1) _____ solvent concentration to the

(2) _____ solvent concentration. A semipermeable membrane separates 5% and 10% sucrose

solutions. The (3) _____% solution has the greater osmotic pressure. Water will move from

the (4) _____% solution into the (5) _____% solution. The compartment that

contains the (6) _____% solution increases in volume.

Answers   (1) higher   (2) lower   (3) 10
                     (4) 5   (5) 10   (6) 10

◆ Learning Exercise 8.8B

A 2% (A) and a 10% (B) starch solution are separated by a semipermeable membrane.

Semipermeable membrane

2% starch | 10% starch

A   B

a. Water will flow from side _____ to side _____.

b. The volume in compartment _____ will increase and decrease in compartment _____.

c. The final concentration of the solutions in both compartments will be _____.

Answers   **a.** A, B   **b.** B, A   **c.** 6%

◆ Learning Exercise 8.8C

Fill in the blanks:

A (1) _____% NaCl solution and a (2) _____% glucose solution are isotonic to the body fluids.

A red blood cell placed in these solutions does not change in volume because these solutions are (3)

_____ tonic. When a red blood cell is placed in water, it undergoes (4) _____ because water is

(5) _____ tonic. A 20% glucose solution will cause a red blood cell to undergo (6) _____

because the 20% glucose solution is (7) _____ tonic.

Answers   (1) 0.9   (2) 5   (3) iso   (4) hemolysis
                (5) hypo   (6) crenation   (7) hyper

◆ Learning Exercise 8.8D

Indicate whether the following solutions are

A. hypotonic   **B.** hypertonic   **C.** isotonic

a. _____ 5% (m/v)glucose   **b.** _____ 3% (m/v) NaCl   **c.** _____ 2% (m/v) glucose

d. _____ water   **e.** _____ 0.9% (m/v)NaCl   **f.** _____ 10% (m/v) glucose

Answers   **a.** C   **b.** B   **c.** A   **d.** A   **e.** C   **f.** B

◆ **Learning Exercise 8.8E**

Indicate whether the following solutions will cause a red blood cell to undergo

A. crenation   **B.** hemolysis   **C.** no change (stays the same)

a. _____ 10% (m/v) NaCl   **b.** _____ 1% (m/v) glucose   **c.** _____ 5% (m/v) glucose

d. _____ 0.5% (m/v) NaCl   **e.** _____ 10% (m/v) glucose   **f.** _____ water

Answers   **a.** A   **b.** B   **c.** C
                 d. B   **e.** A   **f.** B

◆ **Learning Exercise 8.8F**

A dialysis bag contains starch, glucose, NaCl, protein, and urea.

a. When the dialysis bag is placed in water, which of the components would you expect to dialyze through the bag? Why?

b. Which components will stay inside the dialysis bag? Why?

Answers   **a.** Glucose, NaCl, urea; they are solution particles.
                 b. Starch, protein; they are colloids and retained by semipermeable membranes.

Check List for Chapter 8

You are ready to take the practice test for Chapter 8. Be sure that you have accomplished the following learning goals for this chapter. If you are not sure, review the section listed at the end of the goal. Then apply your new skills and understanding to the practice test.

After studying Chapter 8, I can successfully:

_____ Describe hydrogen bonding in water (8.1).

_____ Identify the solute and solvent in a solution (8.1).

_____ Describe the process of dissolving an ionic solute in water (8.2).

_____ Identify a saturated and an unsaturated solution (8.3)

_____ Identify the components in solutions of electrolytes and nonelectrolytes (8.4).

_____ Calculate the number of equivalents for an electrolyte (8.4).

_____ Describe the effects of temperature and nature of the solute on its solubility in a solvent.

_____ Calculate the percent concentration of a solute in a solution and use percent concentration to calculate the amount of solute or solution (8.5).

_____ Calculate the molarity of a solution and use molarity as a conversion factor to calculate between the mole (or grams) of a solute and the volume of the solution (8.6).

_____ Calculate the diluted volume of a solution (8.6).

_____ Identify a mixture as a solution, a colloid, or a suspension (8.7).

_____ Explain the processes of osmosis and dialysis. Describe the change in a red blood cell when placed in hypotonic, isotonic, and hypertonic solutions. (8.8).

Practice Test for Chapter 8

Indicate if the following are more soluble in (A) water, a polar solvent or (B) benzene, a nonpolar solvent.

1. _____ I_2 (g), nonpolar

2. _____ NaBr(s), polar

3. _____ KI(s), polar

4. _____ C_6H_{12}, nonpolar

5. When dissolved in water, $Ca(NO_3)_2$ dissociates into

    A. $Ca^{2+} + (NO_3)_2^{2-}$ **B.** $Ca^+ + NO_3^-$ **C.** $Ca^{2+} + 2\,NO_3^-$
    D. $Ca^{2+} + 2\,N^{5+} + 2\,O_3^{6-}$ **E.** $CaNO_3^+ + NO_3^-$

6. What is the number of equivalents in 2 moles of Mg^{2+}?

    A. 0.50 equiv   **B.** 1 equiv   **C.** 1.5 equiv
    D. 2 equiv   **E.** 4 equiv

7. CH_3CH_2OH, ethyl alcohol, is a nonelectrolyte. When placed in water it

    A. dissociates completely.   **B.** dissociates partially.   **C.** does not dissociate.
    D. makes the solution acidic.   **E.** makes the solution basic.

8. The solubility of NH_4Cl is 46 g in 100 g of water at 40°C. How much NH_4Cl can dissolve in 500 g of water at 40°C?

    A. 9.2 g   **B.** 46 g   **C.** 100 g
    D. 184 g   **E.** 230 g

9. A solution containing 1.20 g sucrose in 50.0 mL of solution has a percent concentration of

    A. 0.600 %   **B.** 1.20%   **C.** 2.40%
    D. 30.0%   **E.** 41.6%

10. The amount of lactose in 250 mL of a 3.0% lactose solution of infant formula is

    A. 0.15 g   **B.** 1.2 g   **C.** 6.0 g
    D. 7.5 g   **E.** 30 g

11. The volume needed to obtain 0.40 g of glucose from a 5.0 % glucose solution is

    A. 1.0 mL   **B.** 2.0 mL   **C.** 4.0 mL
    D. 5.0 mL   **E.** 8.0 mL

12. The amount of NaCl needed to prepare 50.0 mL of a 4.00% NaCl solution is

    A. 20.0 g   **B.** 15.0 g   **C.** 10.0 g
    D. 4.00 g   **E.** 2

13. A solution containing 6.0 g NaCl in 1500 mL of solution has a mass-volume percent concentration of

    A. 0.40 (m/v)%   **B.** 0.25(m/v)%   **C.** 4.0(m/v)%
    D. 0.90(m/v)%   **E.** 2.5(m/v)%

For questions 14 through 18, indicate whether each statement describes a

A. solution   B. colloid   C. suspension

14. _____ Contains single atoms, ions, or small molecules of solute.
15. _____ Settles out upon standing.
16. _____ Can be separated by filtering.
17. _____ Can be separated by semipermeable membranes.
18. _____ Passes through semipermeable membranes.

19. The separation of colloids from solution particles by use of a membrane is called

   A. osmosis   B. dispersion   C. dialysis
   D. hemolysis   E. collodian

20. Any two solutions that have identical osmotic pressures are

   A. hypotonic   B. hypertonic   C. isotonic
   D. isotopic   E. blue

21. In osmosis, water flows

   A. between solutions of equal concentrations.
   B. from higher solute concentrations to lower solute concentrations.
   C. from lower solute concentrations to higher solute concentrations.
   D. from colloids to solutions of equal concentrations.
   E. from lower solvent concentrations to higher solvent concentrations.

22. A normal red blood cell will shrink when placed in a solution that is

   A. isotonic   B. hypotonic   C. hypertonic
   D. colloidal   E. semitonic

23. A red blood cell undergoes hemolysis when placed in a solution that is

   A. isotonic   B. hypotonic   C. hypertonic
   D. colloidal   E. semitonic

24. A solution that has the same osmotic pressure as body fluids is

   A. 0.1% NaCl   B. 0.9 % NaCl   C. 5% NaCl
   D. 10% glucose   E. 15% glucose

25. Which of the following is hypertonic to red blood cells?
   A. 0.5% NaCl   B. 0.9% NaCl   C. 1% glucose
   D. 5% glucose   E. 10% glucose

26. Which of the following is hypotonic to red blood cells?

   A. 2.0% NaCl   B. 0.9% NaCl   C. 1% glucose
   D. 5% glucose   E. 10% glucose

For questions 27 through 31, select the correct term from the following:

A. isotonic   B. hypertonic   C. hypotonic
D. osmosis   E. dialysis

27. _____ A solution with a higher osmotic pressure than the blood.

28. _____ A solution of 10% NaCl surrounding a red blood cell.

29. _____ A 1% glucose solution.

30. _____ The cleansing process of the artificial kidney.

31. _____ The flow of water up the stem of a plant.

32. In dialysis,

   A. dissolved salts and small molecules are separated from colloids.
   B. nothing but water passes through the membrane.
   C. only ions pass through a membrane.
   D. two kinds of colloids are separated.
   E. colloids are separated from suspensions.

33. A dialyzing membrane

   A. is a semipermeable membrane.
   B. allows only water and true solution particles to pass through.
   C. does not allow colloidal particles to pass through.
   D. all of the above
   E. none of the above

34. Which substance will remain inside a dialysis bag?

   A. water   **B.** NaCl   **C.** starch
   D. glucose   **E.** Mg^{2+}

35. Waste removal in hemodialysis is based on

   A. concentration gradients between the bloodstream and the dialysate.
   B. a pH difference between the bloodstream and the dialysate.
   C. use of an osmotic membrane.
   D. greater osmotic pressure in the bloodstream.
   E. renal compensation.

36. The moles of KOH needed to prepare 2400 mL of a 2.0 M KOH solution is

   A. 1.2 moles   **B.** 2.4   **C.** 4.8
   D. 12 moles   **E.** 48 moles

37. The amount in grams of NaOH needed to prepare 7.5 mL of a 5.0 M NaOH is

   A. 1.5 g   **B.** 3.8 g   **C.** 6.7 g
   D. 15 g   **E.** 38 g

For questions 38 through 40, consider a 20.0 mL sample of a solution that contains 2.0 g NaOH.

38. The % concentration of the solution is

   A. 1.0 %   **B.** 4.0 %   **C.** 5%
   D. 10%   **E.** 20%

39. The number of moles of NaOH in the sample is

   A. 0.050 mole   **B.** 0.40 mole   **C.** 1.0 mole
   D. 2.5 moles   **E.** 4.0 moles

40. The molarity of the sample is

A. 0.10 M	**B.** 0.5 M	**C.** 1.0 M
D. 1.5 M	**E.** 2.5 M	

Answers to the Practice Test

1. B	**2.** A	**3.** A	**4.** B	**5.** C
6. E	**7.** C	**8.** E	**9.** C	**10.** D
11. E	**12.** E	**13.** A	**14.** A	**15.** C
16. C	**17.** B	**18.** A	**19.** C	**20.** C
21. C	**22.** C	**23.** B	**24.** B	**25.** E
26. C	**27.** B	**28.** B	**29.** C	**30.** E
31. D	**32.** A	**33.** D	**34.** C	**35.** A
36. C	**37.** A	**38.** D	**39.** A	**40.** E

Answers and Solutions to Selected Problems

8.1 The component present in the smaller amount is the solute; the larger amount is the solvent.

  a. Sodium chloride, solute; water, solvent
  b. Water, solute; ethanol, solvent
  c. Oxygen, solute; nitrogen, solvent

8.3 The K^+ and I^- ions at the surface of the solid are pulled into solution by the polar water molecules where the hydration process surrounds separate ions with water molecules.

8.5 **a.** Potassium chloride, an ionic solute, would be soluble in water (a polar solvent).
  b. Iodine, a nonpolar solute would be soluble in carbon tetrachloride (a nonpolar solvent).
  c. Sugar, a polar solute, would be soluble in water, which is a polar solvent.
  d. Gasoline, a nonpolar solute, would be soluble in carbon tetrachloride, which is a nonpolar solvent.

8.7 **a.** The solution must be saturated because no additional solute dissolves.
  b. The solution was unsaturated because the sugar cube dissolves.

8.9 **a.** In general, the solubility of solid ionic solutes increases as temperature is increased.
  b. The solubility of a gaseous solute (CO_2) decreases as the temperature is increased.
  c. The solubility of a gaseous solute is lowered as temperature increases. When the can of warm soda is opened, more CO_2 is released producing more spray.

8.11 The salt KF dissociates into ions when it dissolves in water. The weak acid HF exists as mostly molecules along with some ions when it dissolves in water.

8.13 Strong electrolytes dissociate into ions.

  a. $KCl \xrightarrow{H_2O} K^+ + Cl^-$

  b. $CaCl_2 \xrightarrow{H_2O} Ca^{2+} + 2Cl^-$

  c. $K_3PO_4 \xrightarrow{H_2O} 3 K^+ + PO_4^{3-}$

  d. $Fe(NO_3)_3 \xrightarrow{H_2O} Fe^{3+} + 3NO_3^-$

8.15 **a.** In solution, a weak electrolyte exists mostly as molecules with a few ions.
  b. Sodium bromide is a strong electrolyte and forms ions in solution.
  c. A nonelectrolyte does not dissociate and forms only molecules in solution.

8.17 a. Strong electrolyte because only ions are present in the K_2SO_4 solution.
   b. Weak electrolyte because both ions and molecules are present in the NH_4OH solution.
   c. Nonelectrolyte because only molecules are present in the $C_6H_{12}O_6$ solution.

8.19 a. $1 \text{ mole K}^+ \times \dfrac{1 \text{ Eq K}^+}{1 \text{ mole K}^+} = 1 \text{ equivalent K}^+$

   b. $2 \text{ moles OH}^- \times \dfrac{1 \text{ Eq OH}^-}{\text{mole OH}^-} = 2 \text{ equivalents OH}^-$

   c. $1 \text{ mole Ca}^{2+} \times \dfrac{2 \text{ Eq Ca}^{2+}}{1 \text{ mole Ca}^{2+}} = 2 \text{ equivalents Ca}^{2+}$

   d. $3 \text{ moles CO}_3^{2-} \times \dfrac{2 \text{ Eq CO}_3^{2-}}{1 \text{ mole CO}_3^{2-}} = 6 \text{ equivalents CO}_3^{2-}$

8.21 $1.0 \text{ O} \times \dfrac{154 \text{ mEq}}{1 \text{ L}} \times \dfrac{1 \text{ Eq}}{1000 \text{ mEq}} \quad \dfrac{1 \text{ mole Na}^+}{1 \text{ Eq}} = 0.154 \text{ mole}$

   $1.0 \text{ O} \times \dfrac{154 \text{ mEq}}{1 \text{ L}} \times \dfrac{1 \text{ Eq}}{1000 \text{ mEq}} \quad \dfrac{1 \text{ mole Cl}^-}{1 \text{ Eq}} = 0.154 \text{ mole Cl}^-$

8.23 The total equivalents of anions must be equal to the equivalents of cations in any solution.

   mEq of anions = 40 mEq Cl^-/L + 15 mEq HPO_4^{2-} /L = 55 mEq/L
   mEq Na^+ = mEq anions = 55 mEq Na^+ /L

8.25 A 5% (m/m) glucose solution contains 5 g glucose in 100 g of solution (5 g glucose + 95 g water), while a 5% (m/v) glucose solution contains 5 g glucose in 100 mL solution.

8.27 a. $\dfrac{25 \text{ g of KCl}}{150 \text{ g solution}} \times 100 = 17\% \text{ (m/m)}$

   b. $\dfrac{12 \text{ g sugar}}{225 \text{ g solution}} \times 100 = 5.3\% \text{ (m/m)}$

8.29 a. $\dfrac{75 \text{ g Na}_2SO_4}{250 \text{ mL solution}} \times 100 = 30.\% \text{ (m/v)}$

   b. $\dfrac{39 \text{ g sucrose}}{355 \text{ mL solution}} \times 100 = 11\% \text{ (m/v)}$

8.31 a. $50.0 \text{ mL solution} \quad \dfrac{5.0 \text{ g KCl}}{100 \text{ mL solution}} = 2.5 \text{ g KCl}$

   b. $1250 \text{ mL solution} \quad \dfrac{4.0 \text{ g NH}_4Cl}{100 \text{ mL solution}} = 50.\text{g NH}_4Cl$

8.33 $355 \text{ mL solution} \dfrac{22.5 \text{ mL alcohol}}{100 \text{ mL solution}} = 79.9 \text{ mL alcohol}$

8.35 a. $1 \text{ hr} \times \dfrac{100 \text{ mL solution}}{1 \text{ hr}} \times \dfrac{20 \text{ g mannitol}}{100 \text{ mL solution}} = 20 \text{ g mannitol}$

    b. $15 \text{ hr} \times \dfrac{100 \text{ mL solution}}{1 \text{ hr}} \times \dfrac{20 \text{ g mannitol}}{100 \text{ mL solution}} = 300 \text{ g mannitol}$

8.37 $100 \text{ g glucose} \times \dfrac{100 \text{ mL solution}}{5 \text{ g glucose}} \times \dfrac{1 \text{ L}}{1000 \text{ mL}} = 2 \text{ L solution}$

8.39 Molarity = moles of solute/L of solution

    a. $\dfrac{2.0 \text{ mole glucose}}{4.0 \text{ L solution}} = 0.50 \text{ M glucose}$

    b. $\dfrac{4.0 \text{ g KOH}}{2.0 \text{ L solution}} \times \dfrac{1 \text{ mole KOH}}{56.1 \text{ g KOH}} = 0.036 \text{ M KOH}$

8.41 a $1.0 \text{ L solution} \times \dfrac{3.0 \text{ mole NaCl}}{1 \text{ L solution}} = 3.0 \text{ mole NaCl}$

    b. $0.40 \text{ L solution} \times \dfrac{1.0 \text{ mole KBr}}{1 \text{ L solution}} = 0.40 \text{ mole KBr}$

8.43 a. $2.0 \text{ L} \times \dfrac{1.5 \text{ mole NaOH}}{1 \text{ L}} \times \dfrac{40.0 \text{ g NaOH}}{1 \text{ mole NaOH}} = 120 \text{ g NaOH}$

    b. $4.0 \text{ L} \times \dfrac{0.20 \text{ mole KCl}}{1 \text{ L}} \times \dfrac{74.6 \text{ g KCl}}{1 \text{ mole KCl}} = 60.\text{g KCl}$

8.45 a. $3.0 \text{ moles NaOH} \times \dfrac{1 \text{ L}}{2 \text{ moles NaOH}} = 1.5 \text{ L NaOH}$

    b. $15 \text{ moles NaCl} \times \dfrac{1 \text{ L}}{1.5 \text{ moles NaCl}} = 10 \text{ L NaCl}$

8.47 Adding water (solvent) to the soup increases the volume and dilutes the tomato concentration.

8.49. a. 2.0 M HCL   **b.** 2.0 M NaOH
     c. 2.5% (m/v) KOH   **d.** 3.0% (m/v) H_2SO_4

8.51 a. 0.60 L   **b.** 0.25 L   **c.** 6.0 L

8.53 a. A solution cannot be separated by a semipermeable membrane.
    b. A suspension settles as time passes.

8.55 a. Water in the soil diffuses through the plant's root membranes to dilute the solutions in these cells. Because the plant's cells above these root-cells contain more concentrated solutions than the root-cells, water moves up from the roots to dilute the more concentrated cell solutions.
    b. The pickling (brine) solution contains more solutes and less solvent than the pickle's cells. Thus, solvent flows out of the cells of the cucumber and into the brine solution, and the cucumber shrivels and becomes a pickle.

8.57 a. The 10% (m/v) starch solution has a higher osmotic pressure than pure water.
    b. The water will initially flow into the starch solution to dilute solute concentration.
    c. The volume of the starch solution will increase due to inflow of water.

8.59 Water flows out of the solution with the higher solvent concentration (which corresponds to a lower solute concentration) to the solution with a lower solvent concentration (which corresponds to a higher solute concentration).

 a. Water flows into compartment B, which contains the 10% (m/v) glucose solution.
 b. Water flows into compartment B, which contains the 8% (m/v) albumin solution.
 c. Water flows into compartment B, which contains the 10% (m/v) NaCl solution.

8.61 A red blood cell has osmotic pressure of a 5 (m/v) glucose solution or a 0.90% (m/v) NaCl solution. In a hypotonic solution (lower osmotic pressure), solvent flows from the hypotonic into the red blood cell. When a red blood cell is placed in a hypertonic solution (higher osmotic pressure), solvent (water) flows from the red blood cell to the hypertonic solution. Isotonic solutions have the same osmotic pressure, and a red blood cell in an isotonic solution will not change volume because the flow of solvent into and out of the cell is equal.

 a. Distilled water is a hypotonic solution when compared to a red blood cell's contents.
 b. A 1% (m/v) glucose solution is a hypotonic solution.
 c. A 0.90% (m/v) NaCl solution is isotonic with a red blood cell's contents.
 d. A 5% (m/v) glucose solution is an isotonic solution.

8.63 Colloids cannot pass through the semipermeable dialysis membrane; water and solutions freely pass through semipermeable membranes.

 a. Sodium and chloride ions will both pass through the membrane into the distilled water.
 b. The amino acid alanine can pass through a dialysis membrane; the colloid starch will not.
 c. Sodium and chloride ions will both be present in the water surrounding the dialysis bag; the colloid starch will not.
 d. Urea will diffuse through the dialysis bag into the water.

8.65 Iodine is a nonpolar molecule and needs a nonpolar solvent such as hexane. Iodine does not dissolve in water because water is a polar solvent.

8.67 $\dfrac{15.5 \text{ g Na}_2\text{SO}_4}{15.5 \text{ g Na}_2\text{SO}_4 + 75.5 \text{ g water}} \times 100 = 17.0\%$ m/m

8.69 a. $24 \text{ hr} \times \dfrac{750 \text{ mL solution}}{12 \text{ hr}} \times \dfrac{4 \text{ g amino acids}}{100 \text{ mL solution}} = 60 \text{ g amino acids}$

 $24 \text{ hr} \times \dfrac{750 \text{ mL solution}}{12 \text{ hr}} \times \dfrac{25 \text{ g glucose}}{100 \text{ mL solution}} = 380 \text{ g glucose}$

 $24 \text{ hr} \times \dfrac{500 \text{ mL solution}}{12 \text{ hr}} \times \dfrac{10 \text{ g lipid}}{100 \text{ mL solution}} = 100 \text{ g lipid}$

 b. $60 \text{ g amino acids (protein)} \times \dfrac{4 \text{ kcal}}{1 \text{ g protein}} = 200 \text{ kcal}$

 $375 \text{ g glucose (carbohydrate)} \times \dfrac{4 \text{ kcal}}{1 \text{ g carbohydrate}} = 1500 \text{ kcal}$

 $100 \text{ g lipid (fat)} \times \dfrac{9 \text{ kcal}}{1 \text{ g fat}} = 900 \text{ kcal}$

 For a total of: 200 kcal + 1500 kcal + 900 kcal = 2600 kcal per day

8.71 $4.5 \text{ mL propyl alcohol} \times \dfrac{100 \text{ mL solution}}{12 \text{ mL propyl alcohol}} = 38 \text{ mL of solution}$

8.73 $250 \text{ mL} \times \dfrac{1 \text{ L}}{1000 \text{ mL}} \times \dfrac{2 \text{ moles KCl}}{1 \text{ L}} \times \dfrac{74.6 \text{ g KCl}}{1 \text{ mole KCl}} = 37.3 \text{ g KCl}$

8.75 Mass of solution: 70.0 g solute + 130.0 g solvent = 200.0 g

a. $250 \text{ mL} \times \dfrac{1 \text{ L}}{1000 \text{ mL}} \times \dfrac{2 \text{ moles KCl}}{1 \text{ L}} \times \dfrac{74.6 \text{ g KCl}}{1 \text{ mole KCl}} = 37.3 \text{ g KCl}$

b. $200.0 \text{ g solution} \times \dfrac{1 \text{ mL solution}}{1.21 \text{ g solution}} = 165 \text{ mL solution}$

c. $\dfrac{70.0 \text{ g HNO}_3}{165 \text{ mL solution}} \times 100 = 42.4\% \text{ (m/v) HNO}_3$

d. $\dfrac{70.0 \text{ g HNO}_3}{0.165 \text{ L solution}} \times \dfrac{1 \text{ mole HNO}_3}{63.0 \text{ g HNO}_3} = 6.73 \text{ M HNO}_3$

8.77 **a.** $2.5 \text{ L} \times \dfrac{3.0 \text{ moles Al(NO}_3)_3}{1 \text{ L}} \times \dfrac{213 \text{ g Al(NO}_3)_3}{1 \text{ mole Al(NO}_3)_3} = 1600 \text{ g Al(NO}_3)_3$

b. $75 \text{ mL} \times \dfrac{1 \text{ L}}{1000 \text{ mL}} \times \dfrac{0.50 \text{ mole C}_6\text{H}_{12}\text{O}_6}{1 \text{ L}} \times \dfrac{180 \text{ g C}_6\text{H}_{12}\text{O}_6}{1 \text{ mole C}_6\text{H}_{12}\text{O}_6} = 6.8 \text{ g of C}_6\text{H}_{12}\text{O}_6$

8.79 A solution with a high salt (solute) concentration will dry flowers because water (solvent) flows out of the flowers' cells and into the salt solution to dilute the salt concentration.

8.81 Drinking seawater, which is hypertonic, will cause water to flow out of the body cells and dehydrate the body's cells.

8.83 Water will flow from the solution with the higher solvent concentration (lower solute concentration) into the solution with the higher solute concentration.

a. B
b. B
c. stay the same
d. stay the same
e. A

Acids and Bases

Study Goals

- Describe the characteristics of acids and bases.
- Identify conjugate acid-base pairs in Brønsted-Lowry acids and bases.
- Use the ion product of water to calculate $[H_3O^+]$, $[OH^-]$, and pH.
- Write balanced equations for reactions of an acid with metals, carbonates, and bases.
- Describe the function of a buffer.

Think About It

1. Why do a lemon, grapefruit, and vinegar taste sour?

2. What do antacids do? What are some bases listed on the labels of antacids?

3. Why are some aspirin products buffered?

Key Terms

A. Acid   **B.** Base   **C.** pH   **D.** Neutralization   **E.** Buffer

1. _____ A substance that forms hydroxide ions (OH^-) in water and/or accepts protons (H^+).

2. _____ A reaction between an acid and a base to form a salt and water.

3. _____ A substance that forms hydrogen ions (H^+) in water.

4. _____ A mixture of a weak acid (or base) and its salt that maintains the pH of a solution.

5. _____ A measure of the acidity (H_3O^+) of a solution.

Answers   **1.** B   **2.** D   **3.** A   **4.** E   **5.** C

9.1 Acids and Bases

- In water, an Arrhenius acid produces H_3O^+, and an Arrhenius base produces OH^-.
- According to the Brønsted-Lowry theory, acids are proton (H^+) donors and bases are proton acceptors.
- Protons form hydronium ions, H_3O^+, in water when they bond to polar water molecules.

◆ Learning Exercise 9.1A

Indicate if the following characteristics describe an (A) acid or (B) base.

1. _____ Turns blue litmus red   2. _____ Tastes sour

3. _____ Contains more OH⁻ ions than H₃O⁺ ions   4. _____ Neutralizes bases

5. _____ Tastes bitter   6. _____ Turns red litmus blue

7. _____ Contains more H₃O⁺ ions than OH⁻ ions   8. _____ Neutralizes acids

Answers   1. A   2. A   3. B   4. A   5. B   6. B   7. A   8. B

◆ Learning Exercise 9.1B

Fill in the blanks with the formula or name of an acid or base:

1. HCl   Hydrochloric acid
2. NaOH   sodium hydroxide
3. H₂SO₃   sulfurous acid
4. HNO₃   nitric acid
5. Ca(OH)₂   Calcium hydroxide
6. H₂CO₃   Carbonic acid
7. Al(OH)₃   Aluminium hydroxide
8. KOH   potassium hydroxide

Answers   1. hydrochloric acid   2. NaOH   3. H₂SO₃
        4. HNO₃   5. calcium hydroxide   6. carbonic acid
        7. aluminum hydroxide   8. KOH

9.2 Brønsted–Lowry Acids and Bases

- According to the Brønsted-Lowry theory, acids donate protons (H⁺) to bases.
- Conjugate acid-base pairs are molecules or ions linked by the loss and gain of a proton.

Study Note

Identify the conjugate acid-base pairs in the following equation:

$$HCl + H_2O \longrightarrow H_3O^+ + Cl^-$$

Solution: HCl (proton donor) and Cl⁻ (proton acceptor)
      H₂O (proton acceptor) and H₃O⁺ (proton donor)

◆ Learning Exercise 9.2A

Complete the following conjugate acid-base pairs:

Conjugate Acid	Conjugate Base
1. H_2O	_OH⁻_
2. HSO_4^-	_SO_4^{2-}_
3. _H_	F^-
4. _H_	CO_3^{2-}
5. HNO_3	_NO_3^-_
6. NH_4^+	_NH_3_
7. _H_2S_	HS^-
8. _H_3PO_4_	$H_2PO_4^-$

Answers   1. OH^- 2. SO_4^{2-} 3. HF   4. HCO_3^-
                 5. NO_3^- 6. NH_3 7. H_2S 8. H_3PO_4

◆ Learning Exercise 9.2B

Identify the conjugate acid-base pairs in each of the following:

1. $HF + H_2O \rightleftharpoons H_3O^+ + F^-$ HF/F⁻ & H_2O/H_3O^+

2. $NH_4^+ + SO_4^{2-} \rightleftharpoons NH_3^+ + HSO_4^-$ NH_4^+/NH_3^+ & SO_4^{2-}/HSO_4^-

3. $NH_3 + H_2O \rightleftharpoons NH_4^+ + OH^-$ NH_3/NH_4^+ & H_2O/OH^-

4. $HNO_3 + OH^- \rightleftharpoons H_2O^+ + NO_3^-$ HNO_3/NO_3^- & OH^-/H_2O

Answers   1. HF/F^- and H_2O/H_3O^+ 2. NH_4/NH_3 and SO_4^{2-}/HSO_4^-
                 3. NH_3/NH_4^+ and H_2O/OH^- 4. HNO_3/NO_3^- and OH^-/H_2O

9.3 Strengths of Acids and Bases

- In aqueous solution, a strong acid donates nearly all of its protons to water, whereas a weak acid donates only a small percentage of protons to water.
- Most hydroxides of Groups 1A and 2A are strong bases, which dissociate nearly completely in water. In an aqueous ammonia solution, NH_3, which is a weak base, accepts only a small percentage of protons to form NH_4^+.

Study Note

Only six common acids are strong acids: other acids are considered as weak acids.

HCl	HNO_3
HBr	H_2SO_4 (first H)
HI	$HClO_4$

Example: Is H_2S a strong or weak acid?

Solution: H_2S is a weak acid because it is not one of the six strong acids.

◆ **Learning Exercise 9.3A**

Identify each of the following as a strong or weak acid or base:

1. HNO_3 ___S___   2. H_2CO_3 ___W___   3. $H_2PO_4^-$ ___W___

4. NH_3 ___W___   5. LiOH ___S___   6. H_3BO_3 ___W___

7. $Ca(OH)_2$ ___S___   8. H_2SO_4 ___S___

Answers   1. strong acid   2. weak acid   3. weak acid   4. weak base
              5. strong base   6. weak acid   7. strong base   8. strong acid

◆ **Learning Exercise 9.3B**

Using Table 9.3, identify the stronger acid in each of the following pairs of acids:

1. HCl or H_2CO_3 ___HCl___   2. HNO_2 or HCN ___HNO$_2$___

3. H_2S or HBr ___HBr___   4. H_2SO_4 or HSO_4^- ___H$_2$SO$_4$___

5. HF or H_3PO_4 ___H$_3$PO$_4$___

Answers   1. HCl   2. HNO_2 3. HBr   4. H_2SO_4 5. H_3PO_4

9.4 Ionization of Water

- In pure water, a few water molecules transfer a proton to other water molecules producing small but equal amounts of $[H_3O^+]$ and $[OH^-] = 1 \times 10^{-7}$ moles/L.
- K_w, the ion product, $[H_3O^+][OH^-] = [1 \times 10^{-7}][1 \times 10^{-7}] = 1 \times 10^{-14}$, applies to all aqueous solutions.
- In acidic solutions, the $[H_3O^+]$ is greater than the $[OH^-]$. In basic solutions, the $[OH^-]$ is greater than the $[H_3O^+]$.

Study Note

Example: What is the $[H_3O^+]$ in a solution that has $[OH^-] = 2.0 \times 10^{-9}$ M?

Solution: $[H_3O^+] = \dfrac{1.0 \times 10^{-14}}{2.0 \times 10^{-9}} = 5.0 \times 10^{-6}$ M $\dfrac{1 \times 10^{-14}}{2 \times 10^{-9}} = 5.0 \times 10^{-6}$

◆ **Learning Exercise 9.4**

Write the $[H_3O^+]$ when the $[OH^-]$ has the following values:

a. $[OH^-] = 1.0 \times 10^{-10}$ M $[H_3O^+] =$

b. $[OH^-] = 2.0 \times 10^{-5}$ M $[H_3O^+] =$

c. $[OH^-] = 4.5 \times 10^{-7}$ M $[H_3O^+] =$

d. $[OH^-] = 8.0 \times 10^{-4}$ M $[H_3O^+] =$

e. $[OH^-] = 5.5 \times 10^{-8}$ M $[H_3O^+] =$

Answers   a. 1.0×10^{-4} M   b. 5.0×10^{-10} M   c. 2.2×10^{-8} M
              d. 1.3×10^{-11} M   e. 1.8×10^{-7} M

9.5 The pH Scale

- The pH scale is a range of numbers from 0 to 14 related to the $[H_3O^+]$ of the solution.
- A neutral solution has a pH of 7. In acidic solutions, the pH is below 7, and in basic solutions the pH is above 7.
- Mathematically, pH is the negative logarithm of the hydronium ion concentration:

$$pH = -\log [H_3O^+].$$

◆ Learning Exercise 9.5A

State whether the following pH values are acidic, basic or neutral:

1. _____ plasma, pH = 7.4
2. _____ soft drink, pH = 2.8
3. _____ maple syrup, pH = 6.8
4. _____ beans, pH = 5.0
5. _____ tomatoes, pH = 4.2
6. _____ lemon juice, pH = 2.2
7. _____ saliva, pH = 7.0
8. _____ eggs, pH = 7.8
9. _____ lime, pH = 12.4
10. _____ strawberries, pH = 3.0

Answers   1. basic   2. acidic   3. acidic   4. acidic   5. acidic
6. acidic   7. neutral   8. basic   9. basic   10. acidic

◆ Learning Exercise 9.5B

Calculate the pH of each of the following solutions.

a. $[H_3O^+] = 1 \times 10^{-8}$ M _____
b. $[OH^-] = 1 \times 10^{-12}$ M _____
c. $[H_3O^+] = 1 \times 10^{-3}$ M _____
d. $[OH^-] = 1 \times 10^{-10}$ M _____

Answers   a. 8.0   b. 2.0   c. 3.0   d. 4.0

◆ Learning Exercise 9.5C

Calculate the pH of each of the following solutions.

a. $[H_3O^+] = 1.0 \times 10^{-3}$ M
b. $[OH^-] = 1.9 \times 10^{-6}$ M

c. $[H_3O^+] = 1 \times 10^{-8}$ M
d. $[OH^-] = 1 \times 10^{-10}$ M

Answers   a. 3.0   b. 8.0   c. 8.0   d. 4.0

◆ **Learning Exercise 9.5D**

Complete the following table:

	$[H_3O^+]$	$[OH^-]$	pH
a.	_____	1×10^{-12} M	_____
b.	_____	_____	8.0
c.	1×10^{-10} M	_____	_____
d.	_____	_____	7.0
e.	_____	_____	1.0

Answers	$[H_3O^+]$	$[OH^-]$	pH
a.	1×10^{-2} M	1×10^{-12} M	2.0
b.	1×10^{-8} M	1×10^{-6} M	8.0
c.	1×10^{-10} M	1×10^{-4} M	10.0
d.	1×10^{-7} M	1×10^{-7} M	7.0
e.	1×10^{-1} M	1×10^{-13} M	1.0

9.6 Reactions of Acids and Bases

- Acids react with many metals to yield hydrogen gas (H_2) and the salt of the metal.
- Acids react with carbonates and bicarbonates to yield CO_2, H_2O, and the salt of the metal.
- Acids neutralize bases in a reaction that produces water and a salt.
- The net ionic equation for any neutralization is $H^+ + OH^- \longrightarrow H_2O$.
- In a balanced neutralization equation, an equal number of moles of H^+ and OH^- must react.

◆ **Learning Exercise 9.6A**

Complete and balance each of the following reactions of acids:

1. _____ Zn(s) + _____ HCl $\longrightarrow$ _____ ZnCl$_2$ + _____

2. _____ HCl + _____ Li$_2$CO$_3$ $\longrightarrow$ _____ + _____

3. _____ HCl + _____ NaHCO$_3$ $\longrightarrow$ _____ CO$_2$ + _____
   H$_2$O + _____ NaCl

4. _____ Al + _____ H$_2$SO$_4$ $\longrightarrow$ _____ Al$_2$(SO$_4$)$_3$ + _____

Answers	
1.	1 Zn(s) + 2 HCl $\longrightarrow$ 1 ZnCl$_2$ + H$_2$
2.	2 HCl + 1 Li$_2$CO$_3$ $\longrightarrow$ 1 CO$_2$ + 1 H$_2$O + 2 LiCl
3.	1 HCl + 1 NaHCO$_3$ $\longrightarrow$ 1 CO$_2$ + 1 H$_2$O + 1 NaCl
4.	2 Al + 3 H$_2$SO$_4$ $\longrightarrow$ 1 Al$_2$(SO$_4$)$_3$ + 3 H$_2$

◆ **Learning Exercise 9.6B**

Balance each of the following neutralization reactions:

1. ____ NaOH + ____ H_2SO_4 ⟶ ____ Na_2SO_4 + ____ H_2O

2. ____ $Mg(OH)_2$ + ____ HCl ⟶ ____ $MgCl_2$ + ____ H_2O

3. ____ $Al(OH)_3$ + ____ HNO_3 ⟶ ____ $Al(NO_3)_3$ + ____ H_2O

4. ____ $Ca(OH)_2$ + ____ H_3PO_4 ⟶ ____ $Ca_3(PO_4)_2$ + ____ H_2O

Answers   1.   2 NaOH + 1 H_2SO_4 ⟶ 1 Na_2SO_4 + 2 H_2O

2.   1 $Mg(OH)_2$ + 2HCl ⟶ 1$MgCl_2$ + 2 H_2O

3.   1 $Al(OH)_3$ + 3HNO_3 ⟶ 1 $Al(NO_3)_3$ + 3 H_2O

4.   3 $Ca(OH)_2$ + 2H_3PO_4 ⟶ 1$Ca_3(PO_4)_2$ + 6 H_2O

◆ **Learning Exercise 9.6C**

Complete each of the following neutralization reactions and then balance:

a.   ____ KOH + ____ H_3PO_4 ⟶ _____ + ____ H_2O

b.   ____ NaOH + _____ ⟶ ____ Na_2SO_4 + _____

c.   _____ + _____ ⟶ ____ $AlCl_3$ + _____

d.   _____ + _____ ⟶ ____ $Fe_2(SO_4)_3$ + _____

Answers   a.   3 KOH + 1 H_3PO_4 ⟶ K_3PO_4 + 3 H_2O

b.   2 NaOH + 1 H_2SO_4 ⟶ 1 Na_2SO_4 + 2H_2O

c. $Al(OH)_3$ + 3 HCl ⟶ 1 $AlCl_3$ + 3H_2O

d.   2 $Fe(OH)_3$ + 3H_2SO_4 ⟶ 1 $Fe_2(SO_4)_3$ + 6H_2O

9.7 Buffers

- A buffer solution resists a change in pH when small amounts of acid or base are added.
- A buffer contains either (1) a weak acid and its salt, or (2) a weak base and its salt. The weak acid picks up excess OH^-, and the anion of the salt picks up excess H_3O^+.
- The pH of a buffer can be calculated by rearranging the K_a for $[H_3O^+]$.

◆ **Learning Exercise 9.7A**

State whether each of the following represents a buffer system or not.

a. HCl + NaCl   b. K_2SO_4 c. H_2CO_3 d. H_2CO_3 + $NaHCO_3$

Answers **a.** No. A strong acid is not a buffer.
b. No. A salt alone cannot act as a buffer.
c. No. A weak acid alone cannot act as a buffer.
d. Yes. A weak acid and its salt act as a buffer system.

Check List for Chapter 9

You are ready to take the practice test for Chapter 9. Be sure that you have accomplished the following learning goals for this chapter. If you are not sure, review the section listed at the end of the goal. Then apply your new skills and understanding to the practice test.

After studying Chapter 9, I can successfully:

_____ Describe the properties of Arrhenius acids and bases and write their names (9.1).

_____ Describe the Brønsted-Lowry concept of acids and bases; write conjugate acid-base pairs for an acid-base reaction (9.2).

_____ Write equations for the ionization of strong and weak acids and bases (9.3).

_____ Use the ion product of water to calculate $[H_3O^+]$ and $[OH^-]$ (9.4).

_____ Calculate pH from the $[H_3O^+]$ or $[OH^-]$ of a solution (9.5).

_____ Write a balanced equation for the reactions of acids with metals, carbonates, and/or bases (9.6).

_____ Describe the role of buffers in maintaining the pH of a solution and calculate the pH of a buffer solution. (9.7).

Practice Test for Chapter 9

1. An acid is a compound which when placed in water yields this characteristic ion:

   A. H_3O^+ **B.** OH^- **C.** Na^+
   D. Cl^- **E.** CO_3^{2-}

2. $MgCl_2$ would be classified as a(n)

   A. acid   **B.** base   **C.** salt
   D. buffer   **E.** nonelectrolyte

3. $Mg(OH)_2$ would be classified as a

   A. weak acid   **B.** strong base   **C.** salt
   D. buffer   **E.** nonelectrolyte

4. In the K_w expression for pure H_2O, the $[H_3O^+]$ has the value

   A. 1×10^{-7} M   **B.** 1×10^{-1} M   **C.** 1×10^{-14} M
   D. 1×10^{-6} M   **E.** 1×10^{-12} M

5. Of the following pH values, which is the most acidic?

   A. 8.0   **B.** 5.5   **C.** 1.5
   D. 3.2   **E.** 9.0

6. Of the following pH values, which is the most basic pH?

   A. 10.0   **B.** 4.0   **C.** 2.2
   D. 11.5   **E.** 9.0

For questions 7 through 9, consider a solution with $[H_3O^+] = 1 \times 10^{-11}$ M.

7. The pH of the solution is
   A. 1.0
   B. 2.0
   C. 3.0
   D. 11.0
   E. 14.0

8. The hydroxide ion concentration is
   A. 1×10^{-1} M
   B. 1×10^{-3} M
   C. 1×10^{-4} M
   D. 1×10^{-7} M
   E. 1×10^{-11} M

9. The solution is
   A. acidic
   B. basic
   C. neutral
   D. a buffer
   E. neutralized

For questions 10 through 12, consider a solution with a $[OH^-] = 1 \times 10^{-5}$ M.

10. The hydrogen ion concentration of the solution is
    A. 1×10^{-5} M
    B. 1×10^{-7} M
    C. 1×10^{-9} M
    D. 1×10^{-10} M
    E. 1×10^{-14} M

11. The pH of the solution is
    A. 2.0
    B. 5.0
    C. 9.0
    D. 11
    E. 14

12. The solution is
    A. acidic
    B. basic
    C. neutral
    D. a buffer
    E. neutralized

13. Acetic acid is a weak acid because
    A. it forms a dilute acid solution.
    B. it is isotonic.
    C. it is less than 50% ionized in water.
    D. it is a nonpolar molecule.
    E. it can form a buffer.

14. A weak base when added to water
    A. makes the solution slightly basic.
    B. does not affect the pH.
    C. dissociates completely.
    D. does not dissociate.
    E. makes the solution slightly acidic.

15. Which is an equation for neutralization?
    A. $CaCO_3 \longrightarrow CaO + CO_2$
    B. $Na_2SO_4\ (s) \longrightarrow 2Na^+ + SO_4^{2-}$
    C. $H_2SO_4 + 2\ NaOH \longrightarrow Na_2SO_4 + 2H_2O$
    D. $Na_2O + SO_3 \longrightarrow Na_2SO_4$
    E. $H_2CO_3 \longrightarrow CO_2 + H_2O$

16. What is the name given to components in the body that keep blood pH within its normal 7.35 to 7.45 range?
    A. nutrients
    B. buffers
    C. metabolites
    D. regufluids
    E. neutralizers

17. What is true of a typical buffer system?

    A. It maintains a pH of 7.0.
    B. It contains a weak base.
    C. It contains a salt.
    D. It contains a strong acid and its salt.
    E. It maintains the pH of a solution.

18. Which of the following would act as a buffer system?

    A. HCl **B.** Na_2CO_3 **C.** $NaOH + NaNO_3$
    D. NH_4OH **E.** $NaHCO_3 + H_2CO_3$

19. Which of the following pairs is a conjugate acid-base pair?

    A. HCl/HNO_3 **B.** HNO_3/NO_3^- **C.** $NaOH/KOH$
    D. HSO_4^-/HCO_3^- **E.** Cl^-/F^-

20. The conjugate base of HSO_4^- is

    A. SO_4^{2-} **B.** H_2SO_4 **C.** HS^-
    D. H_2S **E.** SO_3^{2-}

21. In which reaction does H_2O act as an acid?

    A. $H_3PO_4 + H_2O \longrightarrow H_3O^+ + H_2PO_4^-$
    B. $H_2SO_4 + H_2O \longrightarrow H_3O^+ + HSO_4^-$
    C. $H_2O + HS^- \longrightarrow H_3O^+ + S^{2-}$
    D. $NaOH + HCl \longrightarrow NaCl + H_2O$
    E. $NH_3 + H_2O \longrightarrow NH_4^+ + OH^-$

Answers to the Practice Test

1. A	**2.** C	**3.** B	**4.** A	**5.** C
6. D	**7.** D	**8.** B	**9.** B	**10.** C
11. C	**12.** B	**13.** C	**14.** A	**15.** C
16. B	**17.** E	**18.** E	**19.** B	**20.** A
21. E				

Answers and Solutions to Selected Text Problems

9.1 According to the Arrhenius theory:

    a. acids taste sour.
    b. acids neutralize bases.
    c. acids produce H_3O^+ ions in water.
    d. potassium hydroxide is the name of a base.
    e. a base is a proton acceptor.

9.3 The names of nonoxy acids begin with *hydro-,* followed by the name of the anion. The names of oxyacids use the element root with *–ic acid.* Acids with one oxygen less than the common *–ic acid* name are named as *–ous acids.*

    a. hydrochloric acid   **b.** calcium hydroxide   **c.** carbonic acid
    d. nitric acid   **e.** sulfurous acid

9.5   **a.** $Mg(OH)_2$ **b.** HF **c.** H_3PO_4
         d. $LiOH$ **e.** $Cu(OH)_2$

9.7   The acid donates a proton (H^+), while the base accepts a proton.

    a. Acid (proton donor) HI   proton acceptor (base) H_2O
    b. Acid (proton donor) H_2O proton acceptor (base) F^-

9.9   To form the conjugate base, remove a proton (H^+) from the acid.

    a. F^-, fluoride ion   **b.** OH^-, hydroxide ion
    c. HCO_3^-, bicarbonate ion   **d.** SO_4^{2-}, sulfate ion

9.11   To form the conjugate acid, add a proton (H^+) to the base.

    a. HCO_3^-, bicarbonate ion   **b.** H_3O^+, hydronium ion
    c. H_3PO_4, phosphoric acid   **d.** HBr, hydrobromic acid

9.13   The conjugate acid is a proton donor and the conjugate base is a proton acceptor.

    a. acid H_2CO_3; conjugate base HCO_3^-; base H_2O; conjugate acid H_3O^+
    b. acid NH_4^+; conjugate base NH_3; base H_2O; conjugate acid H_3O^+
    c. acid HCN; conjugate base CN^-; base NO_2^- conjugate acid HNO_2

9.15   Use Table 9.3 to answer.

    a. HBr   **b.** HSO_4^- **c.** H_2CO_3

9.17   Use Table 9.3 to answer.

    a. HSO_4^- **b.** HF   **c.** HCO_3^-

9.19   In pure water, a small fraction of the water molecules break apart to form H^+ and OH^-. The H^+ combines with H_2O to form H_3O^+. Every time a H^+ is formed a OH^- is also formed. Therefore, the concentration of the two must be equal in pure water.

9.21   In an acidic solution, $[H_3O^+]$ is greater than $[OH^-]$, which means that the $[H_3O^+]$ is greater than 1×10^{-7} M and the $[OH^-]$ is less than 1×10^{-7} M.

9.23   A neutral solution has $[OH^-] = [H_3O^+] = 1.0 \times 10^{-7}$ M. If $[OH^-]$ is greater than 1×10^{-7}, the solution is basic; if $[H_3O^+]$ is greater than 1×10^{-7} M, the solution is acidic.

    a. Acidic; $[H_3O^+]$ is greater than 1×10^{-7} M.
    b. Basic; $[H_3O^+]$ is less than 1×10^{-7} M.
    c. Basic; $[OH^-]$ is greater than 1×10^{-7} M.
    d. Acidic; $[OH^-]$ is less than 1×10^{-7} M.

9.25   The $[H_3O^+]$ multiplied by the $[OH^-]$ is equal to K_w, which is 1.0×10^{-14}. When $[H_3O^+]$ is known, the $[OH^-]$ can be calculated.

Rearranging the K_w gives $[OH^-] = K_w/[H_3O^+]$.

    a. 1.0×10^{-9} M   **b.** 1.0×10^{-6} M
    c. 2.0×10^{-5} M   **d.** 4.0×10^{-13} M

9.27   The value of the $[H_3O^+]$ multiplied by the value of the $[OH^-]$ is always equal to K_w, which is 1×10^{-14}. When $[H_3O^+]$ is known, the $[OH^-]$ can be calculated.

Rearranging the K_w gives $[OH^-] = K_w/[H_3O^+]$.

    a. 1.0×10^{-11} M   **b.** 2.0×10^{-9} M
    c. 5.6×10^{-3} M   **d.** 2.5×10^{-2} M

9.29   In neutral solutions, the $[H_3O^+]$ is equal to 1.0×10^{-7} M. The pH is the $-\log [H_3O^+]$ and the $-\log [1.0 \times 10^{-7}] = 7.00$. Note that the pH has two *decimal places* because the coefficient 1.0 has two significant figures.

9.31 An acidic solution has a pH less than 7. A neutral solution has a pH equal to 7. A basic solution has a pH greater than 7.

   a. basic   **b.** acidic   **c.** basic   **d.** acidic

9.33 The value of $[H_3O^+][OH^-]$ is equal to K_w, which is 1.0×10^{-14}. Rearranging the K_w gives $[H_3O^+] = K_w / [OH^-]$.

   a. 4.00   **b.** 8.52   **c.** 9.00   **d.** 3.40

9.35 On a calculator, pH is calculated by entering –log, followed by the coefficient EE (EXP) key and the power of 10 follow by the change sign (+/–) key. On some calculators the concentration is entered first (coefficient EXP – power) followed by log and +/– key.

$[H_3O^+]$	$[OH^-]$	pH	Acidic, Basic, or Neutral?
1×10^{-8} M	1×10^{-6} M	8.	Basic
1×10^{-3} M	1×10^{-11} M	3.0	Acidic
2×10^{-5} M	5×10^{-10} M	4.75	Acidic
1×10^{-12} M	1×10^{-2} M	12.0	Basic

9.37 Acids react with active metals to form H_2 and a salt of the metal. The reaction of acids with carbonates yields CO_2, H_2O, and a salt of the metal. In a neutralization, an acid and a base form a salt and H_2O.

   a. $ZnCO_3 + 2HCl \longrightarrow ZnCl_2 + CO_2 + H_2O$
   b. $Zn + 2HCl \longrightarrow ZnCl_2 + H_2$
   c. $HCl + NaHCO_3 \longrightarrow NaCl + H_2O + CO_2$
   d. $2 HNO_3 + Mg(OH)_2 \longrightarrow Mg(NO_3)_2 + 2 H_2O$

9.39 In balancing a neutralization equation, the number of H^+ and OH^- must be equalized by placing coefficients in front of the formulas for the acid and base.

   a. $2HCl + Mg(OH)_2 \longrightarrow MgCl_2 + 2 H_2O$
   b. $H_3PO_4 + 3 LiOH \longrightarrow Li_3PO_4 + 3 H_2O$

9.41 In balancing a neutralization equation, the number of H^+ and OH^- must be equalized by placing coefficients in front of the formulas for the acid and base.

   a. $H_2SO_4 + 2 NaOH \longrightarrow Na_2SO_4 + 2 H_2O$
   b. $3 HCl + Fe(OH)_3 \longrightarrow FeCl_3 + 3 H_2O$
   c. $H_2CO_3 + Mg(OH)_2 \longrightarrow MgCO_3 + 2 H_2O$

9.43 A buffer system contains a weak acid and its salt, or a weak base and its salt.
   a. This is not a buffer system, because it only contains a strong acid.
   b. This is a buffer system; it contains the weak acid H_2CO_3 and its salt $NaHCO_3$.
   c. This is a buffer system; it contains HF, a weak acid, and its salt KF.
   d. This is not a buffer system because it contains the salts KCl and NaCl.

9.45   **a.** A buffer system keeps the pH of a solution constant.
   b. The salt of the acid in a buffer is needed to neutralize any acid added.
   c. When H^+ is added to the buffer, the F^-, which is the salt of the weak acid, reacts with the acid to neutralize it.
   d. When OH^- is added to the buffer solution, HF (weak acid) reacts to neutralize the OH^-.

9.47   The name of an acid from a simple nonmetallic anion is formed by adding the prefix *hydro-* to the name of the anion and changing the anion ending to *-ic acid*. If the acid has polyatomic anion, the name of the acid uses the name of the polyatomic anion and ends in *–ic acid* or *–ous acid*. There is no prefix *hydro*. Bases are named as ionic compounds containing hydroxide anions.

     a. sulfuric acid, acid   **b.** potassium hydroxide, base
     c. calcium hydroxide, base   **d.** hydrochloric acid, acid   **e.** nitrous acid, acid

9.49   Both strong and weak acids dissolve in water to give H_3O^+. They both neutralize bases, turn litmus red and phenolphthalein clear. Both taste sour and are electrolytes in solution. However, weak acids are only slightly dissociated in solution and are weak electrolytes. Strong acids, which are nearly completely dissociated in solution, are strong electrolytes.

9.51   **a.** $Mg(OH)_2$ is a strong base because all the base that dissolves is dissociated in aqueous solution.
     b. $Mg(OH)_2 + 2\ HCl \rightarrow 2\ H_2O + MgCl_2$

9.53   The pOH = $-\log [OH^-]$, which means that pH + pOH = 14.0.

     a. pH 7.70, pOH 6.30   **b.** pH 1.30, pOH 12.70
     c. pH 10.54, pOH 3.46   **d.** pH 11.7, pOH 2.3

9.55   If the pH is given, the $[H_3O^+]$ can be found by using the relationship $[H_3O^+] = 1.0 \times 10^{-pH}$. The $[OH^-]$ can be found from $[H_3O^+][OH^-] = 1 \times 10^{-14}$.

     a. $[H_3O^+] = 1 \times 10^{-3}\ M$ $[OH^-] = 1 \times 10^{-11}\ M$
     b. $[H_3O^+] = 1 \times 10^{-6}\ M$ $[OH^-] = 1 \times 10^{-8}\ M$
     c. $[H_3O^+] = 1 \times 10^{-8}\ M$ $[OH^-] = 1 \times 10^{-6}\ M$
     d. $[H_3O^+] = 1 \times 10^{-11}\ M$ $[OH^-] = 1 \times 10^{-3}\ M$

9.57   In a buffer, the anion accepts H^+ and the cation provides H^+.
     a. $H_2PO_4^- + H_3O^+ \longrightarrow H_3PO_4 + H_2O$
     b. $H_3PO_4 + OH^- \longrightarrow H_2PO_4^- + H_2O$
     c. $[H_3O^+] = 7.5 \times 10^{-3} = [0.10\ M]/[0.10\ M] = 7.5 \times 10^{-3}$ pH = $-\log (7.5 \times 10^{-3}) = 2.12$

9.59   **a.** When acidic compounds enter the blood, the body reacts by restoring the blood pH. The pH of blood is controlled by the carbonic acid equilibrium.

$$CO_2 + H_2O \rightleftarrows H_2CO_3 \rightleftarrows H^+ + HCO_3^-$$

The body responds to excess H^+ by hyperventilating, which lowers the CO_2 and causes the equilibrium to shift to the left.
     b. The underlying cause of the increased acidity should be treated. In the meanwhile, sodium bicarbonate is given.

149

Introduction to Organic Chemistry

Study Goals

- Identify the number of bonds for carbon and other atoms in organic compounds.
- Describe the tetrahedral shape of carbon with single bonds in organic compounds.
- Draw expanded and condensed structural formulas for alkanes.
- Write the IUPAC names for alkanes.
- Write the IUPAC and common names for haloalkanes; draw the condensed structural formulas.
- Write the IUPAC names, and draw the structural formulas for cycloalkanes.
- Describe the physical properties of alkanes.
- Write equations for the combustion of alkanes and cycloalkanes.
- Describe the properties that are characteristic of organic compounds.
- Identify the functional groups in organic compounds.
- Write condensed structural formulas for organic compounds.

Think About It

1. What is the meaning of the term "organic"?

2. What two elements are found in all organic compounds?

3. In a salad dressing, why is there a layer of vegetable oil floating on the vinegar and water layer?

Key Terms

1. Match the statements shown below with the following key terms.

a. alkene	**b.** isomers	**c.** hydrocarbon
d. alcohol	**e.** functional group	

1. _____ An atom or group of atoms that influences the chemical reactions of an organic compound

2. _____ A class of organic compounds with one or more hydroxyl (—OH) groups

3. _____ A type of hydrocarbon with one or more carbon–carbon double bonds

4. _____ Organic compound consisting of only carbon and hydrogen atoms

5. _____ Compounds having the same molecular formula but a different arrangements of atoms

Answers   **1.** e   **2.** d   **3.** a   **4.** c   **5.** b

2. Match the statements shown below with the correct key term.

a. alkane	**b.** condensed structural formula	**c.** main chain
d. combustion	**e.** cycloalkane	

1. _____ A hydrocarbon that contains only carbon–carbon single bonds

2. _____ An alkane that exists as a cyclic structure

3. _____ The chemical reaction of an alkane and oxygen that yields CO_2, H_2O, and heat

4. _____ The type of formula that shows the arrangement of the carbon atoms grouped with their attached H atoms

5. _____ The longest continuous chain of carbon atoms in a structural formula

Answers   **1.** a   **2.** e   **3.** d   **4.** b   **5.** c

10.1 Organic Compounds

- Organic compounds are compounds of carbon and hydrogen that have covalent bonds, low melting and boiling points, burn vigorously, are nonelectrolytes, and are usually more soluble in nonpolar solvents than in water.

◆ Learning Exercise 10.1

Identify the following as typical of organic (O) or inorganic (I) compounds.

1. _____ have covalent bonds   2. _____ have low boiling points

3. _____ burn in air   4. _____ are soluble in water

5. _____ have high melting points   6. _____ are soluble in nonpolar solvents

7. _____ have ionic bonds   8. _____ form long chains

9. _____ contain carbon   10. _____ are not very combustible

11. _____ have a formula of Na_2SO_4 12. _____ have a formula of CH_3—CH_2—CH_3

Answers   **1.** O   **2.** O   **3.** O   **4.** I   **5.** I   **6.** O
                     7. I   **8.** O   **9.** O   **10.** I   **11.** I   **12.** O

10.2 Bonding in Organic Compounds

- Each carbon in an alkane has four bonds arranged so that the bonded atoms are in the corners of a tetrahedron.

◆ Learning Exercise 10.2

Consider the following three-dimensional structure for methane.

1. Complete the structure by adding hydrogen atoms.

2. What is indicated by the solid lines, wedge, and dashed line used in the three-dimensional structure?

3. What is the shape of this structure?

4. What is the angle between each C—H bond?

Answers

1.

2. The straight lines are in the plane of the page, the wedge comes forward from the page, and the dashed line goes behind the page.

3. Tetrahedron

4. 109.5°

10.3 Alkanes

- In an IUPAC name, the stem indicates the number of carbon atoms, and the suffix describes the family of the compound. For example, in the name *propane,* the stem *prop* indicates a chain of three carbon atoms and the ending *ane* indicates single bonds (alkane). The names of the first six alkanes follow:

Name	Carbon atoms	Condensed structural formula
Methane	1	CH_4
Ethane	2	CH_3—CH_3
Propane	3	CH_3—CH_2—CH_3
Butane	4	CH_3—CH_2—CH_2—CH_3
Pentane	5	CH_3—CH_2—CH_2—CH_2—CH_3
Hexane	6	CH_3—CH_2—CH_2—CH_2—CH_2—CH_3

- An expanded structural formula shows a separate line to each bonded atom; a condensed structural formula depicts each carbon atom and its attached hydrogen atoms as a group. A molecular formula gives the total numbers of atoms.

Expanded Structural Formula	**Condensed Structural Formula**	**Molecular Formula**

```
   H  H  H
   |  |  |
H—C——C——C—H        CH3—CH2—CH3
   |  |  |
   H  H  H          or                      C3H8

                    CH3CH2CH3
```

◆ **Learning Exercise 10.3A**

Indicate if each of the following is a molecular formula (M), an expanded structural formula (E), or a condensed structural formula (C).

1. _____ CH_3—CH_3 **2.** _____ C_5H_{12} **3.** _____ CH_3—CH_2—CH_3

```
          H  H  H
          |  |  |                     CH3
4. ____ H—C——C——C—H     5. ____ CH3—CH—CH2—CH3     6. ____ C8H18
          |  |  |
          H  H  H
```

Answers   **1.** C   **2.** M   **3.** C   **4.** E   **5.** C   **6.** M

◆ Learning Exercise 10.3B

Write the condensed formulas for the following structural formulas.

1.

```
    H  H
    |  |
H—C—C—H
    |  |
    H  H
```

2.

```
    H  H  H
    |  |  |
H—C—C—C—H
    |  |  |
    H  H  H
```

3.

```
    H  H  H  H
    |  |  |  |
H—C—C—C—C—H
    |  |  |  |
    H  H  H  H
```

4.

```
            H
            |
          H—C—H
    H     |  H  H
    |     |  |  |
H—C—C—C—C—H
    |  |  |  |
    H  H  |  H
          H—C—H
            |
            H
```

Answers   **1.** CH₃—CH₃   **2.** CH₃—CH₂—CH₃

3. CH₃— CH₂—CH₂—CII₃

4.
```
          CH₃
          |
CH₃—CH—CH—CH₃
          |
          CH₃
```

◆ Learning Exercise 10.3C

Write the condensed structure and name for the straight-chain alkane of each of the following formulas.

1. C₂H₆ _____

2. C₃H₈ _____

3. C₄H₁₀ _____

4. C₅H₁₂ _____

5. C₆H₁₄ _____

Answers   **1.** CH₃—CH₃, ethane
2. CH₃—CH₂—CH₃, propane
3. CH₃—CH₂—CH₂—CH₃, butane
4. CH₃—CH₂—CH₂—CH₂—CH₃, pentane
5. CH₃—CH₂—CH₂—CH₂—CH₂—CH₃, hexane

◆ Learning Exercise 10.3D

Write the IUPAC name for each of the following cycloalkanes.

1. △

2. (cyclobutane with CH₃)

3. (cyclohexane with CH₃)

4. (cyclopentane)

5. (cyclopentane with CH₂CH₃)

Answers   **1.** cyclopropane   **2.** methylcyclobutane   **3.** methylcyclohexane
          4. cyclopentane   **5.** ethylcyclopentane

10.4 Naming Branched Alkanes

- The IUPAC system is a set of rules used to name organic compounds in a systematic manner.
- Each substituent is numbered and listed alphabetically in front of the name of the longest chain.
- Carbon groups that are substituents are named as alkyl groups or alkyl substituents. An alkyl group is named by replacing the *ane* of the alkane name with *yl*. For example, CH_3— is named as methyl (from CH_4 methane), and CH_3—CH_2— is named as an ethyl group (from CH_3—CH_3 ethane).
- Structural isomers have the same molecular formula, but differ in the sequence of atoms in each of their structural formulas.

Study Note

Example: Write the IUPAC name for the compound

$$CH_3$$
$$|$$
$$CH_3\text{—}CH_2\text{—}CH\text{—}CH_3$$

Solution: The four-carbon chain *butane* is numbered from the end nearest the side group, which places the *methyl* substituent on carbon 2: *2-methylbutane*.

◆ Learning Exercise 10.4A

Provide a correct IUPAC name for each of the following compounds.

1. CH_3
    $|$
    $CH_3\text{—}CH\text{—}CH_3$ _____

2. CH_3 CH_3
    $|$ $|$
    $CH_3\text{—}CH\text{—}CH_2\text{—}CH\text{—}CH_2\text{—}CH_3$ _____

$$\begin{array}{c} \quad\quad CH_3 \quad\quad\quad\quad\quad CH_3 \\ \quad\quad | \quad\quad\quad\quad\quad\quad\quad | \end{array}$$

3. $CH_3—CH—CH_2—CH_2—CH—CH_2—CH_3$ _____

$$\begin{array}{c} CH_3 \\ | \end{array}$$

4. $CH_3—C—CH_2—CH_3$ _____

$$\begin{array}{c} | \\ CH_3 \end{array}$$

Answers   **1.** 2-methylpropane   **2.** 2,4-dimethylhexane   **3.** 2,5-dimethylheptane
4. 2,2-dimethylbutane

Study Note

Example: Write the structural isomers of C_4H_{10}. Solution: Write the first isomer as a main chain of four carbons. Then use a main chain of three carbon atoms and attach the other carbon atom as a substituent.

$$\begin{array}{c} \quad\quad\quad\quad\quad\quad\quad\quad\quad\quad\quad\quad CH_3 \\ \quad\quad\quad\quad\quad\quad\quad\quad\quad\quad\quad\quad | \end{array}$$

$CH_3—CH_2—CH_2—CH_3$ and $CH_3—CH—CH_3$

◆ **Learning Exercise 10.4B**

Write the condensed formula for each of the following compounds:

1. hexane   **2.** methane

3. 2,4-dimethylpentane   **4.** propane

Answers

1. $CH_3—CH_2—CH_2—CH_2—CH_2—CH_3$ **2.** CH_4

$$\begin{array}{c} CH_3 \quad\quad\quad CH_3 \\ | \quad\quad\quad\quad\quad | \end{array}$$

3. $CH_3—CH—CH_2—CH—CH_3$ **4.** $CH_3—CH_2—CH_3$

◆ **Learning Exercise 10.4C**

Write the condensed structural formula for each of the following alkanes.

1. pentane

2. 2-methylpentane

3. 4-ethyl-2-methylhexane

4. 2,2,4-trimethylhexane

Answers

1. $CH_3-CH_2-CH_2-CH_3-CH_3$

2.
$$
\begin{array}{c}
CH_3 \\
| \\
CH_3-CH-CH_2-CH_3-CH_3
\end{array}
$$

3.
$$
\begin{array}{ccc}
CH_3 & & CH_2-CH_3 \\
| & & | \\
CH_3-CH-CH_2- & CH-CH_2-CH_3
\end{array}
$$

4.
$$
\begin{array}{ccc}
CH_3 & & CH_3 \\
| & & | \\
CH_3-C-CH_2- & CH-CH_2-CH_3 \\
| \\
CH_3
\end{array}
$$

10.5 Haloalkanes

- In a haloalkane, a halogen atom, F, Cl, Br, or I replace a hydrogen atom in an alkane.
- A halogen atom is named as a substituent (fluoro, chloro, bromo, iodo) attached to the alkane chain.

◆ **Learning Exercise 10.5A**

Write a correct IUPAC (or common name) for the following.

1. CH_3-CH_2-Br

2.
$$
\begin{array}{c}
Cl \\
| \\
CH_3-CH_2-C-CH_2-CH_3 \\
| \\
Cl
\end{array}
$$

3.
$$
\begin{array}{ccc}
Cl & & Br \\
| & & | \\
CH_3-CH_2-CH-CH_2- & CH-CH_3
\end{array}
$$

4.
$$
\begin{array}{c}
F \\
| \\
CH_3-CH_2-CH_2-CH-Cl
\end{array}
$$

Answers   **1.** bromoethane (ethyl bromide)   **2.** 3,3-dichloropentane
            3. 2-bromo-4-chlorohexane   **4.** 1-chloro-1-fluorobutane

◆ Learning Exercise 10.5B

Write the condensed formula for each of the following haloalkanes.

1. ethyl chloride

2. bromomethane

3. 3-bromo-1-chloropentane

4. 1,1-dichlorohexane

5. 2,2,3-trichlorobutane

6. 2,4-dibromo-2,4-dichloropentane

Answers 1. CH_3-CH_2-Cl

2. CH_3-Br

3. $Cl-CH_2-CH_2-\underset{\underset{Br}{|}}{CH}-CH_2-CH_3$

4. $Cl-\underset{\underset{Cl}{|}}{CH}-CH_2-CH_2-CH_2-CH_2-CH_3$

5. $CH_3-\underset{\underset{Cl}{|}}{\overset{\overset{Cl}{|}}{C}}-\overset{\overset{Cl}{|}}{CH}-CH_3$

6. $CH_3-\underset{\underset{Cl}{|}}{\overset{\overset{Br}{|}}{C}}-CH_2-\underset{\underset{Cl}{|}}{\overset{\overset{Br}{|}}{C}}-CH_3$

10.6 Properties of Alkanes

- The alkanes are nonpolar, less dense than water, and mostly unreactive, except that they burn vigorously.
- Alkanes are found in natural gas, gasoline, and diesel fuels.
- In combustion, an alkane or cycloalkane at a high temperature reacts rapidly with oxygen to produce carbon dioxide, water, and a great amount of heat.

Study Note

Example: Write the equation for the combustion of methane.

Solution: Write the molecular formulas for the reactants: methane (CH_4) and oxygen (O_2). Write the products CO_2 and H_2O and balance the equation.

$$CH_4(g) + O_2(g) \longrightarrow CO_2(g) + H_2O(g) + Heat$$
$$CH_4(g) + 2O_2(g) \longrightarrow CO_2(g) + 2H_2O(g) + Heat \text{ (balanced)}$$

◆ Learning Exercise 10.6A

For each of the following pairs of hydrocarbons, indicate the one that has the higher boiling point.

1. butane or propane _____

2. 3-methylpentane or hexane _____

Answers 1. butane 2. hexane

◆ **Learning Exercise 10.6B**

Write a balanced equation for the complete combustion of the following:

1. propane   _____

2. hexane   _____

3. pentane   _____

4. cyclobutane_____

Answers
1. $C_3H_8 + 5O_2 \longrightarrow 3CO_2 + 4H_2O + Heat$ **2.** $2C_6H_{14} + 19O_2 \longrightarrow 12CO_2 + 14H_2O + Heat$
3. $C_5H_{12} + 8O_2 \longrightarrow 5CO_2 + 6H_2O + Heat$ **4.** $C_4H_8 + 6O_2 \longrightarrow 4CO_2 + 4H_2O + Heat$

10.7 Functional Groups

- Organic compounds are classified by *functional groups*, which are atoms or groups of atoms where specific chemical reactions occur.
- Alkenes are hydrocarbons that contain one or more double bonds (C=C); alkynes contain a triple bond (C≡C).
- Alcohols contain a hydroxyl (—OH) group; ethers have an oxygen atom (—O—) between two alkyl groups.
- Aldehydes contain a carbonyl group (C=O) bonded to at least one H atom; ketones contain the carbonyl group bonded to two alkyl groups.
- Carboxylic acids have a carboxyl group attached to hydrogen (—COOH); esters contain the carboxyl groups attached to an alkyl group.
- Amines are derived from ammonia (NH_3) in which alkyl groups replace one or more of the H atoms.

◆ **Learning Exercise 10.7A**

Classify the organic compounds shown below according to their functional groups:

a. alkane   **b.** alkene   **c.** alcohol   **d.** ether   **e.** aldehyde

1._____ CH_3—CH_2—CH=CH_2 **2.**_____CH_3—CH_2—CH_3

                        O
                        ‖
3._____CH_3—CH_2—C—H   **4.**_____CH_3—CH_2—CH_2—OH

5._____CH_3—CH_2—O—CH_2—CH_3 **6.**_____CH_3—CH_2—CH_2—CH_3

Answers   **1.** b   **2.** a   **3.** e   **4.** c   **5.** d   **6.** a

◆ **Learning Exercise 10.7B**

Classify the following compounds according to their functional groups:
a. alcohol **b.** aldehyde **c.** ketone **d.** ether **e.** amine

$$\overset{\displaystyle O}{\overset{\displaystyle \|}{}}$$

1. ____ $CH_3-CH_2-CH_2-\overset{\displaystyle O}{\overset{\displaystyle \|}{C}}-H$ **2.** ____ $CH_3-CH_2-CH_2-NH_2$

3. ____ $CH_3-CH_2-\overset{\displaystyle O}{\overset{\displaystyle \|}{C}}-CH_2-CH_3$ **4.** ____ $CH_3-CH_2-O-CH_3$

5. ____ $CH_3-\overset{\displaystyle O}{\overset{\displaystyle \|}{C}}-CH_2-CH_3$ **6.** ____ $CH_3-\overset{\displaystyle O}{\overset{\displaystyle \|}{C}}-H$

7. ____ $CH_3-CH_2-\overset{\displaystyle NH_2}{\overset{\displaystyle |}{C}H}-CH_3$ **8.** ____ $CH_3-CH_2-\overset{\displaystyle OH}{\overset{\displaystyle |}{C}H}-CH_3$

Answers   **1.** b   **2.** e   **3.** c   **4.** d
　　　　　 5. c   **6.** b   **7.** e   **8.** a

Check List for Chapter 10

You are ready to take the practice test for Chapter 10. Be sure that you have accomplished the following learning goals for this chapter. If you are not sure, review the section listed at the end of the goal. Then apply your new skills and understanding to the practice test.

After studying Chapter 10, I can successfully:

_____ Identify properties as characteristic of organic or inorganic compounds (10.1).

_____ Identify the number of bonds for carbon (10.2).

_____ Describe the tetrahedral shape of carbon in carbon compounds (10.2).

_____ Draw the complete structural formula and the condensed structural formula for an alkane (10.3).

_____ Use the IUPAC system to write the names for branched and unbranched alkanes (10.4).

_____ Draw the structural formulas of alkanes from the name. (10.4).

_____ Name or draw the structural formula of a cycloalkane (10.4).

_____ Name or draw the structural formula of a haloalkane (10.5).

_____ Describe physical properties of alkanes (10.6).

_____ Identify the functional groups in organic compounds (10.7).

Practice Test for Chapter 10

For problems 1 through 8, indicate whether the following characteristics are typical of (O) organic compounds or (I) inorganic compounds.

1. _____ higher melting points   2. _____ fewer compounds

3. _____ covalent bonds   4. _____ soluble in water

5. _____ ionic bonds   6. _____ combustible

7. _____ low boiling points   8. _____ soluble in nonpolar solvents

Match the name of the hydrocarbon with each of the following structures.

A. methane   **B.** ethane   **C.** propane   **D.** pentane   **E.** heptane

9. _____ CH_3—CH_2—CH_3 10. _____ CH_3—CH_2—CH_2—CH_2—CH_2—CH_2—CH_3

11. _____ CH_4 12. _____ CH_3—CH_2—CH_2—CH_2—CH_3

13. _____ CH_3—CH_3

Match the name of the hydrocarbons with each of the following structures.

A. butane   **B.** methylcyclohexane   **C.** cyclopropane
D. 3,5-dimethylhexane   **E.** 2,4-dimethylhexane

14. _____ CH_3—CH_2—CH_2—CH_3

15. _____ CH_3—$\overset{\displaystyle CH_3}{\overset{|}{CH}}$—$CH_2$—$\overset{\displaystyle CH_3}{\overset{|}{CH}}$—$CH_2$—$CH_3$

16. _____ △

17. _____ (cyclohexane with —CH_3)

Match the name of the hydrocarbon with each of the following structures.

A. methylcyclopentane   **B.** cyclobutane
C. cyclohexane   **D.** ethylcyclopentane

18. _____ (cyclohexane)   19. _____ (cyclopentane with CH_3)   20. _____ (cyclopentane with CH_2-CH_3)

Match each of the following compounds with the correct name.

A. 2,4-dichloropentane   **B.** chlorocyclopentane
C. 1,2-dichloropentane   **D.** 4,5-dichloropentane

21. _____ CH_3—CH_2—CH_2—$\overset{\displaystyle Cl}{\overset{|}{CH}}$—$CH_2$—$Cl$ 22. _____ (cyclopentane with Cl)

160

23. _____ $$\overset{\displaystyle \text{Cl} \quad\quad\quad \text{Cl}}{\underset{}{|}\quad\quad\quad\underset{}{|}}$$
   CH₃—CH—CH₂—CH—CH₃

24. The correctly balanced equation for the complete combustion of ethane is

A. $C_2H_6 + O_2 \longrightarrow 2CO + 3H_2O$.   **B.** $C_2H_6 + O_2 \longrightarrow CO_2 + H_2O$.
C. $C_2H_6 + 2O_2 \longrightarrow 2CO_2 + 3H_2O$.   **D.** $2C_2H_6 + 7O_2 \longrightarrow 4CO_2 + 6H_2O$.
E. $2C_2H_6 + 4O_2 \longrightarrow 4CO_2 + 6H_2O$.

25. The hydrocarbon with the highest boiling point is

A. pentane.   **B.** cyclopentane.   **C.** cyclohexane.
D. 2-Methylbutane.   **E.** hexane.

Classify the compounds in problems 26 through 33 by the functional groups.

A. alkane   **B.** alkene   **C.** alcohol   **D.** aldehyde
E. ketone   **F.** ether   **G.** amine

26. _____ $$\overset{\displaystyle \text{O}}{\underset{}{\|}}$$
   CH₃—CH₂—C—CH₃   27. _____   CH₃—CH₂—CH₂—OH

28. _____ $$\overset{\displaystyle \text{CH}_3}{\underset{}{|}}$$
   CH₃—CH₂—CH—CH₃   29. _____   CH₃—CH₂—O—CH₃

30. _____ $$\overset{\displaystyle \text{NH}_2}{\underset{}{|}}$$
   CH₃—CH—CH₂—CH₃   31. _____ $$\overset{\displaystyle \text{O}}{\underset{}{\|}}$$ CH₃—C—H

32. _____ $$\overset{\displaystyle \text{CH}_3}{\underset{}{|}}$$
   CH₃—CH₂—CH—CH₃   33. _____ $$\overset{\displaystyle \text{OH}}{\underset{}{|}}$$ CH₃—CH₂—CH—CH₃

Indicate whether the pairs of compounds in problems 34 through 38 are isomers (I), the same compound (S), or different compounds (D).

34. _____   CH₃—CH₂—CH₂—CH₃ and $$\overset{\displaystyle \text{CH}_3}{\underset{}{|}}$$ CH₃—CH—CH₃

35. _____   CH₃—CH₂—OH and $$\overset{\displaystyle \text{O}}{\underset{}{\|}}$$ CH₃—C—H

36. _____   CH₃—CH₂—NH₂ and $$\overset{\displaystyle \text{H}}{\underset{}{|}}$$ CH₃—N—CH₂—CH₃

37 _____ $$\overset{\displaystyle \text{O}}{\underset{}{\|}}$$ CH₃—CH₂—C—OH and $$\overset{\displaystyle \text{O}}{\underset{}{\|}}$$ CH₃—C—O—CH₃

38. _____   CH₃—CH₂—CH₂—CH₃ and   CH₃—C≡C—CH₃

Answers to Practice Test

1. I	**2.** I	**3.** O	**4.** I	**5.** I
6. O	**7.** O	**8.** O	**9.** C	**10.** E
11. A	**12.** D	**13.** B	**14.** A	**15.** E
16. C	**17.** B	**18.** D	**19.** A	**20.** E
21. C	**22.** B	**23.** A	**24.** D	**25.** E
26. E	**27.** C	**28.** A	**29.** F	**30.** G
31. D	**32.** A	**33.** C	**34.** I	**35.** D
36. D	**37.** I	**38.** D		

Answers to Selected Problems

10.1 Organic compounds contain C and H and sometimes O, N, or a halogen atom. Inorganic compounds usually contain elements other than C and H.

    a. inorganic   **b.** organic   **c.** organic
    d. inorganic   **e.** inorganic   **f.** organic

10.3   **a.** Inorganic compounds are usually soluble in water.
        b. Organic compounds have lower boiling points than most inorganic compounds.
        c. Organic compounds often burn in air.
        d. Inorganic compounds are more likely to be solids at room temperature.

10.5   **a.** ethane   **b.** ethane   **c.** NaBr   **d.** NaBr

10.7 VSEPR theory predicts that the four bonds in CH_4 will be as far apart as possible, which means that the hydrogen atoms are at the corners of a tetrahedron.

10.9   **a.** Pentane is a carbon chain of five (5) carbon atoms.
        b. Ethane is a carbon chain of two (2) carbon atoms.
        c. Hexane is a carbon chain of six (6) carbon atoms.

10.11   **a.** CH_4 **b.** $CH_3{-}CH_3$ **c.** $CH_3{-}CH_2{-}CH_2{-}CH_2{-}CH_3$ **d.** △

10.13 Isomers have the same molecular formula, but different structural formulas. The same structure occurs when rotation about a single bond moves the attached groups into different positions, but does not change the arrangement of atoms.

    a. The same molecule.
    b. Same molecular formula, but different structures, which are isomers of C_5H_{12}.
    c. Same molecular formula, but different structures, which are isomers of C_6H_{14}.

10.15 The alkyl name for a hydrocarbon substituent uses the name of the alkane, but changes the ending to –yl.

    a. propyl (from propane)   **b.** methyl (from methane)

10.17   **a.** 2-methylbutane   **b.** 2,2-dimethylpropane
        c. 2,3-dimethylpentane   **d.** 4-ethyl-dimethylhexane

10.19   **a.** A ring of four carbon atoms is cyclobutane.
        b. A ring of five carbon atoms with one methyl group is chlorocyclopentane.
        c. A ring of six carbon atoms with an ethyl group is ethylcyclohexane.

10.21 Draw the main chain with the number of carbon atoms in the ending. For example, butane has a main chain of 4 carbon atoms, and hexane has a main chain of 6 carbon atoms. Attach substituents on the carbon atoms indicated. For example, in 3-methylpentane, a $CH_3{-}$ group is bonded to carbon 3 of a five-carbon chain.

162

a. CH₃—CH—CH₂—CH₃
      |
      CH₃

b. CH₃—CH₂—C—CH₂—CH₃
            |
            CH₃
(with CH₃ above the C)

c. CH₃—CH—CH—CH₂—CH—CH₃
         | | |
         CH₃ CH₃   CH₃

d. CH₃—CH—CH—CH₂—CH—CH₂—CH₂—CH₃
         | | |
         CH₃ CH₂—CH₃   CH₃

10.23

a.

b.

10.25 In the IUPAC system, the halogen substituent in haloalkanes is named as a halo- on the main chain of carbon atom.

a. bromoethane
c. 2-chloropropane

b. 1-fluoropropane
d. trichloromethane

10.27
a. CH₃—CH—CH₃
         |
         Cl
c. CH₃Br

b. CH₃—CH—CH—CH₃
         | |
         Br   Cl

10.29 Alkanes are nonpolar and less dense than water.

a. CH₃—CH₂—CH₂—CH₂—CH₂—CH₂—CH₃
c. Insoluble in water
e. Lower

b. liquid
d. Float

10.31 Longer carbon chains have higher boiling points. The boiling points of branched alkanes are usually lower than the same number of carbon atoms in a continuous chain. Cycloalkanes have higher boiling points than continuous-chain alkanes.

a. Heptane has a longer carbon chain.
b. The continuous chain hexane has a higher boiling point than its branched chain isomer.

10.33 In combustion, a hydrocarbon reacts with oxygen to yield CO_2 and H_2O.

a. $2C_2H_6 + 7O_2 \longrightarrow 4CO_2 + 6H_2O$
c. $2C_8H_{18} + 25O_2 \longrightarrow 16CO_2 + 18H_2O$

b. $2C_3H_6 + 9O_2 \longrightarrow 6CO_2 + 6H_2O$
d. $C_6H_{12} + 9O_2 \longrightarrow 6CO_2 + 6H_2O$

10.35
a. alcohol
c. aldehyde

b. alkene
d. ester

10.37
a. Ethers have an —O— group.
b. Alcohols have a —OH group.
c. Ketones have a C=O group between alkyl groups.
d. Carboxylic acids have a —COOH group.
e. Amines contain a N atom.

163

10.39 **a.** Organic compounds have covalent bonds; inorganic compounds have ionic as well as polar covalent and a few have nonpolar covalent bonds.
b. Most organic compounds are insoluble in water; inorganic compounds are soluble in water.
c. Most organic compounds have low melting points; inorganic compounds have high melting points.
d. Most organic compounds are flammable; inorganic compounds are not flammable.

10.41 **a.** butane; organic compounds have low melting points
b. butane; organic compounds burn vigorously in air
c. potassium chloride; inorganic compounds have high melting points
d. potassium chloride; inorganic compounds (ionic) produce ions in water
e. butane; organic compounds are more likely to be gases at room temperature

10.43 **a.**

```
    H  H
    |  |
H—C—C—H
    |  |
    H  H
```

b.

```
    H  H
    |  |
H—C—C—O—H
    |  |
    H  H
```

c.

```
    H  H  O
    |  |  ‖
H—C—C—C—H
    |  |
    H  H
```

d.

```
    H     H  H
    |     |  |
H—C—O—C—C—H
    |     |  |
    H     H  H
```

10.45 The alkyl name for a hydrocarbon substituent uses the name of the alkane, but changes the ending to –yl.

  a. methyl   **b.** propyl   **c.** isopropyl   **d.** ethyl

10.47 Write the carbon atom in the main chain first. Attach the substituents listed in front of the alkane name or use the alkyl group indicated.

a.
```
                CH₂—CH₃
                 |
    CH₃—CH₂—CH—CH₂—CH₂—CH₃
```

b.
```
        CH₃  CH₃
         |    |
    CH₃—CH—CH—CH₂—CH₃
```

c.
```
                Cl
                 |
    Cl—CH₂—CH₂—C—CH₂—CH₂—CH₂—CH₃
                 |
                CH₃
```

10.49 Condensed structural formula
```
             CH₃     CH₃
              |       |
    CH₃—C—CH₂—CH—CH₃
              |
             CH₃
```
molecular formula of C_8H_{18}

The combustion reaction: $2C_8H_{18} + 25O_2 \rightarrow 16CO_2 + 18H_2O$

10.51 **a.** $C_3H_8 + 5O_2 \longrightarrow 3CO_2 + 4H_2O$ **b.** $C_5H_{12} + 8O_2 \longrightarrow 5CO_2 + 6H_2O$
c. $C_4H_8 + 6O_2 \longrightarrow 4CO_2 + 4H_2O$ **d.** $2C_8H_{18} + 25O_2 \longrightarrow 16CO_2 + 18H_2O$

10.53   **a.** $C_5H_{12} + 8O_2 \longrightarrow 5CO_2 + 6H_2O$

b. 72.0 g/mole

c. 1 ~~gal~~ $\times$ $\dfrac{3.78 \text{ L}}{1 \text{ gal}}$ $\times$ $\dfrac{1000 \text{ mL}}{1 \text{ L}}$ $\times$ $\dfrac{0.63 \text{ g}}{1 \text{ mL}}$ $\times$ $\dfrac{1 \text{ mole } C_5H_{12}}{72.0 \text{ g}}$ $\times$ $\dfrac{845 \text{ kcal}}{1 \text{ mole}}$ = 2.8 x 10^4 kcal

d. 1 ~~gal~~ $\times$ $\dfrac{3.78 \text{ L}}{1 \text{ gal}}$ $\times$ $\dfrac{1000 \text{ mL}}{1 \text{ L}}$ $\times$ $\dfrac{0.63 \text{ g}}{1 \text{ mL}}$ $\times$ $\dfrac{1 \text{ mole } C_5H_{12}}{72.0 \text{ g}}$ $\times$ $\dfrac{5 \text{ moles } CO_2}{1 \text{ mole } C_5H_{12}}$ $\times$ $\dfrac{22.4 \text{ L}}{1 \text{ mole}}$ = 3700 L

10.55   **a.** alcohol   **b.** alkene   **c.** aldehyde
        d. alkane   **e.** carboxylic acid   **f.** amine
        g. tetrahedral   **h.** isomers   **i.** ester
        j. ether   **k..** alkyne   **l.** functional group
        m. ketone

Unsaturated Hydrocarbons

Study Goals

- Classify unsaturated compounds as alkenes, cycloalkenes, and alkynes.
- Write IUPAC and common names for alkenes and alkynes.
- Write structural formulas and names for cis-trans isomers of alkenes.
- Write equations for hydration and hydrogenation of alkenes and alkynes.
- Describe the formation of a polymer from alkene monomers.
- Describe the bonding in benzene.
- Write structural formulas and give the names of aromatic compounds.

Think About It

1. The label on a bottle of vegetable oil says the oil is unsaturated. What does this mean?

2. What are polymers?

3. A margarine is partially hydrogenated. What does that mean?

Key Terms

Match the statements shown below with the following key terms.

a. alkene **b.** hydrogenation **c.** alkyne **d.** hydration **e.** polymer

1. _____ A long-chain molecule formed by linking many small molecules

2. _____ The addition of H_2 to a carbon-carbon double bond

3. _____ An unsaturated hydrocarbon containing a carbon-carbon double bond

4. _____ The addition of H_2O to a carbon-carbon double bond

5. _____ A compound that contains a triple bond

Answers   **1.** e   **2.** b   **3.** a   **4.** d   **5.** c

11.1 Alkenes and Alkynes

- Alkenes are unsaturated hydrocarbons that contain one or more carbon—carbon double bonds
- Alkynes are unsaturated hydrocarbons that contain a carbon—carbon triple bond.

◆ **Learning Exercise 11.1**

Classify the following structural formulas as alkane, alkene, cycloalkene, or alkyne.

1. _____ CH₃—CH₂—CH₃

2. _____
$$CH_3-CH_2-CH=\overset{\overset{\displaystyle CH_3}{\displaystyle |}}{C}-CH_2-CH_3$$

3. _____ CH₃—C≡C—CH₃

Answers   **1.** alkane   **2.** alkyne   **3.** alkene

11.2 Naming Alkenes and Alkynes

- The IUPAC names of alkenes are derived by changing the *ane* ending of the parent alkane to *ene*.
- For example, the IUPAC name of H₂C=CH₂ is ethene. It has a common name of ethylene.
- In alkenes, the longest carbon chain containing the double bond is numbered from the end nearest the double bond.

CH₃—CH=CH₂   CH₂=CH—CH₂—CH₃ $$CH_3-CH=\overset{\overset{\displaystyle CH_3}{\displaystyle |}}{C}-CH_3$$
Propene (propylene)   1-Butene   2-Methylbutene

- The alkynes are a family of unsaturated hydrocarbons that contain a triple bond. They use naming rules similar to the alkenes, but the parent chain ends with *yne*.

HC≡CH   CH₃—C≡CH
ethyne   propyne

◆ **Learning Exercise 11.2A**

Write the IUPAC (and common name, if one) for each of the following alkenes:

1. CH₃CH=CH₂

2. CH₃—CH=CH—CH₃

3.

4. $$CH_2=CH\overset{\overset{\displaystyle Cl}{\displaystyle |}}{C}HCH_2\overset{\overset{\displaystyle CH_3}{\displaystyle |}}{C}HCH_3$$

5. $$CH_3-CH=\overset{\overset{\displaystyle CH_3}{\displaystyle |}}{C}-CH_2-CH_3$$

6. $$CH_3-CH_2-\overset{\overset{\displaystyle CH_2}{\displaystyle ||}}{C}H$$

Answers   **1.** propene (propylene)   **2.** 2-butene   **3.** cyclohexene
              4. 3-chloro-5-methyl-1-hexene   **5.** 3-methyl-2-pentene   **6.** 1-butene

167

◆ **Learning Exercise 11.2B**

Write the IUPAC and common name (if any) of each of the following alkynes.

1. HC≡CH

2. CH₃—C≡CH

3. CH₃—CH₂—C≡CH

4.
$$CH_3-CH-C\equiv C-CH_3$$
with CH₃ above the CH.

Answers
1. ethyne (acetylene)
2. propyne
3. 1-butyne
4. 4-methyl-2-pentyne

◆ **Learning Exercise 11.2C**

Draw the condensed structural formula for each of the following:

1. 2-pentyne

2. 2-chloro-2-butene

3. 3-bromo-2-methyl-2-pentene

4. cyclohexene

Answers

1. CH₃—C≡C—CH₂—CH₃

2. CH₃—CH=C—CH₃ with Cl above the third carbon

3. CH₃—C=C—CH₂—CH₃ with Br above the second carbon and CH₃ below the second carbon

4.

11.3 Cis–Trans Isomers

- Cis–trans isomers are possible for alkenes because there is no rotation around the rigid double bond.
- In the cis isomer, groups are attached on the same side of the double bond, whereas in the trans isomer, they are attached on the opposite sides of the double bond.

168

◆ **Learning Exercise 11.3A**

Write the cis–trans isomers of 2,3-dibromo-2-butene and name each.

Answers

cis-2,3-dibromo-2-butene   trans-2,3-dibromo-2-butene

In the cis isomer, the bromine atoms are attached on the same side of the double bond; in the trans isomer, they are on opposite sides.

◆ **Learning Exercise 11.3B**

Name the following alkenes using the cis–trans where isomers are possible.

Answers   1. *cis*-1,2-dibromoethene   2. *trans*-2-butene
3. 2-chloropropene (not a cis–trans isomer)   4. *trans*-2-pentene

11.4 Addition Reactions

- The addition of small molecules to the double bond is a characteristic reaction of alkenes.
- Hydrogenation adds hydrogen atoms to the double bond of an alkene or the triple bond of an alkyne to yield an alkane.

$$CH_2{=}CH_2 + H_2 \xrightarrow{\text{Pt}} CH_3{-}CH_3$$

$$HC{\equiv}CH + 2H_2 \xrightarrow{\text{Pt}} CH_3{-}CH_3$$

- Hydration adds water to a double bond. The H from water (HOH) bonds to the carbon in the double bond that has the greater number of hydrogen atoms.

$$CH_2{=}CH_2 + HOH \xrightarrow{H^+} CH_3{-}CH_2{-}OH$$

◆ Learning Exercise 11.4A

Write the products of the following addition reactions.

1. $CH_3{-}CH_2{-}CH{=}CH_2 + H_2 \xrightarrow{Pt}$

2. $+\ H_2 \xrightarrow{Pt}$

3. $CH_3CH{=}CHCH_2CH_3 + H_2 \xrightarrow{Pt}$

4. $CH_3CH{=}CH_2 + H_2 \xrightarrow{Pt}$

5. $CH_3CH{=}CHCH_3 + H_2 \xrightarrow{Pt}$

Answers

1. $CH_3{-}CH_2{-}CH_2{-}CH_3$ 2.

3. $CH_3{-}CH_2{-}CH_2{-}CH_2{-}CH_3$ 4. $CH_3{-}CH_2{-}CH_3$ 5. $CH_3{-}CH_2{-}CH_2{-}CH_3$

◆ Learning Exercise 11.4B

1. $CH_3{-}CH{=}CH{-}CH_3 + HOH \xrightarrow{H^+}$

2. $CH_3\overset{\displaystyle CH_3}{\overset{|}{C}}{=}CH_2 + HOH \xrightarrow{H^+}$

3. $CH_3CH{=}CH_2 + HOH \xrightarrow{H^+}$

4. $CH_3{-}CH_2{-}CH{=}\overset{\displaystyle CH_3}{\overset{|}{C}}{-}CH_3 + HOH \xrightarrow{H^+}$

5. $+\ H_2O \xrightarrow{H^+}$

Answers

1. CH₃—CH₂—CH—CH₃ with OH above the CH

$$CH_3-CH_2-\overset{\overset{\displaystyle OH}{|}}{CH}-CH_3$$

2. $$CH_3-\overset{\overset{\displaystyle CH_3}{|}}{\underset{\underset{\displaystyle OH}{|}}{C}}-CH_3$$

3. $$CH_3-\overset{\overset{\displaystyle OH}{|}}{CH}-CH_3$$

4. $$CH_3-CH_2-CH_2-\overset{\overset{\displaystyle CH_3}{|}}{\underset{\underset{\displaystyle OH}{|}}{C}}-CH_3$$

5. cyclopentane with OH

11.5 Polymers of Alkenes

- *Polymers* are large molecules prepared from the bonding of many small units called *monomers*.
- Many synthetic polymers are made from small alkene monomers.

◆ Learning Exercise 11.5A

Write the formula of the alkene monomer that would be used for each of the following polymers.

1. polyethylene chain (all H)

2. chain with CH₃ groups

3. chain with all F

Answers   1. H₂C=CH₂   2. $H_2C=\overset{\overset{\displaystyle CH_3}{|}}{CH}$ 3. F₂C=CF₂

◆ Learning Exercise 11.5B

Write three sections of the polymer that would result when 1,1-difluoroethene is the monomer unit.

Answer

chain: —C—C—C—C—C—C— with F,H alternating

171

11.6 Aromatic Compounds

- Most aromatic compounds contain benzene, a cyclic structure containing six CH units. The structure of benzene is represented as a hexagon with a circle in the center.
- The names of many aromatic compounds use the parent name benzene, although many common names were retained as IUPAC names, such as toluene, phenol, and aniline.

◆ Learning Exercise 11.6

Write the IUPAC (or common name) for each of the following.

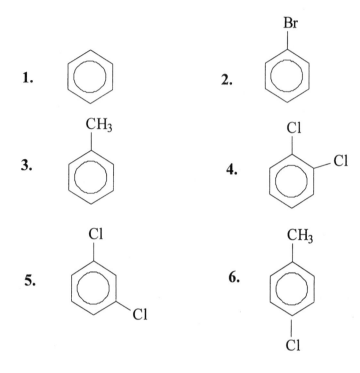

1.

2. Br

3. CH₃

4. Cl, Cl

5. Cl, Cl

6. CH₃, Cl

Answers   **1.** benzene   **2.** bromobenzene   **3.** methylbenzene; toluene
4. 1,2-dichlorobenzene **5.** 1,3-dichlorobenzene **6.** 4-chlorotoluene

Check List for Chapter 11

You are ready to take the practice test for Chapter 11. Be sure that you have accomplished the following learning goals for this chapter. If you are not sure, review the section listed at the end of the goal. Then apply your new skills and understanding to the practice test.

After studying Chapter 11, I can successfully:

_____ Identify the structural features of alkenes and alkynes (11.1).

_____ Name alkenes and alkynes using IUPAC rules and write their structural formulas (11.2).

_____ Identify alkenes that exist as cis–trans isomers; write their structural formulas and names (11.3).

_____ Write the structural formulas and names for the products of the addition of hydrogen and water to alkenes (11.4).

_____ Describe the process of forming polymers from alkene monomers (11.5).

_____ Write the names and structures for compounds that contain a benzene ring (11.6).

Practice Test for Chapter 11

Questions 1 through 4 refer to $H_2C=CH-CH_3$ and

$$\begin{array}{c} CH_2 \\ \diagup\ \diagdown \\ H_2C-CH_2 \end{array}$$

(A)   (B)

1.   These compounds are

    A. aromatic.   **B.** alkanes.   **C.** isomers.
    D. alkenes.   **E.** cycloalkanes.

2.   Compound (A) is a(n)

    A. alkane.   **B.** alkene.   **C.** cycloalkane.
    D. alkyne.   **E.** aromatic.

3.   Compound (B) is named

    A. propane.   **B.** propylene.   **C.** cyclobutane.
    D. cyclopropane.   **E.** cyclopropene.

4.   Compound (A) is named

    A. propane.   **B.** propene.   **C.** 2-propene.
    D. propyne.   **E** 1-butene.

In questions 5 through 8, match the name of the alkene with the structural formula.

A.   cyclopentene   **B.**   methylpropene   **C.**   cyclohexene
D.   ethene

5. $CH_2=CH_2$ 6. $CH_3-\overset{\displaystyle CH_3}{\overset{\displaystyle |}{C}}=CH_2$

7.   8.

9.   The *cis* isomer of 2-butene is

    A. $CH_2=CH-CH_2-CH_3$ **B.** $CH_3-CH=CH-CH_3$

    C. $\begin{array}{c} CH_3 \quad\quad H \\ \diagdown\quad\diagup \\ C=C \\ \diagup\quad\diagdown \\ H \quad\quad CH_3 \end{array}$ **D.** $\begin{array}{c} CH_3 \quad\quad CH_3 \\ \diagdown\quad\diagup \\ C=C \\ \diagup\quad\diagdown \\ H \quad\quad H \end{array}$

    E. $\begin{array}{c} CH_3 \;\; CH_3 \\ | \quad\; | \\ CH=CH \end{array}$

10.   The name of this compound is:

$$\begin{array}{c} Cl \quad\quad\quad H \\ \diagdown\quad\quad\diagup \\ C=C \\ \diagup\quad\quad\diagdown \\ H \quad\quad\quad Cl \end{array}$$

    A. dichloroethene   **B.** *cis*-1,2-dichloroethene   **C.** *trans*-1,2-dichloroethene
    D. *cis*-chloroethene   **E.** *trans*-chloroethene

11. Hydrogenation of CH_3—CH=CH_2 gives
  A. $3CO_2 + 6H_2$ **B.** CH_3—CH_2—CH_3.   **C.** CH_2=CH—CH_3.
  D. no reaction.   **E.** CH_3—CH_2—CH_2—CH_3.

12. Hydration of 2-butene gives
  A. CH_3—CH_2—CH_2—CH_3 **B.** CH_3—CH_2—CH_2—CH_2—OH

  OH
  |
  C. CH_3—CH—CH_2—CH_3 **D.**   **E.**

13. What is the common name of methylbenzene?
  A. aniline   **B.** phenol   **C.** toluene
  D. xylene   **E.** toluidine

14. What is the IUPAC name of CH_3—CH_2—C≡CH?
  A. methylacetylene   **B.** propyne   **C.** propylene
  D. 4-butyne   **E.** 1-butyne

15. The reaction CH_3—CH=$CH_2 + H_2O \longrightarrow CH_3$—$\overset{\overset{\displaystyle OH}{|}}{CH}$—$CH_3$ is called a
  A. hydrogenation.   **B.** halogenation.   **C.** hydrohalogenation of an alkene
  D. hydration of an alkene.   **E.** combustion.

For questions 16 through 19 identify the family for each compound as

A. alkane   **B.** alkene   **C.** alkyne   **D.** cycloalkene

16. CH_3—CH=CH_2 **17.**

  CH$_3$
  |
18. CH_3—CH_2—CH—CH_2—CH_3

19. CH_3—CH_2—C≡CH

Match the name of each of the following aromatic compounds with the correct structure.

A.   **B.**   **C.**

D.   **E.**

20. ____ chlorobenzene   **21.** ____ benzene

22. ____ toluene   **23.** ____ 4-chlorotoluene

24. ____ 3-bromotoluene

Answers to the Practice Test

1. C	**2.** B	**3.** D	**4.** B	**5.** D
6. B	**7.** A	**8.** C	**9.** D	**10.** C
11. B	**12.** C	**13.** C	**14.** E	**15.** D
16. B	**17.** D	**18.** A	**19.** C	**20.** D
21. A	**22.** B	**23.** E	**24.** C	

Answers and Solutions to Selected Text Problems

11.1. **a.** An alkene has a double bond.
   b. An alkyne has a triple bond.
   c. A cycloalkene has a double bond in a ring.

11.3 Propene contains three carbon atoms with a carbon-carbon double bond. Propyne contains three carbon atoms with a carbon-carbon triple bond.

11.5 **a.** The two-carbon compound with a double bond is ethene.
   b. methylpropene
   c. 2-pentyne
   d. This four-carbon cyclic structure with a double bond is cyclobutene.

11.7 **a.** Propene is the three-carbon alkene. $H_2C=CH—CH_3$
   b. 1-pentene is the five-carbon compound with a double bond between carbon1 and carbon 2.

   $H_2C=CH—CH_2—CH_2—CH_3$

   c. 2-methyl-1-butene has a four-carbon chain with a double bond between carbon 1 and carbon 2 and a methyl attached to carbon 2.

   d.

11.9 **a.** *cis*-2-butene. This is a four-carbon compound with a double bond between carbon 2 and carbon 3. Both methyl groups are on the same side of the double bond; it is cis.
   b. *trans*-3-octene This compound has eight carbons with a double bond between carbon 3 and carbon 4. The alkyl groups are on opposite sides of the double bond; it is trans.
   c. *cis*-3-heptene. This is a seven-carbon compound with a double bond between carbon 3 and carbon 4. Both alkyl groups are on the same side of the double bond; it is cis.

11.11 **a.** *trans*-2-butene has a four-carbon chain with a double bond between carbon 2 and carbon 3. The trans isomer has the two methyl groups on opposite sides of the double bond.

b. *cis*-2-pentene has a five-carbon chain with a double bond between carbon 2 and carbon 3. The cis isomer has the alkyl groups on the same side of the double bond.

c. *trans*-3-heptene has a seven-carbon chain with a double bond between carbon 3 and carbon 4. The trans isomer has the alkyl groups on opposite sides of the double bond.

11.13 **a.** $CH_3—CH_2—CH_2—CH_2—CH_3$ pentane

b.
$$CH_3—CH—CH_2—CH_3$$
with OH on the second carbon   2-butanol

c. When water is added to an alkene, the product is an alcohol. The name is cyclobutanol.

d. When H_2 is added to a cycloalkene the product is a cycloalkane. Cyclopentene would form cyclopentane.

cyclopentene   cyclopentane

e. $CH_3—CH_2—CH_2—CH_2—CH_3$ pentane

11.15 A polymer is a long-chain molecule consisting of many repeating smaller units. These smaller units are called monomers.

11.17 Teflon is a polymer of the monomer tetrafluoroethene.

11.19 Cyclohexane, C_6H_{12}, is a cycloalkane in which six carbon atoms are linked by single bonds in a ring. In benzene, C_6H_6, an aromatic system links the six carbon atoms in a ring.

11.21 **a.** 2-chlorotoluene
b. ethylbenzene
c. 1,3,5-trichlorobenzene
d. 3-bromo-5-chlorotoluene

11.23 a.

CH₃

b.

Cl

Cl

c.

CH₂CH₃

CH₃

d.

CH₃

Cl

11.25 Propane is the three-carbon alkane. All the carbon–carbon bonds in propane are single bonds. Cyclopropane is the three carbon cycloalkane. All the carbon–carbon bonds in cyclopropane are single bonds. Propene is the three-carbon compound which has a carbon–carbon double bond. Propyne is the three-carbon compound with a carbon–carbon triple bond.

11.27 a. This compound contains a five-carbon chain with a double bond between carbon 1 and carbon 2 and a methyl group attached to carbon 2. The IUPAC name is: 2-methyl-1-pentene.
   b. This compound contains a five-carbon chain with a triple bond between carbon 2 and carbon 3. The IUPAC name is: 2-pentyne.
   c. This compound is a five-carbon cycloalkene. The IUPAC name is cyclopentene.
   d. This compound contains a five-carbon chain with a double bond between carbon 2 and carbon 3. The alkyl groups are on opposite sides of the double bond. The IUPAC name is: *trans*-2-pentene.
   e. This compound is a six-carbon ring with a double bond. The IUPAC name is: cyclohexene.

11.29 a. These structures represent a pair of constitutional isomers. In one isomer, the chlorine is attached to one of the carbons in the double bond; in the other isomer, the carbon bonded to the chlorine is not part of the double bond.
   b. These structures are cis–trans isomers. In the cis isomer, the two methyl groups are on the same side of the double bond. In the trans isomer, the methyl groups are on opposite sides of the double bond.
   c. These structures are identical and not isomers. Both have five-carbon chains with a double bond between carbon 1 and carbon 2.
   d. These structures represent a pair of isomers. Both have the molecular formula C_7H_{16}. One isomer has a six-carbon chain with a methyl group attached, the other has a five-carbon chain with two methyl groups attached.

11.31 a.

CH₃   CH₂CH₃

C═C

H   H

CH₃   H

C═C

H   CH₂CH₃

cis-2-pentene; both alkyl groups are on the same side of the double bond

trans-2-pentene; both alkyl groups are on opposite sides of the double bond

b.

CH₃CH₂   CH₂CH₃

C═C

H   H

CH₃CH₂   H

C═C

H   CH₂CH₃

cis-3-hexene; both alkyl groups are on the same side of the double bond

trans-3-hexene; both alkyl groups are on opposite sides of the double bond

177

c.

cis-2-butene; both alkyl groups are on the same side of the double bond

trans-2-butene; both alkyl groups are on opposite sides of the double bond

d.

cis-2-hexene; both alkyl groups are on the same side of the double bond

trans-2-hexene; both alkyl groups are on opposite sides of the double bond

11.33 **a.** toluene
      b. 2-chlorotoluene
      c. 4-ethyltoluene
      d. 1,3-diethylbenzene

Organic Compounds with Oxygen and Sulfur

Study Goals

- Classify alcohols as primary, secondary, or tertiary.
- Name and write the condensed structural formulas for alcohols, phenols, and thiols.
- Identify the uses of some alcohols and phenols.
- Name and write the condensed structural formulas for ethers.
- Describe the solubility in water and boiling points of alcohols, phenols, and ethers.
- Write equations for combustion, dehydration, and oxidation of alcohols.
- Name and write the condensed structural formulas for aldehydes and ketones.
- Describe some important aldehydes and ketones.
- Identify the chiral carbon atoms in organic molecules.
- Write equations for the oxidation of aldehydes and for the reduction of aldehydes and ketones.

Think About It

1. What are the functional groups of alcohols, phenols, ethers, and thiols?

2. Phenol is sometime used in mouthwashes. Why does it form a solution with water?

3. What reaction of ethanol takes place when you make a fondue dish or a flambé dessert?

4. What are the functional groups of an aldehyde and ketone?

5. How is an alcohol changed to an aldehyde or ketone?

Key Terms

Match the following terms with the statements shown below.

a. primary alcohol   **b.** thiol   **c.** ether   **d.** phenol   **e.** tertiary alcohol

f. chiral carbon   **g.** aldehyde   **h.** ketone

1. _____ An organic compound with one alkyl group bonded to the carbon with the —OH group
2. _____ An organic compound that contains an —SH group
3. _____ An organic compound that contains an oxygen atom —O— attached to two alkyl groups
4. _____ An organic compound with three alkyl groups bonded to the carbon with the —OH group
5. _____ An organic compound that contains a benzene ring bonded to a hydroxyl group
6. _____ An organic compound with a carbonyl group attached to two alkyl groups
7. _____ A carbon that is bonded to four different groups
8. _____ An organic compound that contains a carbonyl group and a hydrogen atom at the end of the carbon chain

Answers   **1.** a   **2.** b   **3.** c   **4.** e   **5.** d   **6.** h   **7.** f   **8.** g

12.1 Alcohols, Phenols, and Thiols

- Alcohols are classified according to the number of alkyl groups attached to the carbon bonded to the —OH group.
- In a primary alcohol, there is one alkyl group attached to the carbon atom bonded to the —OH. In a secondary alcohol, there are two alkyl groups, and in a tertiary alcohol there are three alkyl groups attached to the carbon atom with the —OH functional group.
- An alcohol contains the hydroxyl group —OH attached to a carbon chain.
- In the IUPAC system alcohols are named by replacing the *ane* of the alkane name with *ol*. The location of the —OH group is given by numbering the carbon chain. Simple alcohols are generally named by their common names with the alkyl name preceding the term alcohol. For example, CH_3—OH is methyl alcohol, and CH_3—CH_2—OH is ethyl alcohol.

CH_3—OH	CH_3—CH_2—OH	CH_3—CH_2—CH_2—OH
methanol	ethanol	1-propanol
(methyl alcohol)	(ethyl alcohol)	(propyl alcohol)

- When a hydroxyl group is attached to a benzene ring, the compound is a phenol.
- Thiols are similar to alcohols, except they have an —SH functional group in place of the —OH group, R—SH.

Study Note

Example: Identify the following as primary, secondary, or tertiary alcohols.

Solution: Determine the number of alkyl groups attached to the hydroxyl carbon atom.

$$CH_3—CH_2—OH \qquad CH_3—\overset{\overset{\textstyle CH_3}{|}}{C}H—OH \qquad CH_3—\overset{\overset{\textstyle CH_3}{|}}{\underset{\underset{\textstyle CH_3}{|}}{C}}—OH$$

Primary (1°)   Secondary (2°)   Tertiary (3°)

◆ Learning Exercise 12.1A

Give the correct IUPAC and common name (if any) for each of the following compounds.

1. CH_3—CH_2—OH

2. CH_3—CH_2—CH_2—OH

3. CH_3—$\overset{\overset{\textstyle OH}{|}}{C}H$—$CH_2$—$CH_2$—$CH_3$

4. CH_3—CH_2—$\overset{\overset{\textstyle CH_3}{|}}{C}H$—$\overset{\overset{\textstyle OH}{|}}{C}H$—$CH_3$

5.

6. (phenol ring with OH)

Answers   **1.** ethanol (ethyl alcohol)   **2.** 1-propanol (propyl alcohol)
3. 2-pentanol   **4.** 3-methyl-2-pentanol
5. cyclopentanol   **6.** phenol

◆ Learning Exercise 12.1B

Write the correct condensed structural formula for each of the following compounds.

1. 2-butanol

2. 2-chloro-1-propanol

3. 2,4-dimethyl-1-pentanol

4. cyclohexanol

5. 3-methylcyclopentanol

6. 2-chlorophenol

Answers

1.
$$\begin{array}{c} \text{OH} \\ | \\ \text{CH}_3\text{—CH—CH}_2\text{—CH}_3 \end{array}$$

2.
$$\begin{array}{c} \text{Cl} \\ | \\ \text{CH}_3\text{—CH—CH}_2\text{—OH} \end{array}$$

3.
$$\begin{array}{c} \text{CH}_3 \qquad \text{CH}_3 \\ | \qquad\quad | \\ \text{CH}_3\text{—CH—CH}_2\text{—CH—CH}_2\text{—OH} \end{array}$$

4.

5.

6.

◆ Learning Exercise 12.1C

Classify each of the following alcohols as primary (1°), secondary (2°), or tertiary (3°).

1. CH₃—CH₂—OH ____

2.
$$\begin{array}{c} \text{OH} \\ | \\ \text{CH}_3\text{—CH}_2\text{—CH—CH}_3 \end{array}$$ ____

3.
$$\begin{array}{c} \text{OH} \\ | \\ \text{CH}_3\text{—C—CH}_2\text{—CH}_3 \\ | \\ \text{CH}_3 \end{array}$$ ____

4.
$$\begin{array}{c} \text{OH} \\ | \\ \text{CH}_3\text{—C—CH}_2\text{—CH}_2\text{—CH}_3 \\ | \\ \text{CH}_3 \end{array}$$ ____

181

5. CH₃—C(CH₃)(CH₃)—CH₂—OH _____

$$\begin{array}{c}\quad\;\; CH_3 \\ \quad\;\; | \\ CH_3\!-\!C\!-\!CH_2\!-\!OH \\ \quad\;\; | \\ \quad\;\; CH_3 \end{array}$$

6. (cyclopentane ring with OH) _____

Answers
1. primary (1°) 2. secondary (3°) 3. tertiary (3°)
4. tertiary (3°) 5. primary (1°) 6. secondary (2°)

12.2 Some Important Alcohols and Phenols

- Methanol CH_3—OH, the simplest alcohol, and ethanol, CH_3—CH_2—OH are found in many solvents and paint removers.
- Glycerol, a trihydroxy alcohol, is obtained from oils and fats and used as a skin softener.
- Derivatives of phenol such as resorcinol are used as antiseptics in throat lozenges and mouthwashes.

◆ Learning Exercise 12.2

Identify the alcohol or phenol that matches each of the following descriptions.

1. Used to make alcoholic beverages _____

2. Used to clean the skin before giving an injection or drawing a blood sample _____

3. Forms an insoluble salt that damages the kidneys _____

Answers   1. ethanol   2. isopropyl alcohol   3. 1,2-ethanediol (ethylene glycol)

12.3 Ethers

- In ethers, an oxygen atom is connected by single bonds to two alkyl or aromatic groups, R—O—R.
- In the common names of ethers, the alkyl groups are listed alphabetically followed by the name *ether*.

Study Note

Example: Write the common names for CH_3—CH_2—O—CH_3.
Solution: The common name lists the alkyl groups alphabetically before the name *ether*.

ethyl group   methyl group
CH_3—CH_2—O—CH_3
Common: ethyl methyl ether

◆ Learning Exercise 12.3A

Write the common name for each of the following ethers.

1. CH_3—O—CH_3

2. CH_3—CH_2—O—CH_2—CH_3

3. CH_3—CH_2—CH_2—CH_2—O—CH_3

4. CH_3—O—CH_2—CH_3

5. —OCH_3

Answers
1. (di)methyl ether
3. butyl methyl ether
5. methyl phenyl ether

2. (di)ethyl ether
4. ethyl methyl ether

◆ Learning Exercise 12.3B

Write the structural formula for each of the following ethers.

1. ethyl propyl ether

2. ethyl methyl ether

Answers
1. CH_3—CH_2—O—CH_2—CH_2—CH_3
2. CH_3—O—CH_2—CH_3

12.4 Properties of Alcohols, Phenols, and Ethers

- The polar —OH group gives alcohols higher boiling points than alkanes and ethers of similar mass.
- Alcohols with one to four carbons are soluble in water because the —OH group forms hydrogen bonds with water molecules.
- Phenol is soluble in water and acts as a weak acid.
- Because ethers are less polar than alcohols, they have boiling points similar to alkanes. Ethers are soluble in water due to hydrogen bonding. Ethers are widely used as solvents but can be dangerous to use because their vapors are highly flammable.

◆ Learning Exercise 12.4A

Circle the compound in each pair that is the more soluble in water.

1. _____ CH_3—CH_3 or CH_3—CH_2—OH

2. _____ CH_3—CH_2—CH_2—OH or CH_3—CH_2—CH_2—CH_2—CH_2—OH

3. _____ CH_3—CH_2—CH_2—CH_3 or CH_3—CH_2—CH_2—CH_2—OH

4. _____ Benzene or phenol

Answers
1. CH_3—CH_2—OH
3. CH_3—CH_2—CH_2—CH_2—OH

2. CH_3—CH_2—CH_2—OH
4. phenol

◆ **Learning Exercise 12.4B**

Select the compound in each pair with the higher boiling point.

1. $CH_3—CH_2—CH_3$ or $CH_3—CH_2—OH$

2. 2-butanol or 2-hexanol

3. $CH_3—O—CH_2—CH_3$ or $CH_3—CH_2—CH_2—OH$

4. $CH_3—CH_2—CH_2—OH$ or $CH_3—CH_2—CH_2—CH_3$

Answers   1. $CH_3—CH_2—OH$ 2. 2-hexanol
              3. $CH_3—CH_2—CH_2—OH$ 4. $CH_3—CH_2—CH_2—OH$

12.5 Reactions of Alcohols and Thiols

- At high temperatures, an alcohol dehydrates in the presence of an acid to yield an alkene and water.

$$CH_3—CH_2—OH \xrightarrow[\text{Heat}]{H^+} H_2C{=}CH_2 + H_2O$$

- Using an oxidizing agent[O], primary alcohols oxidize to aldehydes, which usually oxidize further to carboxylic acids. Secondary alcohols are oxidized to ketones, but tertiary alcohols do not oxidize.

$$\underset{1° \text{ alcohol}}{CH_3—CH_2—OH} \xrightarrow{[O]} \underset{\text{aldehyde}}{CH_3—\overset{\overset{\displaystyle O}{\|}}{C}—H} + H_2O$$

$$\underset{2° \text{ alcohol}}{CH_3—\overset{\overset{\displaystyle OH}{|}}{C}H—CH_3} \xrightarrow{[O]} \underset{\text{ketone}}{CH_3—\overset{\overset{\displaystyle O}{\|}}{C}—CH_3} + H_2O$$

◆ **Learning Exercise 12.5A**

Write the condensed structural formulas of the products expected from dehydration of each of the following reactants:

1. $CH_3—CH_2—CH_2—CH_2—OH \xrightarrow{H^+,\ heat}$

2.
$$\begin{array}{c} OH \\ | \\ \bigcirc \end{array} \xrightarrow{H^+,\ heat}$$

3. $CH_3—\overset{\overset{\displaystyle OH}{|}}{C}H—CH_3 \xrightarrow{H^+,\ heat}$

4. $CH_3—CH_2—\overset{\overset{\displaystyle OH}{|}}{C}H—CH_2—CH_3 \xrightarrow{H^+,\ heat}$

184

Answers

1. CH_3—CH_2—$CH=CH_2$ 2.

3. CH_3—$CH=CH_2$

4. CH_3—CH_2—$CH=CH$—CH_3

◆ **Learning Exercise 12.5B**

Write the condensed structural formulas of the products expected in the oxidation reaction of each of the following reactants.

1. CH_3—CH_2—CH_2—CH_2—$OH \xrightarrow{[O]}$

2.

   OH

   $\xrightarrow{[O]}$

3.

   OH

   CH_3—CH—$CH_3 \xrightarrow{[O]}$

4.

   OH

   CH_3—CH_2—CH—CH_2—$CH_3 \xrightarrow{[O]}$

Answers

1.
$$CH_3-CH_2-CH_2-\overset{\overset{\displaystyle O}{\|}}{C}-H$$

2.

3.
$$CH_3-\overset{\overset{\displaystyle O}{\|}}{C}-CH_3$$

4.
$$CH_3-CH_2-\overset{\overset{\displaystyle O}{\|}}{C}-CH_2-CH_3$$

12.6 Aldehydes and Ketones

- In an aldehyde, the carbonyl group appears at the end of a carbon chain attached to at least one hydrogen atom.
- In a ketone, the carbonyl group occurs between carbon groups and has no hydrogens attached to it.
- In the IUPAC system, aldehydes and ketones are named by replacing the *e* in the longest chain containing the carbonyl group with *al* for aldehydes, and *one* for ketones. The location of the carbonyl group in a ketone is given if there are more than four carbon atoms in the chain.

$$CH_3-\overset{\overset{\displaystyle O}{\|}}{C}-H$$
ethanal
(acetaldehyde)

$$CH_3-\overset{\overset{\displaystyle O}{\|}}{C}-CH_3$$
propanone
(dimethyl ketone)

185

◆ Learning Exercise 12.6A

Classify each of the following compounds.

A. alcohol   **B.** aldehyde   **C.** ketone   **D.** ether   **E.** thiol

$$\overset{\displaystyle O}{\overset{\displaystyle \|}{}}$$

_____ **1.** CH_3—CH_2—CH_2—C—H

_____ **2.** CH_3—CH_2—CH_2—OH

$$\overset{\displaystyle O}{\overset{\displaystyle \|}{}}$$

_____ **3.** CH_3—CH_2—C—CH_2—CH_3

_____ **4.** CH_3—CH_2—O—CH_3

$$\overset{\displaystyle O}{\overset{\displaystyle \|}{}}$$

_____ **5.** CH_3—C—CH_2—CH_3

$$\overset{\displaystyle O}{\overset{\displaystyle \|}{}}$$

_____ **6.** CH_3—C—H

$$\overset{\displaystyle SH}{\overset{\displaystyle |}{}}$$

_____ **7.** CH_3—CH_2—CH—CH_3

$$\overset{\displaystyle OH}{\overset{\displaystyle |}{}}$$

_____ **8.** CH_3—CH_2—CH—CH_3

Answers   **1.** B   **2.** A   **3.** C   **4.** D
　　　　　　5. C   **6.** B   **7.** E   **8.** A

◆ Learning Exercise 12.6B

Write the correct IUPAC (or common name) for the following aldehydes.

$$\overset{\displaystyle O}{\overset{\displaystyle \|}{}}$$

1. CH_3—C—H

$$\overset{\displaystyle O}{\overset{\displaystyle \|}{}}$$

2. CH_3—CH_2—CH_2—CH_2—C—H

$$\overset{\displaystyle CH_3}{\overset{\displaystyle |}{}} \qquad \overset{\displaystyle O}{\overset{\displaystyle \|}{}}$$

3. CH_3—CH_2—CH—CH_2—CH_2—C—H

$$\overset{\displaystyle O}{\overset{\displaystyle \|}{}}$$

4. CH_3—CH_2—CH_2—C—H

$$\overset{\displaystyle O}{\overset{\displaystyle \|}{}}$$

5. H—C—H

Answers   **1.** ethanal; acetaldehyde   **2.** pentanal   **3.** 4-methylhexanal
　　　　　　4. butanal; butyraldehyde   **5.** methanal; formaldehyde

◆ **Learning Exercise 12.6C**

Write the IUPAC (or common name) for the following ketones.

1. $CH_3-\overset{\overset{\textstyle O}{\|}}{C}-CH_3$

2. $CH_3-CH_2-CH_2-\overset{\overset{\textstyle O}{\|}}{C}-CH_3$

3. $CH_3-CH_2-\overset{\overset{\textstyle O}{\|}}{C}-CH_2-CH_3$

4.

5.

Answers

1. propanone; dimethyl ketone, acetone
2. 2-pentanone; methyl propyl ketone
3. 3-pentanone; diethyl ketone
4. cyclopentanone
5. cyclohexyl methyl ketone

◆ **Learning Exercise 12.6D**

Write the correct condensed formulas for the following.

1. ethanal

2. 2-methylbutanol

3. 2-chloropropanal

4. ethylmethylketone

5. 3-hexanone

6. benzaldehyde

Answers

1. $CH_3-\overset{\overset{\textstyle O}{\|}}{C}-H$

2. $CH_3-CH_2-\overset{\overset{\textstyle CH_3}{|}}{CH}-\overset{\overset{\textstyle O}{\|}}{C}-H$

3. $CH_3-\overset{\overset{\textstyle Cl}{|}}{CH}-\overset{\overset{\textstyle O}{\|}}{C}-H$

4. $CH_3-CH_2-\overset{\overset{\textstyle O}{\|}}{C}-CH_3$

5. $CH_3-CH_2-\overset{\overset{\textstyle O}{\|}}{C}-CH_2-CH_2-CH_3$

6.

12.7 Some Important Aldehydes and Ketones

Match each of the following important aldehydes and ketones with a characteristic or use of that compound.

a. acetone   **b.** formaldehyde   **c.** butanedione   **d.** benzaldehyde

1. _____ 40% solution is used to preserve biological specimens

2. _____ provides the flavor of butter in margarine

3. _____ a solvent used to remove paint and nail polish

4. _____ provides the odor and flavor of almonds

5. _____ produced in uncontrolled diabetes or fasting

Answers   **1.** b   **2.** c   **3.** a   **4.** d   **5.** a

12.8 Properties of Aldehydes and Ketones

- The polarity of the carbonyl group makes aldehydes and ketones of one to four carbon atoms soluble in water.
- Using an oxidizing agent, aldehydes oxidize to carboxylic acids. Ketones do not oxidize further.

$$CH_3-\overset{\overset{\text{O}}{\|}}{C}-H \xrightarrow{[O]} CH_3-\overset{\overset{\text{O}}{\|}}{C}-OH$$
aldehyde   *carboxylic acid*

$$CH_3-\overset{\overset{\text{O}}{\|}}{C}-CH_3 \xrightarrow{[O]} \text{No reaction}$$
ketone

◆ Learning Exercise 12.8A

Indicate the compound with the highest boiling point in each of the following groups of compounds.

1. $CH_3-CH_2-\overset{\overset{\text{O}}{\|}}{C}-H$, $CH_3-CH_2-CH_2-OH$, or $CH_3-\overset{\overset{\text{O}}{\|}}{C}-CH_3$

2. acetaldehyde or propionaldehyde

3. propanone or butanone

4. methylcyclohexane or cyclohexanone

Answers   **1.** CH_3—CH_2—CH_2—OH   **2.** propionaldehyde
3. butanone   **4.** cyclohexanone

◆ Learning Exercise 12.8B

Indicate whether each of the following compounds is soluble (S) or not soluble (NS) in water.

1. _____ 3-hexanone   **2.** _____ propanal   **3.** _____ acetaldehyde

4. _____ butanal   **5.** _____ cyclohexanone

Answers   **1.** NS   **2.** S   **3.** S   **4.** S   **5.** NS

◆ Learning Exercise 12.8C

Indicate the compound in each of the following pairs that will oxidize.

1. propanal or propanone   _____

2. butane or butanal   _____

3. ethane or acetaldehyde   _____

Answers   **1.** propanal   **2.** butanal   **3.** acetaldehyde

12.9 Chiral Molecules

- Chiral molecules have mirror images that cannot be superimposed.
- In a chiral molecule, there is one or more carbon atoms attached to four different atoms or groups.
- The mirror images of a chiral molecule represent two different molecules called enantiomers.
- In a Fischer projection (straight chain), the prefixes D- and L- are used to distinguish between the mirror images. In D-glyceraldehyde, the —OH is on the right of the chiral carbon; it is on the left in L-glyceraldehyde.

L-Glyceraldehyde   D-Glyceraldehyde

◆ Learning Exercise 12.9A

Indicate whether the following objects would be chiral or not.

1. a piece of plain computer paper _____
2. weight-lifting glove _____
3. a baseball cap _____
4. a volleyball net _____
5. your left foot _____

Answers 1. not chiral 2. chiral 3. not chiral 4. not chiral 5. chiral

◆ Learning Exercise 12.9B

State whether each of the following molecules is chiral or not chiral.

1. $\underset{\text{CH}_3}{\overset{\text{Cl}}{\text{H}-\text{C}-\text{Cl}}}$
    _____

2. $\underset{\text{CH}_3}{\overset{\text{Cl}}{\text{H}-\text{C}-\text{OH}}}$
    _____

3. $\underset{\text{CH}_3}{\overset{\text{CHO}}{\text{H}-\text{C}-\text{OH}}}$
    _____

Answers 1. not chiral 2. chiral 3. chiral

◆ Learning Exercise 12.9C

Identify the following as a feature that is characteristic of a chiral compound or not.

1. the central atom is attached to two identical groups _____
2. contains a carbon attached to four different groups _____
3. has identical mirror images _____

Answers 1. not chiral 2. chiral 3. not chiral

◆ Learning Exercise 12.9D

Indicate whether each pair of Fischer projections represents enantiomers (E) or identical structures (I).

a. HO—|—H and H—|—OH (COOH top, CH₂OH bottom)

b. Cl—|—H and Cl—|—H (CH₃ top, CH₂OH bottom)

c. Cl—|—Br and Br—|—Cl (CHO top, CH₃ bottom)

d. H—|—OH and HO—|—H (COOH top, COOH bottom)

190

Answers   1. E   2. I   3. E   4. I

Check List for Chapter 12

You are ready to take the practice test for Chapter 12. Be sure that you have accomplished the following learning goals for this chapter. If you are not sure, review the section listed at the end of the goal. Then apply your new skills and understanding to the practice test.

After studying Chapter 12, I can successfully:

_____ Classify an alcohol as primary, secondary, or tertiary (12.1).

_____ Give the IUPAC or common name of an alcohol or phenol and draw the condensed structural formula from the name. (12.1).

_____ Identify the uses of some important alcohols and phenols (12.2).

_____ Write the common name of an ether; write the condensed structural formula from the name (12.3).

_____ Describe the solubility of alcohols, phenols, and ethers in water; compare their boiling points (12.4).

_____ Write the products of alcohols that undergo dehydration or oxidation (12.5).

_____ Write the structural formulas for reactants and products of the oxidation of alcohols (12.6).

_____ Identify structural formulas as aldehydes and ketones (12.6).

_____ Give the IUPAC and common names of an aldehyde or ketone; draw the condensed structural formula from the name (12.6).

_____ Identify the uses of some common aldehydes and ketones (12.7).

_____ Compare the physical properties of aldehydes and ketones with alcohols and alkanes (12.8).

_____ Identify a molecule as a chiral or not: write the D- and L-Fischer projections (12.9).

Practice Test for Chapter 12

Match the names of the following compounds with their structures.

A. 1-propanol   B. cyclobutanol   C. 2-propanol   D. ethyl methyl ether   E. diethyl ether

1.

2. $CH_3—CH_2—CH_2—OH$

3. $CH_3—O—CH_2—CH_3$

4.

5. $CH_3—CH_2—O—CH_2—CH_3$

6. The compound is formed by the oxidation of

    A. 2-propanol.   **B.** propane.   **C.** 1-propanol.
    D. dimethyl ether.   **E.** methyl ethyl ketone.

7. Why are short-chain alcohols water soluble?

    A. They are nonpolar.   **B.** They can hydrogen bond.   **C.** They are organic.
    D. They are bases.   **E.** They are acids.

8.   Phenol is

   A. the alcohol of benzene.   **B.** the aldehyde of benzene.
   C. the phenyl group of benzene.   **D.** the ketone of benzene.   **E.** cyclohexanol.

9. $CH_3—CH_2—OH \xrightarrow{[O]}$

   A. an alkane   **B.** an aldehyde   **C.** a ketone
   D. an ether   **E.** a phenol

10.   The dehydration of cyclohexanol gives

   A. cyclohexane.   **B.** cyclohexene.   **C.** cyclohexyne.
   D. benzene.   **E.** phenol.

11.   The formula of the thiol of ethane is

   A. $CH_3—SH$.   **B.** $CH_3—CH_2—OH$.   **C.** $CH_3—CH_2—SH$.
   D. $CH_3—CH_2—S—CH_3$ **E.** $CH_3—S—OH$.

In questions 12 through 16, classify each alcohol as

A.   primary (1°)   **B.**   secondary (2°)   **C.**   tertiary (3°)

12. $CH_3—CH_2—CH_2—OH$ 13.   14.

15. $CH_3—\underset{\underset{CH_3}{|}}{\overset{\overset{OH}{|}}{C}}—CH_2—CH_2—CH_3$ 16. $CH_3—\overset{\overset{OH}{|}}{CH}—CH_2—CH_2—CH_2—CH_3$

Complete questions 17 through 20 by indicating one of the products (A–E) formed in each of the following reactions.

A.   primary alcohol   **B.**   secondary alcohol   **C.**   aldehyde   **D.**   ketone   **E.**   carboxylic acid

17.   _____ Oxidation of a primary alcohol

18.   _____ Oxidation of a secondary alcohol

19.   _____ Oxidation of an aldehyde

20.   _____ Hydration of ethene

In 21-25, match the following compounds with the names given.

A. dimethyl ether   **B.** acetaldehyde   **C.** methanal   **D.** dimethyl ketone   **E.** propanal

21. _____ $H—\overset{\overset{O}{||}}{C}—H$ 22. _____ $CH_3—O—CH_3$

23. _____ $CH_3—\overset{\overset{O}{||}}{C}—CH_3$ 24. _____ $CH_3—\overset{\overset{O}{||}}{C}—H$

25. _____ CH_3—CH_2—$\overset{\overset{\displaystyle O}{\|}}{C}$—H

26. The compound with the higher boiling point is

    A. CH_3—CH_2—CH_2—CH_3 **B.** CH_3—CH_2—CH_2—OH

    C. CH_3—$\overset{\overset{\displaystyle O}{\|}}{C}$—$CH_3$ **D.** CH_3—CH_2—$\overset{\overset{\displaystyle O}{\|}}{C}$—H

    E. CH_3—CH_2—O—CH_3

Complete questions 27 through 29 by indicating one of the products (A–E) formed in each of the following reactions.

    A. primary alcohol   **B.** secondary alcohol   **C.** aldehyde
    D. ketone   **E.** carboxylic acid

27. _____ Oxidation of a primary alcohol   28. _____ Oxidation of a secondary alcohol

29. _____ Oxidation of an aldehyde

30. Benedict's reagent will oxidize

    A. CH_3—$\overset{\overset{\displaystyle O}{\|}}{C}$—$CH_3$ **B.** CH_3—$\overset{\overset{\displaystyle OH}{|}}{CH}$—$CH_2$—OH

    C. CH_3—$\overset{\overset{\displaystyle O}{\|}}{C}$—$CH_2$—OH   **D.** CH_3—CH_2—$\overset{\overset{\displaystyle O}{\|}}{C}$—H

    E. CH_3—$\overset{\overset{\displaystyle OH}{|}}{CH}$—$\overset{\overset{\displaystyle O}{\|}}{C}$—OH

31. In the Tollen's test
    A. an aldehyde is oxidized and Ag^+ reduced.
    B. an aldehyde is reduced and Ag^+ oxidized.
    C. a ketone is oxidized and Ag^+ reduced.
    D. a ketone is reduced and Ag^+ oxidized.
    E. all of these

Identify each of the following structural formulas as

32. alcohol   33. ether

    A. CH_3—CH_2—$\overset{\overset{\displaystyle OH}{|}}{CH}$—$CH_3$

    B. CH_3—$\overset{\overset{\displaystyle O-CH_3}{|}}{\underset{\underset{\displaystyle CH_3}{|}}{C}}$—$CH_3$

193

34. The structural formula for 4-bromo-3-methylcyclohexanone is

Identify each of the following as enantiomers (E), identical (I), or different (D) compounds.

35. HO—[COOH | H]—CH$_2$OH and H—[COOH | OH]—CH$_2$OH

36. Cl—[CH$_3$ | H]—CH$_2$OH and Cl—[CH$_3$ | H]—CH$_2$OH

37. Cl—[CHO | Cl]—CH$_3$ and Cl—[CHO | Cl]—CH$_3$

38. H—[COOH | OH]—COOH and HO—[COOH | H]—COOH

39. Cl—[CHO | Br]—CH$_3$ and Br—[COOH | Cl]—CH$_3$

Answers to Practice Test

1. C	2. A	3. D	4. B	5. E
6. A	7. B	8. A	9. B	10. B
11. C	12. A	13. B	14. C	15. C
16. B	17. C	18. D	19. E	20. A
21 C	22. A	23. D	24. B	25. E
26. B	27. C,E	28. D	29. E	30. D
31. A	32. A	33. B	34. B	35. E
36. E	37. I	38. I	39. D	

Answers and Solutions to Selected Text Problems

12.1 a. This compound has a two-carbon chain (ethane). The final –e is dropped and –ol added to indicate an alcohol. The IUPAC name is ethanol.

b. This compound has a four-carbon chain with a hydroxyl attached to carbon 2. The IUPAC name is 2-butanol.

c. This compound has a four-carbon chain with a hydroxyl attached to carbon 1and a methyl attached to carbon 3. The IUPAC name is 3-methyl-1-butanol.

d. This compound is a six-carbon cycloalkane with a hydroxyl attached to carbon 1 and a methyl group attached to carbon 4. Since the hydroxyl is always attached to carbon 1, the number 1 is omitted in the name. The IUPAC name is 4-methylcyclohexanol.

12.3 a. 1-propanol has a three-carbon chain with a hydroxyl attached to carbon 1.

CH_3—CH_2—CH_2—OH

b. Methyl alcohol has a hydroxyl attached to a one-carbon alkane. CH_3—OH.

c. 3-pentanol has a five-carbon chain with a hydroxyl attached to carbon 3.

$$\underset{\displaystyle CH_3-CH_2-\underset{\textstyle |}{C}H-CH_2-CH_3}{\overset{\textstyle OH}{\overset{\textstyle |}{}}}$$

d. 2-methyl-2-butanol has a four-carbon chain with a methyl and hydroxyl attached to carbon 2.

$$\begin{array}{c} OH \\ | \\ CH_3-\overset{\textstyle |}{\underset{\textstyle |}{C}}-CH_2-CH_3 \\ CH_3 \end{array}$$

12.5 A benzene ring with a hydroxyl group is called *phenol*. Substituents are numbered from the carbon bonded to the hydroxyl group as carbon 1.
a. phenol
b. 2-bromophenol
c. 3-bromophenol

12.7 In a primary (1°) alcohol, the carbon bonded to the hydroxyl group (—OH) is attached to one alkyl group (except for methanol); to two alkyl groups in a secondary alcohol (2°); and to three alkyl groups in a tertiary alcohol (3°).

   a. 1°   **b.** 1°   **c.** 3°   **d.** 2°   **e.** 3°

12.9 a. ethanol   **b.** menthol   **c.** 2-phenylphenol

12.11 a. ethyl methyl ether
     b. cyclohexyl methyl ether
     c. cyclobutyl ethyl ether
     d. methyl propyl ether

12.13 a. Ethyl propyl ether has a two-carbon group and a three-carbon group attached to oxygen by single bonds. CH_3—CH_2—O—CH_2—CH_2—CH_3
     b. Ethyl cyclopropyl ether has a two-carbon group and a three-carbon cyclo alkyl group attached to oxygen by single bonds.

CH_3—CH_2—O—▷

   c. CH_3—CH_2–O–CH_3

12.15 **a.** methanol; hydrogen bonding of alcohols gives higher boiling points than alkanes.
  b. 1-butanol; alcohols hydrogen bond, but ethers cannot.
  c. 1-butanol; hydrogen bonding of alcohols gives higher boiling points than alkanes.

12.17 **a.** yes, alcohols with 1-4 carbon atoms hydrogen bond with water
  b. yes; the water can hydrogen bond to the O in ether
  c. no; a carbon chain longer than 4 carbon atoms diminishes the effect of the —OH group.
  d. no; alkanes are nonpolar and do not hydrogen bond
  e. yes; the —OH in phenol ionizes in water, which makes it soluble.

12.19 Dehydration is the removal of an —OH and a —H from adjacent carbon atoms.

  a. CH_3—CH_2—CH=CH_2 **b.**

  c. CH_3—CH_2—CH=CH—CH_3

12.21 **a.** A primary alcohol oxidizes to an aldehyde and then to a carboxylic acid.

  b. A secondary alcohol oxidizes to a ketone. CH_3—CH_2—$\overset{\overset{\textstyle O}{\|}}{C}$—$CH_3$

  c. A secondary alcohol oxidizes to a ketone.

  d. A secondary alcohol oxidizes to a ketone. CH_3—$\overset{\overset{\textstyle O}{\|}}{C}$—$CH_2$—$\overset{\overset{\textstyle CH_3}{|}}{CH}$—$CH_3$

12.23 **a.** ketone   **b.** ketone   **c.** aldehyde

12.25 **a.** acetaldehyde   **b.** methyl propyl ketone   **c.** formaldehyde

12.27 **a.** propanal   **b.** 2-methyl-3-pentanone
  c. 3-methylcyclohexanone   **d.** benzaldehyde

12.29 **a.** CH_3—$\overset{\overset{\textstyle O}{\|}}{C}$—H   **b.** CH_3—$\overset{\overset{\textstyle O}{\|}}{C}$—$CH_2$—$CH_2$—$CH_3$

  c. CH_3—$\overset{\overset{\textstyle O}{\|}}{C}$—$CH_2$—$CH_2$—$CH_2$—$CH_3$

  d. CH_3—CH_2—$\overset{\overset{\textstyle CH_3}{|}}{CH}$—$CH_2$—$\overset{\overset{\textstyle O}{\|}}{C}$—H

12.31 **a.** benzaldehyde   **b.** acetone; propanone   **c.** formaldehyde

$$\begin{array}{c}O\\\parallel\end{array}$$

12.33 **a.** CH_3—CH_2—C—H has a polar carbonyl group.
   b. pentanal has more carbons and thus a higher molar mass.
   c. 1-butanol can hydrogen bond with other 1-butanol molecules.

$$\begin{array}{cc}O & O\\\parallel & \parallel\end{array}$$

12.35 **a.** CH_3—C—C—CH_3: more hydrogen bonding
   b. acetone; lower number of carbon atoms

12.37 **a.** A primary alcohol will be oxidized to an aldehyde and then to a carboxylic acid.

$$\begin{array}{cc}O & O\\\parallel & \parallel\end{array}$$

CH_3—CH_2—CH_2—CH_2—C—H then CH_3—CH_2—CH_2—CH_2—C—OH

   b. A secondary alcohol will be oxidized to a ketone. CH_3—CH_2—C—CH_3 (with O double-bonded to C)

   c. A secondary alcohol will be oxidized to a ketone.

   d. A secondary alcohol will be oxidized to a ketone. CH_3—C—CH_2—CH—CH_3 (with O double-bonded to the second C and CH_3 branch on the CH)

   e. A primary alcohol will be oxidized to an aldehyde and then to a carboxylic acid.

CH_3—CH—CH_2—C—H then CH_3—CH—CH_2—C—OH (with CH_3 branches and O double-bonded carbonyls)

12.39 **a.** achiral   **b.** chiral CH_3—CH—CH_2CH_3 with *chiral carbon* Br

   c. chiral CH_3—CH—C—H (with Br and *chiral carbon*, O double-bonded)   **d.** achiral

12.41 **a.** CH_3 CH_3 *chiral carbon*

CH_3—C=CH—CH_2—CH_2—CH—CH_2—CH_2—OH

   b. CH_3 O

H_2N—CH—C—OH

   chiral carbon

12.43

a.   HO— C —Br (with H on top, CH₃ on bottom)

b.   Cl— C —Br (with CH₃ on top, OH on bottom)

c.   HO— C —H (with CHO on top, CH₂CH₃ on bottom)

12.45 **a.** identical   **b.** enantiomers
          c. enantiomers   **d.** enantiomers

12.47 **a.** 2° **b.** 1° **c.** 1° **d.** 2° **e.** 1° **f.** 3°

12.49 **a.** alcohol   **b.** ether   **c.** thiol   **d.** alcohol
          e. ether   **f.** alcohol   **g.** phenol

12.51

a. (cyclopentane ring with OH at top and CH₃ on lower carbon)

b. (benzene ring with OH at top and Cl at bottom)

c. H_3C—CH—CH—CH_2—CH_3 (with CH_3 and OH substituents)

d. (benzene ring with O—CH_2—CH_3)

e. CH_3—CH_2—C(=O)—CH_2—CH_3

f. (benzene ring with OH at top, Br on side, Br at bottom)

12.53 **a.** Glycerol is used in skin lotions.

b. 1,2-ethanediol; ethylene glycol is used in antifreeze

c. Ethanol is produced by fermentation of grains and sugars.

12.55 **a.** 1-propanol; hydrogen bonding   **b.** 1-propanol; hydrogen bonding
          c. 1-butanol; larger molar mass

12.57 **a.** soluble; hydrogen bonding

b. soluble; hydrogen bonding

c. insoluble; carbon chains over four carbon atoms diminishes effect of polar —OH on hydrogen bonding

12.59 **a.** CH_3—CH=CH_2 **b.** CH_3—CH_2—C(=O)—H

c. CH_3—CH_2—C(=O)—CH_3 **d.** (cyclohexene ring)   **e.** (cyclohexanone ring)

12.61 Testosterone contains cycloalkene, alcohol and ketone functional groups.

12.63 **a.** 2,5-dichlorophenol is a benzene ring with a hydroxyl on carbon 1 and chlorine atoms on carbons 2 and 5.

OH
Cl
Cl

b. CH$_3$—CH—CH$_2$—CH$_2$—SH
       |
       CH$_3$

c.

OH
Cl   Cl
Cl   Cl
    Cl

12.65 **a.** 2-bromo-4-chlorocyclopentanone   **b.** 4-chloro-3-hydroxybenzaldehyde
c. 3-chloropropanal   **d.** 2-chloro-3-pentanone
e. 3-methylcyclohexanone

12.67 **a.** 3-methylcyclopentanone is a five-carbon cyclic structure with a methyl group located two carbons from the carbonyl group.

CH$_3$

b. 4-chlorobenzaldehyde is a benzene with an aldehyde group and a chlorine on carbon 4.

CHO

Cl

c. 3–chloropropionaldehyde is a three carbon aldehyde with a chlorine located two carbons from the carbonyl.

O
||
Cl—CH$_2$—CH$_2$—C—H

d. Ethyl methyl ketone has a carbonyl bonded to a methy and an ethyl group.

O
||
CH$_3$—C—CH$_2$—CH$_3$

e. This is a six-carbon aldehyde with a methyl group on carbon 3.

$$CH_3-CH_2-CH_2-\underset{\underset{CH_3}{|}}{CH}-CH_2-\underset{\overset{O}{\|}}{C}-H$$

f. This has a seven-carbon chain with a carbonyl group on carbon 2.

$$CH_3-\underset{\overset{O}{\|}}{C}-CH_2-CH_2-CH_2-CH_2-CH_3$$

12.69 Compounds b, c, and d with oxygen atoms and less than five carbon atoms can hydrogen bond to be soluble.

12.71 a. CH_3-CH_2-OH; polar —OH group can hydrogen bond

b. $CH_3-CH_2-\underset{\overset{O}{\|}}{C}-H$; polar carbonyl group can hydrogen bond

c. $CH_3-CH_2-CH_2-OH$; polar —OH group can hydrogen bond

12.73 A chiral carbon is bonded to four different groups.

a. $H-\underset{\underset{Cl}{|}}{\overset{\overset{Cl}{|}}{C}}-\underset{\underset{H}{|}}{\overset{\overset{Cl}{|}}{\textcircled{C}}}-O-H$ **b.** None.   **c.** None.

d. $CH_3-\underset{\overset{NH_2}{|}}{\textcircled{CH}}-\underset{\overset{O}{\|}}{C}-H$ **e.** $CH_3-CH_2-\underset{\overset{Br}{|}}{\textcircled{CH}}-CH_2-CH_2-CH_3$

f. None.

12.75 Enantiomers are mirror images

a. identical   **b.** enantiomers
c. enantiomers (turn 180°)   **d.** identical (two –OH groups)

12.77 Primary alcohols oxidize to aldehydes and then to carboxylic acids. Secondary alcohols oxidize to ketones.

a. $CH_3-CH_2-\underset{\overset{O}{\|}}{C}-H \xrightarrow{\substack{\text{further}\\\text{oxidation}}} CH_3-CH_2-\underset{\overset{O}{\|}}{C}-OH$

b. $CH_3-\underset{\overset{O}{\|}}{C}-CH_2-CH_2-CH_3$

c. $CH_3-CH_2-CH_2-\underset{\overset{O}{\|}}{C}-OH$

d.

Carboxylic Acids, Esters, Amines, and Amides

Study Goals

- Name and write structural formulas of carboxylic acids and esters.
- Describe the boiling points and solubility of carboxylic acids.
- Write equations for the ionization of carboxylic acids in water.
- Write equations for the esterification, hydrolysis, and saponification of esters.
- Name and write structural formulas of amines and amides.
- Describe the ionization of amines in water.
- Describe the boiling points of amines and amides compared to alkanes and alcohols.
- Describe the solubility of amines and amides in water.
- Write equations for the neutralization and amidation of amines.
- Describe acid and base hydrolysis of amides.

Think About It

1. Why do vinegar and citrus juices taste sour?

2. What type of compound gives flowers and fruits their pleasant aromas?

3. Fish smell "fishy," but lemon juice removes the "fishy" odor. Why?

4. What functional groups are often found in tranquilizers and hallucinogens?

Key Terms

Match the key term with the correct statement shown below.

a. carboxylic acid	b. saponification	c. esterification
d. hydrolysis	e. ester	f. amine
g. amide	h. alkaloid	

1. _____ An organic compound containing the carboxyl group (—COOH)

2. _____ A reaction of a carboxylic acid and an alcohol in the presence of an acid catalyst

3. _____ A type of organic compound that produces pleasant aromas in flowers and fruits

4. _____ The hydrolysis of an ester with a strong base producing a salt of the carboxylic acid and an alcohol

5. _____ The splitting of a molecule such as an ester by the addition of water in the presence of an acid

6. _____ A nitrogen-containing compound that is active physiologically

7. _____ The hydrolysis of this compound produces a carboxylic acid and an amine.

8. _____ An organic compound that contains an amino group

Answers   **1.** a   **2.** c   **3.** e   **4.** b   **5.** d   **6.** h   **7.** g   **8.** f

13.1 Carboxylic Acids

- In the IUPAC system, a carboxylic acid is named by replacing the *ane* ending with *oic acid*. Simple acids usually are named by the common naming system using the prefixes: **form** (1C), **acet** (2C), **propion** (4C), **butyr** (4C), followed by *ic acid*.

$$\underset{\substack{\text{methanoic acid} \\ \text{(formic acid)}}}{\overset{\overset{\displaystyle O}{\|}}{H-C-OH}} \qquad \underset{\substack{\text{ethanoic acid} \\ \text{(acetic acid)}}}{\overset{\overset{\displaystyle O}{\|}}{CH_3-C-OH}} \qquad \underset{\substack{\text{butanoic acid} \\ \text{(butyric acid)}}}{\overset{\overset{\displaystyle O}{\|}}{CH_3-CH_2-CH_2-C-OH}}$$

- A carboxylic acid is prepared by the oxidation of a primary alcohol or an aldehyde.

$$CH_3-CH_2-OH \xrightarrow{[O]} \overset{\overset{\displaystyle O}{\|}}{CH_3-C-H} \xrightarrow{[O]} \overset{\overset{\displaystyle O}{\|}}{CH_3-C-OH}$$

◆ Learning Exercise 13.1A

Give the IUPAC name for each of the following carboxylic acids.

1. $\overset{\overset{\displaystyle O}{\|}}{CH_3-C-OH}$

2. $CH_3-\overset{\overset{\displaystyle OH}{|}}{CH}-\overset{\overset{\displaystyle O}{\|}}{C}-OH$

3. $CH_3-\overset{\overset{\displaystyle CH_3}{|}}{CH}-CH_2-\overset{\overset{\displaystyle O}{\|}}{C}-OH$

4. [structure: benzene ring with COOH at top and Cl at bottom (para)]

Answers
1. ethanoic acid
2. 2-hydroxypropanoic acid
3. 3-methylbutanoic acid
4. 4-chlorobenzoic acid

◆ Learning Exercise 13.1B

A. Write the formulas for the following carboxylic acids.

1. acetic acid

2. 2-ketobutanoic acid

3. benzoic acid

4. 3-hydroxyproponoic acid

5. formic acid   **6.** 3-methylpentanoic acid

Answers

1.
$$CH_3—\overset{\overset{\displaystyle O}{\|}}{C}—OH$$

2.
$$CH_3—CH_2—\overset{\overset{\displaystyle O}{\|}}{C}—\overset{\overset{\displaystyle O}{\|}}{C}—OH$$

3.

4.
$$HO—CH_2—CH_2—\overset{\overset{\displaystyle O}{\|}}{C}—OH$$

5.
$$H—\overset{\overset{\displaystyle O}{\|}}{C}—OH$$

6.
$$CH_3—CH_2—\overset{\overset{\displaystyle CH_3}{|}}{C}H—CH_2—\overset{\overset{\displaystyle O}{\|}}{C}—OH$$

13.2 Properties of Carboxylic Acids

- Carboxylic acids have higher boiling points than other polar compounds such as alcohols.
- Because they have two polar groups, two carboxylic acids form a dimer, which contains two sets of hydrogen bonds.
- Carboxylic acids with one to four carbon atoms are very soluble in water.

◆ Learning Exercise 13.2A

Indicate whether each of the following carboxylic acids are soluble in water.

1. _____ hexanoic acid   **2.** _____ acetic acid   **3.** _____ propanoic acid

4. _____ benzoic acid   **5.** _____ formic acid   **6.** _____ octanoic acid

Answers   **1.** no   **2.** yes   **3.** yes   **4.** no   **5.** yes   **6.** no

◆ Learning Exercise 13.2B

Identify the compound in each pair that has the higher boiling point.

1. acetic acid or butyric acid   **2.** propanoic acid or 2-propanol

3. propanoic acid or propanone   **4.** acetic acid or acetaldehyde

Answers   **1.** butyric acid   **2.** propanoic acid
              3. propanoic acid   **4.** acetic acid

13.3 Acidity of Carboxylic Acids

- As weak acids, carboxylic acids ionize slightly in water to form acidic solutions of H_3O^+ and a carboxylate ion.
- When bases neutralize carboxylic acids, the products are carboxylic acid salts and water.

◆ Learning Exercise 13.3A

Write the products for the ionization of the following carboxylic acids in water.

$$\text{O}$$
$$\|$$
1. $CH_3-CH_2-C-OH + H_2O \rightleftharpoons$

2. benzoic acid + $H_2O \rightleftharpoons$

Answers   **1.** $CH_3-CH_2-\overset{\displaystyle O}{\overset{\|}{C}}-O^- + H_3O^+$ **2.**

                                          $+$ H_3O^+

◆ Learning Exercise 13.3B

Write the products and names for each of the following reactions.

$$\text{O}$$
$$\|$$
1. $CH_3-CH_2-C-OH + NaOH \longrightarrow$

2. formic acid + KOH $\longrightarrow$

Answers   **1.** $CH_3-CH_2-\overset{\displaystyle O}{\overset{\|}{C}}-O^-Na^+ + H_2O$ **2.** $H-\overset{\displaystyle O}{\overset{\|}{C}}-O^-\,K^+ + H_2O$
                           Sodium propanoate   potassium methanoate
                           (sodium propionate)   (potassium formate)

204

13.4 Esters

- In the presence of a strong acid, carboxylic acids react with alcohols to produce esters and water.
- The names of esters consist of two words, one from the alcohol and the other from the carboxylic acid with the *ic* ending replaced by *ate*.

$$CH_3-\overset{\overset{\displaystyle O}{\|}}{C}-O-CH_3 \quad \text{methyl ethanoate (IUPAC) or methyl acetate (common)}$$

◆ **Learning Exercise 13.4A**

Write the products of the following reactions.

1. $CH_3-\overset{\overset{\displaystyle O}{\|}}{C}-OH + CH_3-OH \xrightarrow{\text{H}^+}$

2. $H-\overset{\overset{\displaystyle O}{\|}}{C}-OH + CH_3-CH_2-OH \xrightarrow{\text{H}^+}$

3.

$+ \quad HO-CH_3 \xrightarrow{\text{H}^+}$

4. propanoic acid and ethanol $\xrightarrow{\text{H}^+}$

Answers

1. $CH_3-\overset{\overset{\displaystyle O}{\|}}{C}-O-CH_3 + H_2O$

2. $H-\overset{\overset{\displaystyle O}{\|}}{C}-O-CH_2-CH_3 + H_2O$

3.

$+ \ H_2O$

4. $CH_3-CH_2-\overset{\overset{\displaystyle O}{\|}}{C}-O-CH_2-CH_3 + H_2O$

◆ **Learning Exercise 13.4B**

Name each of the following esters.

1. $CH_3-\overset{\overset{\displaystyle O}{\|}}{C}-O-CH_2-CH_3$

2. $CH_3-CH_2-CH_2-\overset{\overset{\displaystyle O}{\|}}{C}-O-CH_3$

3.

$$
\begin{matrix} & \overset{\text{O}}{\underset{\parallel}{}} & & \overset{\text{OH}}{\underset{|}{}} \\ \text{CH}_3\text{—CH}_2\text{—C—O—CH}_2\text{—CH—CH}_3 \end{matrix}
$$

4.

$$
\overset{\text{O}}{\underset{\parallel}{\text{C}}}\text{—O—CH}_3
$$

(benzene ring attached)

Answers
1. ethyl ethanoate (ethyl acetate)
2. methylbutanoate (methylbutyrate)
3. 2-hydroxypropylpropanoate (2-hydroxypropylpropionate)
4. methylbenzoate

◆ Learning Exercise 13.4C

Write structural formulas for each of the following esters.

1. propylacetate

2. ethylbutyrate

3. ethylpropanoate

4. ethylbenzoate

Answers

1. $\text{CH}_3\overset{\text{O}}{\underset{\parallel}{\text{—C}}}\text{—O—CH}_2\text{—CH}_2\text{—CH}_3$

2. $\text{CH}_3\text{—CH}_2\text{—CH}_2\overset{\text{O}}{\underset{\parallel}{\text{—C}}}\text{—O—CH}_2\text{—CH}_3$

3. $\text{CH}_3\text{—CH}_2\overset{\text{O}}{\underset{\parallel}{\text{—C}}}\text{—O—CH}_2\text{—CH}_3$

4. $\overset{\text{O}}{\underset{\parallel}{\text{C}}}\text{—O—CH}_2\text{—CH}_3$ (benzene ring attached)

13.5 Properties of Esters

- Esters have higher boiling points than alkanes, but lower than alcohols and carboxylic acids of similar mass.
- In hydrolysis, esters are split apart by a reaction with water. When the catalyst is an acid, the products are a carboxylic acid and an alcohol.

$$
\underset{\text{methyl acetate}}{\text{CH}_3\overset{\text{O}}{\underset{\parallel}{\text{—C}}}\text{—O—CH}_3} + \text{H}_2\text{O} \xrightarrow{\text{H}^+} \underset{\text{acetic acid}}{\text{CH}_3\overset{\text{O}}{\underset{\parallel}{\text{—C}}}\text{—OH}} + \underset{\text{methyl alcohol}}{\text{HO—CH}_3}
$$

206

- In saponification, long-chain fatty acids from fats react with strong bases to produce salts of the fatty acids, which are soaps.

- Saponification is the hydrolysis of an ester in the presence of a base, which produces a carboxylate salt and an alcohol.

$$
\underset{\textit{methyl acetate}}{CH_3-\overset{\overset{\displaystyle O}{\|}}{C}-O-CH_3} + NaOH \longrightarrow \underset{\textit{sodium acetate}}{CH_3-\overset{\overset{\displaystyle O}{\|}}{C}-O^-Na^+} + \underset{\textit{methyl alcohol}}{HO-CH_3}
$$

◆ Learning Exercise 13.5A

Identify the compound with the higher boiling point in each of the following pairs of compounds.

1. CH_3-CH_2-OH or $H-\overset{\overset{\displaystyle O}{\|}}{C}-O-CH_3$

2. $CH_3-\overset{\overset{\displaystyle O}{\|}}{C}-O-CH_3$ or $CH_3-\overset{\overset{\displaystyle OH}{|}}{CH}-CH_2-CH_3$

3. $CH_3-\overset{\overset{\displaystyle O}{\|}}{C}-O-CH_3$ or $CH_3-CH_2-CH_2-CH_2-CH_3$

Answers 1. CH_3-CH_2-OH 2. $CH_3-\overset{\overset{\displaystyle OH}{|}}{CH}-CH_2-CH_3$

3. $CH_3-\overset{\overset{\displaystyle O}{\|}}{C}-O-CH_3$

◆ Learning Exercise 13.5B

Write the products of hydrolysis or saponification for the following esters:

1. $CH_3-CH_2-CH_2-\overset{\overset{\displaystyle O}{\|}}{C}-O-CH_3 + H_2O \overset{H^+}{\longrightarrow}$

2. $CH_3-\overset{\overset{\displaystyle O}{\|}}{C}-O-CH_3 + NaOH \longrightarrow$

3. $\langle\bigcirc\rangle-\overset{\overset{\displaystyle O}{\|}}{C}-O-CH_2-CH_3 + KOH \longrightarrow$

4. $\langle\bigcirc\rangle-\overset{\overset{\displaystyle O}{\|}}{C}-O-CH_2-CH_2-CH_3 + H_2O \overset{H^+}{\longrightarrow}$

Answers

1. $CH_3{-}CH_2{-}CH_2{-}\overset{\overset{\displaystyle O}{\|}}{C}{-}OH + HO{-}CH_3$

2. $CH_3{-}\overset{\overset{\displaystyle O}{\|}}{C}{-}O^- Na^+ + CH_3{-}OH$

3. $\langle\!\bigcirc\!\rangle{-}\overset{\overset{\displaystyle O}{\|}}{C}{-}O^- K^+ \quad + \quad HO{-}CH_2{-}CH_3$

4. $\langle\!\bigcirc\!\rangle{-}\overset{\overset{\displaystyle O}{\|}}{C}{-}OH \quad + \quad HO{-}CH_2{-}CH_2{-}CH_3$

13.6 Amines

- Amines are derivatives of ammonia (NH_3), in which alkyl or aromatic groups replace one or more hydrogen atoms.
- Amines are classified as primary, secondary, or tertiary when the nitrogen atom is bonded to one, two, or three alkyl or aromatic groups.

$CH_3{-}NH_2$
Primary (1°)

$CH_3{-}\overset{\overset{\displaystyle CH_3}{|}}{N}{-}H$
Secondary (2°)

$CH_3{-}\overset{\overset{\displaystyle CH_3}{|}}{N}{-}CH_3$
Tertiary (3°)

◆ **Learning Exercise 13.6A**

Classify each of the following as a primary (1°), secondary (2°), or tertiary (3°) amine.

1. ____ $CH_3{-}\overset{\overset{\displaystyle H}{|}}{N}{-}CH_2CH_3$

2. ____ (cyclohexane with NH_2)

3. ____ $CH_3{-}CH_2{-}\overset{\overset{\displaystyle CH_3}{|}}{N}{-}CH_3$

4. ____ $CH_3{-}CH_2{-}CH_2{-}CH_2{-}\overset{\overset{\displaystyle H}{|}}{N}{-}CH_2{-}CH_3$

5. ____ (benzene with NH_2 and CH_3)

Answers   1. 2°   2. 1°   3. 3°   4. 2°   5. 1°

208

◆ **Learning Exercise 13.6B**

Name each of the amines in problem 13.6A.

1. _____ 2. _____

3. _____ 4. _____

5. _____

Answers
1. ethylmethylamine; *N*-methylethanamine
2. cyclohexanamine
3. ethyldimethylamine; *N,N*-dimethylethanamine
4. butylethylamine; *N*-ethyl-1-butanamine
5. 3-methylaniline

◆ **Learning Exercise 13.6C**

Write the structural formulas of the following amines.

1. 2-propanamine   2. *N*-ethyl-*N*-methyl-1-aminobutane

3. 3-bromoaniline   4. *N*-methylaniline

Answers

1.
$$\underset{\displaystyle CH_3-\underset{\displaystyle |}{\overset{\displaystyle |}{CH}}-CH_3}{\overset{\displaystyle NH_2}{}}$$

2.
$$CH_3CH_2-\underset{\displaystyle |}{\overset{\displaystyle CH_3}{N}}-CH_2CH_2CH_2CH_3$$

3. (benzene ring with NH₂ and Br substituents)

4. (benzene ring with NHCH₃ substituent)

13.7 Physical Properties of Amines

- The N—H bonds in primary and secondary amines form hydrogen bonds.
- Amines have higher boiling points than hydrocarbons, but lower than alcohols of similar mass because the N atom is not as electronegative as the O atoms in alcohols.
- Hydrogen bonding allows amines with up to six carbon atoms to be soluble in water.
- In water, amines act as weak bases by accepting protons from water to produce ammonium and hydroxide ions.

$$CH_3-NH_2 + H_2O \rightleftharpoons CH_3-NH_3^+ + OH^-$$
methylamine   *methylammonium hydroxide*

- Strong acids neutralize amines to yield ammonium salts.

$$CH_3-NH_2 + HCl \longrightarrow CH_3-NH_3^+ + Cl^-$$
methylamine   *methylammonium chloride*

◆ **Learning Exercise 13.7A**

Indicate the compound in each pair that has the higher boiling point.

1. CH_3—NH_2 and CH_3—OH _____

2. CH_3—CH_2—CH_2 and CH_3—CH_2—NH_2 _____

3. CH_3—CH_2—NH_2 and CH_3—CH_2—CH_2—NH_2 _____

4. CH_3—$\overset{\overset{\displaystyle H}{|}}{N}$—$CH_3$ and CH_3—CH_2—NH_2 _____

Answers 1. CH_3—OH 2. CH_3—CH_2—NH_2
           3. CH_3—CH_2—CH_2—NH_2 4. CH_3—CH_2—NH_2

◆ **Learning Exercise 13.7B**

Write the products of the following reactions.

1. CH_3—CH_2—$NH_2 + H_2O \rightleftarrows$

2. CH_3—CH_2—CH_2—$NH_2 + HCl \longrightarrow$

3. CH_3CH_2—NH—$CH_3 + HCl \longrightarrow$

4.

$\qquad NH_2$

$\qquad + \quad HBr \quad \longrightarrow$

5. $\qquad NH_2$

$\qquad + \quad H_2O \quad \rightleftarrows$

6. CH_3—CH_2—$NH_3^+ Cl^- + NaOH \longrightarrow$

Answers

1. CH_3—CH_2—$NH_3^+ OH^-$ 2. CH_3—CH_2—CH_2—$NH_3^+ Cl^-$ 3. CH_3—CH_2—$\overset{+}{N}H_2$—$CH_3 \, Cl^-$

4. $NH_3^+ Br^-$

5. $NH_3^+ OH^-$

6. CH_3—CH_2—$NH_2 + NaCl + H_2O$

13.8 Amides

- Amides are derivatives of carboxylic acids in which an amine group replaces the —OH group in the acid.
- Amides are named by replacing the *ic acid* or *oic acid* ending by *amide*.

$$CH_3-\overset{\overset{\displaystyle O}{\|}}{C}-NH_2 \qquad \text{ethanamide (acetamide)}$$

- Amides undergo acid and base hydrolysis to produce the carboxylic acid (or carboxylate salt) and the amine (or amine salt).

$$CH_3-\overset{\overset{\displaystyle O}{\|}}{C}-NH_2 + HCl + H_2O \longrightarrow CH_3-\overset{\overset{\displaystyle O}{\|}}{C}-OH + NH_4^+ Cl^-$$

$$CH_3-\overset{\overset{\displaystyle O}{\|}}{C}-NH_2 + NaOH \longrightarrow CH_3-\overset{\overset{\displaystyle O}{\|}}{C}-O^- Na^+ + NH_3$$

◆ Learning Exercise 13.8A

Write the structural formula(s) of the amides formed in each of the following reactions.

1. $CH_3-CH_2-\overset{\overset{\displaystyle O}{\|}}{C}-OH + NH_3 \xrightarrow{\text{Heat}}$

2. $\langle\bigcirc\rangle-\overset{\overset{\displaystyle O}{\|}}{C}-OH + CH_3-NH_2 \xrightarrow{\text{Heat}}$

3. $CH_3-\overset{\overset{\displaystyle O}{\|}}{C}-OH + \overset{\overset{\displaystyle CH_3}{|}}{NH}-CH_3 \xrightarrow{\text{Heat}}$

Answers

1. $CH_3-CH_2-\overset{\overset{\displaystyle O}{\|}}{C}-NH_2$

2.

3. $CH_3-\overset{\overset{\displaystyle O}{\|}}{C}-\overset{\overset{\displaystyle CH_3}{|}}{N}-CH_3$

◆ Learning Exercise 13.8B

Name the following amides.

1. $CH_3-CH_2-\overset{\overset{\displaystyle O}{\|}}{C}-NH_2$ _____

2. $\langle\bigcirc\rangle-\overset{\overset{\displaystyle O}{\|}}{C}-NH_2$ _____

3. $CH_3{-}CH_2{-}CH_2{-}CH_2{-}\overset{\overset{\displaystyle O}{\|}}{C}{-}NH_2$ _____

4. $CH_3{-}\overset{\overset{\displaystyle O}{\|}}{C}{-}NH_2$ _____

Answers   **1.** propanamide (propionamide)   **2.** benzamide
            3. pentanamide   **4.** ethanamide (acetamide)

◆ Learning Exercise 13.8C

Write the structural formulas for each of the following amides.

1. propanamide

2. butanamide

3. 3-chloropentanamide

4. benzamide

Answers   **1.** $CH_3{-}CH_2{-}\overset{\overset{\displaystyle O}{\|}}{C}{-}NH_2$ **2.** $CH_3{-}CH_2{-}CH_2{-}\overset{\overset{\displaystyle O}{\|}}{C}{-}NH_2$

3. $CH_3{-}CH_2{-}\overset{\overset{\displaystyle Cl}{|}}{C}H{-}CH_2{-}\overset{\overset{\displaystyle O}{\|}}{C}{-}NH_2$ **4.**

◆ Learning Exercise 13.8D

Write the structural formulas for the hydrolysis of each of the following with HCl and NaOH.

1. $CH_3{-}CH_2{-}\overset{\overset{\displaystyle O}{\|}}{C}{-}NH_2$

2. $CH_3{-}\overset{\overset{\displaystyle O}{\|}}{C}{-}NH_2$

Answers

1. (HCl) $CH_3—CH_2—\overset{\overset{\displaystyle O}{\|}}{C}—OH + NH_4^+\ Cl^-$ (NaOH)$CH_3—CH_2—\overset{\overset{\displaystyle O}{\|}}{C}—O^-\ Na^+ + NH_3$

2. (HCl) $CH_3—\overset{\overset{\displaystyle O}{\|}}{C}—OH + \overset{+}{N}H_4Cl^-$ (NaOH) $CH_3—\overset{\overset{\displaystyle O}{\|}}{C}—O^-\ Na^+ + NH_3$

Check List for Chapter 13

You are ready to take the practice test for Chapter 13. Be sure that you have accomplished the following learning goals for this chapter. If you are not sure, review the section listed at the end of the goal. Then apply your new skills and understanding to the practice test.

After studying Chapter 13, I can successfully:

_____ Write the IUPAC and common names and draw condensed structural formulas of carboxylic acids (13.1).

_____ Describe the solubility and ionization of carboxylic acids in water (13.2).

_____ Describe the behavior of carboxylic acids as weak acids and write the structural formulas for the products of neutralization (13.3).

_____ Write equations for the preparation of esters (13.4).

_____ Write the IUPAC or common names, and condensed structural formulas of esters (13.4).

_____ Write equations for the hydrolysis and saponification of esters (13.5).

_____ Classify amines as primary, secondary, or tertiary (13.6).

_____ Write the IUPAC and common names of amines and draw their condensed structural formulas (13.6).

_____ Compare the boiling points and solubility of amines to alkanes and alcohols of similar mass (13.7).

_____ Write equations for the ionization and neutralization of amines (13.7).

_____ Write the IUPAC and common names of amides and draw their condensed structural formulas (13.8).

_____ Write equations for the hydrolysis of amides (13.8).

Practice Test for Chapter 13

Match each structure to its functional group.

A. alcohol   **B.** aldehyde   **C.** carboxylic acid   **D.** ester   **E.** ketone

1. _____ $CH_3—\overset{\overset{\displaystyle CH_3}{|}}{CH}—CH_2—OH$ 2. _____ $CH_3—CH_2—\overset{\overset{\displaystyle O}{\|}}{C}—H$

3. _____ $CH_3—\overset{\overset{\displaystyle O}{\|}}{C}—CH_2—CH_3$ 4. _____ $CH_3—CH_2—\overset{\overset{\displaystyle O}{\|}}{C}—OH$

5. _____ $CH_3—\overset{\overset{\displaystyle O}{\|}}{C}—O—CH_3$

Match the names of the following compounds with their structures.

A. CH_3—$\overset{\overset{\displaystyle O}{\|}}{C}$—O—$CH_2$—$CH_3$ B. CH_3—CH_2—CH_2—$\overset{\overset{\displaystyle O}{\|}}{C}$—$O^-$ Na^+ C. CH_3—$\overset{\overset{\displaystyle O}{\|}}{C}$—$O^-$ Na^+

D. CH_3—CH_2—$\overset{\overset{\displaystyle CH_3}{|}}{CH}$—$\overset{\overset{\displaystyle O}{\|}}{C}$—OH   E. CH_3—CH_2—$\overset{\overset{\displaystyle O}{\|}}{C}$—O—$CH_3$

6. _____ 2-methylbutanoic acid

7. _____ methylpropanoate

8. _____ sodium butanoate

9. _____ ethyl acetate

10. _____ sodium acetate

11. An aldehyde can be oxidized to give a(n)

    A. alcohol.   B. ketone.   C. carboxylic acid.
    D. ester.   E. no reaction

12. What is the product when a carboxylic acid reacts with sodium hydroxide?

    A. carboxylic acid salt   B. alcohol   C. ester
    D. aldehyde   E. no reaction

13. Carboxylic acids are water soluble due to their

    A. nonpolar nature.   B. ionic bonds.   C. ability to lower pH.
    D. ability to hydrogen bond.   E. high melting points.

Questions 14 through 17 refer to the following reactions:

A. CH_3—$\overset{\overset{\displaystyle O}{\|}}{C}$—OH + CH_3—OH $\overset{H^+}{\longrightarrow}$ CH_3—$\overset{\overset{\displaystyle O}{\|}}{C}$—O—$CH_3$ + H_2O

B. CH_3—$\overset{\overset{\displaystyle O}{\|}}{C}$—OH + NaOH $\longrightarrow$ CH_3—$\overset{\overset{\displaystyle O}{\|}}{C}$—$O^-$ Na^+ + H_2O

C. CH_3—$\overset{\overset{\displaystyle O}{\|}}{C}$—O—$CH_3$ + H_2O $\overset{H^+}{\longrightarrow}$ CH_3—$\overset{\overset{\displaystyle O}{\|}}{C}$—OH + CH_3—OH

D. CH_3—$\overset{\overset{\displaystyle O}{\|}}{C}$—O—$CH_3$ + NaOH $\longrightarrow$ CH_3—$\overset{\overset{\displaystyle O}{\|}}{C}$—$O^-$ Na^+ + CH_3—OH

14. _____ is an ester hydrolysis.   15. _____ is a neutralization

16. _____ is a saponification.   17. _____ is an esterification.

18. What is the name of the organic product of reaction A?

    A. methyl acetate   B. acetic acid   C. methyl alcohol
    D. acetaldehyde   E. ethyl methanoate

19. The compound with the highest boiling point is

   A. formic acid.   **B.** acetic acid.   **C.** propanol.
   D. propanoic acid.   **E.** ethyl acetate.

20. The ester produced from the reactions of 1-butanol and propanoic acid is

   A. butyl propanoate.   **B.** butyl propanone.   **C.** propyl butyrate.
   D. propyl butanone.   **E.** heptanoate.

21. The reaction of methyl acetate with NaOH produces

   A. ethanol and formic acid
   B. ethanol and sodium formate
   C. ethanol and sodium ethanoate
   D. methanol and acetic acid
   E. methanol and sodium acetate

22. Identify the carboxylic acid and alcohol needed to produce

$$CH_3-CH_2-CH_2-\overset{\overset{\textstyle O}{\|}}{C}-O-CH_2-CH_3$$

   A. propanoic acid and ethanol   **B.** acetic acid and 1-pentanol
   C. acetic acid and 1-butanol   **D.** butanoic acid and ethanol
   E. hexanoic acid and methanol

23. When butanal is oxidized, the product is

   A. butanone.   **B.** 1-butanol.   **C.** 2-butanol.
   D. butanoic acid.   **E.** butane.

24. The name of $CH_3-CH_2-\overset{\overset{\textstyle O}{\|}}{C}-O-CH_2-CH_3$ is

   A. ethyl acetate.   **B.** ethyl ethanoate.   **C.** ethyl propanoate.
   D. propyl ethanoate.   **E.** ethyl butyrate.

25. Soaps are

   A. long chain fatty acids.   **B.** fatty acid salts.
   C. esters of acetic acid.   **D.** alcohols with 10 carbon atoms.
   E. aromatic compounds.

26. In a hydrolysis reaction,

   A. an acid reacts with an alcohol.
   B. an ester reacts with NaOH.
   C. an ester reacts with H_2O.
   D. an acid neutralizes a base.
   E. water is added to an alkene.

27. Esters

   A. have pleasant odors.
   B. can undergo hydrolysis.
   C. are formed from alcohols and carboxylic acids.
   D. have a lower boiling point than the corresponding acid.
   E. all of the above

28. The products of $H-\overset{\overset{\displaystyle O}{\|}}{C}-OH + H_2O$ are

A. $H-\overset{\overset{\displaystyle O}{\|}}{C}-O^- + H_3O^+$

B. $H-\overset{\overset{\displaystyle O}{\|}}{C}-\overset{+}{O}H_2 + OH^-$

C. $H-\overset{\overset{\displaystyle O}{\|}}{C}-O-CH_3$

D. $CH_3-\overset{\overset{\displaystyle O}{\|}}{C}-OH$

E. $H-\overset{\overset{\displaystyle O}{\|}}{C}-O^- Na^+ + H_2O$

Classify the amines in questions 29 through 32 as

A. primary amine   B. secondary amine   C. tertiary amine

29. _____ $CH_3-\overset{\overset{\displaystyle CH_3}{|}}{CH}-NH_2$

30. _____ $CH_3-CH_2-\overset{\overset{\displaystyle CH_3}{|}}{N}-CH_3$

31. _____ $CH_3-CH_2-\overset{\overset{\displaystyle NH_2}{|}}{CH}-CH_2-CH_3$

32. _____ $CH_3-\overset{\overset{\displaystyle H}{|}}{N}-CH_2-CH_3$

Match the amines and amides in questions 33–35 with the following names.

A. ethyl dimethyl amine   B. butanamide   C. N-methylacetamide
D. benzamide   E. N-ethylbutyramide

33. $CH_3-CH_2-\overset{\overset{\displaystyle CH_3}{|}}{N}-CH_3$

34. $CH_3-CH_2-CH_2-\overset{\overset{\displaystyle O}{\|}}{C}-NH_2$

35.

Use the following products to complete the reactions in questions 36 through 39.

A. $CH_3-CH_2-\overset{\overset{\displaystyle O}{\|}}{C}-OH + NH_3$

B. $CH_3-CH_2-NH_3^+ Cl^-$

C. $CH_3-CH_2-CH_2-NH_3^+ OH^-$

D. $CH_3-\overset{\overset{\displaystyle O}{\|}}{C}-NH_2$

36. _____ ionization of 1-propanamine in water

37. _____ hydrolysis of propanamide

38. _____ reaction of ethanamine and hydrochloric acid

39. _____ amidation of acetic acid

40. Amines used in drugs are converted to their amine salt because the salt is

    A. a solid at room temperature.   **B.** soluble in water.   **C.** odorless.
    D. soluble in body fluids.   **E.** all of these.

Match the following alkaloids with their sources

    A. caffeine   **B.** nicotine   **C.** morphine   **E.** quinine

41. a painkiller from the Oriental poppy plant

42. obtained from the bark of the cinchona tree and used in the treatment of malaria

43. a stimulant obtained from the leaves of tobacco plants

44. a stimulant obtained from coffee beans and tea

Answers to the Practice Test

1. A	**2.** B	**3.** E	**4.** C	**5.** D
6. D	**7.** E	**8.** B	**9.** A	**10.** C
11. C	**12.** A	**13.** D	**14.** C	**15.** B
16. D	**17.** A	**18.** A	**19.** D	**20.** A
21. E	**22.** D	**23.** D	**24.** C	**25.** B
26. C	**27.** E	**28.** A	**29.** A	**30.** C
31. A	**32.** B	**33.** A	**34.** B	**35.** D
36. C	**37.** A	**38.** B	**39.** D	**40.** E
41. C	**42.** E	**43.** B	**44.** A	

Answers and Solutions To Selected Text Problems

13.1 Methanoic acid (formic acid) is the carboxylic acid that is responsible for the pain associated with ant stings.

13.3 Each compound contains three carbon atoms. They differ because propanal, an aldehyde, contains a carbonyl group bonded to a hydrogen. In propanoic acid, the carbonyl group connects to a hydroxyl group.

13.5 a. Ethanoic acid (acetic acid) is the carboxylic acid with two carbons.
    b. propanoic acid (propionic acid) is a three-carbon carboxylic acid.
    c. 4-hydroxybenzoic acid has a carboxylic acid group on benzene and a hydroxyl group on carbon 4.
    d. 4-bromopentanoic acid is a five-carbon carboxylic acid with a –Br atom on carbon 4.

13.7

a. $CH_3-CH_2-\overset{\overset{\displaystyle O}{\|}}{C}-OH$ Propionic acid has three carbons.

b.

           Benzoic acid is the carboxylic acid of benzene.

c. $Cl-CH_2-\overset{\overset{\displaystyle O}{\|}}{C}-OH$ 2-chloroethanoic acid is a carboxylic acid that has a two-carbon chain with a chlorine atom on carbon 2.

d. $HO-CH_2-CH_2-\overset{\overset{\displaystyle O}{\|}}{C}-OH$ 3-hydroxypropanoic acid is a carboxylic acid that has a three-carbon chain with a hydroxyl on carbon 3.

e. $CH_3-CH_2-CH_2-\overset{\overset{\displaystyle O}{\|}}{C}-OH$ butyric acid is a carboxylic acid that has a four-carbon chain.

f. $CH_3-CH_2-CH_2-CH_2-CH_2-CH_2-\overset{\overset{\displaystyle O}{\|}}{C}-OH$ heptanoic acid is a carboxylic acid that has a seven-carbon chain.

13.9 a. Butanoic acid has a higher molar mass and would have a higher boiling point.
b. Propanoic acid can form more hydrogen bonds and would have a higher boiling point.
c. Butanoic acid can form more hydrogen bonds and would have a higher boiling point.

13.11   **a.** Propanoic acid has three carbon atoms and the lowest molar mass of the group.
  b. Propionic acid forms the most hydrogen bonds of the three compounds.

13.13   **a.** $H-\overset{\overset{\displaystyle O}{\|}}{C}-OH + H_2O \longrightarrow H-\overset{\overset{\displaystyle O}{\|}}{C}-O^- + H_3O^+$

    b. $CH_3-CH_2-\overset{\overset{\displaystyle O}{\|}}{C}-OH + H_2O \longrightarrow CH_3-CH_2-\overset{\overset{\displaystyle O}{\|}}{C}-O^- + H_3O^+$

    c. $CH_3-\overset{\overset{\displaystyle O}{\|}}{C}-OH + H_2O \longrightarrow CH_3-\overset{\overset{\displaystyle O}{\|}}{C}-O^- + H_3O^+$

13.15   **a.** $H-\overset{\overset{\displaystyle O}{\|}}{C}-OH + NaOH \longrightarrow H-\overset{\overset{\displaystyle O}{\|}}{C}-O^-\ Na^+ + H_2O$

    b. $CH_3-CH_2-\overset{\overset{\displaystyle O}{\|}}{C}-OH + NaOH \longrightarrow CH_3-CH_2-\overset{\overset{\displaystyle O}{\|}}{C}-O^-\ Na^+ + H_2O$

c.

$$+ \text{ NaOH} \longrightarrow$$

$$+ \text{ H}_2\text{O}$$

13.17 **a.** This is an *aldehyde* since it has a carbonyl bonded to carbon and hydrogen.
  b. This is an *ester* since it has a carbonyl bonded to oxygen that is also bonded to a carbon.
  c. This is a *ketone* since it has a carbonyl bonded to two carbon atoms.
  d. This is a *carboxylic acid* since it has a carboxylic group; a carbonyl bonded to a hydroxyl.

13.19 **a.**
$$\text{CH}_3-\overset{\overset{\displaystyle O}{\|}}{\text{C}}-\text{O}-\text{CH}_3$$
The carbonyl portion of the ester has two carbons bonded to a one-carbon methyl group.

  b.
$$\text{CH}_3-\text{CH}_2-\text{CH}_2-\overset{\overset{\displaystyle O}{\|}}{\text{C}}-\text{OCH}_3$$
The carbonyl portion of the ester is a four-carbon chain bonded to a one-carbon methyl group.

  c.

13.21 A carboxylic acid and an alcohol react to give an ester with the elimination of water.

  a.
$$\text{CH}_3-\text{CH}_2-\overset{\overset{\displaystyle O}{\|}}{\text{C}}-\text{O}-\text{CH}_2-\text{CH}_2-\text{CH}_3$$

  b.
$$\text{CH}_3-\text{CH}_2-\text{CH}_2-\text{CH}_2-\overset{\overset{\displaystyle O}{\|}}{\text{C}}-\text{O}-\overset{\overset{\displaystyle \text{CH}_3}{|}}{\text{CH}}-\text{CH}_3$$

13.23 **a.** The name of this ester is methyl methanoate (methyl formate). The carbonyl portion of the ester contains one carbon, the name is derived from methanoic (formic) acid. The alkyl portion has one carbon; it is methyl.
  b. The name of this ester is methyl ethanoate (methyl acetate). The carbonyl portion of the ester contains two carbons; the name is derived from ethanoic (acetic) acid. The alkyl portion has one carbon; it is methyl.
  c. The name of this ester is methyl butanoate (methyl butyrate). The carbonyl portion of the ester contains four carbons; the name is derived from butanoic (butyric) acid. The alkyl portion has one carbon; it is methyl.
  d. The name of this ester is ethyl butanoate (ethyl butyrate). The carbonyl portion of the ester has a four-carbon chain. The alkyl portion with two carbons is an ethyl.

13.25 **a.**
$$\text{CH}_3-\overset{\overset{\displaystyle O}{\|}}{\text{C}}-\text{O}-\text{CH}_3$$
Acetic acid is the two-carbon carboxylic acid. Methanol gives a one-carbon alkyl group.

13.25 **a.** CH_3—$\overset{\displaystyle O}{\overset{\displaystyle \|}{C}}$—O—$CH_3$ Acetic acid is the two-carbon carboxylic acid. Methanol gives a one-carbon alkyl group.

b. H—$\overset{\displaystyle O}{\overset{\displaystyle \|}{C}}$—O—$CH_2$—$CH_2$—$CH_2$—$CH_3$ Formic acid is the carboxylic acid bonded to the four-carbon 1-butanol.

c. CH_3—CH_2—CH_2—CH_2—$\overset{\displaystyle O}{\overset{\displaystyle \|}{C}}$—O—$CH_2$—$CH_3$ Pentanoic acid is the carboxylic acid bonded to ethanol.

d.
CH_3—CH_2—$\overset{\displaystyle O}{\overset{\displaystyle \|}{C}}$—O—$CH_2$—$CH_2$—$CH_3$ Propanoic acid is the carboxylic acid bonded to propanol.

13.27 **a.** The flavor and odor of bananas is pentyl ethanoate (pentyl acetate).
b. The flavor and odor of oranges is octyl ethanoate (octyl acetate).
c. The flavor and odor of apricots is pentyl butanoate (pentyl butyrate).

13.29 Acid hydrolysis of an ester adds water in the presence of acid and gives a carboxylic acid and an alcohol.

13.31 Acid hydrolysis of an ester gives the carboxylic acid and the alcohol, which were combined to form the ester; basic hydrolysis of an ester gives the salt of carboxylic acid and the alcohol, which combine to form the ester.

a. CH_3—CH_2—$\overset{\displaystyle O}{\overset{\displaystyle \|}{C}}$—$O^-$ Na^+ and CH_3—OH

b. CH_3—$\overset{\displaystyle O}{\overset{\displaystyle \|}{C}}$—OH and CH_3—CH_2—CH_2—OH

c. CH_3—CH_2—CH_2—$\overset{\displaystyle O}{\overset{\displaystyle \|}{C}}$—OH and CH_3—CH_2—OH

d.

$\langle\!\!\bigcirc\!\!\rangle$—$COO^-$ Na^+ and CH_3CH_2OH

13.33 **a.** This is a primary (1°) amine; there is only one alkyl group attached to the nitrogen atom.
b. This is a secondary (2°) amine; there are two alkyl groups attached to the nitrogen atom.
c. This is a tertiary (3°) amine; there are three alkyl groups attached to the nitrogen atom.
d. This is a tertiary (3°) amine; there are three alkyl groups attached to the nitrogen atom.

13.35 The common name of an amine consists of naming the alkyl groups bonding to the nitrogen atom in alphabetical order. In the IUPAC name, the *e* in the alkane chain is replaced with *amine*.

a. An ethyl group attached to —NH_2 is ethylamine. In the IUPAC name, the *e* in ethane is replaced by *amine*: ethanamine.
b. Two alkyl groups attach to nitrogen as methyl and propyl for methylpropylamine. The IUPAC name based on the longer chain of propane with a methyl group attached to the nitrogen atoms is *N*-methyl-1-propanamine
c. Diethylmethylamine; *N*-methyl-*N*-ethylethanamine
d. Isopropylamine; 2-propanamine

13.37 **a.** CH_3—CH_2—NH_2

  b.

NHCH$_3$

  c. CH_3—CH_2—CH_2—CH_2—$\overset{\overset{\displaystyle H}{|}}{N}$—$CH_2$—$CH_2$—$CH_3$

13.39 Amines have higher boiling points than hydrocarbons, but lower than alcohols of similar mass.

  a. CH_3—CH_2—OH **b.** CH_3—CH_2—CH_2—NH_2 **c.** CH_3—CH_2—CH_2—NH_2

13.41 Amines with one to five carbon atoms are soluble. The solubility in water of amines with longer carbon chains decreases.

  a. yes   **b.** yes   **c.** no   **d.** yes

13.43 Amines, which are weak bases, bond with a proton from water to give a hydroxide ion and an ammonium ion.

  a. CH_3—$NH_2 + H_2O \rightleftarrows CH_3$—$NH_3^+ + OH^-$

  b. CH_3—$\overset{\overset{\displaystyle CH_3}{|}}{N}H + H_2O \rightleftarrows CH_3$—$\overset{\overset{\displaystyle CH_3}{|}}{N}H_2^+ + OH^-$

  c.

13.45 **a.** H_2N—⬡—$\overset{\overset{\displaystyle O}{\|}}{C}$—$O$—$CH_2$—$CH_2$—$\overset{\overset{\displaystyle CH_2CH_3}{|}}{\underset{\underset{\displaystyle CH_2CH_3}{|}}{\overset{+}{N}}}$—$H$ Cl^-

  b. Amine salts are soluble in body fluids.

13.47 **a.** Ethanamide (Acetamide) tells us that this amide has two carbon atoms.
  b. Butanamide (butyramide) is a chain a four carbon atoms bonded to an amino group.
  c. Methanamide (formamide)

13.49 **a.** This is an amide of propionic acid, which has three carbon atoms.

  CH_3—CH_2—$\overset{\overset{\displaystyle O}{\|}}{C}$—$NH_2$

  b. 2-methyl indicates that a methyl is bonded to carbon 2 in an amide chain of five carbon atoms.

  CH_3—CH_2—CH_2—$\overset{\overset{\displaystyle CH_3}{|}}{C}H$—$\overset{\overset{\displaystyle O}{\|}}{C}$—$NH_2$

  c. H—$\overset{\overset{\displaystyle O}{\|}}{C}$—$NH_2$

13.51 Acid hydrolysis of amides gives the carboxylic acid and the amine salt.

  a. $CH_3-COOH + NH_4^+ Cl^-$

  b. $CH_3-CH_2-COOH + NH_4^+ Cl^-$

  c. $CH_3-CH_2-CH_2-COOH + CH_3-NH_3^+ Cl^-$

  d. $-COOH + NH_4^+ Cl^-$

  e. $CH_3-CH_2-CH_2-CH_2-COOH + CH_3-CH_2-NH_3^+ Cl^-$

13.53 **a.** 3-methylbutanoic acid
  b. ethyl benzoate
  c. ethyl propanoate; ethylpropionate
  d. 2-chlorobenzoic acid
  e. pentanoic acid

13.55 **a.**
$$CH_3-O-\overset{\overset{\displaystyle O}{\|}}{C}-CH_3$$

  b.
$$CH_3-CH_2-O-\overset{\overset{\displaystyle O}{\|}}{C}-CH_2-CH_2-CH_3$$

  c.
$$CH_3-CH_2-\overset{\overset{\displaystyle CH_3}{|}}{CH}-CH_2-\overset{\overset{\displaystyle O}{\|}}{C}-OH$$

  d.
$$\overset{\overset{\displaystyle O}{\|}}{C}-O-CH_2-CH_3$$
(attached to benzene ring)

13.57 **a.** $CH_3-\overset{\overset{\displaystyle O}{\|}}{C}-OH$ **b.** $CH_3-CH_2-\overset{\overset{\displaystyle O}{\|}}{C}-OH$ **c.** $CH_3-CH_2-CH_2-\overset{\overset{\displaystyle O}{\|}}{C}-OH$

13.59 b and c are soluble in water

13.61

  a. $CH_3-CH_2-\overset{\overset{\displaystyle O}{\|}}{C}-O^- K^+ + H_2O$

  b. $CH_3-CH_2-\overset{\overset{\displaystyle O}{\|}}{C}-O-CH_3 + H_2O$

  c. $\overset{\overset{\displaystyle O}{\|}}{C}-O-CH_2-CH_3 + H_2O$
(attached to benzene ring)

13.63 **a.** CH₃—CH₂—C(=O)—OH and HO—CH(CH₃)—CH₃

$$\text{CH}_3\text{—CH}_2\overset{\text{O}}{\overset{\|}{\text{—C}}}\text{—OH} \quad \text{and} \quad \text{HO—}\overset{\text{CH}_3}{\overset{|}{\text{CH}}}\text{—CH}_3$$

b. $$\overset{\text{CH}_3}{\overset{|}{\text{CH}_3\text{—CH}}}\overset{\text{O}}{\overset{\|}{\text{—C}}}\text{—OH} \quad \text{and} \quad \text{HO—CH}_2\text{—CH}_2\text{—CH}_3$$

13.65 **a.** $$\text{CH}_3\text{—CH}_2\overset{\text{NH}_2}{\overset{|}{\text{—CH}}}\text{—CH}_2\text{—CH}_3$$

b.

c. This is an ammonium salt with two methyl groups bonded to the nitrogen atom.

$$\overset{\text{CH}_3}{\overset{|}{\text{CH}_3\text{—NH}_2^+}}\text{ Cl}^-$$

d. Three ethyl groups are bonded to a nitrogen atom

$$\text{CH}_3\text{—CH}_2\overset{\text{CH}_2\text{—CH}_3}{\overset{|}{\text{—N—}}}\text{CH}_2\text{—CH}_3$$

e. This six-carbon chain has a —NH₂ group on carbon 3 and an —OH on carbon 2.

$$\text{CH}_3\text{—CH}_2\overset{\text{NH}_2}{\overset{|}{\text{—CH}}}\text{—CH}_2\text{—CH}_2\text{—CH}_3$$

13.67 The smaller amines are more soluble in water.

a. ethylamine	**b.** trimethylamine
c. butylamine	**d.** NH₂—CH₂—CH₂—CH₂—NH₂

13.69 **a.** An amine in water accepts a proton from water, which produces an ammonium ion and OH⁻.

CH₃—CH₂—NH₃⁺ OH⁻

b. The amine accepts a proton to give an ammonium salt: CH₃—CH₂—NH₃⁺ Cl⁻

c. CH₃—CH₂—N⁺H₂—CH₃ OH⁻

d. CH₃—CH₂—N⁺H₂—CH₃ Cl⁻

e. An ammonium salt and a strong base produce the amine, a salt, and water.

CH₃—CH₂—CH₂—NH₂ + NaCl + H₂O

13.71 carboxylic acid salt, aromatic, amine

13.73 **a.** aromatic, amine, amide, carboxylic acid, cycloalkene
  b. aromatic, ether, alcohol, amine
  c. aromatic, carboxylic acid
  d. phenol, amine, carboxylic acid
  e. aromatic, ether, alcohol, amine, ketone
  f. aromatic, amine

Study Goals

- Identify the common carbohydrates in the diet.
- Distinguish between monosaccharides, disaccharides, and polysaccharides.
- Identify the chiral carbons in a carbohydrate.
- Label the Fischer projection for a monosaccharide as the D- or L- enantiomer.
- Write Haworth structures for monosaccharides.
- Describe the structural units and bonds in disaccharides and polysaccharides.

Think About It

1. What are some foods you eat that contain carbohydrates?

2. What elements are found in carbohydrates?

3. What carbohydrates are present in table sugar, milk, and wood?

4. What is meant by a "high-fiber" diet?

Key Terms

Match the following key terms with the descriptions shown below.

A. carbohydrate   **B.** glucose   **C.** disaccharide   **D.** Haworth structure   **E.** cellulose

1. _____ A simple or complex sugar composed of a carbon chain with an aldehyde or ketone group and several hydroxyl groups

2. _____ A cyclic structure that represents the closed chain form of a monosaccharide

3. _____ An unbranched polysaccharide that cannot be digested by humans

4. _____ An aldohexose that is the most prevalent monosaccharide in the diet

5. _____ A carbohydrate that contains two monosaccharides linked by a glycosidic bond

Answers   **1.** A   **2.** D   **3.** E   **4.** B   **5.** C

14.1 Carbohydrates

- Carbohydrates are classified as monosaccharides (simple sugars), disaccharides (two monosaccharide units), and polysaccharides (many monosaccharide units).

◆ Learning Exercise 14.1A

Complete and balance the equations for the photosynthesis of

1. glucose: _____ + _____ $\longrightarrow C_6H_{12}O_6 +$ _____

2. ribose: _____ + _____ $\longrightarrow C_5H_{10}O_5 +$ _____

Answers   **1.** $6CO_2 + 6H_2O \longrightarrow C_6H_{12}O_6 + 6O_2$
       2. $5CO_2 + 5H_2O \longrightarrow C_5H_{10}O_5 + 5O_2$

◆ Learning Exercise 14.1B

Indicate the number of monosaccharide units (1, 2, or many) in each of the following carbohydrates.

1. Sucrose, a disaccharide _____   **2.** Cellulose, a polysaccharide _____

3. Glucose, a monosaccharide _____   **4.** Amylose, a polysaccharide _____

5. Maltose, a disaccharide _____

Answers   **1.** two   **2.** many   **3.** one   **4.** many   **5.** two

14.2 Classification of Monosaccharides

- In a chiral molecule, there is one or more carbon atoms attached to four different atoms or groups.
- Monosaccharides are polyhydroxy alddehyes (aldoses) or ketones (ketoses).
- Monosaccharides are classified by the number of carbon atoms as *trioses, tetroses, pentoses, or hexoses.*

◆ Learning Exercise 14.2

Identify the following monosaccharides as aldo- or ketotrioses, tetroses, pentoses, or hexoses.

1. CH$_2$OH
   C=O
   CH$_2$OH

2. H O
   \ //
   C
   H—C—OH
   H—C—OH
   HO—C—H
   CH$_2$OH

3. CH$_2$OH
   C=O
   HO—C—H
   HO—C—H
   H—C—OH
   CH$_2$OH

4. H O
   \ //
   C
   H—C—OH
   HO—C—H
   H—C—OH
   H—C—OH
   CH$_2$OH

5. H O
   \ //
   C
   H—C—OH
   H—C—OH
   CH$_2$OH

1. _____   **2.** _____

3. _____   **4.** _____

5. _____

Answers   **1.** ketotriose   **2.** aldopentose   **3.** ketohexose
            4. aldohexose   **5.** aldotetrose

14.3 D and L Notations from Fischer Projections

- In a Fischer projection (straight chain), the prefixes D- and L- are used to distinguish between the mirror images. In D-glyceraldehyde, the —OH is on the right of the chiral carbon; it is on the left in L-glyceraldehyde.
- In the Fischer projection of a monosaccharide, the chiral —OH farthest from the carbonyl group (C=O) is on the left side in the L-isomer, and on the right side in the D-isomer.

◆ **Learning Exercise 14.3A**

Identify each of the following sugars as the D- or L- isomer.

1. CH_2OH
  |
  $C=O$
  |
  $HOCH$
  |
  $HCOH$
  |
  CH_2OH

  ____-Xylulose

2. CHO
  |
  $HCOH$
  |
  $HCOH$
  |
  $HOCH$
  |
  $HOCH$
  |
  CH_2OH

  ____-Mannos

3. CHO
  |
  $HOCH$
  |
  $HCOH$
  |
  CH_2OH

  ____-Threose

4. CH_2OH
  |
  $C=O$
  |
  $HOCH$
  |
  $HOCH$
  |
  CH_2OH

  ____-Ribulose

Answers **1.** D-Xylulose **2.** L-Mannose **3.** D-Threose **4.** L-Ribulose

◆ **Learning Exercise 14.3B**

Write the mirror image of each of the sugars in learning exercise 14.3A and give the D- or L-name.

1. **2.** **3.** **4.**

Answers

1. CH_2OH
  |
  $C=O$
  |
  $HCOH$
  |
  $HOCH$
  |
  CH_2OH

  L-Xylulose

2. CHO
  |
  $HOCH$
  |
  $HOCH$
  |
  $HCOH$
  |
  $HCOH$
  |
  CH_2OH

  D-Mannose

3. CHO
  |
  $HCOH$
  |
  $HOCH$
  |
  CH_2OH

  L-Threose

4. CH_2OH
  |
  $C=O$
  |
  $HCOH$
  |
  $HCOH$
  |
  CH_2OH

  D-Ribulose

14.4 Structures of Some Important Monosaccharides

- Important monosaccharides are the aldohexoses glucose and galactose and the ketohexose fructose.

◆ Learning Exercise 14.4A

Identify the monosaccharide (glucose, fructose, or galactose) that fits the following description.

1. obtained as a hydrolysis product of amylose   _____

2. also known as fruit sugar   _____

3. accumulates in the disease known as *galactosemia*   _____

4. the monosaccharide unit in cellulose   _____

5. also known as blood sugar   _____

Answers   **1.** glucose   **2.** fructose   **3.** galactose   **4.** glucose   **5.** glucose

◆ Learning Exercise 14.4B

Draw the open-chain structure for the following monosaccharides:

D-Glucose   D-Galactose   D-Fructose

Answers

D-glucose   D-Galactose   D-Fructose

14.5 Cyclic Structures of Monosaccharides

- The predominant form of monosaccharides is the cyclic form of five or six atoms called the Haworth structure. The cyclic structure forms by a reaction between an OH on carbon 5 in hexoses with the carbonyl group of the same molecule.
- The formation of a new hydroxyl group on carbon 1 (or 2 in fructose) gives α and β anomers of the cyclic monosaccharide. Because the molecule opens and closes continuously (mutarotation) while in solution, both anomers are present.

◆ Learning Exercise 14.5

Write the Haworth structures (α-anomers) for the following.

1. D-Glucose
2. D-Galactose
3. D-Fructose

Answers

α-D-Glucose   α-D-Galactose   α-D-Fructose

14.6 Chemical Properties of Monosaccharides

- Monosaccharides contain functional groups that undergo oxidation or reduction.
- Monosaccharides are called *reducing sugars* because the aldehyde group (also available in ketoses) is oxidized by a metal ion such as Cu^{2+} in Benedict's solution, which is reduced.
- Monosaccharides are also reduced to give sugar alcohols.

◆ Learning Exercise 14.6

What changes occur when a reducing sugar reacts with Benedict's reagent?

Answers   The carbonyl group of the reducing sugar is oxidized to a carboxylic acid group; the Cu^{2+} ion in Benedict's reagent is reduced to Cu^+, which forms a brick-red solid of Cu_2O.

14.7 Disaccharides

- Disaccharides are glycosides, two monosaccharide units joined together by a glycosidic bond:

$$\text{monosaccharide(1)} + \text{monosaccharide (2)} \longrightarrow \text{disaccharide} + H_2O$$

- In the most common disaccharides, maltose, lactose, and sucrose, there is at least one glucose unit.
- In the disaccharide maltose, two glucose units are linked by an α-1,4-glycosidic bond. The α-1,4 indicates that the —OH of the alpha anomer at carbon 1 was bonded to the —OH on carbon 4 of the other glucose molecule.
- When a disaccharide is hydrolyzed by water, the products are a glucose unit and one other monosaccharide.

$$\text{Maltose} + H_2O \longrightarrow \text{Glucose} + \text{Glucose}$$
$$\text{Lactose} + H_2O \longrightarrow \text{Glucose} + \text{Galactose}$$
$$\text{Sucrose} + H_2O \longrightarrow \text{Glucose} + \text{Fructose}$$

◆ **Learning Exercise 14.7**

a. What is a glycosidic bond?

b. For the following disaccharides, state (a) the monosaccharide units, (b) the type of glycosidic bond, and (c) the name of the disaccharide.

	a. Monosaccharide(s)	b. Type of glycosidic bond	c. Name of dissacharide
1.			
2.			

3.

4.

	a. Monosaccharide units	b. Type of glycosidic bond	c. Name of disaccharide
3.			
4.			

Answers   **a.** A glycosidic bond forms between the OH of a sugar with the —OH of another compound, usually another sugar.

    b. **1.** (**a**) two glucose units   (**b**) α-1,4-glycosidic bond   (**c**) β-maltose

    2. (**a**) galactose + glucose   (**b**) β-1,4-glycosidic bond   (**c**) α-lactose

    3. (**a**) fructose + glucose   (**b**) α-1, β-2 glycosidic bond   (**c**) sucrose

    4. (**a**) two glucose units   (**b**) α-1,4-glycosidic bond   (**c**) α-maltose

14.8 Polysaccharides

- Polysaccharides are polymers of monosaccharide units.
- Starches consist of amylose, an unbranched chain of glucose; amylopectin is a branched polymer of glucose. Glycogen, the storage form of glucose in animals, is similar to amylopectin with more branching.
- Cellulose is also a polymer of glucose, but in cellulose the glycosidic bonds are β bonds rather than α bonds as in the starches. Humans can digest starches to obtain energy, but not cellulose. However, cellulose is important as a source of fiber in our diets.

◆ Learning Exercise 14.8

List the monosaccharides and describe the glycosidic bonds in each of the following carbohydrates:

	Monosaccharides	Type(s) of glycosidic bonds
1. amylose	_____	_____
2. amylopectin	_____	_____
3. glycogen	_____	_____
4. cellulose	_____	_____

Answers 1. glucose; α-1,4-glycosidic bonds   2. glucose; α-1,4- and α-1,6-glycosidic bonds
3. glucose; α-1,4- and α-1,6-glycosidic bonds   4. glucose; β-1,4-glycosidic bonds

Check List for Chapter 14

You are ready to take the practice test for Chapter 14. Be sure that you have accomplished the following learning goals for this chapter. If you are not sure, review the section listed at the end of the goal. Then apply your new skills and understanding to the practice test.

After studying Chapter 14, I can successfully:

_____ Classify carbohydrates as monosaccharides, disaccharides, and polysaccharides (14.1).

_____ Classify a monosaccharide as an aldose or ketose and indicate the number of carbon atoms (14.2).

_____ Draw and identify D- and L- Fischer projections for carbohydrate molecules (14.3).

_____ Draw the open-chain structures for D-glucose, D-galactose, and D-fructose (14.4).

_____ Draw or identify the cyclic structures of monosaccharides (14.5).

_____ Describe some chemical properties of carbohydrates (14.6).

_____ Describe the monosaccharide units and linkages in disaccharides (14.7).

_____ Describe the structural features of amylose, amylopectin, glycogen, and cellulose (14.8).

Practice Test for Chapter 14

1. The requirements for photosynthesis are

   A. sun.   B. sun and water.   C. water and carbon dioxide.
   D. sun, water, and carbon dioxide.   E. carbon dioxide and sun.

2. What are the products of photosynthesis?

   A. carbohydrates   B. carbohydrates and oxygen
   C. carbon dioxide and oxygen   D. carbohydrates and carbon dioxide
   E. water and oxygen

3. The name "carbohydrate" came from the fact that

   A. carbohydrates are hydrates of water.
   B. carbohydrates contain hydrogen and oxygen in a 2:1 ratio.
   C. carbohydrates contain a great quantity of water.
   D. all plants produce carbohydrates.
   E. carbon and hydrogen atoms are abundant in carbohydrates.

4. What functional groups are in the open chains of monosaccharides?

   A. hydroxyl groups
   B. aldehyde groups
   C. ketone groups
   D. hydroxyl and aldehyde or ketone groups
   E. hydroxyl and ether groups

5. What is the classification of the following sugar?

CH_2OH

$C=O$

CH_2OH

   A. aldotriose   B. ketotriose   C. aldotetrose   D. ketotetrose   E. ketopentose

Questions 6 through 10 refer to

CH_2OH

O   OH

OH

HO

OH

6. It is the cyclic structure of an

   A. aldotriose.   B. ketopentose.   C. aldopentose.
   D. aldohexose.   E. aldoheptose.

7. This is a Haworth structure of

   A. fructose.   B. glucose.   C. ribose.
   D. glyceraldehyde.   E. galactose.

8. It is at least one of the products of the complete hydrolysis of

   A. maltose.   B. sucrose.   C. lactose.
   D. glycogen.   E. all of these

9. A Benedict's test with this sugar would

   A. be positive.   B. be negative.   C. produce a blue precipitate.
   D. give no color change. E. produce a silver mirror.

10. It is the monosaccharide unit used to build polymers of

   A. amylose.   B. amylopectin.   C. cellulose.
   D. glycogen   E. all of these

Identify each of the carbohydrates described in 11 through 15 as:

A. maltose   B. sucrose   C. cellulose
D. amylopectin   E. glycogen

11. _____ A disaccharide that is not a reducing sugar

12. _____ A disaccharide that occurs as a breakdown product of amylose

13. _____ A carbohydrate that is produced as a storage form of energy in plants

14. _____ The storage form of energy in humans

15. _____ A carbohydrate that is used for structural purposes by plants

For questions 16 through 20 select answers from:

A. amylose   **B.** cellulose   **C.** glycogen   **D.** lactose   **E.** sucrose

16. _____ A polysaccharide composed of many glucose units linked by α-1,4-glycosidic bonds.

17. _____ A sugar containing both glucose and galactose.

18. _____ A sugar composed of glucose units joined by both α-1,4- and α-1,6-glycosidic bonds.

19. _____ A sugar that has no anomeric forms.

20. _____ A carbohydrate composed of glucose units joined by β-1,4-glycosidic bonds.

For questions 21 through 25, select answers from the following:

A. amylose   **B.** lactose   **C.** sucrose   **D.** maltose

21. _____ A sugar composed of glucose and fructose

22. _____ Gives a positive Benedict's test, but is negative for fermentation

23. _____ Gives a negative Benedict's test and a positive fermentation test

24. _____ Gives a positive iodine test

25. _____ Gives galactose upon hydrolysis

Answers to the Practice Test

1. D	**2.** B	**3.** B	**4.** D	**5.** B
6. D	**7.** B	**8.** E	**9.** A	**10.** E
11. B	**12.** A	**13.** D	**14.** E	**15.** C
16. A	**17.** D	**18.** C	**19.** E	**20.** B
21. C	**22.** B	**23.** C	**24.** A	**25.** B

Answers and Solutions to Selected Text Problems

14.1   Photosynthesis requires CO_2, H_2O, and the energy from the sun. Respiration requires O_2 from the air and glucose from our foods.

14.3   A monosaccharide cannot be split into smaller carbohydrates. A disaccharide is composed of two monosaccharide units.

14.5   Hydroxyl groups and a carbonyl are found in all monosaccharides.

14.7   The name ketopentose tells us that the compound contains a ketone functional group and has five carbon atoms. In addition, all monosaccharides contain hydroxyl groups.

14.9
  a. This monosaccharide is a ketose; it has a carbonyl between two carbon atoms.
  b. This monosaccharide is an aldose; it has a CHO, an aldehyde group.
  c. This monosaccharide is a ketose; it has a carbonyl between two carbon atoms.
  d. This monosaccharide is an aldose; it has a CHO, an aldehyde group.
  e. This monosaccharide is an aldose; it has a CHO, an aldehyde group.

14.11   A Fischer projection is a two-dimensional representation of the three-dimensional structure of a molecule.

14.13
  a. This structure is a D-isomer since the hydroxyl on the chiral carbon farthest from the carbonyl is on the right.
  b. This structure is a D-isomer since the hydroxyl on the chiral carbon farthest from the carbonyl is on the right.
  c. This structure is an L-isomer since the hydroxyl on the chiral carbon farthest from the carbonyl is on the left.

d. This structure is a D-isomer since the hydroxyl on the chiral carbon farthest from the carbonyl is on the right.

14.15

a.

b..

c.

d.

CHO
HO——H
HO——H
HO——H
HO——H
CH₂OH

14.17 L-glucose is the mirror image of D-glucose.

D-glucose   L-glucose

14.19 In D-galactose the hydroxyl on carbon four extends to the left; in glucose this hydroxyl group goes to the right.

14.21 **a.** Glucose is also called blood sugar.
b. Galactose is not metabolized in the condition called galactosemia.
c. Another name for fructose is fruit sugar.

14.23 In the cyclic structure of glucose, there are five carbon atoms and an oxygen atom in the ring.

14.25 In the α anomer, the hydroxyl (—OH) on carbon 1 is down; the β anomer has the hydroxyl (—OH) on carbon 1 up;

α-D-Glucose   β-D-Glucose

14.27 **a.** This is the α-anomer because the —OH on carbon 1 is down.
   b. This is the α-anomer because the —OH on carbon 1 is down.

14.29

```
        CH₂OH
          |
   H —— C —— OH
          |
  HO —— C —— H
          |
   H —— C —— OH
          |
        CH₂OH
        Xylitol
```

14.31 Oxidation product:

```
          O
          ‖
          C —— OH
          |
  HO —— C —— H
          |
   H —— C —— OH
          |
   H —— C —— OH
          |
        CH₂OH
```

Reduction product:

```
        CH₂OH
          |
  HO —— C —— H
          |
   H —— C —— OH
          |
   H —— C —— OH
          |
        CH₂OH
       D-arabitol
```

14.33

α-anomer β-anomer

14.35 **a.** When this disaccharide is hydrolyzed, galactose and glucose are produced. The glycosidic bond is a β-1,4 bond since the ether bond is up from the 1 carbon of the galactose, which is on the left in the drawing to the 4 carbon of the glucose on the right. β-lactose is the name of this disaccharide since the free hydroxyl is up.

b. When this disaccharide is hydrolyzed, two molecules of glucose are produced. The glycosidic bond is an α-1,4 bond since the ether bond is down from the 1 carbon of the glucose on the left to the 4 carbon of the glucose on the right. α-maltose is the name of this disaccharide since the free hydroxyl is down.

14.37 **a.** Can be oxidized
      b. Can be oxidized

14.39 **a.** Another name for table sugar is sucrose.
      b. Lactose is the disaccharide found in milk and milk products.
      c. Maltose is also called malt sugar.
      d. When lactose is hydrolyzed, the products are the monosaccahrides galactose and glucose.

14.41 **a.** Amylose is an unbranched polymer of glucose units joined by α-1,4 bonds; amylopectin is a branched polymer of glucose joined by α-1,4 and α-1,6 bonds.
      b. Amylopectin, produced by plants, is a branched polymer of glucose joined by α-1,4 and α-1,6 bonds. Glycogen, which is made by animals, is a highly branched polymer of glucose joined by α-1,4 and α-1,6 bonds.

14.43 **a.** Cellulose is not digestible by humans since we do not have the enzymes necessary to break the β-1,4-glycosidic bonds in cellulose.
      b. Amylose and amylopectin are the storage forms of carbohydrates in plants.
      c. Amylose is the polysaccharide, which contains only α-1,4 glycosidic bonds.
      d. Glycogen contains many α-1,4 and α-1,6 bonds and is the most highly branched polysaccharide.

14.45 They differ only at carbon 4; the —OH in D-glucose is on the right side and in D-galactose it is on the left side.

14.47 D-galactose is the mirror image of L-galactose. In D-galactose, the —OH group on carbon 5 is on the right side whereas in L-galactose, the —OH group on carbon 5 is on the left side.

14.49 **a.**

L-Gulose

b.

α-D-Gulose   β-D-Gulose

14.51   Since sorbitol can be oxidized to D-glucose, it must contain the same number of carbons with the same groups attached as glucose. The difference is that sorbitol has only hydroxyls while glucose has an aldehyde group. In sorbitol, the aldehyde group is changed to a hydroxyl.

14.53   The α-galactose forms an open chain structure and when the chain closes, it can form both α- and β-galactose.

14.55

β-1,4-glycosidic bond. The bond from the glucose on the left is up (β).

14.57   **a.**

b. Yes. The cyclic structure on the right side can open up to form the open chain with an aldehyde.

Study Goals

- Describe the properties and types of lipids.
- Write the structures of triacylglycerols obtained from glycerol and fatty acids.
- Draw the structure of the product from hydrogenation, hydrolysis, and saponification of triacylglycerols.
- Describe glycerophospholipids.
- Describe steroids and their role in bile salts, vitamins, and hormones.
- Describe the lipid bilayer in a cell.

Think About It

1. What are fats used for in the body?

2. What foods are high in fat?

3. What oils are used to produce margarines?

4. What kind of lipid is cholesterol?

Key Terms

Match the key terms with the correct statement shown below.

a. lipid   **b.** fatty acid   **c.** triacylglycerol
d. saponification   **e.** glycerophospholipid   **f.** steroid

1. _____ A lipid consisting of glycerol bonded to two fatty acids and a phosphate group attached to an amino group

2. _____ A type of compound that is not soluble in water but is soluble in nonpolar solvents

3. _____ The hydrolysis of a triacylglycerol with a strong base producing salts called soaps and glycerol

4. _____ A lipid consisting of glycerol bonded to three fatty acids

5. _____ A lipid composed of a multicyclic ring system

6. _____ Long-chain carboxylic acid found in triacylglycerols

Answers   **1.** e   **2.** a   **3.** d   **4.** c   **5.** f   **6.** b

15.1 Lipids

- Lipids are nonpolar compounds that are not soluble in water.
- Classes of lipids include waxes, triacylglycerols, glycerophospholipids, and steroids.

◆ Learning Exercise 15.1

Match one of the classes of lipids with the composition of lipids below:

a. wax   **b.** triacylglycerol   **c.** glycerophospholipid
d. steroid

1. _____ A fused structure of four cycloalkanes.

2. _____ A long chain alcohol and a fatty acid

3. _____ Glycerol and three fatty acids

4. _____ Glycerol, two fatty acids, phosphate and choline

Answers   **1.** d   **2.** a   **3.** b   **4.** c

15.2 Fatty Acids

- Fatty acids are unbranched carboxylic acids that typically contain an even number (12–18) of carbon atoms.
- Fatty acids may be saturated, monounsaturated with one double bond, or polyunsaturated with two or more double bonds. The double bonds in unsaturated fatty acids are almost always cis.

◆ Learning Exercise 15.2

Draw the structural formulas of linoleic acid, stearic acid, and oleic acid.

A. linoleic acid

B. stearic acid

C. oleic acid

Which of these three fatty acids

1. _____ is the most saturated?   **2.** _____ is the most unsaturated?

3. _____ has the lowest melting point?   **4.** _____ has the highest melting point?

5. _____ is found in vegetables?   **6.** _____ is from animal sources?

Answers

linoleic acid CH_3—$(CH_2)_4$—CH=CH—CH_2—CH=CH—$(CH_2)_7$—$\overset{\overset{\displaystyle O}{\|}}{C}$—$OH$

stearic acid CH_3—$(CH_2)_{16}$—$\overset{\overset{\displaystyle O}{\|}}{C}$—$OH$

oleic acid CH_3—$(CH_2)_7$—CH=CH—$(CH_2)_7$—$\overset{\overset{\displaystyle O}{\|}}{C}$—$OH$

1. B   2. A   3. A   4. B   5. A and C   6. B

15.3 Waxes, Fats, and Oils

- A wax is an ester of a long-chain fatty acid and a long-chain alcohol.
- The triacylglycerols in fats and oils are esters of glycerol with three long-chain fatty acids.
- Fats from animal sources contain more saturated fatty acids and have higher melting points than fats found in most vegetable oils.

◆ Learning Exercise 15.3A

Write the formula of the wax formed by the reaction of palmitic acid, CH_3—$(CH_2)_{14}$—$COOH$, and cetyl alcohol, CH_3—$(CH_2)_{14}$—CH_2—OH.

Answer CH_3—$(CH_2)_{14}$—$\overset{\overset{\displaystyle O}{\|}}{C}$—$O$—$CH_2$—$(CH_2)_{14}$—$CH_3$

◆ Learning Exercise 15.3B

Consider the following fatty acid called oleic acid.

1. Why is the compound an acid?

2. Is it a saturated or unsaturated compound? Why?

3. Is the double bond cis or trans?

4. Is it likely to be a solid or a liquid at room temperature?

5. Why is it not soluble in water?

Answers   1. contains a carboxylic acid group   2. unsaturated; double bond
                   3. cis   4. liquid
                   5. it has a long hydrocarbon chain

◆ Learning Exercise 15.3C

Write the structure and name of the triacylglycerol formed from the following.

1. Glycerol and three palmitic acids, CH_3—$(CH_2)_{14}$—COOH

2. Glycerol and three myristic acids, CH_3—$(CH_2)_{12}$—COOH

Answers

1.

$$
\begin{array}{l}
\quad\quad\quad\quad O \\
\quad\quad\quad\quad \| \\
CH_2\!-\!O\!-\!C\!-\!(CH_2)_{14}\!-\!CH_3 \\
\quad|\quad\quad O \\
\quad|\quad\quad \| \\
HC\!-\!O\!-\!C\!-\!(CH_2)_{14}\!-\!CH_3 \\
\quad|\quad\quad O \\
\quad|\quad\quad \| \\
CH_2\!-\!O\!-\!C\!-\!(CH_2)_{14}\!-\!CH_3
\end{array}
$$

Glyceryl tripalmitate
(Tripalmitin)

2.

$$
\begin{array}{l}
\quad\quad\quad\quad O \\
\quad\quad\quad\quad \| \\
CH_2\!-\!O\!-\!C\!-\!(CH_2)_{12}\!-\!CH_3 \\
\quad|\quad\quad O \\
\quad|\quad\quad \| \\
HC\!-\!O\!-\!C\!-\!(CH_2)_{12}\!-\!CH_3 \\
\quad|\quad\quad O \\
\quad|\quad\quad \| \\
CH_2\!-\!O\!-\!C\!-\!(CH_2)_{12}\!-\!CH_3
\end{array}
$$

Glyceryl trimyristate
(Trimyristin)

◆ Learning Exercise 15.3D

Write the structural formulas of the following triacylglycerols:

1. Glyceryl tristearate (Tristearin)

2. Glyceryl trioleate (Triolein)

Answers

1. $CH_2-O-\overset{\overset{\displaystyle O}{\|}}{C}-(CH_2)_{16}-CH_3$

$HC-O-\overset{\overset{\displaystyle O}{\|}}{C}-(CH_2)_{16}-CH_3$

$CH_2-O-\overset{\overset{\displaystyle O}{\|}}{C}-(CH_2)_{16}-CH_3$

Glyceryl tristearate
(Tristearin)

2. $CH_2-O-\overset{\overset{\displaystyle O}{\|}}{C}-(CH_2)_7-CH=CH-(CH_2)_7-CH_3$

$HC-O-\overset{\overset{\displaystyle O}{\|}}{C}-(CH_2)_7-CH=CH-(CH_2)_7-CH_3$

$CH_2-O-\overset{\overset{\displaystyle O}{\|}}{C}-(CH_2)_7-CH=CH-(CH_2)_7-CH_3$

Glyceryl trioleate
(Triolein)

15.4 Chemical Properties of Triacylglycerols

- The hydrogenation of unsaturated fatty acids converts double bonds to single bonds.
- The hydrolysis of the ester bonds in fats or oils produces glycerol and fatty acids.
- In saponification, a fat heated with a strong base produces glycerol and the salts of the fatty acids or soaps. The dual polarity of soap permits its solubility in both water and oil.

◆   **Learning Exercise 15.4**

Write the equations for the following reactions of glyceryl trioleate (triolein)

1.   hydrogenation with a nickel catalyst

2.   acid hydrolysis with HCl

3.   saponification with NaOH

Answers

1.
$$
\begin{array}{l}
\text{CH}_2\text{—O—}\overset{\displaystyle O}{\overset{\|}{\text{C}}}\text{—(CH}_2)_7\text{—CH}=\text{CH—(CH}_2)_7\text{—CH}_3 \\[2mm]
\text{HC—O—}\overset{\displaystyle O}{\overset{\|}{\text{C}}}\text{—(CH}_2)_7\text{—CH}=\text{CH—(CH}_2)_7\text{—CH}_3 + 3\text{H}_2 \xrightarrow{\text{Ni}} \\[2mm]
\text{CH}_2\text{—O—}\overset{\displaystyle O}{\overset{\|}{\text{C}}}\text{—(CH}_2)_7\text{—CH}=\text{CH—(CH}_2)_7\text{—CH}_3
\end{array}
$$

$$
\begin{array}{l}
\text{CH}_2\text{—O—}\overset{\displaystyle O}{\overset{\|}{\text{C}}}\text{—(CH}_2)_{16}\text{—CH}_3 \\[2mm]
\text{HC—O—}\overset{\displaystyle O}{\overset{\|}{\text{C}}}\text{—(CH}_2)_{16}\text{—CH}_3 \\[2mm]
\text{CH}_2\text{—O—}\overset{\displaystyle O}{\overset{\|}{\text{C}}}\text{—(CH}_2)_{16}\text{—CH}_3
\end{array}
$$

2.
$$
\begin{array}{l}
\text{CH}_2\text{—O—}\overset{\displaystyle O}{\overset{\|}{\text{C}}}\text{—(CH}_2)_7\text{—CH}=\text{CH—(CH}_2)_7\text{—CH}_3 \\[2mm]
\text{HC—O—}\overset{\displaystyle O}{\overset{\|}{\text{C}}}\text{—(CH}_2)_7\text{—CH}=\text{CH—(CH}_2)_7\text{—CH}_3 + 3\text{H}_2\text{O} \xrightarrow{\text{H}^+} \\[2mm]
\text{CH}_2\text{—O—}\overset{\displaystyle O}{\overset{\|}{\text{C}}}\text{—(CH}_2)_7\text{—CH}=\text{CH—(CH}_2)_7\text{—CH}_3
\end{array}
$$

$$
\begin{array}{l}
\text{CH}_2\text{—OH} \\
\text{HC—OH} \\
\text{CH}_2\text{—OH}
\end{array}
$$

$$
+ 3\ \text{HO—}\overset{\displaystyle O}{\overset{\|}{\text{C}}}\text{—(CH}_2)_7\text{—CH}=\text{CH—(CH}_2)_7\text{—CH}_3
$$

3.
$$
\begin{array}{l}
\text{CH}_2\text{—O—}\overset{\displaystyle O}{\overset{\|}{\text{C}}}\text{—(CH}_2)_7\text{—CH}=\text{CH—(CH}_2)_7\text{—CH}_3 \\[2mm]
\text{HC—O—}\overset{\displaystyle O}{\overset{\|}{\text{C}}}\text{—(CH}_2)_7\text{—CH}=\text{CH—(CH}_2)_7\text{—CH}_3 + 3\text{NaOH} \longrightarrow \\[2mm]
\text{CH}_2\text{—O—}\overset{\displaystyle O}{\overset{\|}{\text{C}}}\text{—(CH}_2)_7\text{—CH}=\text{CH—(CH}_2)_7\text{—CH}_3
\end{array}
$$

$$
\begin{array}{l}
\text{CH}_2\text{—OH} \\
\text{HC—OH} \\
\text{CH}_2\text{—OH}
\end{array}
$$

$$
+ 3\ \text{Na}^+ \ ^-\text{O—}\overset{\displaystyle O}{\overset{\|}{\text{C}}}\text{—(CH}_2)_7\text{—CH}=\text{CH—(CH}_2)_7\text{—CH}_3
$$

15.5 Glycerophospholipids

- Glycerophospholipids are esters of glycerol with two fatty acids and a phosphate group attached to an amino alcohol.
- The fatty acids are a nonpolar region, whereas the phosphate group and the amino alcohol make up a polar region.

◆ Learning Exercise 15.5A

Draw the structure of a glycerophospholipid that is formed from two molecules of palmitic acid and serine, an amino alcohol.

$$
\text{CH}_3\text{—(CH}_2)_{14}\text{—}\overset{\displaystyle O}{\overset{\|}{\text{C}}}\text{OH}
$$
Palmitic acid

$$
\text{HO—CH}_2\text{—}\overset{\overset{\displaystyle \overset{+}{\text{NH}_3}}{|}}{\text{CH}}\text{—}\overset{\displaystyle O}{\overset{\|}{\text{C}}}\text{—O}^-
$$
Serine

Answer

◆ Learning Exercise 15.5B

Consider the following glycerophospholipid.

On the above structure, indicate the

A. two fatty acids.
C. the phosphate section.
E. the nonpolar region.

B. the part from the glycerol molecule.
D. the amino alcohol group.
F. the polar region.

1. What is the name of the amino alcohol group? _____

2. Why is a glycerophospholipid more soluble in water than most lipids? _____

Answers
(B) Glycerol

1. ethanolamine
2. The polar portion is attracted to water, which makes this type of lipid more soluble in water than other lipids.

244

15.6 Steroids: Cholesterol, and Steroid Hormones

- Steroids are lipids containing the steroid nucleus, which is a fused structure of four rings.
- Steroids include cholesterol, bile salts, and vitamin D.
- The steroid hormones are closely related in structure to cholesterol and depend on cholesterol for their synthesis. The sex hormones such as estrogen and testosterone are responsible for sexual characteristics and reproduction. The adrenal corticosteroids such as aldosterone and cortisone regulate water balance and glucose levels in the cells.

◆ **Learning Exercise 15.6A**

1. Write the structure of the steroid nucleus.

2. Write the structure of cholesterol.

Answers

1.

2.

◆ **Learning Exercise 15.6B**

Identify one of these compounds with the following statements.

a. estrogen   b. testosterone   c. cortisone   d. aldosterone

1. _____ Increases the blood level of glucose

2. _____ Increases the reabsorption of Na^+ in the blood

3. _____ Stimulates development of secondary sex characteristics in females

4. _____ Stimulates reabsorption of water by the kidneys

5. _____ Stimulates the secondary sex characteristics in males

Answers   1. c   2. d   3. a   4. d   5. b

15.7 Cell Membranes

- Cell membranes surround all of our cells and separate the cellular contents from the external liquid environment.
- A cell membrane is a lipid bilayer composed of two rows of phospholipids such that the nonpolar hydrocarbon tails are in the center and the polar sections are aligned along the outside.
- The inner portion of the lipid bilayer consists of nonpolar chains of the fatty acids, with the polar heads at the outer and inner surfaces.
- Molecules of cholesterol, proteins, and carbohydrates are embedded in the lipid bilayer.

◆ Learning Exercise 15.7

a. What is the function of the lipid bilayer in cell membranes?

b. What type of lipid makes up the lipid bilayer?

c. What is the general arrangement of the lipids in a lipid bilayer?

Answers
a. The lipid bilayer separates the contents of a cell from the surrounding aqueous environment.
b. The lipid bilayer is composed of phospholipids.
c. The nonpolar hydrocarbon tails are in the center of the bilayer, while the polar sections are aligned along the outside of the bilayer.

Check List for Chapter 15

You are ready to take the practice test for Chapter 15. Be sure that you have accomplished the following learning goals for this chapter. If you are not sure, review the section listed at the end of the goal. Then apply your new skills and understanding to the practice test.

After studying Chapter 15, I can successfully:

_____ Describe the classes of lipids (15.1).

_____ Identify a fatty acid as saturated or unsaturated (15.2).

_____ Write the structural formula of a wax or triacylglycerol produced by the reaction of a fatty acid and an alcohol or glycerol (15.3).

_____ Draw the structure of the product from the reaction of a triacylglycerol with hydrogen, an acid or base, or an oxidizing agent (15.4).

_____ Describe the components of glycerolphospholipids (15.5).

_____ Describe the structure of a steroid and cholesterol (15.6).

_____ Describe the function of the lipid bilayer in cell membranes (15.7).

Practice Test for Chapter 15

1. An ester of a fatty acid is called a

    A. carbohydrate   **B.** lipid   **C.** protein   **D.** oxyacid   **E.** soap

2. A fatty acid that is unsaturated is usually from

    A. animal sources and liquid at room temperature.
    B. animal sources and solid at room temperature.
    C. vegetable sources and liquid at room temperature.
    D. vegetable sources and solid at room temperature.
    E. both vegetable and animal sources and solid at room temperature.

3. CH_3—$(CH_2)_{16}$—$\overset{\overset{\displaystyle O}{\|}}{C}$—OH is a

    A. unsaturated fatty acid   **B.** saturated fatty acid   **C.** wax
    D. triacylglycerol   **E.** steroid

For questions 4 through 7, consider the following compound.

$$CH_2\text{—}O\text{—}\overset{\overset{\displaystyle O}{\|}}{C}\text{—}(CH_2)_{16}\text{—}CH_3$$
$$HC\text{—}O\text{—}\overset{\overset{\displaystyle O}{\|}}{C}\text{—}(CH_2)_{16}\text{—}CH_3$$
$$CH_2\text{—}O\text{—}\overset{\overset{\displaystyle O}{\|}}{C}\text{—}(CH_2)_{16}\text{—}CH_3$$

4. This compound belongs in the family called

    A. wax.   **B.** triacylglycerol.   **C.** glycerophospholipid.
    D. fatty acid   **E.** steroid.

5. The molecule shown above was formed by

    A. esterification.   **B.** hydrolysis (acid).   **C.** saponification.
    D. emulsification.   **E.** oxidation.

6. If this molecule were reacted with a strong base such as NaOH, the products would be

    A. glycerol and fatty acids.   **B.** glycerol and water.
    C. glycerol and soap.   **D.** an ester and salts of fatty acids.
    E. an ester and fatty acids.

7. The compound would be expected to be

    A. saturated, and a solid at room temperature.
    B. saturated, and a liquid at room temperature.
    C. unsaturated, and a solid at room temperature.
    D. unsaturated, and a liquid at room temperature.
    E. supersaturated, and a liquid at room temperature.

8. Which are found in glycerophospholipids?

    A. fatty acids   **B.** glycerol   **C.** a nitrogen compound
    D. phosphate   **E.** all of these

For questions 9 and 10, consider the following reaction:

$$\text{Triacylglycerol} + 3\text{NaOH} \longrightarrow 3 \text{ sodium salts of fatty acids and glycerol}$$

9. The reaction of a triacylglycerol with a strong base such as NaOH is called

      A. esterification.   **B.** lipogenesis.   **C.** hydrolysis.
      D. saponification.   **E.** oxidation.

10. What is another name for the sodium salts of the fatty acids?

      A. margarines   **B.** fat substitutes   **C.** soaps
      D. perfumes   **E.** vitamins

For questions 11 through 16, consider the following glycerophospholipid.

Match the labels in the glycerophospholipid with the following:

11. _____ The glycerol portion   12. _____ The phosphate portion   13. _____ The amino alcohol

14. _____ The polar region   15. _____ The nonpolar region

16. Type of glycerophospholipid

      A. choline   **B.** cephalin   **C.** fat
      D. steroid   **E.** cerebroside

Classify the lipids in 17 through 20 as
      A. wax   **B.** triacylglycerol   **C.** glycerophospholipid
      D. steroid   **E.** fatty acid

17. _____ cholesterol

18. _____ $\underset{\displaystyle \|}{\overset{\displaystyle O}{}}$ $CH_3{-}(CH_2)_{14}{-}C{-}OH$

19. _____ $\underset{\displaystyle \|}{\overset{\displaystyle O}{}}$ $CH_3{-}(CH_2)_{14}{-}C{-}O{-}(CH_2)_{30}{-}CH_3$

20. _____ an ester of glycerol with three palmitic acids

Select answers for 21 through 25 from the following:

      A. testosterone   **B.** estrogen   **C.** prednisone
      D. cortisone   **E.** aldosterone

21. ____ Stimulates the female sexual characteristics

22. ____ Increases the retention of water by the kidneys

23. ____ Stimulates the male sexual characteristics

24. ____ Increases the blood glucose level

25. ____ Used medically to reduce inflammation and treat asthma

26. This compound is a

    A. cholesterol.   **B** triacylglycerol.   **C.** prostaglandin.
    D. glycerophospholipid.   **E.** steroid.

27. The lipid bilayer of a cell is composed of

    A. cholesterol.   **B** glycerophospholipids. **C.** proteins.
    D. carbohydrate side chains.   **E.** all of these.

28. The type of lipoprotein that transports cholesterol to the liver for elimination is called

    A. chylomicron.   **B.** high density lipoprotein   **C.** low density lipoprotein.
    D. very low density lipoprotein. **E.** all of these.

Answers to the Practice Test

1. B	**2.** C	**3.** B	**4.** B	**5.** A
6. C	**7.** A	**8.** E	**9.** D	**10.** C
11. A	**12.** D	**13.** C	**14.** C, D	**15.** B
16. B	**17.** D	**18.** E	**19.** A	**20.** B
21. B	**22.** E	**23.** A	**24.** D	**25.** C
26. C	**27.** E	**28.** B		

Answers and Solutions to Selected Text Problems

15.1 Lipids provide energy, protection, and insulation for the organs in the body.

15.3 Since lipids are not soluble in water, they are nonpolar molecules.

15.5. All fatty acids contain a long chain of carbon atoms with a carboxylic acid group. Saturated fats contain only carbon-to-carbon single bonds; unsaturated fats contain one or more double bonds. More saturated fats are from animal sources, while vegetable oils contain more unsaturated fatty acids.

15.7.

    a. palmitic acid

    b. oleic aicd

15.9   **a.** Lauric acid has only carbon–carbon single bonds; it is saturated.
        b. Linolenic acid has three carbon–carbon double bonds; it is unsaturated.
        c. Palmitoleic acid has one carbon–carbon double bond; it is unsaturated.
        d. Stearic acid has only carbon–carbon single bonds; it is saturated.

15.11 In a cis double bond, the alkyl groups are on the same side of the double bond, whereas in trans fatty acids, the alkyl groups are on opposite sides.

15.13 In an omega-3 fatty acid, the first double bond occurs at carbon 3 counting from the methyl. In an omega-6 fatty acid, the first double bond occurs at carbon 6.

15.15 Arachidonic acid contains four double bonds and no side groups. In PGE_2, a part of the chain forms cyclopentane and there are hydroxyl and ketone functional groups.

15.17 Prostaglandins affect blood pressure, stimulate contraction and relaxation of smooth muscle.

15.19 Palmitic acid is the 16-carbon saturated fatty acid.

$$CH_3-(CH_2)_{14}-\overset{\overset{\displaystyle O}{\|}}{C}-O-(CH_2)_{29}-CH_3$$

15.21 Fats are composed of fatty acids and glycerol. In this case, the fatty acid is stearic acid, an 18-carbon saturated fatty acid.

$$
\begin{array}{l}
CH_2-O-\overset{\overset{\displaystyle O}{\|}}{C}-(CH_2)_{16}-CH_3\\[4pt]
\;\;|\qquad\;\; \overset{\displaystyle O}{}\\
HC-O-\overset{\overset{\displaystyle \|}{}}{C}-(CH_2)_{16}-CH_3\\[4pt]
\;\;|\qquad\;\; \overset{\displaystyle O}{}\\
CH_2-O-\overset{\overset{\displaystyle \|}{}}{C}-(CH_2)_{16}-CH_3
\end{array}
$$

15.23 Tripalmitin has three palmitic acids (16-carbon saturated fatty acid) forming ester bonds with glycerol.

$$
\begin{array}{l}
CH_2-O-\overset{\overset{\displaystyle O}{\|}}{C}-(CH_2)_{14}CH_3\\[4pt]
\;\;|\qquad\;\; \overset{\displaystyle O}{}\\
HC-O-\overset{\overset{\displaystyle \|}{}}{C}-(CH_2)_{14}-CH_3\\[4pt]
\;\;|\qquad\;\; \overset{\displaystyle O}{}\\
CH_2-O-\overset{\overset{\displaystyle \|}{}}{C}-(CH_2)_{14}-CH_3
\end{array}
$$

15.25 Safflower oil contains fatty acids with two or three double bonds; olive oil contains a large amount of oleic acid, which has a single (monounsaturated) double bond.

15.27 Although coconut oil comes from a vegetable source, it has large amounts of saturated fatty acids and small amounts of unsaturated fatty acids. Since coconut oil contains the same kinds of fatty acids as animal fat, coconut oil has a melting point similar to the melting point of animal fats.

15.29

$$\underset{\text{triacylglycerol (unsaturated)}}{\begin{array}{l} CH_2-O-\overset{\displaystyle O}{\overset{\|}{C}}-(CH_2)_7-CH=CH-(CH_2)_7-CH_3 \\[2mm] HC-O-\overset{\displaystyle O}{\overset{\|}{C}}-(CH_2)_7-CH=CH-(CH_2)_7-CH_3 \;+\; 3H_2 \\[2mm] CH_2-O-\overset{\displaystyle O}{\overset{\|}{C}}-(CH_2)_7-CH=CH-(CH_2)_7-CH_3 \end{array}} \xrightarrow{\text{Ni}} \begin{array}{l} CH_2-O-\overset{\displaystyle O}{\overset{\|}{C}}-(CH_2)_{16}-CH_3 \\[2mm] HC-O-\overset{\displaystyle O}{\overset{\|}{C}}-(CH_2)_{16}-CH_3 \\[2mm] CH_2-O-\overset{\displaystyle O}{\overset{\|}{C}}-(CH_2)_{16}-CH_3 \end{array}$$

15.31 Acid hydrolysis of a fat gives glycerol and the fatty acids. Basic hydrolysis (saponification) of fat gives glycerol and the salts of the fatty acids.

a.

$$\begin{array}{l} CH_2-O-\overset{\displaystyle O}{\overset{\|}{C}}-(CH_2)_{12}-CH_3 \\[2mm] CH-O-\overset{\displaystyle O}{\overset{\|}{C}}-(CH_2)_{12}-CH_3 \\[2mm] CH_2-O-\overset{\displaystyle O}{\overset{\|}{C}}-(CH_2)_{12}-CH_3 \end{array} \;+\;3H_2O \xrightarrow{H^+} \begin{array}{l} CH_2OH \\[2mm] CHOH \;+\; 3\; HO-\overset{\displaystyle O}{\overset{\|}{C}}-(CH_2)_{12}-CH_3 \\[2mm] CH_2OH \end{array}$$

b.

$$\begin{array}{l} CH_2-O-\overset{\displaystyle O}{\overset{\|}{C}}-(CH_2)_{12}-CH_3 \\[2mm] CH-O-\overset{\displaystyle O}{\overset{\|}{C}}-(CH_2)_{12}-CH_3 \\[2mm] CH_2-O-\overset{\displaystyle O}{\overset{\|}{C}}-(CH_2)_{12}-CH_3 \end{array} \;+\;3NaOH \longrightarrow \begin{array}{l} CH_2OH \\[2mm] CHOH \;+\; 3\; Na^+\;O-\overset{\displaystyle O}{\overset{\|}{C}}-(CH_2)_{12}-CH_3 \\[2mm] CH_2OH \end{array}$$

15.33 A triacylglycerol is a combination of three fatty acids bonded to glycerol by ester bonds. Olestra is sucrose bonded to six to eight fatty acids by ester bonds. Olestra cannot be digested because digestive enzymes cannot break down the molecule.

15.35

$$\begin{array}{l} CH_2-O-\overset{\displaystyle O}{\overset{\|}{C}}-(CH_2)_{16}-CH_3 \\[2mm] HC-O-\overset{\displaystyle O}{\overset{\|}{C}}-(CH_2)_{16}-CH_3 \\[2mm] CH_2-O-\overset{\displaystyle O}{\overset{\|}{C}}-(CH_2)_{16}-CH_3 \end{array}$$

15.37 A triacylglycerol consists of glycerol and three fatty acids. A glycerophospholipid consists of glycerol, two fatty acids, a phosphate group, and an amino alcohol.

15.39

$$\begin{array}{l} \text{CH}_2\text{—O—}\overset{\displaystyle\overset{O}{\|}}{\text{C}}\text{—(CH}_2)_{14}\text{—CH}_3 \\[2pt] \text{HC—O—}\overset{\displaystyle\overset{O}{\|}}{\text{C}}\text{—(CH}_2)_{14}\text{—CH}_3 \qquad \text{This is a cephalin.} \\[2pt] \text{CH}_2\text{—O—}\overset{\displaystyle\overset{O}{\|}}{\underset{\displaystyle\underset{O^-}{|}}{\text{P}}}\text{—O—CH}_2\text{—CH}_2\text{—}\overset{+}{\text{N}}\text{H}_3 \end{array}$$

15.41 This phospholipid is a cephalin. It contains glycerol, oleic acid, stearic acid, phosphate, and ethanolamine.

15.43

15.45 Lipoproteins are large, spherically-shaped molecules that transport lipids in the bloodstream. They consist of an outer layer of phospholipids and proteins surrounding an inner core of hundreds of nonpolar lipids and cholesterol esters.

15.47 Chylomicrons have a lower density than VLDLs. They pick up triacylglycerols from the intestine, whereas VLDLs transport triacylglycerols synthesized in the liver.

15.49 "Bad" cholesterol is the cholesterol carried by LDLs to the tissues where it can form deposits called plaque, which can narrow the arteries.

15.51 Both estradiol and testosterone contain the steroid nucleus and a hydroxyl group. Testosterone has a ketone group, a double bond, and an extra methyl group. Estradiol has a benzene ring and a second hydroxyl group.

15.53 Testosterone is a male sex hormone.

15.55 Cell membranes contain a number of lipids: phospholipids that contain fatty acids with cis double bonds, glycolipids which are on the outside of the cell membrane and in animal membranes, cholesterol.

15.57 The function of the lipid bilayer in the plasma membrane is to keep the cell contents separated from the outside environment and to allow the cell to regulate the movement of substances into and out of the cell.

15.59 The peripheral proteins in the membrane emerge on the inner or outer surface only, whereas the integral proteins extend through the membrane to both surfaces.

15.61 The carbohydrates, as glycoproteins and glycolipids on the surface of cells, act as receptors for cell recognition and chemical messengers such as neurotransmitters.

15.63 Beeswax and carnauba are waxes. Vegetable oil and capric triacylglycerol are triacylglycerols.

$$CH_2-O-\overset{\displaystyle O}{\overset{\|}{C}}-(CH_2)_8-CH_3$$
$$CH-O-\overset{\displaystyle O}{\overset{\|}{C}}-(CH_2)_8-CH_3 \qquad \text{Capric triacylglycerol}$$
$$CH_2-O-\overset{\displaystyle O}{\overset{\|}{C}}-(CH_2)_8-CH_3$$

15.65 **a.** A typical monounsaturated fatty acid has a cis double bond.

b. A trans fatty acid has a trans double bond with the alkyl groups on opposite sides of the double bond.

c.

$$\underset{CH_3(CH_2)_6CH_2}{\overset{H}{\diagdown}}C=C\underset{H}{\overset{CH_2(CH_2)_6\overset{\displaystyle O}{\overset{\|}{C}}OH}{\diagup}}$$

15.67

$$CH_2-O-\overset{\displaystyle O}{\overset{\|}{C}}-(CH_2)_{16}-CH_3$$
$$CH-O-\overset{\displaystyle O}{\overset{\|}{C}}-(CH_2)_{16}-CH_3 \qquad \text{glyceryl tristearate}$$
$$CH_2-O-\overset{\displaystyle O}{\overset{\|}{C}}-(CH_2)_{16}-CH_3$$

$$CH_2-O-\overset{\displaystyle O}{\overset{\|}{C}}-(CH_2)_{14}-CH_3$$
$$CH-O-\overset{\displaystyle O}{\overset{\|}{C}}-(CH_2)_{14}-CH_3 \quad \text{lecithin}$$
$$CH_2-O-\overset{\displaystyle O}{\overset{\|}{\underset{\underset{\displaystyle O^-}{|}}{P}}}-O-CH_2-CH_2-\overset{\overset{\displaystyle CH_3}{|}}{\underset{\underset{\displaystyle CH_3}{|}}{N^+}}-CH_3$$

15.69 **a.** wax **b.** steroid **c.** glycerophospholipid **d.** triacylglycerol
e. soap **f.** triacylglycerol **g.** triacylglycerol **h.** triacylglycerol
i. steroid **j.** steroid **k.** fatty acid

15.71 **a.** 5 **b.** 1, 2, 3, 4 **c.** 2
d. 1, 2 **e.** 1, 2, 3, 4

15.73 **a.** 4 **b.** 3 **c.** 1
d. 4 **e.** 4 **f.** 3
g. 2 **h.** 1

Amino Acids, Proteins, and Enzymes

Study Goals

- Classify proteins by their functions in the cells.
- Draw the structures of amino acids.
- Draw the zwitterion forms of amino acids.
- Write the structural formulas of di- and tripeptides.
- Identify the structural levels of proteins as primary, secondary, tertiary, and quaternary.
- Describe the effects of denaturation on the structure of proteins.
- Classify enzymes according to the type of reaction they catalyze.
- Describe the lock-and-key and induced-fit models of enzyme action.
- Discuss the effect of changes in temperature, pH, and concentration of substrate on enzyme action.
- Describe the competitive and noncompetitive inhibition of enzymes.
- Identify the types of cofactors that are necessary for enzyme action.

Think About It

1. What are some uses of protein in the body?

2. What are the units that make up a protein?

3. How do you obtain protein in your diet?

4. What are some functions of enzymes in the cells of the body?

5. Why are enzymes sensitive to high temperatures and low or high pH levels?

Key Terms

1. Match the following key terms with the correct statement shown below.

a. amino acid   **b.** peptide bond   **c.** denaturation
d. primary structure   **e.** zwitterion

1. _____ The order of amino acids in a protein

2. _____ The ionized structure of an amino acid has a net charge of zero

3. _____ The bond that connects amino acids in peptides and proteins

4. _____ The loss of secondary and tertiary protein structure caused by agents such as heat and acid

5. _____ The building block of proteins

Answers   1. d   2. e   3. b   4. c   5. a

2. Match the following key terms with the correct statement shown below.

a. lock-and-key theory   **b.** vitamin   **c.** inhibitor   **d.** enzyme   **e.** active site

1. _____ The portion of an enzyme structure where a substrate undergoes reaction

2. _____ A protein that catalyzes a biological reaction in the cells

3. _____ A model of enzyme action in which the substrate exactly fits the shape of an enzyme like a key fits into a lock

4. _____ A substance that makes an enzyme inactive by interfering with its ability to react with a substrate

5. _____ An organic compound essential for normal health and growth that must be obtained from the diet

Answers   **1.** e   **2.** d   **3.** a   **4.** c   **5.** b

16.1 Functions of Proteins

- Some proteins are enzymes or hormones, while others are important in structure, transport, protection, storage, and contraction of muscles.

◆ Learning Exercise 16.1

Match one of the following functions of a protein with the examples below.

a. structural   **b.** contractile   **c.** storage   **d.** transport
e. hormonal   **f.** enzyme   **g.** protection

1. _____ hemoglobin carries oxygen in blood   **2.** _____ amylase hydrolyzes starch

3. _____ egg albumin, a protein in egg white   **4.** _____ hormone that controls growth

5. _____ collagen makes up connective tissue   **6.** _____ immunoglobulin

7. _____ keratin, a major protein of hair   **8.** _____ lipoprotein carries lipids in blood

Answers   **1.** d   **2.** f   **3.** c   **4.** e
                5. a   **6.** g   **7.** a   **8.** d

16.2 Amino Acids

- A group of 20 amino acids provides the molecular building blocks of proteins.
- In an amino acid, a central (alpha) carbon is attached to an amino group, a carboxyl group, and a side chain or R group, which is a characteristic group for each amino acid.
- The particular R group makes each amino acid polar, nonpolar, acidic, or basic. Nonpolar amino acids contain hydrocarbon side chains, while polar amino acids contain electronegative atoms such as oxygen (—OH) or sulfur (—SH). Acidic side chains contain a carboxylic acid group and basic side chains contain an amino group (—NH_2).

◆ **Learning Exercise 16.2**

Using the appropriate R group, complete the structural formula of each of the following amino acids. Indicate whether the amino acid would be polar, nonpolar, acidic, or basic.

glycine (R = —H)

$$H_3\overset{+}{N}—\overset{\Box}{\underset{\underset{H}{|}}{C}}—\overset{O}{\underset{}{\overset{||}{C}}}—O^-$$

_____

alanine (R = —CH_3)

$$H_3\overset{+}{N}—\overset{\Box}{\underset{\underset{H}{|}}{C}}—\overset{O}{\underset{}{\overset{||}{C}}}—O^-$$

_____

serine (R = –CH_2—OH)

$$H_3\overset{+}{N}—\overset{\Box}{\underset{\underset{H}{|}}{C}}—\overset{O}{\underset{}{\overset{||}{C}}}—O^-$$

_____

aspartic acid (R = –CH_2—$\overset{O}{\overset{||}{C}}$—$O^-$)

$$H_3\overset{+}{N}—\overset{\Box}{\underset{\underset{H}{|}}{C}}—\overset{O}{\underset{}{\overset{||}{C}}}—O^-$$

_____

Answers

$$H_3\overset{+}{N}—\overset{\overset{H}{|}}{\underset{\underset{H}{|}}{C}}—\overset{O}{\overset{||}{C}}—O^-$$
nonpolar

$$H_3\overset{+}{N}—\overset{\overset{CH_3}{|}}{\underset{\underset{H}{|}}{C}}—\overset{O}{\overset{||}{C}}—O^-$$
nonpolar

$$H_3\overset{+}{N}—\overset{\overset{CH_2—OH}{|}}{\underset{\underset{H}{|}}{C}}—\overset{O}{\overset{||}{C}}—O^-$$
polar

$$H_3\overset{+}{N}—\overset{\overset{CH_2—\overset{O}{\overset{||}{C}}—O^-}{|}}{\underset{\underset{H}{|}}{C}}—\overset{O}{\overset{||}{C}}—O^-$$
acidic

16.3 Amino Acids as Acids and Bases

• Amino acids exist as dipolar ions called zwitterions, which are neutral at the isoelectric point (pI).
• A zwitterion has a positive charge at pH levels below its pI and a negative charge at pH levels higher than its pI.

Study Note
Example: Glycine has an isoelectric point at a pH of 6.0. Write the zwitterion of glycine at its isoelectric point (pI), and at pH levels above and below its isoelectric point.
Solution: In more acidic solutions, glycine has a net positive charge, and in more basic solutions, a net negative charge.

$$\underset{below\ pI}{H_3N^+—CH_2—COOH} \overset{H^+}{\longleftarrow} \underset{zwitterion\ of\ glycine}{H_3N^+—CH_2—COO^-} \overset{OH^-}{\longrightarrow} \underset{above\ pI}{H_2N—CH_2—COO^-}$$

256

◆ **Learning Exercise 16.3**

Write the structure of the amino acids under the given conditions.

Zwitterion	H⁺	OH⁻
Alanine		
Serine		

Answers

Zwitterion	H⁺	OH⁻
Alanine CH₃ | H₃N⁺—CH—COO⁻	CH₃ | H₃N⁺—CH—COOH	CH₃ | H₂N—CH—COO⁻
Serine CH₂OH | H₃N⁺—CH—COO⁻	CH₂OH | H₃N⁺—CH—COOH	CH₂OH | H₂N—CH—COO⁻

16.4 Formation of Peptides

- A peptide bond is an amide bond between the carboxyl group of one amino acid and the amino group of the second.

$$H_3\overset{+}{N}-CH_2-\overset{\overset{\displaystyle R_1}{|}}{}\overset{\overset{\displaystyle O}{\|}}{C}-\overset{\overset{\displaystyle H}{|}}{N}-\overset{\overset{\displaystyle R_2}{|}}{CH}-COO^-$$

peptide bond

- Short chains of amino acids are called peptides. Long chains of amino acids are called proteins.

◆ Learning Exercise 16.4

Draw the structural formulas of the following di- and tripeptides.

1. serylglycine

2. cystylvaline

3. Gly-Ser-Cys

Answers

1.
$$
\begin{array}{c}
\overset{\text{HOCH}_2}{|} \quad \overset{O}{||} \quad \overset{H}{|} \\
\overset{+}{\text{H}_2\text{N}}\text{—CH—C—N—CH}_2\text{—COO}^-
\end{array}
$$

2.
$$
\begin{array}{c}
\text{CH}_3 \\
| \\
\text{HSCH}_2 \quad O \quad H \quad \text{CH—CH}_3 \\
\overset{+}{\text{H}_3\text{N}}\text{—CH—C—N—CH —COO}^-
\end{array}
$$

3.
$$
\begin{array}{c}
O \quad\quad \text{HOCH}_2 \quad O \quad\quad \text{CH}_2\text{SH} \\
\overset{+}{\text{H}_3\text{N}}\text{—CH}_2\text{—C—N—CH —C—N—CH—COO}^- \\
\quad\quad\quad | \quad\quad\quad\quad\quad | \\
\quad\quad\quad H \quad\quad\quad\quad\quad H
\end{array}
$$

16.5 Levels of Protein Structure

- The primary structure of a protein is the sequence of amino acids.
- In the secondary structure, hydrogen bonds between different sections of the peptide produce a characteristic shape such as an α-helix, β-pleated sheet, or a triple helix.
- In globular proteins, the polypeptide chain including its α-helical and β-pleated sheet regions folds upon itself to form a tertiary structure.
- In a tertiary structure, hydrophobic R groups are found on the inside and hydrophilic R groups on the outside surface. The tertiary structure is stabilized by interactions between R groups.
- In a quaternary structure, two or more subunits must combine for biological activity. They are held together by the same interactions found in tertiary structures.
- Denaturation of a protein occurs when heat or other denaturing agents destroys the secondary and tertiary structure (but not the primary structure) of the protein until biological activity is lost.

◆ **Learning Exercise 16.5A**

Identify the following descriptions of protein structure as primary or secondary structure.

1. _____ Hydrogen bonding forms an alpha (α)-helix.

2. _____ Hydrogen bonding occurs between C=O and N—H within a peptide chain.

3. _____ The order of amino acids, which are linked by peptide bonds

4. _____ Hydrogen bonds between protein chains form a pleated-sheet structure.

Answers　　**1.** secondary　　**2.** secondary　　**3.** primary　　**4.** secondary

◆ **Learning Exercise 16.5B**

Identify the following descriptions of protein structure as tertiary or quaternary.

1. _____ A disulfide bond joining distant parts of a peptide

2. _____ The combination of four protein subunits

3. _____ Hydrophilic side groups seeking contact with water

4. _____ A salt bridge forms between two oppositely charged side chains.

5. _____ Hydrophobic side groups forming a nonpolar center

Answers　　**1.** tertiary　　**2.** quaternary　　**3.** tertiary　　**4.** tertiary　　**5.** tertiary

◆ **Learning Exercise 16.5C**

Indicate the denaturing agent in the following examples.

A. heat or UV light 　　　　**B.** pH change 　　　　**C.** organic solvent
D. heavy metal ions 　　　　**E.** agitation

1. _____ Placing surgical instruments in a 120°C autoclave

2. _____ Whipping cream to make a desert topping

3. _____ Applying tannic acid to a burn

4. _____ Placing $AgNO_3$ drops in the eyes of newborns

5. _____ Using alcohol to disinfect a wound

6. _____ Using lactobacillus bacteria culture to produce acid that converts milk to yogurt.

Answers　　**1.** A　　**2.** E　　**3.** B　　**4.** D　　**5.** C　　**6.** B

16.6 Enzymes

- Enzymes are globular proteins that act as biological catalysts.
- Enzymes accelerate the rate of biological reactions by lowering the activation energy of a reaction.
- The names of most enzymes are indicated by their *ase* endings.
- Enzymes are classified by the type of reaction they catalyze: oxidoreductase, hydrolase, isomerase, transferase, lyase, or ligase.

◆ **Learning Exercise 16.6A**

Indicate whether each of the following characteristics of an enzyme is *true or false*.

An enzyme

1. _____ is a biological catalyst.

2. _____ functions at a low pH.

3. _____ does not change the equilibrium position of a reaction.

4. _____ is obtained from the diet.

5. _____ greatly increases the rate of a cellular reaction.

6. _____ is needed for every reaction that takes place in the cell.

7. _____ catalyzes at a faster rate at higher temperatures.

8. _____ functions best at mild conditions of pH 7.4 and 37°C.

9. _____ lowers the activation energy of a biological reaction.

10. _____ increases the rate of the forward reaction, but not the reverse.

Answers   1. T   2. F   3. T   4. F   5. T
             6. T   7. F   8. T   9. T   10. F

◆ **Learning Exercise 16.6B**

Match the common name of each of the following enzymes with the description of the reaction.

1. dehydrogenase   2. oxidase   3. peptidase
4. decarboxylase   5. esterase   6. transaminase

a. _____ hydrolyzes the ester bonds in triacylglycerols to yield fatty acids and glycerol

b. _____ removes hydrogen from a substrate

c. _____ removes CO_2 from a substrate

d. _____ decomposes hydrogen peroxide to water and oxygen

e. _____ hydrolyzes peptide bonds during the digestion of proteins

f. _____ transfers an amino (NH_2) group from an amino acid to an α-keto acid

Answers   a. 5   b. 1   c. 4   d. 2   e. 3   f. 6

◆ Learning Exercise 16.6C

Match the IUPAC classification for enzymes with each of the following types of reactions.

1 oxidoreductase   **2.** transferase   **3.** hydrolase
4. lyase   **5.** isomerase   **6.** ligase

a. _____ combines small molecules using energy from ATP

b. _____ transfers phosphate groups

c. _____ hydrolyzes a disaccharide into two glucose units

d. _____ converts a substrate to an isomer of the substrate.

e. _____ adds hydrogen to a substrate

f. _____ removes H_2O from a substrate.

g. _____ adds oxygen to a substrate

h. _____ converts a cis structure to a trans structure

Answers   **a.** 6   **b.** 2   **c.** 3   **d.** 5   **e.** 1   **f.** 4   **g.** 1   **h.** 5

16.7 Enzyme Action

- Within the structure of the enzyme, there is a small pocket called the active site, which has a specific shape that fits a specific substrate.
- In the lock-and-key model or the induced-fit model, an enzyme and substrate form an enzyme-substrate complex so the reaction of the substrate can be catalyzed at the active site.

◆ Learning Exercise 16.7A

Match the terms (A) active site, (B) substrate, (C) enzyme-substrate complex, (D) lock-and-key, and (E) induced-fit with the following descriptions:

1. _____ the combination of an enzyme with a substrate

2. _____ a model of enzyme action in which the rigid shape of the active site exactly fits the shape of the substrate

3. _____ has a tertiary structure that fits the structure of the active site

4. _____ a model of enzyme action in which the shape of the active site adjusts to fit the shape of a substrate

5. _____ the portion of an enzyme that binds to the substrate and catalyzes the reaction

Answers   **1.** C   **2.** D   **3.** B   **4.** E   **5.** A

◆ Learning Exercise 16.7B

Write an equation to illustrate the following:

1. The formation of an enzyme-substrate complex. _____

2. The conversion of enzyme-substrate complex to product. _____

Answers   1. $E + S \rightleftarrows ES$ 2. $ES \longrightarrow E + P$

16.8 Factors Affecting Enzyme Activity

- Enzymes are most effective at optimum temperature and pH. The rate of an enzyme reaction decreases considerably at temperatures and pH above or below the optimum.
- An enzyme can be made inactive by changes in pH, temperature, or by chemical compounds called inhibitors.
- An increase in substrate concentration increases the reaction rate of an enzyme-catalyzed reaction until all the enzyme molecules combine with substrate.
- A competitive inhibitor has a structure similar to the substrate and competes for the active site. When the active site is occupied by a competitive inhibitor, the enzyme cannot catalyze the reaction of the substrate.
- A noncompetitive inhibitor attaches elsewhere on the enzyme changing the shape of both the enzyme and the active site. As long as the noncompetitive inhibitor is attached to the enzyme, the altered active site cannot bind with substrate.

◆ **Learning Exercise 16.8A**

Urease, which has an optimum pH of 5, catalyzes the hydrolysis of urea to ammonia and CO_2 in the liver.

$$H_2N-\overset{\overset{\displaystyle O}{\displaystyle \|}}{C}-NH_2 + H_2O \xrightarrow{\text{urease}} 2NH_3 + CO_2$$

Draw a graph to represent the effects of each of the following on enzyme activity. Indicate the optimum pH and optimum temperature.

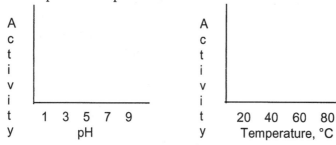

How is the rate of the urease-catalyzed reaction affected by each of the following?

a. increases   **b.** decreases   **c.** not changed

1. ____ adding more urea when an excess of enzyme is present

2. ____ running the reaction at pH 8

3. ____ lowering the temperature to 0°C

4. ____ running the reaction at 85°C

5. ____ increasing the concentration of urea for a specific amount of urease

6. ____ adjusting pH to the optimum

Answers

1. a   **2.** b   **3.** b   **4.** b   **5.** a   **6.** a

◆ **Learning Exercise 16.8B**

Identify each of the following as characteristic of competitive inhibition (C) or noncompetitive inhibition (N).

1. _____ An inhibitor binds to the surface of the enzyme away from the active site.

2. _____ An inhibitor resembling the substrate molecule blocks the active site on the enzyme.

3. _____ The action of this inhibitor can be reversed by adding more substrate.

4. _____ Increasing substrate concentration does not change the effect of this inhibition.

5. _____ Sulfanilamide stops bacterial infections because its structure is similar to PABA (p-aminobenzoic acid), which is essential for bacterial growth.

Answers   **1.** N   **2.** C   **3.** C   **4.** N   **5.** C

16.9 Enzyme Cofactors

- Simple enzymes are biologically active as a protein only, whereas other enzymes require a cofactor.
- A cofactor may be a metal ion such as Cu^{2+} or Fe^{2+}, or an organic compound called a coenzyme, usually a vitamin.
- Vitamins are organic molecules that are essential for proper health.
- Vitamins must be obtained from the diet because they are not synthesized in the body.
- Vitamins B and C are classified as water-soluble; vitamins A, D, E, and K are fat-soluble vitamins.
- Many water-soluble vitamins function as coenzymes.

◆ **Learning Exercise 16.9**

Indicate whether each statement describes a simple enzyme or a protein that requires a cofactor.

1. _____ An enzyme consisting only of protein

2. _____ An enzyme requiring magnesium ion for activity

3 _____ An enzyme containing a sugar group

4. _____ An enzyme that gives only amino acids upon hydrolysis

5. _____ An enzyme that requires zinc ions for activity

Answers   **1.** simple   **2.** requires a cofactor   **3.** requires a cofactor
    4. simple   **5.** requires a cofactor

Check List for Chapter 16

You are ready to take the practice test for Chapter 16 Be sure that you have accomplished the following learning goals for this chapter. If you are not sure, review the section listed at the end of the goal.

After studying Chapter 16, I can successfully:

_____ Classify proteins by their functions in the cells (16.1).

_____ Draw the structure for an amino acid (16.2).

_____ Draw the zwitterion at the isoelectric point (pI), above, and below the pI (16.3).

_____ Describe a peptide bond; draw the structure for a peptide (16.4).

_____ Distinguish between the primary and secondary structures of a protein (16.5).

_____ Distinguish between the tertiary and quaternary structures of a protein (16.5).

_____ Describe the ways that denaturation affects the structure of a protein (16.5).

_____ Classify enzymes according to the type of reaction they catalyze (16.6).

_____ Describe the lock-and-key and induced fit models of enzyme action (16.7).

_____ Discuss the effect of changes in temperature, pH, and concentration of substrate on enzyme action (16.8).

_____ Describe the competitive and noncompetitive inhibition of enzymes (16.8).

_____ Identify the types of cofactors that are necessary for enzyme action (16.9).

Practice Test for Chapter 16

1. Which amino acid is nonpolar?

   A. serine   **B.** aspartic acid **C.** valine   **D.** cysteine   **E.** glutamine

2. Which amino acid will form disulfide cross-links in a tertiary structure?

   A. serine   **B.** aspartic acid **C.** valine   **D.** cysteine   **E.** glutamine

3. Which amino acid has a basic side chain?

   A. serine   **B.** aspartic acid **C.** valine   **D.** cysteine   **E.** glutamine

4. All amino acids

   A. have the same side chains.
   B. form zwitterions.
   C. have the same isoelectric points.
   D. show hydrophobic tendencies.
   E. are essential amino acids.

5. Essential amino acids

   A. are the amino acids that must be supplied by the diet.
   B. are not synthesized by the body.
   C. are missing in incomplete proteins.
   D. are present in proteins from animal sources.
   E. all of the above

Use the following to answer questions for the amino acid alanine in questions 6 through 9.

A. $^+H_3N-\overset{\overset{\displaystyle CH_3}{|}}{CH}-COO^-$ B. $H_2N-\overset{\overset{\displaystyle CH_3}{|}}{CH}-COO^-$ C. $^+H_3N-\overset{\overset{\displaystyle CH_3}{|}}{CH}-COOH$

6. ____ Alanine in its zwitterion form

7. ____ Alanine at a low pH

8. ____ Alanine at a high pH

9. ____ Alanine at its isoelectric point

10. The sequence Tyr-Ala-Gly
    A. is a tripeptide.   B. has two peptide bonds.   C. has tyrosine with free $-NH_2$ end
    D. has glycine with the free $-COOH$ end   E. all of these.

11. The type of bonding expected between lysine and aspartic acid is a
    A. ionic bond.   B. hydrogen bond.   C. disulfide bond.
    D. hydrophobic attraction.   E. hydrophilic attraction.

12. What type of bond is used to form the α-helix structure of a protein?
    A. peptide bond   B. hydrogen bond   C. ionic bond
    D. disulfide bond   E. hydrophobic attraction

13. What type of bonding places portions of the protein chain in the center of a tertiary structure?
    A. peptide bonds   B. ionic bonds   C. disulfide bonds
    D. hydrophobic attraction   E. hydrophilic attraction

In questions 14 through 18, identify the protein structural levels that each of the following statements describe.

A. primary   B. secondary   C. tertiary
D. quaternary   E. pentenary

14. ____ peptide bonds   15. ____ a pleated sheet

16. ____ two or more protein subunits   17. ____ an α-helix

18. ____ disulfide bonds

In questions 19 through 23, match the function of a protein with each example.

19. ____ enzyme   A. myoglobin in the muscles
                       B. α-keratin in skin

20. ____ structural   C. peptidase for protein hydrolysis
                       D. casein in milk

21. ____ transport

22. ____ storage

23. Denaturation of a protein
    A. occurs at a pH of 7.
    B. causes a change in protein structure.
    C. hydrolyzes a protein.
    D. oxidizes the protein.
    E. adds amino acids to a protein.

24. Which of the following will not cause denaturation?
    A. 0°C   B. $AgNO_3$ C. 80°C   D. ethanol   E. pH 1

25. Enzymes are ____.

    A. biological catalysts.   B. polysaccharides.   C. insoluble in water.
    D. always contain a cofactor.   E. named with an "ose" ending.

Classify the enzymes described in questions 2 through 5 as (A) simple or (B) require a cofactor

26. ____ An enzyme that yields amino acids and a glucose molecule on analysis

27. ____ An enzyme consisting of protein only

28. ____ An enzyme requiring zinc ion for activation

29. ____ An enzyme containing vitamin K

For problems 30 through 34, select answers from the following: (**E** = enzyme; **S** = substrate; **P** = product)

A. S $\longrightarrow$ P   B. EP $\longrightarrow$ E + P   C. E + S $\longrightarrow$ ES
D. ES $\longrightarrow$ EP   E. EP $\longrightarrow$ ES

30. ____ The enzymatic reaction occurring at the active site

31. ____ The release of product from the enzyme

32. ____ The first step in the lock-and-key theory of enzyme action

33. ____ The formation of the enzyme-substrate complex

34. ____ The final step in the lock-and-key theory of enzyme action

In problems 35 through 39, match the names of enzymes with a reaction they each catalyze.

A. decarboxylase   B. isomerase   C. dehydrogenase
D. lipase   E. sucrase

35. ____ CH_3—CH(OH)—COOH $\longrightarrow$ CH_3—C(=O)—COOH

36. ____ sucrose + H_2O $\longrightarrow$ glucose and fructose

37. ____ CH_3—C(=O)—COOH $\longrightarrow$ $CH_3COOH + CO_2$

38. ____ fructose $\longrightarrow$ glucose

39. ____ triglyceride + $3H_2O$ $\longrightarrow$ fatty acids and glycerol

For problems 40 through 44 select your answers from A, B, or C.

A. Increases the rate of reaction   B. Decreases the rate of reaction
C. Denatures the enzyme and no reaction occurs

40. ____ Setting the reaction tube in a beaker of water at 100°C

41. ____ Adding substrate to the reaction vessel

42. ____ Running the reaction at 10°C

43. ____ Adding ethanol to the reaction system

44. ____ Adjusting the pH to optimum pH

For problems 45 through 47, identify each description of inhibition as

A. competitive   **B.** noncompetitive

45. _____ An alteration in the conformation of the enzyme

46. _____ A molecule closely resembling the substrate interferes with activity

47. _____ The inhibition can be reversed by increasing substrate concentration.

48. _____ The presence of zinc in the enzyme called alcohol dehydrogenase classifies a protein as

A. simple   **B.** requiring a cofactor   **C.** hormonal
D. structural   **E.** secondary

Answers to the Practice Test

1. C	2. D	3. E	4. B	5. E
6. A	7. C	8. B	9. A	10. E
11. A	12. B	13. D	14. A	15. B
16. D	17. B	18. C	19. C	20. B
21. A	22. D	23. B	24. A	25. A
26. B	27. A	28. B	29. B	30. D
31. B	32. C	33. C	34. B	35. C
36. E	37. A	38. B	39. D	40. C
41. A	42. B	43. C	44. A	45. B
46. A	47. A	48. B		

Answers and Solutions to Selected Text Problems

16.1   **a.** Hemoglobin, which carries oxygen in the blood, is a transport protein.
      b. Collagen, which is a major component of tendon and cartilage, is a structural protein.
      c. Keratin, which is found in hair, is a structural protein.
      d. Amylase, which catalyzes the breakdown of starch, is an enzyme.

16.3   All amino acids contain a carboxylic acid group and an amino group on the alpha carbon.

16.5   **a.**   **b.**

    c.   **d.**

16.7   **a.** Alanine, which has a methyl (hydrocarbon) side group, is nonpolar.
      b. Threonine has a side group that contains the polar —OH. Threonine is polar.
      c. Glutamic acid has a side group containing a polar carboxylic acid. Glutamic acid is acidic.
      d. Phenylalanine has a side group with a nonpolar benzene ring. Phenylalanine is nonpolar.

16.9   The abbreviations of most amino acids is derived from the first three letters in the name.

      a. alanine   **b.** valine   **c.** lysine   **d.** cysteine

16.11 In the L isomer, the —NH₂ is on the left side of the horizontal line of the Fischer projection; in D isomer, the —NH₂ group is on the right.

a.
$$
\begin{array}{c}
\text{COOH} \\
| \\
\text{H}_2\text{N}\!-\!\!-\!\text{H} \\
| \\
\text{CH} \\
\diagup \ \diagdown \\
\text{H}_3\text{C} \quad \text{CH}_3
\end{array}
$$

b.
$$
\begin{array}{c}
\text{COOH} \\
| \\
\text{H}\!-\!\!-\!\text{NH}_2 \\
| \\
\text{CH}_2\text{SH}
\end{array}
$$

16.13 A zwitterion is formed when the H from the acid part of the amino acid is transferred to the amine portion of the amino acid. The resulting dipolar ion has an overall zero charge.

a. $\overset{+}{\text{H}_3\text{N}}\!-\!\overset{\overset{\text{H}}{|}}{\text{CH}}\!-\!\overset{\overset{\text{O}}{||}}{\text{C}}\text{O}^-$

b. $\overset{+}{\text{H}_3\text{N}}\!-\!\overset{\overset{\text{SH}}{\overset{|}{\text{CH}_2}}}{\text{CH}}\!-\!\overset{\overset{\text{O}}{||}}{\text{C}}\text{O}^-$

c. $\overset{+}{\text{H}_3\text{N}}\!-\!\overset{\overset{\text{OH}}{\overset{|}{\text{CH}_2}}}{\text{CH}}\!-\!\overset{\overset{\text{O}}{||}}{\text{C}}\text{O}^-$

d. $\overset{+}{\text{H}_3\text{N}}\!-\!\overset{\overset{\text{CH}_3}{|}}{\text{CH}}\!-\!\overset{\overset{\text{O}}{||}}{\text{C}}\text{O}^-$

16.15 At low pH (highly acidic), the –COO⁻ of the zwitterion accepts a proton and the amino acid has a positive charge overall.

a. $\overset{+}{\text{H}_3\text{N}}\!-\!\overset{\overset{\text{H}}{|}}{\text{CH}}\!-\!\overset{\overset{\text{O}}{||}}{\text{C}}\text{OH}$

b. $\overset{+}{\text{H}_3\text{N}}\!-\!\overset{\overset{\text{SH}}{\overset{|}{\text{CH}_2}}}{\text{CH}}\!-\!\overset{\overset{\text{O}}{||}}{\text{C}}\text{OH}$

c. $\overset{+}{\text{H}_3\text{N}}\!-\!\overset{\overset{\text{OH}}{\overset{|}{\text{CH}_2}}}{\text{CH}}\!-\!\overset{\overset{\text{O}}{||}}{\text{C}}\text{OH}$

d. $\overset{+}{\text{H}_3\text{N}}\!-\!\overset{\overset{\text{CH}_3}{|}}{\text{CH}}\!-\!\overset{\overset{\text{O}}{||}}{\text{C}}\text{OH}$

16.17 a. A negative charge means the zwitterion donated a proton from —NH₃⁺, which occurs at pH levels above the isoelectric point

b. A positive charge means the zwitterion accepted a proton (H⁺) from an acidic solution, which occurs at a pH level below the isoelectric point.

c. A zwitterion with a net charge of zero means that the pH level is equal to the isoelectric point.

16.19 In a peptide, the amino acids are joined by peptide bonds (amide bonds). The first amino acid has a free amine group, and the last one has a free carboxyl group.

a. Ala-Cys

b. Ser-Phe

c.

$$\text{H}_3\overset{+}{\text{N}}\text{—CH}_2\text{—}\overset{\overset{\text{O}}{\|}}{\text{C}}\text{—NH—}\overset{\overset{\text{CH}_3}{|}}{\text{CH}}\text{—}\overset{\overset{\text{O}}{\|}}{\text{C}}\text{—NH—}\overset{\overset{\overset{\overset{\text{CH}_3}{|}}{\text{H}_3\text{C—CH}}}{|}}{\text{CH}}\text{—}\overset{\overset{\text{O}}{\|}}{\text{C}}\text{—O}^-$$

Gly-Ala-Val

d.

$$\text{H}_3\overset{+}{\text{N}}\text{—}\overset{\overset{\overset{\text{CH}_3}{|}}{\text{H}_3\text{C—CH}}}{\text{CH}}\text{—}\overset{\overset{\text{O}}{\|}}{\text{C}}\text{—NH—}\overset{\overset{\overset{\overset{\overset{\text{CH}_3}{|}}{\text{CH}_2}}{|}}{\text{H}_3\text{C—CH}}}{\text{CH}}\text{—}\overset{\overset{\text{O}}{\|}}{\text{C}}\text{—NH—}\overset{\overset{\text{CH}_2}{|}}{\text{CH}}\text{—}\overset{\overset{\text{O}}{\|}}{\text{C}}\text{—O}^-$$

Val-Ile-Trp

16.21 The primary structure of a protein is the order of amino acids; the bonds that hold the amino acids together in a protein are amide or peptide bonds.

16.23 The possible primary structure of a tripeptide of one valine and two serines are:

Val-Ser-Ser, Ser-Val-Ser, and Ser-Ser-Val

16.25 The primary structure remains unchanged and intact as hydrogen bonds form secondary structures.

16.27 In an alpha helix, there are hydrogen bonds between the different turns of the helix, which preserves the helical shape of the protein. In a beta-pleated sheet, the hydrogen bonds occur between two protein chains that are side by side or between different parts of a long protein.

16.29
   a. The two cysteine residues have —SH groups, which react to form a disulfide bond.
   b. Glutamic acid is acidic, and lysine is basic; the two groups form an ionic bond, or salt bridge.
   c. Serine has a polar —OH group that can form a hydrogen bond with the carboxyl group of aspartic acid.
   d. Two leucine residues are hydrocarbon and nonpolar. They would have a hydrophobic interaction.

16.31
   a. The R group of cysteine with the —SH group can form disulfide cross-links.
   b. Leucine and valine are found on the inside of the protein since they have nonpolar side groups and are hydrophobic.
   c. The cysteine and aspartic acid are on the outside of the protein since they are polar.
   d. The order of the amino acid (the primary structure) provides the R groups, whose interactions determine the tertiary structure of the protein.

16.33
   a. Placing an egg in boiling water disrupts hydrogen bonds and hydrophobic interactions, which cause a loss of overall shape.
   b. Using an alcohol swab disrupts hydrogen bonds and hydrophobic interactions, which changes the tertiary structure.
   c. The heat from an autoclave will disrupt hydrogen bonds and hydrophobic interactions in bacterial protein.
   d. Cauterization (heating) of a wound helps to close the wound by breaking hydrogen bonds and disrupting hydrophobic interactions.

16.35 The chemical reactions can occur without enzymes, but the rates are too slow. Catalyzed reactions, which are many times faster, provide the amounts of products needed by the cell at a particular time.

16.37 **a.** galactose   **b.** lipid   **c.** aspartic acid

16.39 **a.** A hydrolase enzyme would catalyze the hydrolysis of sucrose.
  b. An oxidase would catalyze the addition of oxygen (oxidation).
  c. An isomerase enzyme would catalyze converting glucose to fructose.
  d. A transaminase enzyme would catalyze moving an amino group.

16.41 **a.** An enzyme has a tertiary structure that recognized the substrate.
  b. The combination of the enzyme and substrate is the enzyme-substrate complex.
  c. The substrate has a structure that complements the structure of the enzyme.

16.43 **a.** The equation for an enzyme-catalyzed reaction is:

$$E + S \rightleftharpoons ES \longrightarrow E + P$$
E = enzyme, S = substrate, ES = enzyme-substrate complex, P = products

  b. The active site is a region or pocket within the tertiary structure of an enzyme that accepts the substrate, aligns the substrate for reaction, and catalyzes the reaction.

16.45 Isoenzymes are slightly different forms of an enzyme that catalyze the same reaction in different organs and tissues of the body.

16.47 A doctor might run tests for the enzymes CK, LDH, and AST to determine if the patient had a heart attack.

16.49 **a.** Decreasing the substrate concentration decreases the rate of reaction.
  b. Running the reaction at a pH below optimum pH will decrease the rate of reaction.
  c. Temperature above 37°C (optimum pH) will denature the enzymes and decrease the rate of reaction.

16.51 pepsin, pH 2; urease, pH 5; trypsin , pH 8

16.53 **a.** If the inhibitor has a structure similar to the structure of the substrate, the inhibitor is competitive
  b. If adding more substrate cannot reverse the effect of the inhibitor, the inhibitor is noncompetitive.
  c. If the inhibitor competes with the substrate for the active site, it is a competitive inhibitor.
  d. If the structure of the inhibitor is not similar to the structure of the substrate, the inhibitor is noncompetitive.
  e. If adding more substrate reverses inhibition, the inhibitor is competitive.

16.55 **a.** Methanol has the structural formula CH_3—OH whereas ethanol is CH_3—CH_2—OH.
  b. Ethanol has a structure similar to methanol and could compete for the active site.
  c. Ethanol is a competitive inhibitor of methanol oxidation.

16.57 **a.** The active form of this enzyme requires a cofactor.
  b. The active form of this enzyme requires a cofactor.
  c. A simple enzyme is active as a protein.

16.59 **a.** Pantothenic acid (vitamin B_5) is part of coenzyme A.
  b. Tetrahydrofolate (THF) is a reduced form of folic acid.
  c. Niacin (vitamin B_3) is a component of NAD^+.

16.61 **a.** Yes; a combination of rice and garbanzo beans contains all the three essential amino acids.

        b. Yes; a combination of lima beans and cornmeal beans contains all the three essential amino acids.

        c. No; a salad of garbanzo beans and lima beans does not contain all the three essential amino acids; it is deficient in tryptophan.

        d. Yes; combination of rice and lima beans contains all the three essential amino acids in lysine.

        e. No; a combination of rice and oatmeal does not contain all the essential amino acids, it is deficient in lysine.

        f. Yes; a combination of oatmeal and lima beans contains the three essential amino acids.

16.63 **a.** The secondary structure of a protein depends on hydrogen bonds to form a helix or a pleated sheet. The tertiary structure is determined by the interaction of R groups and determines the three dimensional structure of the protein.

        b. Nonessential amino acids are synthesized by the body, but essential amino acids must be supplied by the diet.

        c. Polar amino acids have hydrophilic side groups while nonpolar amino acids have hydrophobic side groups.

        d. Dipeptides contain two amino acids, while tripeptides contain three.

        e. An ionic bond is an interaction between a basic and acidic side group, a disulfide bond links the sulfides of two cysteines.

        f. Fibrous proteins consist of three to seven alpha helixes coiled like a rope. Globular proteins form a compact spherical shape.

        g. The alpha helix is the secondary shape like a spiral staircase or corkscrew. The beta-pleated sheet is a secondary structure that is formed by many proteins side by side, like a pleated sheet.

        h. The tertiary structure of a protein is its three dimensional structure. In the quaternary structure, two or more peptide subunits are grouped.

16.65 **a.**

$$\overset{+}{H_3N}-CH-\overset{\overset{\displaystyle O}{\|}}{C}-\overset{\overset{\displaystyle H}{|}}{N}-CH-\overset{\overset{\displaystyle O}{\|}}{C}-\overset{\overset{\displaystyle H}{|}}{N}-CH-\overset{\overset{\displaystyle O}{\|}}{C}-O^{-}$$

with the R groups: CH₂OH ; (CH₂)₄—NH₂ ; CH₂—COOH

        b. This segment contains polar R groups, which would be found on the surface of a globular proteins where they can hydrogen bond with water.

16.67 Serine is a polar amino acid, whereas valine is nonpolar. Valine would be in the center of the tertiary structure. However, serine would pull that part of the chain to the outside surface of the protein where valine forms hydrogen bonds with water.

16.69 When exposed to conditions of strong acids or bases, or high temperatures, enzymatic proteins are denatured rapidly, causing a loss of tertiary structure and catalytic activity.

16.71 **a.** The reactant is lactose and the products are glucose and galactose.

        b.

    c. By lowering the energy of activation, the enzyme furnishes a lower energy pathway by which the reaction can take place.

16.73   **a.** The disaccharide lactose is a substrate.
        b. The –*ase* in lactase indicates that it is an enzyme.
        c. The –*ase* in urease indicates that it is an enzyme.
        d. Trypsin is an enzyme, which hydrolyzes polypeptides.
        e. Pyruvate is a substrate.
        f. The –*ase* in transaminase indicates that it is an enzyme.

16.75   **a.** Urea is the substrate of urease.
        b. Lactose is the substrate of lactase.
        c. Aspartate is the substrate of aspartate transaminase.
        d. Tyrosine is the substrate of tyrosine synthetase.

16.77   Sucrose fits the shape of the active site in sucrase, but lactose does not.

16.79   A heart attack may be the cause. Normally the enzymes LDH and CK are present only in low levels in the blood.

16.81   **a.** An enzyme is saturated if adding more substrate does not increase the rate.
        b. An enzyme is unsaturated when increasing the substrate increases the rate.

16.83   **a.** The oxidation of glycol to an aldehyde and carboxylic acid is catalyzed by an oxidoreductase.
        b. At high concentration, ethanol, which acts as a competitive inhibitor of ethylene glycol, would saturate the enzyme to allow ethylene glycol to be removed from the body without producing oxalic acid.

16.85   **a.** The Mg^{2+} is a cofactor, which is required by this enzyme.
        b. A protein that is catalytically active is a simple enzyme.
        c. The folic acid is a coenzyme, which is required by this enzyme.

Nucleic Acids and Protein Synthesis

Study Goals

- Draw the structures of the nitrogen bases, sugars, and nucleotides in DNA and RNA.
- Describe the structures of DNA and RNA.
- Explain the process of DNA replication.
- Describe the transcription process during the synthesis of mRNA.
- Use the codons in the genetic code to describe protein synthesis.
- Explain how an alteration in the DNA sequence can lead to mutations in proteins.

Think About It

1. Where is DNA in your cells?

2. How does DNA determine your height, or the color of your hair or eyes?

3. What is the genetic code?

4. How does a mutation occur?

Key Terms

Match the statements show below with the following key terms:

a. DNA   **b.** RNA   **c.** double helix   **d.** mutation   **e.** transcription

1. _____ The formation of mRNA to carry genetic information from DNA to protein synthesis

2. _____ The genetic material containing nucleotides and nitrogenous bases adenine, cytosine, guanine, and thymine

3. _____ The shape of DNA with a sugar-phosphate backbone and base pairs linked in the center

4. _____ A change in the DNA base sequence that may alter the shape and function of a protein

5. _____ A type of nucleic acid with a single strand of nucleotides of adenine, cytosine, guanine, and uracil

Answers   **1.** e   **2.** a   **3.** c   **4.** d   **5.** b

17.1 Components of Nucleic Acids

- Nucleic acids are composed of four nitrogenous bases, five-carbon sugars, and a phosphate group.
- In DNA, the nitrogen bases are adenine, thymine, guanine, or cytosine. In RNA, uracil replaces thymine.
- In DNA, the sugar is deoxyribose; in RNA the sugar is ribose.
- A nucleoside is composed of a nitrogen base and a sugar.
- A nucleotide is composed of three parts: a nitrogen base, a sugar, and a phosphate group.
- Deoxyribonucleic acid (DNA) and ribonucleic acid (RNA) are polymers of nucleotides.

◆ **Learning Exercise 17.1A**

1. Write the names and abbreviations for the nitrogen bases in each of the following.

   DNA _____

   RNA _____

2. Write the name of the sugar in each of the following nucleotides.

   DNA _____

   RNA _____

Answers
1. DNA: adenine (A), thymine (T), guanine (G), cytosine (C)
   RNA: adenine (A), uracil (U), guanine (G), cytosine (C)
2. DNA: deoxyribose   RNA: ribose

◆ **Learning Exercise 17.1B**

Name each of the following and classify it as a purine or a pyrimidine.

Answers   **1.** cytosine; pyrimidine   **2.**   adenine; purine
            3. guanine; purine   **4.**   thymine, pyrimidine

◆ Learning Exercise 17.1C

Identify the nucleic acid (DNA or RNA) in which each of the following are found.

1. _____ adenosine-5′-monophosphate _____   **2.** _____ dCMP

3. _____ deoxythymidine-5′-monophosphate   **4.** _____ dGMP

5. _____ guanosine-5′-monophosphate   **6.** _____ cytidine-5′-monophosphate

7. _____ UMP   **8.** _____ deoxyadenosine-5′-monophosphate

Answers   **1.** RNA   **2.** DNA   **3.** DNA   **4.** DNA
            5. RNA   **6.** RNA   **7.** RNA   **8.** DNA

◆ Learning Exercise 17.1D

Write the structural formula for deoxyadenosine-5′-monophosphate. Indicate the 5′- and the 3′-carbon atoms on the sugar.

Answer

Deoxyadenosine 5′-monophosphate (dAMP)

17.2 Primary Structure of Nucleic Acids

- Nucleic acids are polymers of nucleotides in which the —OH group on the 3′-carbon of a sugar in one nucleotide bonds to the phosphate group attached to the 5′-carbon of a sugar in the adjacent nucleotide.

◆ Learning Exercise 17.2A

In the following dinucleotide, identify each nucleotide, the phosphodiester bond, the 5′-free phosphate group, and the free 3′-hydroxyl group.

Answer

◆ Learning Exercise 17.2B

Consider the following sequence of nucleotides in RNA: —A—G—U—C—

1. What are the names of the nucleotides in this sequence?

2. Which nucleotide has the free 5′-phosphate group? _____

3. Which nucleotide has the free 3′-hydroxyl group? _____

Answer
1. adenosine 5′-monophosphate, guanosine 5′-monophosphate, uridine 5′-monophosphate, cytosine 5′-monophosphate
2. adenosine 5′-monophosphate (AMP)
3. cytosine 5′-monophosphate (CMP)

17.3 DNA Double Helix

- The two strands in DNA are held together by hydrogen bonds between complementary base pairs, A with T, and G with C.
- During DNA replication, DNA polymerase makes new DNA strands along each of the original DNA strands that serve as templates.
- Complementary base pairing ensures the correct pairing of bases to give identical copies of the original DNA.

◆ Learning Exercise 17.3A

Complete the following statements.

1. The structure of the two strands of nucleotides in DNA is called a _____.

2. In one strand of DNA, the sugar-phosphate backbone runs in the 5′-3′ direction, whereas the opposite strand goes in the _____ direction.

3. The only combinations of base pairs that connect the two DNA strands are _____ and _____.

4. The base pairs along one DNA strand are _____ to the base pairs on the opposite strand.

Answers   1. double helix   2. 3′-5′   3. A—T; G—C   5. complementary

◆ Learning Exercise 17.3B

Complete each DNA section by writing the complementary strand:

1. —ATGCTTGGCTCC—

2. —AAATTTCCCGGG—

3. —GCGCTCAAATGC—

Answers   1. —TACGAACCGAGG—   2. —TTTAAAGGGCCC—
3. —CGCGAGTTTAC.

◆ Learning Exercise 17.3C

How does the replication of DNA produce identical copies of the DNA?

Answer   In the replication process, the bases on each strand of the separated parent DNA are paired with their complementary bases. Because each complementary base is specific for a base in DNA, the new DNA strands exactly duplicate the original strands of DNA.

17.4 RNA and the Genetic Code

- The three types of RNA differ by function in the cell: ribosomal RNA makes up most of the structure of the ribosomes, messenger RNA carries genetic information from the DNA to the ribosomes, and transfer RNA places the correct amino acids in the protein.
- Transcription is the process by which RNA polymerase produces mRNA from one strand of DNA.
- The bases in the mRNA are complementary to the DNA, except U is paired with A in DNA.
- The production of mRNA occurs when certain proteins are needed in the cell.
- The genetic code consists of a sequence of three bases (triplet) that specifies the order for the amino acids in a protein.
- There are 64 codons for the 20 amino acids, which means there are several codons for most amino acids.
- The codon AUG signals the start of transcription and codons UAG, UGA, and UAA signal stop.

◆ Learning Exercise 17.4A

Match each of the following characteristics with a specific type of RNA: mRNA, tRNA, or rRNA.

1. the most abundant type of RNA in a cell _____

2. the RNA that has the shortest chain of nucleotides _____

3. the RNA that carries information from DNA to the ribosomes for protein synthesis _____

4. the RNA that is the major component of ribosomes _____

5. the RNA that carries specific amino acids to the ribosome for protein synthesis _____

6. the RNA that consists of a large and a small subunit _____

Answers   1. rRNA   2. tRNA   3. mRNA
             4. rRNA   5. tRNA   6. rRNA

◆ Learning Exercise 17.4B

Fill in the blanks with a word or phrase that answers each of the following questions:

1. Where in the cell does transcription take place? _____

2. How many strands of the DNA molecules are involved? _____

3. The abbreviations for the four nucleotides in mRNA are _____

4. Write the corresponding section of a mRNA produced from each of the following questions.

    A. —C—A—T—T—C—G—G—T—A—

    B. —G—T—A—C—C—T—A—A—C—G—T—C—C—G—

Answers   **1.** nucleus   **2.** one   **3.** A, U, G, C
                 4. **A.** —G—U—A—A—G—C—C—A—U—
                      B. —C—A—U—G—G—A—U—U—G—C—A—G—G—C—

◆ Learning Exercise 17.4C

Indicate the amino acid coded for by the following mRNA codons.

1. UUU _____   **2.** GCG _____

3. AGC _____   **4.** CCA _____

5. GGA _____   **6.** ACA _____

7. AUG _____   **8.** CUC _____

9. CAU _____   **10.** GUU _____

Answers   **1.** Phe   **2.** Ala   **3.** Ser   **4.** Pro   **5.** Gly
              6. Thr   **7.** Start/Met **8.** Leu   **9.** His   **10.** Val

17.5 Protein Synthesis: Translation

- Proteins are synthesized at the ribosomes in a translation process that includes three steps: initiation, elongation, and termination.
- During translation, the different tRNA molecules bring the appropriate amino acids to the ribosome where the amino acid is bonded by a peptide bond to the growing peptide chain.
- When the polypeptide is released, it takes on its secondary and tertiary structures to become a functional protein in the cell.

◆ Learning Exercise 17.5A

Match the following components of the translation process with the following.

a. initiation   **b.** activation   **c.** anticodon   **d.** translocation   **e.** termination

1. ____ The three bases in each tRNA that complement a codon on the mRNA

2. ____ The combining of an amino acid with a specific tRNA

3. ____ The placement of methionine on the large ribosome

4. ____ The shift of the ribosome from one codon on mRNA to the next

5. ____ The process that occurs when the ribosome reaches a UAA or UGA codon on mRNA

◆ **Learning Exercise 17.5B**

Write the mRNA that would form for the following section of DNA. For each codon in the mRNA, write the amino acid that would be placed in the protein by a tRNA.

1. DNA strand: —CCC—TCA—GGG—CGC—

    mRNA: —_____—_____—_____—_____—

    amino acid order: _____—_____—_____—_____

2. DNA: —ATA—GCC—TTT—GGC—AAC—

    mRNA: —_____—_____—_____—_____—_____—

    amino acid order: —_____—_____—_____—_____—_____—_____

Answers   **1.** mRNA: —GGG—AGU—CCC—GCG—
                          —Gly—Ser—Pro—Ala—
           2. mRNA: —UAU—CGG—AAA—CCG—UUG—
                          — Tyr—Arg—Lys—Pro—Leu—

◆ **Learning Exercise 17.5C**

A segment of DNA that codes for a protein contains 270 nucleic acids. How many amino acids would be present in the protein for this DNA segment?

Answer   Assuming that the entire segment codes for a protein, there would be 90
                $(270 \div 3)$ amino acids in the protein produced.

17.6 Genetic Mutations

- A genetic mutation is a change of one or more bases in the DNA sequence that may alter the structure and ability of the resulting protein to function properly.
- In a substitution, one base is altered, which codes for a different amino acid.
- In a frame shift mutation, the insertion or deletion of one base alters all the codons following the base change, which affects the amino acid sequence that follows the mutation.

◆ **Learning Exercise 17.6**

Consider the DNA template of —AAT—CCC—GGG—.

1. Write the mRNA produced.

    _____—_____—_____

2. Write the amino acid order for the mRNA codons.

_____—_____—_____

3. Suppose thymine in the DNA template is replaced with a guanine. Write the mRNA it produces.

_____—_____—_____

4. What is the new amino acid order?

_____—_____—_____

5. What are some possible causes of genetic mutations?

Answers **1.** —UUA—GGG—CCC—   **2.** Leu-Gly-Pro
3. —UUC—GGG—CCC—   **4.** Phe-Gly-Pro
5. X-rays, UV light, chemicals called mutagens, and some viruses are possible causes of mutations.

17.7 Viruses

* Viruses are small particles of 3-200 genes that cannot replicate unless they invade a host cell.
* A viral infection involves using the host cell machinery to replicate the viral DNA.
* A retrovirus contains RNA and a reverse transcriptase enzyme that synthesizes a viral DNA in a host cell.

◆ Learning Exercise 17.7

Match the key terms with the statements shown below

A. host cell   **B.** retrovirus   **C.** vaccine   **D.** protease   **E.** virus

1. _____ The enzyme inhibited by drugs that prevent the synthesis of viral proteins

2. _____ A small, disease-causing particle that contains either DNA or RNA as its genetic material

3. _____ A type of virus that must use reverse transcriptase to make a viral DNA

4. _____ Required by viruses to replicate

5. _____ Inactive form of viruses that boosts the immune response by causing the body to produce antibodies

Answers   **1.** D   **2.** E   **3.** B   **4.** A   **5.** C

Check List for Chapter 17

You are ready to take the practice test for Chapter 17. Be sure that you have accomplished the following learning goals for this chapter. If you are not sure, review the section listed at the end of the goal. Then apply your new skills and understanding to the practice test.

After studying Chapter 17, I can successfully:

_____ Identify the components of nucleic acids RNA and DNA (17.1).

_____ Describe the nucleotides contained in DNA and RNA (17.1).

_____ Describe the primary structure of nucleic acids (17.2).

_____ Describe the structures of RNA and DNA; show the relationship between the bases in the double helix (17.3).

_____ Explain the process of DNA replication (17.3)

_____ Describe the structures and characteristics of the three types of RNA (17.4).

_____ Describe the synthesis of mRNA (transcription) (17.4).

_____ the function of the codons in the genetic code (17.4).

_____ Describe the role of translation in protein synthesis (17.5).

_____ Describe some ways in which DNA is altered to cause mutations (17.6).

_____ Explain how retroviruses use reverse transcription to synthesize DNA (17.7)

Practice Test for Chapter 17

1. A nucleotide contains

    A. a nitrogen base.   B. a nitrogen base and a sugar.
    C. a phosphate and a sugar.   D. a nitrogen base and a deoxyribose.
    E. a nitrogen base, a sugar, and a phosphate.

2. The double helix in DNA is held together by

    A. hydrogen bonds.   B. ester linkages.   C. peptide bonds.
    D. salt bridges.   E. disulfide bonds.

3. The process of producing DNA in the nucleus is called

    A. complementation.   B. replication.   C. translation.
    D. transcription.   E. mutation.

4. Which occurs in RNA but **NOT** in DNA?

    A. thymine   B. cytosine   C. adenine
    D. phosphate   E. uracil

5. Which molecule determines protein structure in protein synthesis?

    A. DNA   B. mRNA   C. tRNA   D. rRNA   E. ribosomes

6. Which type of molecule carries amino acids to the ribosomes?

    A. DNA   B. mRNA   C. tRNA   D. rRNA   E. protein

For questions 7 through 15, select answers from the following nucleic acids.

A. DNA   **B.** mRNA   **C.** tRNA   **D.** rRNA

7. _____ Along with protein, it is a major component of the ribosomes.

8. _____ A double helix consisting of two chains of nucleotides held together by hydrogen bonds between nitrogen bases.

9. _____ A nucleic acid that uses deoxyribose as the sugar.

10. _____ A nucleic acid produced in the nucleus that migrates to the ribosomes to direct the formation of a protein.

11. _____ It can place the proper amino acid into the peptide chain.

12. _____ It has nitrogen bases of adenine, cytosine, guanine, and thymine.

13. _____ It contains the codons for the amino acid order.

14. _____ It contains a triplet called an anticodon loop.

15. _____ This nucleic acid is replicated during cellular division.

For questions 16 through 20, select answers from the following.

A. —A—G—C—C—T—A—
      | | | | | |
     —T—C—G—G—A—T—

B. —A—U—U—G—C—U—C—

C. —A—G—T—U—G—U—
      | | | | | |
     —T—C—A—A—C—A—

D. —G—U—A—

E. —A—T—G—T—A—T—

16. _____ A section of a mRNA

17. _____ An impossible section of DNA

18. _____ A codon

19. _____ A section from a DNA molecul

20. _____ A single strand that would not be possible for mRNA

Read the following statements.

A. tRNA assembles the amino acids at the ribosomes.
B. DNA forms a complementary copy of itself called mRNA.
C. Protein is formed and breaks away.
D. tRNA picks up specific amino acids.
E. mRNA goes to the ribosomes.

Of the statements above, select the order in which they occur during protein synthesis.

21. _____ First step   22. _____ Second step   23. _____ Third step

24. _____ Fourth step   25. _____ Fifth step

Answers to the Practice Test

1. E	2. A	3. B	4. E	5. A
6. C	7. D	8. A	9. A	10. B
11. C	12. A	13. B	14. C	15. A
16. B, D	17. C	18. D	19. A	20. E
21. B	22. E	23. D	24. A	25. C

Answers and Solutions to Selected Text Problems

17.1 DNA contains two purines, adenine (A) and guanine (G) and two pyrimidines, cytosine (C) and thymine (T). RNA contains the same bases, except thymine (T) is replaced by the pyrimidine uracil (U).

    a. Pyrimidine   **b.** Pyrimidine

17.3 DNA contains two purines, adenine (A) and guanine (G) and two pyrimidines, cytosine (C) and thymine (T). RNA contains the same bases, except thymine (T) is replaced by the pyrimidine uracil (U).

    a. DNA   **b.** Both DNA and RNA

17.5 Nucleotides contain a base, a sugar, and a phosphate group. The nucleotides found in DNA would all contain the sugar deoxyribose. The four nucleotides are: deoxyadenosine-5′-monophosphate (dAMP), deoxythymidine-5′-monophosphate (dTMP), deoxycytidine-5′-monophosphate (dCMP), and deoxyguanosine-5′-monophosphate (dGMP).

17.7   **a.** Adenosine is a nucleoside found in RNA.
       b. Deoxycytidine is a nucleoside found in DNA.
       c. Uridine is a nucleoside found in RNA.
       d. Cytidine-5′-monophosphate is a nucleotide found in RNA.

17.9

17.11 The nucleotides in nucleic acids are held together by phosphodiester bonds between the 3′ OH of a sugar (ribose or deoxyribose) and the 5′ OH of another sugar.

17.13

17.15 The two DNA strands are held together by hydrogen bonds between the bases in each strand.

17.17 **a.** Since T pairs with A, if one strand of DNA has the sequence —AAAAAA—, the second strand would be: —TTTTTT—.
   b. Since C pairs with G, if one strand of DNA has the sequence —GGGGGG—, the second strand would be: —CCCCCC—.
   c. Since T pairs with A, and C pairs with G, if one strand of DNA has the sequence —AGTCCAGGT—, the second strand would be —TCAGGTCCA—.
   d. Since T pairs with A, and C pairs with G, if one strand of DNA has the sequence —CTGTATACGTTA, the second strand would be: —GACATATGCAAT—.

17.19 Ribosomal RNA (rRNA) is found in the ribosomes, which are the sites for protein synthesis. Transfer RNA (tRNA) brings specific amino acids to the ribosomes for protein synthesis. Messenger RNA (mRNA) carries the information needed for protein synthesis from the DNA in the nucleus to the ribosomes.

17.21 In transcription, the sequence of nucleotides on a DNA template (one strand) is used to produce the base sequences of a messenger RNA. The DNA unwinds and one strand is copied as complementary bases are placed in the mRNA molecule. In RNA, U (uracil) is paired with A in DNA.

17.23 In mRNA, C, G, and A pair with G, C, and T in DNA. However, in mRNA U will pair with A in DNA. The strand of mRNA would have the following sequence:
   —GGC—UUC—CAA—GUG—.

17.25 A codon is the three-base sequence (triplet) in mRNA that codes for a specific amino acid in a protein.

17.27 **a.** The codon CUU in mRNA codes for the amino acid leucine.
   b. The codon UCA in mRNA codes for the amino acid serine.
   c. The codon GGU in mRNA codes for the amino acid glycine.
   d. The codon AGG in mRNA codes for the amino acid arginine.

17.29 When AUG is the first codon, it signals the start of protein synthesis and incorporates methionine as the first amino acid in the peptide. Eventually the initial methionine is removed as the protein forms its secondary and tertiary protein structure. In the middle of an mRNA sequence AUG codes for methionine.

17.31 A codon is a base triplet in the mRNA template. An anticodon is the complementary triplet on a tRNA for a specific amino acid.

17.33 The mRNA must be divided into triplets and the amino acid coded for by each triplet read from the table.
   a. The codon AAA in mRNA codes for lysine: —Lys—Lys—Lys—
   b. The codon UUU codes for phenylalanine and CCC for proline: —Phe—Pro—Phe—Pro—
   c. —Tyr—Gly—Arg—Cys—

17.35 After a tRNA attaches to the first binding site on the ribosome, its amino acid forms a peptide bond with the amino acid on the tRNA attached to the second binding site. The ribosome moves along the mRNA and a new tRNA with its amino acid occupies the open binding site.

17.37 **a.** By using the pairing: DNA bases   C   G   T   A
                                                    ↓   ↓   ↓   ↓
                                      mRNA bases   G   C   A   U
   the mRNA sequence can be determined: —CGA—AAA—GUU—UUU—.
   b. The tRNA triplet anticodons would be as follows: GCU, UUU, CAA, AAA.

c. The mRNA is divided into triplets and the amino acid coded for by each triplet read from the table. Using codons in mRNA: Arg—Lys—Val—Phe.

17.39 In a substitution mutation an incorrect base replaces a base in DNA.

17.41 If the resulting codon still codes for the same amino acid, there is no effect. If the new codon codes for a different amino acid, there is a change in the order of amino acids in the polypeptide.

17.43 The normal triplet TTT in DNA transcribes to AAA in mRNA. AAA codes for lysine. The mutation TTC in DNA transcribes to AAG in mRNA, which also codes for lysine. Thus, there is no effect on protein synthesis.

17.45
  a. —Thr—Ser—Arg—Val— is the amino acid sequence produced by normal DNA.
  b. —Thr—Thr—Arg—Val— is the amino acid sequence produced by a mutation.
  c. —Thr—Ser—Gly—Val— is the amino acid sequence produced by a mutation.
  d. —Thr—STOP   Protein synthesis would terminate early. If this mutation occurs early in the formation of the polypeptide, the resulting protein will probably be nonfunctional.
  e. The new protein will contain the sequence —Asp—Ile—Thr—Gly—.
  f. The new protein will contain the sequence —His—His—Gly—.

17.47
  a. Both codons GCC and GCA code for alanine.
  b. A vital ionic cross-link in the tertiary structure of hemoglobin cannot be formed when the polar glutamine is replaced by valine, which is nonpolar. The resulting hemoglobin is malformed and less capable of carrying oxygen.

17.49 A virus contains either DNA or RNA, but not both, inside a protein coating.

17.51
  a. An RNA-containing virus must make viral DNA from the RNA, a process called reverse transcription.
  b. A virus that uses reverse transcription is a retrovirus.

17.53 Nucleoside analogs like AZT or ddI mimic the structures of nucleosides that the HIV virus uses for DNA synthesis. These analogs are incorporated into the new viral DNA chain, but the lack of a hydroxyl group in position 3' of the sugar stops the chain from growing any longer and prevents replication of the virus.

17.55
  a. pyrimidine   **b.** purine   **c.** pyrimidine
  d. pyrimidine   **e.** purine

17.57
  a. thymine and deoxyribose   **b.** adenine and ribose
  c. cytosine and ribose   **d.** guanine and deoxyribose

17.59 They are both pyrimidines, but thymine has a methyl group.

17.61 They are both polymers of nucleotides connected through phosphodiester bonds between alternating sugar and phosphate groups with bases extending out from each sugar.

17.63
  a. —CTGAATCCG—
  b. —ACGTTTGATCGT—
  c. —TAGCTAGCTAGC—

17.65 **a.** tRNA   **b.** rRNA   **c.** mRNA

17.67
  a. ACU, ACC, ACA, and ACG
  b. UAU, UCC, UCA, and UCG
  c. UGU and UGC
  d.

17.69 **a.** AAG codes for lysine   **b.** AUU codes for isoleucine   **c.** CGG codes for arginine

17.71 Using the genetic code the codons indicate the following:
start(methionine) —Tyr—Gly—Gly—Phe—Leu—stop

17.73 The anticodon consists of the three complementary bases to the codon.
a. UCG   **b.** AUA   **c.** GGU

17.75 Three nucleotides are needed for each amino acid plus a start and stop triplet, which makes a minimum total of 33 nucleotides.

17.77 A DNA virus attaches to a cell and injects viral DNA that uses the host cell to produce copies of DNA to make viral RNA. A retrovirus injects viral RNA from which complementary DNA is produced by reverse transcription.

Metabolic Pathways and Energy Production

Study Goals

- Explain the role of ATP in anabolic and catabolic reactions.
- Compare the structures and function of the coenzymes NAD^+, FAD, and coenzyme A.
- Give the sites, enzymes, and products for the digestion of carbohydrates, triacylglycerols, and proteins.
- Describe the key reactions in the degradation of glucose in glycolysis.
- Describe the pathways for pyruvate.
- Describe the reactions in the citric acid cycle that oxidize acetyl CoA.
- Explain how electrons from NADH and H^+ and FAD move along the electron transport chain to form H_2O.
- Describe the role of oxidative phosphorylation in ATP synthesis.
- Calculate the ATP produced by the complete combustion of glucose.
- Describe the oxidation of fatty acids via β-oxidation.
- Calculate the ATP produced by the complete oxidation of a fatty acid.
- Explain the role of transamination and oxidative deamination in the degradation of amino acids.

Think About It

1. Why do you need ATP in your cells?

2. What monosaccharides are produced when carbohydrates undergo digestion?

3. What is meant by *aerobic* and *anaerobic* conditions in the cells?

4. Why is the citric acid cycle considered a central pathway in metabolism?

5. How is the citric acid cycle connected to electron transport?

6. Which stage of metabolism produces most of the ATP for the cells?

7. What are the products from the digestion of triacylglycerols and proteins?

8. When do you utilize fats and proteins for energy?

Key Terms

1. Match the key terms with the correct statement shown below.

a. ATP   **b.** anabolic reaction   **c.** glycolysis
d. catabolic reaction   **e.** mitochondria

1. _____ A metabolic reaction that uses energy to build large molecules.

2. _____ A metabolic reaction that produces energy for the cell by degrading large molecules

3. _____ A high-energy compound produced from energy-releasing processes that provides energy for energy-producing reactions

4. _____ The degradation reactions of glucose that yield two pyruvate molecules

5. _____ The organelles in the cells where energy-producing reactions take place

Answers   **1.** b   **2.** d   **3.** a   **4.** c   **5.** e

2. Match the key terms with the correct statement shown below.

a. citric acid cycle   **b.** oxidative phosphorylation   **c.** coenyzme Q
d. cytochromes   **e.** proton pump

1. _____ A mobile carrier that passes electrons from NADH and $FADH_2$ to cytochrome b in complex III

2. _____ Proteins containing iron as Fe^{3+} or Fe^{2+} that transfer electrons from QH_2 to oxygen

3. _____ A function of complexes I, II, and III whereby protons move from the matrix into the intermembrane space to create a proton gradient

4. _____ The synthesis of ATP from ADP and P_i using energy generated from electron transport

5. _____ Oxidation reactions that convert acetyl CoA to CO_2 producing reduced coenzymes for energy production via the electron chain transport system.

Answers   **1.** c   **2.** d   **3.** e   **4.** b   **5.** a

18.1 Metabolism and ATP Energy

- Metabolism is all the chemical reactions that provide energy and substances for cell growth.
- Catabolic reactions degrade large molecules to produce energy.
- Anabolic reactions utilize energy in the cells to build large molecules for the cells.
- Energy is stored in ATP, a high-energy compound that is hydrolyzed when energy is required for the anabolic reactions that do work in the cells.
- The hydrolysis of ATP, which releases energy, is linked with many anabolic reactions in the cell.

◆ Learning Exercise 18.1A

Identify the stages of metabolism for each of the following processes.

a. Stage 1   **b.** Stage 2   **c.** Stage 3

1. _____ Oxidation of two-carbon acetyl CoA enters a series of reactions that provide most of the energy for ATP synthesis.

2. _____ Polysaccharides undergo digestion to monosaccharides such as glucose.

3. _____ Digestion products such as glucose are degraded to two- or three-carbon compounds.

Answers   **1.** c   **2.** a   **3.** b

◆ Learning Exercise 18.1B

Complete the following statements for ATP.

The ATP molecule is composed of a nitrogen-base (1)_____, a (2) _____ sugar, and three (3) _____. ATP undergoes (4)_____, which cleaves a (5) _____ and releases (6) _____. For this reason,

ATP is called a (7)_____ compound. The resulting phosphate group, called

inorganic phosphate, is abbreviated as (8) _____. This equation can be written as

(9)_____. The energy from ATP is

linked to cellular reactions that are (10)_____.

Answers   **1.** adenine **2.** ribose **3.** phosphate groups **4.** hydrolysis
5. phosphate **6.** energy **7.** high-energy **8.** P_i
9. $ATP + H_2O \longrightarrow ADP + P_i + Energy$ (7.3 kcal/mole) **10.** energy requiring

18.2 Digestion: Stage 1

- Digestion is a series of reactions that break down large food molecules of carbohydrates, lipids, and proteins into smaller molecules that can be absorbed and used by the cells.
- The end products of digestion of polysaccharides are the monosaccharides glucose, fructose, and galactose.
- Proteins begin digestion in the stomach, where HCl denatures proteins and activates peptidases that hydrolyze peptide bonds.
- In the small intestine trypsin and chymotrypsin complete the hydrolysis of peptides to amino acids.
- Dietary fats begin digestion in the small intestine where they are emulsified by bile salts.
- Pancreatic lipases hydrolyze the triacylglycerols to yield monoacylglycerols and free fatty acids.
- The triacylglycerols reformed in the intestinal lining combine with proteins to form chylomicrons for transport through the lymph system and bloodstream.
- In the cells, triacylglycerols hydrolyze to glycerol and fatty acids, which can be used for energy.

◆ Learning Exercise 18.2A

Complete the table to describe sites, enzymes, and products for the digestion of carbohydrates.

Food	Digestion site(s)	Enzyme	Products
1. amylose			
2. amylopectin			
3. maltose			
4. lactose			
5. sucrose			

Answers

Food	Digestion site(s)	Enzyme	Products
1. amylose	**a.** mouth **b.** small intestine	**a.** salivary amylase **b.** pancreatic amylase	**a.** smaller polysaccharides (dextrins), some maltose and glucose **b.** maltose, glucose
2. amylopectin	**a.** mouth **b.** small intestine	**a.** salivary amylase **b.** pancreatic amylase	**a.** smaller polysaccharides (dextrins), some maltose and glucose **b.** maltose, glucose
3. maltose	small intestine	maltase	glucose and glucose
4. lactose	small intestine	lactase	glucose and galactose
5. sucrose	small intestine	sucrase	glucose and fructose

◆ Learning Exercise 18.2B

Match each of the following terms with the correct description.

   a. stomach   **b.** small intestine

1. _____ HCl activates enzymes that hydrolyzes peptide bonds in proteins

2. _____ trypsin and chymotrypsin convert peptides to amino acids

Answers   **1.** a   **2.** b

18.3 Important Coenzymes in Metabolic Pathways

- Coenzymes such as FAD and NAD^+ pick up hydrogen and electrons during oxidative processes.
- Coenzyme A is a coenzyme that carries acetyl (two-carbon) groups produced when glucose, fatty acids, and amino acids are degraded.

◆ Learning Exercise 18.3

Select the coenzyme that matches each of the following descriptions of coenzymes.

  a. NAD^+ **b.** NADH   **c.** FAD   **d.** $FADH_2$ **e.** coenzyme A

1. _____ participates in reactions that convert a hydroxyl group to a $C{=}O$ group

2. _____ contains riboflavin (vitamin B_2)

3. _____ reduced form of nicotinamide adenine dinucleotide

4. _____ contains the vitamin niacin

5. _____ oxidized form of flavin adenine dinucleotide

6. _____ contains the vitamin pantothenic acid, ADP, and an aminoethanethiol

7. _____ participates in oxidation reactions that produce a carbon–carbon double bond (C=C)

8. _____ transfers acyl groups such as the two-carbon acetyl group

9. _____ reduced form of flavin adenine dinucleotide

Answers	**1.** a	**2.** c, d	**3.** b	**4.** a, b	**5.** c
	6. e	**7.** c	**8.** e	**9.** d	

18.4 Glycolysis: Stage 2

- Glycolysis is the primary anaerobic pathway for the degradation of glucose to yield pyruvic acid.
- Glucose is converted to fructose-1,6-diphosphate that is split into two triose phosphate molecules.
- The oxidation of the three-carbon sugars yields the reduced coenzyme 2 NADH and 2 ATP.
- In the absence of oxygen, pyruvate is reduced to lactate and NAD^+ is regenerated for the continuation of glycolysis.
- Under aerobic conditions, pyruvate is oxidized in the mitochondria to acetyl CoA, which enters the citric acid cycle.

◆ Learning Exercise 18.4A

Match each of the following terms of glycolysis with the best description.

a. 2 NADH	**b.** anaerobic	**c.** glucose	**d.** two pyruvate
e. energy invested	**f.** energy generated	**g.** 2 ATP	**h.** 4 ATP

1. _____ the starting material for glycolysis   **2.** _____ Steps 1–5 of glycolysis

3. _____ operates without oxygen   **4.** _____ net ATP energy produced

5. _____ number of reduced coenzymes produced   **6.** _____ Steps 6–10 of glycolysis

7. _____ end product of glycolysis   **8.** _____ number of ATP required

Answers	**1.** c	**2.** e	**3.** b	**4.** g	**5.** a
	6. f	**7.** d, a	**8.** g		

◆ Learning Exercise 18.4B

Fill in the blanks with the following terms.

lactate	NAD^+	acetyl CoA
NADH	aerobic	anaerobic

When oxygen is available during glycolysis, the three-carbon pyruvate may be oxidized to form

(1)_____ + CO_2. The coenzyme (2)_____ is reduced to (3)_____.

Under (4)_____ conditions, pyruvate is reduced to (5)_____.

Answers   1. acetyl CoA   2. NAD$^+$ 3. NADH
               4. anaerobic   5. lactate

◆ Learning Exercise 18.4C

Essay: Explain how the formation of lactate from pyruvate during anaerobic conditions allows glycolysis to continue.

Answer   Under anaerobic conditions, the oxidation of pyruvate to acetyl CoA to regenerate NAD$^+$ cannot take place. Then, pyruvate is reduced to lactate using NADH in the cytoplasm and regenerating NAD$^+$.

18.5 The Citric Acid Cycle: Stage 3

- Under aerobic conditions, pyruvate is oxidized in the mitochondria to acetyl CoA, which enters the citric acid cycle.
- In a sequence of reactions called the citric acid cycle, acetyl CoA combines with oxaloacetate to yield citrate.
- In one turn of the citric acid cycle, the oxidation of acetyl CoA yields two CO_2, GTP, three NADH, and FADH$_2$. The phosphorylation of ADP by GTP yields ATP.

◆ Learning Exercise 18.5

In each of the following steps of the citric acid cycle, indicate if oxidation occurs (yes/no) and any coenzyme or direct phosphorylation product produced (NADH + H$^+$, FADH$_2$, GTP).

Step in citric acid cycle	Oxidation	Coenzyme
1. acetyl CoA + oxaloacetate ⟶ citrate	_____	_____
2. citrate ⟶ isocitrate	_____	_____
3. isocitrate ⟶ α-ketoglutarate acid	_____	_____
4. α-ketoglutarate ⟶ succinyl CoA	_____	_____
5. succinyl CoA ⟶ succinate	_____	_____
6. succinate ⟶ fumarate	_____	_____
7. fumarate ⟶ malate	_____	_____
8. malate ⟶ oxaloacetate	_____	_____

Answers   1. no   2. no   3. yes, NADH + H$^+$ 4. yes, NADH + H$^+$

5. no, GTP   6. yes, FADH$_2$ 7. no   8. yes, NADH + H$^+$

18.6 Electron Transport

- The reduced coenzymes from glycolysis and the citric acid cycle are oxidized to NAD⁺ and FAD by transferring protons and electrons to the electron transport chain.
- In the electron transport system or respiratory chain, electrons are transferred to electron carriers including flavins, coenzyme Q, iron-sulfur proteins, and cytochromes with Fe^{3+}/Fe^{2+}.
- The final acceptor, O_2, combines with protons and electrons to yield H_2O.

◆ Learning Exercise 18.6A

Write the oxidized and reduced forms of each of the following electron carriers.

1. flavin mononucleotide   oxidized _____   reduced _____

2. coenzyme Q   oxidized _____   reduced _____

3. iron-protein clusters   oxidized _____   reduced _____

4. cytochrome b   oxidized _____   reduced _____

Answers   1. oxidized: FMN   reduced: $FMNH_2$
              2. oxidized: Q   reduced: QH_2
              3. oxidized: Fe^{3+} S cluster   reduced Fe^{2+} S cluster
              4. oxidized: Cyt b (Fe^{3+})   reduced Cyt b (Fe^{2+})

◆ Learning Exercise 18.6B

Identify the protein complexes and mobile carriers in the electron transport chain.

a. cytochrome *c* oxidase (IV)   **b.** NADH dehydrogenase (I)   **c.** cytochrome *c*
d. coenzyme Q-cytochrome *c* reductase (III)   **e.** succinate dehydrogenase (II)   **f.** Q

1. _____ FMN and Fe-S clusters

2. _____ $FADH_2 + Q \longrightarrow FAD + QH_2$

3. _____ mobile carrier from complex I or complex II to complex III

4. _____ electrons are passed from cyt *a* and a_3 to O_2 and $4H^+$ to yield $2H_2O$

5. _____ mobile carrier between complex III and IV

6. _____ cyt b and Fe-S clusters

Answers   1. b   2. e   3. f   4. a   5. c   6. d

◆ Learning Exercise 18.6C

1. Write an equation for the transfer of hydrogen from $FMNH_2$ to Q.

2. What is the function of coenzyme Q in the electron transport chain?

3. What are the end products of the electron transport chain?

Answers
1. $FMNH_2 + Q \longrightarrow FMN + QH_2$
2. Q accepts hydrogen atoms from $FMNH_2$ or $FADH_2$. From QH_2, the hydrogen atoms are separated into protons and electrons with the electrons being passed on to the cytochromes, the electron acceptors in the chain.
3. $CO_2 + H_2O$

18.7 Oxidative Phosphorylation and ATP

- The flow of electrons along the electron chain pumps protons across the inner membrane, which produces a high-energy proton gradient that provides energy for the synthesis of ATP.
- The process of using the energy of the electron transport chain to synthesize ATP is called oxidative phosphorylation.
- The oxidation of NADH yields three ATP molecules, and $FADH_2$ yields two ATP.
- The complete oxidation of glucose yields a total of 36 ATP from direct phosphorylation and the oxidation of the reduced coenzymes NADH and $FADH_2$ by the electron transport chain and oxidative phosphorylation.

◆ Learning Exercise 18.7A

Match the following terms with the correct description below:

a. oxidative phosphorylation   b. ATP synthase
c. proton pumps   d. proton gradient

1. _____ the complexes I, III, and IV through which II^+ ions move out of the matrix into the inner membrane space

2. _____ the protein tunnel where proton flow from the intermembrane space back to the matrix generates energy for ATP synthesis

3. _____ energy from electron transport is used to form a proton gradient that drives ATP synthesis

4. _____ the accumulation of protons in the intermembrane space that lowers pH

Answers   1. c   2. b   3. a   4. d

◆ Learning Exercise 18.7B

Complete the following:

Substrate	Reaction	Products	Amount of ATP
1. glucose	glycolysis (aerobic)		
2. pyruvate	oxidation		
3. acetyl CoA	citric acid cycle		
4. glucose	glycolysis (anaerobic)		
5. glucose	complete oxidation		

Substrate	Reaction	Products	Amount of ATP
1. glucose	glycolysis (aerobic)	2 pyruvate acid	6 ATP
2. pyruvate acid	oxidation	acetyl CoA + CoA	3 ATP
3. acetyl CoA	citric acid cycle	$2CO_2$	12 ATP
4. glucose	glycolysis (anaerobic)	2 lactate	2 ATP
5. glucose	complete oxidation	$6 CO_2 + 6 H_2O$	36 ATP

18.8   Oxidation of Fatty Acids

- When needed for energy, fatty acids link to coenzyme A for transport to the mitochondria where they undergo β-oxidation.
- In β-oxidation, a fatty acyl chain is oxidized to yield a shortened fatty acid, acetyl CoA, and the reduced coenzymes NADH and $FADH_2$.
- The energy obtained from a particular fatty acid depends on the number of carbon atoms.
- Two ATP are required for activation. Then each acetyl CoA produces 12 ATP via citric acid cycle, and the electron transport chain converts each NADH to 3 ATP and each FADH to 2 ATP.

◆ **Learning Exercise 18.8A**

1. Write an equation for the activation of myristic (C_{14}) acid: CH_3—$(CH_2)_{12}$—$\overset{\overset{\displaystyle O}{\|}}{C}$—OH

2. Write an equation for the first oxidation of myristyl CoA.

3. Write an equation for the hydration of the double bond.

4. Write the overall equation for the complete oxidation of myristyl CoA.

5. **a.** How many cycles of β-oxidation will be required?

   b. How many acetyl CoA units will be produced?

Answers

1. $CH_3-(CH_2)_{12}-\overset{\overset{\displaystyle O}{\|}}{C}-OH + HS-CoA + ATP \longrightarrow CH_3-(CH_2)_{12}-\overset{\overset{\displaystyle O}{\|}}{C}-S-CoA + AMP + 2P_i$

2. $CH_3-(CH_2)_{12}-\overset{\overset{\displaystyle O}{\|}}{C}-S-CoA + FAD \longrightarrow CH_3-(CH_2)_{10}-CH=CH-\overset{\overset{\displaystyle O}{\|}}{C}-S-CoA + FADH_2$

3. $CH_3-(CH_2)_{10}-CH=CH-\overset{\overset{\displaystyle O}{\|}}{C}-S-CoA + H_2O \longrightarrow CH_3-(CH_2)_{10}-\overset{\overset{\displaystyle OH}{|}}{CH}-CH_2-\overset{\overset{\displaystyle O}{\|}}{C}-S-CoA$

4. myristyl (C_{14})—CoA + 6CoA + 6 FAD + 6 NAD$^+$ + 6 H$_2$O $\longrightarrow$

$$7 \text{Acetyl CoA} + 6 \text{ FADH}_2 + 6 \text{ NADH} + 6H^+$$

5. **a.** 6 cycles   **b.** 7 acetyl CoA units are produced

◆ Learning Exercise 18.8B

Lauric acid is a 12-carbon fatty acid: $CH_3(CH_2)_{10}COOH$.

1. How much ATP is needed for activation?

2. How many cycles of β-oxidation are required?

3. How many NADH and FADH$_2$ are produced during β-oxidation?

4. How many acetyl CoA units are produced?

5. What is the total ATP produced from the electron transport chain and the citric acid cycle?

Answers   **1.** 2 ATP   **2.** 5 cycles   **3.** 5 cycles produce 5 NADH and 5 FADH$_2$
4. 6 acetyl CoA   **5.** 5 NADH × 3 ATP = 15 ATP; 5 FADH$_2$ × 2 ATP = 10 ATP;
6 acetyl CoA × 12 ATP = 72 ATP; Total ATP = 15 ATP + 10 ATP + 72 ATP –
2 ATP (for activation) = 95 ATP

18.9 Degradation of Amino Acids

- Amino acids are normally used for protein synthesis.
- Amino acids are degraded by transferring an amino group from an amino acid to an α-keto acid to yield a different amino acid and α-keto acid.
- In oxidative deamination, the amino group in glutamate is removed as an ammonium ion, NH_4^+.
- α-Keto acids resulting from transamination can be used as intermediates in the citric acid cycle, in the synthesis of lipids or glucose, or oxidized for energy.

◆ **Learning Exercise 18.9A**

Match each of the following descriptions with transamination (T) or oxidative deamination (D).

1. _____ produces an ammonium ion, NH_4^+

2. _____ transfers an amino group to an α-keto acid

3. _____ usually involves the degradation of glutamate

4. _____ requires NAD^+ or $NADP^+$

5. _____ produces another amino acid and α-keto acid

6. _____ usually produces α-ketoglutarate

Answers   1. D   2. T   3. D
          4. T   5. T   6. D

◆ **Learning Exercise 18.9B**

1. Write an equation for the transamination reaction of serine and oxaloacetate.

2. Write an equation for the oxidation deamination of glutamate.

Answers

$$\underset{\displaystyle |}{\overset{\displaystyle NH_3^+}{}}$$
1. $HO-CH_2-\overset{NH_3^+}{\underset{|}{CH}}-COO^- + {}^-OOC-\overset{O}{\overset{||}{C}}-CH_2-COO^- \longrightarrow$

$HO-CH_2-\overset{O}{\overset{||}{C}}-COO^- + {}^-OOC-\overset{NH_3^+}{\underset{|}{CH}}-CH_2-COO^-$

$$^-OOC-\underset{\underset{\displaystyle NH_3^+}{|}}{CH}-CH_2-CH_2-COO^- + NAD^+ \text{ (or } NADP^+) + H_2O \longrightarrow$$

2.

$$^-OOC-\underset{\underset{\displaystyle \parallel}{O}}{C}-CH_2-CH_2-COO^- + NH_4^+ + NADH \text{ (or } NADPH) + H^+$$

Check List for Chapter 18

You are ready to take the practice test for Chapter 18. Be sure that you have accomplished the following learning goals for this chapter. If you are not sure, review the section listed at the end of the goal. Then apply your new skills and understanding to the practice test.

After studying Chapter 18 I can successfully:

____ Describe the role of ATP in catabolic and anabolic reactions (18.1).

____ Describe the sites, enzymes, and products of digestion for carbohydrates (18.2)

____ Describe the coenzymes NAD^+, FAD, and Coenzyme A (18.3).

.____ Describe the conversion of glucose to pyruvate in glycolysis (18.4).

____ Give the conditions for the conversion of pyruvate to lactate and acetyl coenzyme A (18.4).

____ Describe the oxidation of acetyl CoA in the citric acid cycle (18.5).

____ Identify the electron carriers in the electron transport system (18.6).

____ Describe the process of electron transport (18.6).

____ Explain the chemiosmotic theory whereby ATP synthesis is linked to the energy of the electron transport chain and a proton gradient (18.7).

____ Account for the ATP produced by the complete oxidation of glucose (18.7).

____ Describe the oxidation of fatty acids via β-oxidation (18.8).

____ Calculate the ATP produced by the complete oxidation of a fatty acid (18.8).

____ Explain the role of transamination and oxidative deamination in degrading amino acids (18.9).

Practice Test for Chapter 18

1. The main function of the mitochondria is
    A. energy production.   B. protein synthesis.   C. glycolysis.
    D. genetic instructions.   E. waste disposal.

2. ATP is a(n)
    A. nucleotide unit in RNA and DNA
    B. end product of glycogenolysis
    C. end product of transamination
    D. enzyme
    E. energy storage molecule

Use one or more of the following enzymes and end products for the digestion of each of items 3 through 6.

A. maltase   B. glucose   C. fructose   D. sucrase

E. galactose   F. lactase   G. pancreatic amylase

3. sucrose   _____   4. lactose   _____

5. small polysaccharides _____   6. maltose   _____

7. The digestion of triacylglycerols takes place in the _____

   by enzymes called _____.

   A. small intestine; peptidases   **B.** stomach; lipases   **C.**   stomach; peptidases
   D. small intestine; lipases   **E.** all of these

8. The products of the digestion of triacylglycerols are

   A. fatty acids.   **B.** monoacylglycerols. **C.**   glycerol.
   D. diacylglycerols.   **E.** all of these

9. The digestion of proteins takes place in the _____ by enzymes called _____.

   A. small intestine; peptidases   **B.** stomach; lipases   **C.** stomach; peptidases

   D.   small intestine; lipases   **E.** stomach and small intestine; proteases and peptidases

10. Glycolysis

    A. requires oxygen for the catabolism of glucose.
    B. represents the aerobic sequence for glucose anabolism and ATP production.
    C. represents the splitting off of glucose residues from glycogen.
    D. represents the anaerobic catabolism of glucose to pyruvate.
    E. produces acetyl units and ATP as end products.

Associate each of the following coenzymes with the correct description.

A. NAD^+ **B.** NADH   **C.** FAD   **D.** $FADH_2$ **E.** coenzyme A

11. _____ converts a hydroxyl group to a C=O group

12. _____ reduced form of nicotinamide adenine dinucleotide

13. _____ participates in oxidation reactions that produce a carbon–carbon double bond (C=C)

14. _____ transfers acyl groups such as the two-carbon acetyl group

15. _____ reduced form of flavin adenine dinucleotide

Answer the following questions for glycolysis.

16. _____ Number of ATP invested to oxidation one glucose molecule

17. _____ Number of ATP (net) produced from one glucose molecule

18. _____ Number of NADH produced from the degradation of one glucose molecule

19. Which is true of the citric acid cycle?

    A. Acetyl CoA is converted to CO_2 and H_2O.
    B. Oxaloacetate combines with acetyl units to form citric acid.
    C. The coenzymes are NAD^+ and FAD.
    D. ATP is produced by direct phosphorylation.
    E. all of the above

Match the types of reactions with each of the following.
A. malate   **B.** fumarate   **C.** succinate
D. citrate   **E.** oxaloacetate

20. _____ formed when oxaloacetate combines with acetyl CoA

21. _____ H_2O adds to its double bond to form malate

22. _____ FAD removes hydrogen to form a double bond

23. _____ formed when the hydroxyl group in malate is oxidizes

24. _____ the compound that is regenerated in the citric acid cycle

25. One turn of the citric acid cycle produces

    A. 3 NADH.   **B.** 3 NADH, 1 FADH$_2$.   **C.** 3 FADH$_2$, 1 NADH, 1 ATP.
    D. 3 NADH, 1 FADH$_2$, 1 ATP.   **E.** 1 NADH, 1 FADH$_2$, 1 ATP.

26. How many electron transfers in the electron transport chain provide sufficient energy for ATP synthesis?

    A. none   **B.** 1   **C.** 2   **D.** 3   **E.** 4

27. The electron transport chain

    A. produces most of the body's ATP.
    B. carries oxygen to the cells.
    C. produces $CO_2 + H_2O$.
    D. is only involved in the citric acid cycle.
    E. operates during fermentation.

In questions 28 through 30, match the components of the electron transport system with the following activities.

A. NAD$^+$ **B.** FMN   **C.** FAD   **D.** Q   **E.** cytochromes

28. _____ A mobile carrier that transfers electrons from FMN and FADH$_2$ to cytochromes

29. _____ The coenzyme that accepts hydrogen atoms from NADH

30. _____ The electron acceptors containing iron

Indicate the number of ATP's for the equations in questions 31 through 35. Select answers from below.

A. 2 ATP   **B.** 3 ATP   **C.** 6 ATP   **D.** 12 ATP   **E.** 24 ATP   **F.** 36 ATP

31. one turn of the citric acid cycle (acetyl CoA $\longrightarrow$ 2CO$_2$)

32. complete combustion of glucose (glucose + 6O$_2$ $\longrightarrow$ 6H$_2$O + 6CO$_2$)

33. produced when NADH enters electron transport

34. glycolysis (glucose + O$_2$ $\longrightarrow$ 2 pyruvate + 2H$_2$O)

35. oxidation of 2 pyruvate (2 pyruvate $\longrightarrow$ 2 acetyl CoA + 2CO$_2$)

36. Chylomicrons formed in the intestinal lining

    A. are lipoproteins.
    B. are triacylglycerols coated with proteins.
    C. transport fats into the lymph system and bloodstream.
    D. carry triacylglycerols tp the cells of the heart, muscle, and adipose tissues.
    E. all of these

Consider the β-oxidation of palmitic (C$_{16}$) acid for questions 37 through 40.

37. The number of β-oxidation cycles required for palmitic (C$_{16}$) acid is

    A. 16.   **B.** 9.   **C.** 8.
    D. 7.   **E.** 6.

38. The number of acetyl CoA groups produced by the β-oxidation of palmitic (C_{16}) acid is

    A. 16.   **B.** 9.   **C.** 8.
    D. 7.   **E.** 6.

39. The number of NADH and $FADH_2$ produced by the β-oxidation of palmitic (C_{16}) acid is

    A. 16.   **B.** 9.   **C.** 8.
    D. 7.   **E.** 6.

40. The total ATP produced by the β-oxidation of palmitic (C_{16}) acid is

    A. 96.   **B.** 129.   **C.** 131.
    D. 134.   **E.** 136.

41. The process of transamination

    A. is part of the citric acid cycle.   **B.** converts α-amino acids to β-keto acids.
    C. produces new amino acids.   **D.** is not used in the metabolism of amino acids.
    E. is part of the β-oxidation of fats.

42. The oxidative deamination of glutamate produces

    A. a new amino acid.   **B.** a new β-keto acid.
    C. ammonia, NH_3.   **D.** ammonium ion, NH_4^+.
    E. urea.

43. The purpose of the urea cycle in the liver is to

    A. synthesize urea.
    B. convert urea to ammonium ion, NH_4^+.
    C. convert ammonium ion NH_4^+ to urea.
    D. synthesize new amino acids.
    E. is part of the β-oxidation of fats.

44. The carbon atoms from various amino acids can be used in several ways such as

    A. intermediates of the citric acid cycle   **B.** formation of pyruvate
    C. synthesis of glucose   **D.** formation of ketone bodies
    E. all of these

45. Essential amino acids

    A. are not synthesized by humans   **B.** are required in the diet
    C. are excreted if in excess   **D.** include leucine, lysine, and valine
    E. all of these

Answers to the Practice Test

1. A	**2.** E	**3.** B, C, D	**4.** B, E, F	**5.** G, B
6. A, B	**7.** D	**8.** E	**9.** E	**10.** D
11. A	**12.** B	**13.** C	**14.** E	**15.** D
16. 2	**17.** 2	**18.** 2	**19.** E	**20.** D
21. B	**22.** C	**23.** E	**24.** E	**25.** D
26. E	**27.** A	**28.** D	**29.** B	**30.** E
31. D	**32.** F	**33.** B	**34.** C	**35.** C
36. E	**37.** D	**38.** C	**39.** D	**40.** B
41. C	**42.** D	**43.** C	**44.** E	**45.** E

Answers and Solutions to Selected Text Problems

18.1 The digestion of polysaccharides takes place in stage 1.

18.3 A catabolic reaction breaks down larger molecules to smaller molecules accompanied by the release of energy.

18.5 The phosphoric anhydride bonds (P—O—P) in ATP release energy that is sufficient for energy-requiring processes in the cell.

18.7 Digestion breaks down the large molecules in food into smaller compounds that can be absorbed by the body. Hydrolysis is the main reaction involved in the digestion of carbohydrates.

18.9   **a.** The disaccharide lactose is digested in the small intestine to yield galactose and glucose.
      b. The disaccharide sucrose is digested in the small intestine to yield glucose and fructose.
      c. The disaccharide maltose is digested in the small intestine to yield two glucose.

18.11 The bile salts emulsify fat to give small fat globules for lipase hydrolysis.

18.13 The digestion of proteins begins in the stomach and is completed in the small intestine.

18.15 In biochemical systems, oxidation is usually accompanied by gain of oxygen or loss of hydrogen. Loss of oxygen or gain of hydrogen usually accompanies reduction.
  a. The reduced form of NAD^+ is abbreviated NADH.
  b. The oxidized form of $FADH_2$ is abbreviated FAD.

18.17 The coenzyme FAD accepts hydrogen when a dehydrogenase forms a carbon-carbon double bond.

18.19 Glucose is the starting reactant for glycolysis.

18.21 In the initial reactions of glycolysis, ATP molecules are required to add phosphate groups to glucose.

18.23 ATP is produced directly in glycolysis in two places. In reaction 7, phosphate from 1,3-bisphosphoglycerate is transferred to ADP and yield ATP. In reaction 10, phosphate from phosphoenolpyruvate is transferred directly to ADP.

18.25 **a.** In the phosphorylation of glucose to glucose-6-phosphate 1 ATP is required.
  b. One ATP is required for the conversion of glyceraldehyde-3-phosphate to 1,3-bisphosphoglycerate.
  c. When glucose is converted to pyruvate, two ATP and two NADH are produced.

18.27 A cell converts pyruvate to acetyl CoA only under aerobic conditions when sufficient oxygen is available.

18.29 The overall reaction for the conversion of pyruvate to acetyl CoA is:

$$CH_3\underset{\substack{\| \\ \text{pyruvate}}}{\overset{\overset{\textstyle O}{\|}}{-C}}-COO^- + NAD^+ + HS-CoA \longrightarrow CH_3\underset{\substack{\| \\ \text{acetyl CoA}}}{\overset{\overset{\textstyle O}{\|}}{-C}}-S-CoA + CO_2 + NADH + H^+$$

18.31 The reduction of pyruvate to lactate regenerates NAD^+, which allows glycolysis to proceed.

18.33 One turn of the citric acid cycle converts 1 acetyl CoA to $2CO_2$, 3NADH, $FADH_2$, GTP (ATP), and HS—CoA.

18.35 The reactions in steps 3 and 4 involve oxidative decarboxylation, which reduces the length of the carbon chain by one carbon in each reaction.

18.37 NAD^+ is reduced by the oxidation reactions 3, 4, and 8 of the citric acid cycle.

18.39 In reaction 5, GDP undergoes a direct substrate phosphorylation to yield GTP, which converts ADP to ATP and regenerates GDP for the citric acid cycle.

18.41 **a.** The six-carbon compounds in the citric acid cycle are citrate and isocitrate.

b. Decarboxylation reactions remove carbon atoms as CO_2, which reduces the number of carbon atoms in a chain (reactions 3 and 4).

c. The one five-carbon compound is _-ketoglutarate.

d. Several reactions are oxidation reactions; isocitrate $\longrightarrow$ α-ketoglutarate; α-ketoglutarate $\longrightarrow$ succinyl CoA; succinate $\longrightarrow$ fumarate; malate $\longrightarrow$ oxaloacetate

e. Secondary alcohols are oxidized in reactions 3 and 8.

18.43 The Fe^{3+} is the oxidized form of the iron in cytochrome *c*.

18.45 **a.** The loss of $2H^+$ and $2e^-$ is oxidation.　　　**b.** The gain of $2H^+ + 2e^-$ is reduction.

18.47 NADH and $FADH_2$ produced in glycolysis, oxidation of pyruvate, and the citric acid cycle provide the electrons for electron transport.

18.49 FAD is reduced to $FADH_2$, which provides $2H^+$ and $2e^-$ for coenzyme Q, then cytochrome *b*, and then cytochrome *c*.

18.51 The mobile carrier coenzyme Q (or Q) transfers electrons from complex I to III. It also transfers electrons from complex II to complex III.

18.53 When NADH transfers electrons to FMN in complex I, NAD^+ is produced.

18.55 **a.** $NADH + H^+ + \underline{FMN} \longrightarrow \underline{NAD^+} + FMNH_2$

b. $QH_2 + 2Fe^{3+} \text{ cyt b} \longrightarrow Q + \underline{2Fe^{2+}\text{cyt b}} + 2H^+$

18.57 In oxidative phosphorylation, the energy from the oxidation reactions in the electron transport chain is used to drive ATP synthesis.

18.59 Protons must pass through ATP synthase to return to the matrix. During the process, energy is released to drive the synthesis of ATP.

18.61 The oxidation of the reduced coenzymes NADH and $FADH_2$ by the electron transport chain generates energy to drive the synthesis of ATP.

18.63 **a.** 3 ATP are produced by the oxidation of NADH in electron transport.

b. 2 ATP are produced in glycolysis when glucose degrades to 2 pyruvate.

c. 6 ATP are produced when 2 pyruvate are oxidized to 2 acetyl CoA and $2CO_2$.

d. 12 ATP are produced in one turn of the citric acid cycle as acetyl CoA goes $2CO_2$.

18.65 Fatty acids are activated in the cytosol of the mitochondria.

18.67

a., b. CH_3—$(CH_2)_6$—$\underset{\beta}{CH_2}$—$\underset{\alpha}{CH_2}$—$\overset{\displaystyle O}{\overset{\displaystyle \|}{C}}$—$S$—$CoA$

c.

CH_3—$(CH_2)_8$—$\overset{\displaystyle O}{\overset{\displaystyle \|}{C}}$—$S$—$CoA$ + NAD^+ + FAD + H_2O + SH—CoA $\longrightarrow$

CH_3—$(CH_2)_6$—$\overset{\displaystyle O}{\overset{\displaystyle \|}{C}}$—$S$—$CoA$ + CH_3—$\overset{\displaystyle O}{\overset{\displaystyle \|}{C}}$—$S$—$CoA$ + $NADH$ + H^+ + $FADH_2$

d. CH_3—$(CH_2)_8$—$COOH$ + $5CoA$ + $4FAD$ + $4NAD^+$ + $4H_2O$ $\longrightarrow$
   $5Acetyl\ CoA$ + $4FADH_2$ + $4NADH$ + $4H^+$

18.69 The hydrolysis of ATP to AMP provides the same amount of energy as the hydrolysis of 2 ATP to 2 ADP.

18.71 **a.** The β-oxidation of a chain of 10 carbon atoms produces 5 acetyl CoA units.

   b. A C_{10} fatty acid will go through 4 β-oxidation cycles.

   c. 60 ATP from 5 acetyl CoA (citric acid cycle) + 12 ATP from 4 NADH + 8 ATP from 4 FADH$_2$ –2 ATP (activation) = 80 –2 = 78 ATP

18.73 Ketone bodies are produced from excess acetyl CoA produced when large amount of fats undergo fatty acid oxidation, which occurs when glucose is not available for energy. This occurs in starvation, fasting, and diabetes.

18.75 High levels of ketone bodies lead to ketosis, a condition characterized by acidosis (a drop in blood pH values), and characterized by excessive urination and strong thirst.

18.77 The reactants are an amino acid and an α-keto acid, and the products are a new amino acid and a new α-keto acid.

18.79 In transamination, an amino group replaces a keto group in the corresponding α-keto acid.

a. H—$\overset{\displaystyle O}{\overset{\displaystyle \|}{C}}$—$COO^-$ **b.** CH_3—$\overset{\displaystyle O}{\overset{\displaystyle \|}{C}}$—$COO^-$

18.81 NH_4^+ is toxic if allowed to accumulate in the liver.

18.83 **a.** The three-carbon atom structure of alanine is converted to pyruvate.

   b. The four-carbon structure of aspartate is converted to fumarate or oxaloacetate.
   c. Valine is converted to succinyl CoA.
   d. The five-carbon structure from glutamine can be converted to α-ketoglutarate.

18.85 Humans can synthesize only nonessential amino acids.

18.87 ATP + H_2O $\longrightarrow$ ADP + P_i + 7.3 kcal/mole

18.89 Lactose undergoes digestion in the mucosal cells of the small intestine to yield galactose and glucose.

18.91 Glucose is the reactant and pyruvate is the product of glycolysis.

18.93 Pyruvate is converted to lactate when oxygen is not present in the cell (anaerobic) to regenerate NAD^+ for glycolysis.

18.95 The oxidation reactions of the citric acid cycle produce a source of reduced coenzymes for the electron transport chain and ATP synthesis.

18.97 The electron transport chain regenerates the oxidized forms of the coenzymes NAD^+ and FAD for use again by the citric acid cycle.

18.99 In the chemiosmotic model, energy released by the flow of protons through the ATP synthase is utilized for the synthesis of ATP.

18.101 The oxidation of glucose to pyruvate by glycolysis produces 6 ATP. 2 ATP are formed by direct phosphorylation along with 2 NADH. Because the 2 NADH are produced in the cytosol, the electrons are transferred to form 2 $FADH_2$, which produces an additional 4 ATP. The oxidation of glucose to CO_2 and H_2O produces 36 ATP.

18.103 Lauric acid, CH_3—$(CH_2)_{10}$—COOH, is a C_{12} fatty acid. $(C_{12}H_{24}O_2)$

a. and b. CH_3—$(CH_2)_8$—$\overset{\beta}{CH_2}$—$\overset{\alpha}{CH_2}$—$\overset{\overset{\displaystyle O}{\|}}{C}$——CoA

c. Lauryl-CoA + 5 CoA + 5 FAD + 5 NAD^+ + 5 H_2O ⟶
6 Acetyl CoA + 5 $FADH_2$ + 5 NADH + 5H^+

d. Six acetyl CoA units are produced.

e. Five cycles of _ oxidation are needed.

f.

activation	⟶	-2 ATP
6 acetyl CoA × 12	⟶	72 ATP
5 $FADH_2$ × 2	⟶	10 ATP
5 NADH × 3	⟶	15ATP
Total		95 ATP